STATE OF THE
WORLD
1989

Other Norton/Worldwatch Books

Lester R. Brown et al.
State of the World 1984
State of the World 1985
State of the World 1986
State of the World 1987
State of the World 1988

STATE OF THE WORLD

1989

A Worldwatch Institute Report on Progress Toward a Sustainable Society

PROJECT DIRECTOR
Lester R. Brown

ASSOCIATE PROJECT DIRECTORS
Christopher Flavin
Sandra Postel

EDITOR
Linda Starke

SENIOR RESEARCHERS

Lester R. Brown
Alan Durning
Christopher Flavin
Lori Heise
Jodi Jacobson
Sandra Postel
Michael Renner
Cynthia Pollock Shea

W·W·NORTON & COMPANY

NEW YORK   LONDON

ISBN 0-393-02638-8

ISBN 0-393-30567-8 {PBK}

W. W. Norton & Company, Inc., 500 Fifth Avenue, New York, N.Y. 10110
W. W. Norton & Company Ltd., 37 Great Russell Street, London WC1B 3NU

2 3 4 5 6 7 8 9 0

Acknowledgments

Nine names are inscribed on the cover of *State of the World 1989,* but the book is the fruit of countless others' labor. It is a tribute to years of strong support and sound advice from Chairman Orville Freeman and the entire Worldwatch Board of Directors. They have never ceased to encourage us to ask the hard questions of how to sustain humanity while sustaining the earth. The Rockefeller Brothers Fund, Winthrop Rockefeller Trust, and the George Gund Foundation supply the backbone of financial support for the *State of the World* series.

The Institute receives the bulk of research funding from the Geraldine R. Dodge, William and Flora Hewlett, W. Alton Jones, Andrew W. Mellon, Edward John Noble, and Jessie Smith Noyes Foundations, as well as project support from the Public Welfare Foundation and the United Nations Population Fund. Without them, *State of the World* would still be a concept on a drawing board.

On short notice, ranks of scholars and policy experts outside the institute reviewed chapters to double-check our facts, critique our analysis, and add depth to our vision. We thank Jeff Alson, Sheldon Annis, Deborah Bleviss, James Chin, Douglas Cogan, Clarence Ditlow, Harold Dregne, Martin Foreman, Laurie Greenberg, Jeffrey Harris, John Hoffman, Kevin Healy, Ken Hughes, William Lyerly, Michael Oppenheimer, Mead Over, Philip Patterson, Michael Replogle, Sherwood Rowland, Jane Sisk, Daniel Stiles, Michael Walsh, and Edward Wolf. Any remaining errors fall, of course, to the authors alone.

While the bulk of our research is carried out by mail and telephone from our offices off Dupont Circle in Washington, D.C., members of our research team journeyed to China, Europe, and Latin America during the summer of 1988 to see firsthand the problems and prospects of those regions. We are deeply indebted to those generous individuals, too numerous to name, who shared with us their wisdom, their experience, and often their homes.

Nineteen hundred eighty-eight was a year of growth at Worldwatch Institute. With the launch of our new magazine, *World Watch*, and production beginning on a *State of the World* television series, extraordinary demands have been placed on the staff. The quality of this volume testifies to their sheer tenacity and to the strength of their commitment. Vice President Blondeen Gravely nursed the Institute through its growth pains, while Treasurer Felix Gorrell skillfully maintained the financial health of the organization.

Reah Janise Kauffman not only bore the full responsibility of assisting the president but also managed a fickle and expanding computer system. Linda Doherty and Guy Gorman deftly juggled telephones, incoming orders, and visitors without losing their sense of humor. The editorial duo of Stephen Dujack and James Gorman steered the *Worldwatch*

Papers and *World Watch* magazine through the rapids of *State of the World* production. Lori Eaton and Ann Kip both put in early mornings and late nights to keep our accounts and drafts on track. Ted Wolf, newly independent from the institute, kept us in close contact with the team working from Boston on the television series.

The research business is characterized by an enormous volume of paper, coming in and going out. In that department, three part-timers at the Institute bore the brunt. Chas Chiodo mailed books from our offices to almost every country on earth. Meanwhile, most of the sources cited in the notes reach the authors after photocopying by either our resident distance runner George Brown or our resident whitewater champion Brian Brown.

Those who left the institute for other opportunities since the last *State of the World* include Mary Jo Allen, Cynthia Bainton, Robin Bell, Bill Chandler, and Bruce Goldstein. They are each sorely missed. We also owe an apology to Amy Thein, who was unintentionally omitted from the acknowledgments in *State of the World 1988.* What is closest to the eye is sometimes overlooked.

Talented research assistants are the foundation of Worldwatch's work and this year, in particular, we have had a dedicated team. They each contributed to the entire book with their insightful suggestions, as well as to the particular chapters on which they worked: Susan Fine and Bruce Goldstein (Chapters 5 and 7), Hilary French (Chapter 4), Nick Lenssen (Chapters 1 and 10), Marcia Lowe (Chapters 2 and 10), and John Young (Chapters 1, 3, 6, 8, and 10).

The final and greatest debt is owed to those who do the thankless job of turning 10 disjointed manuscripts into one unified whole. At W.W. Norton & Company in New York, Iva Ashner and Andy Marasia patiently accommodate our last-minute alterations and still produce *State of the World* in record time. And here on Massachusetts Avenue, the book itself is made possible only by the unerring red pen of our editor, Linda Starke, who tirelessly works on draft after draft and then coordinates the project through galleys to final product. The real finale—the index—is once again due to the skills of Bart Brown.

We also all appreciate the ceaseless vigilance of Susan Norris, who manages production of the volume and keeps all the details in mind herself while calming the fears of eight authors. We thank her in particular for years of spirited service.

Lester R. Brown, Christopher Flavin, and Sandra Postel

Contents

List of Tables and Figures

LIST OF TABLES

LIST OF FIGURES

Foreword

This sixth annual *State of the World* report is being released at a time when more people are being affected by environmental change than ever before. The destruction of the world's forests is accelerating and deserts continue to expand. Soil erosion is sapping not just agricultural production, but the livelihoods of millions, while the extinction of plant and animal species is rapidly diminishing our biological heritage. For the first time in history, we are altering the atmosphere itself, destroying the ozone layer that protects us from ultraviolet radiation and raising the level of "greenhouse gases" that are warming the earth.

The deterioration of the earth's physical condition that we have documented in past volumes of this report is now accelerating. And there is nothing in prospect that will reverse it in the foreseeable future. We are now in a race to stop environmental deterioration before it becomes unmanageable, before it leads to economic decline and social disruption.

On the encouraging side, during the past year environmental stories have moved onto the front pages of newspapers, magazine covers, and television talk shows. At the same time, a new commitment to global environmental issues by Soviet leaders and a new administration in Washington present extraordinary opportunities to address environmental problems.

In the United States, devastating heat and drought in 1988 led to the unthinkable—a U.S. grain harvest that fell below consumption. The precipitous fall in the North American grain harvest raised world grain prices by half between mid-1987 and mid-1988. If the North American drought was exacerbated by global warming, which is being driven by the buildup in greenhouse gases, it would mark the first time human-induced environmental change has caused a major shift in a basic economic indicator.

Environmental threats came to light in numerous ways. For vacationers going to many of the beaches along the Baltic or Adriatic seas, the "No Swimming" signs were a disappointing reminder of increasing oceanic pollution. For millions of Chinese living in the Chang Jiang (Yangtze) Valley, it was exposure to the dangerously high July temperatures that caused local hospitals to be overwhelmed with heat-stroke victims.

As the evidence of potentially uncontrollable environmental changes mounted, there were scattered signs of national governments beginning to respond. In late October, President José Sarney of Brazil announced a 90-day suspension of the tax breaks and other incentives that had spurred the clearing and burning of large tracts of Amazon rain forest. In Lagos, the Nigerian government asked couples to limit the number of children to four at most, making it the first African country to call for a limit on family size. The Soviet Union called for a massive international effort *to* shift resources from military security to environmental security. And the Prime Ministers of Canada and Norway publicly endorsed a goal of cutting carbon emissions from fossil fuels by 20 percent by 2005.

Notwithstanding these and other national initiatives, the gap between what needs to be done to protect the planet's habitability and what is being done is growing. That is the bad news. The good news is that more people want to get involved in the effort to save the planet. The question that now dominates our mail is, What can I do?

Record advance sales of *State of the World* indicate a growing hunger for information among people concerned about the fate of their planet and their children's future. This concern is by no means limited to the English-speaking world. *State of the World* now appears in nearly all of the world's major languages—Spanish, Arabic, Chinese, Japanese, Indonesian, German, Polish, Italian, and Russian. In 1987, the Arabic translation was the first to be published, following the English edition by only two months. In 1988, the Italian version, published by Editore Petrini, was available just one month after the English edition. Petrini's 1989 goal, using a team of translators, is to publish the Italian edition simultaneously with the English one.

Although it is too early to tell for sure, it looks as though U.S. sales of *State of the World 1989* will pass the 100,000 mark. All segments of the market—public policymakers, concerned citizens, corporate planners, and the academic community—continue to grow. Last year, *State of the World* was adopted for use in 751 courses in 451 U.S. colleges and universities.

Three years ago, we announced that

we were joining forces with WGBH, the Boston-based producers of "Nova," to produce a major series for public television based on *State of the World.* We are pleased to report that filming began in late 1988, and the series is scheduled to air in 1990.

We conclude this year's report with the notion that the nineties needs to be a "turnaround decade." The looming threats we now face—including climate change, ozone depletion, and population growth—have so much momentum that unless action begins now to reverse them, they will inevitably lead to paralyzingly costly economic consequences and the collapse of social and political institutions. One of these years, we would like to be able to write an upbeat *State of the World,* one in which we can report that the trends undermining the human prospect have been reversed. It now seems that if we cannot write such a report in the nineties, we may not be able to write it at all.

In numerous ways each year, we see how *State of the World* plants the seeds of change. Our goal is to inspire enough people to nourish and spread those seeds that meaningful change begins to occur.

As always, we welcome your comments, reactions, and suggestions.

Lester R. Brown
   Project Director

Christopher Flavin
Sandra Postel
   Associate Project Directors

Worldwatch Institute
1776 Massachusetts Ave., N.W.
Washington, D.C. 20036

December 1988

STATE OF THE
WORLD
1989

1

A World at Risk

Lester R. Brown, Christopher Flavin, and Sandra Postel

Historians looking back on 1988 may well mark it a watershed year both for the environment and the public's concern about it. The earth's deteriorating condition moved into the limelight, as weekly news magazines and television talk shows gave prominent play to unsettling evidence of environmental stress. A collage of the year's headlines would cry out to be captioned "a world at risk." Indeed, the year provided a tangible foretaste of what lies ahead if we continue down the current path—and this glimpse into the global future was disquieting, to say the least.

In June, evidence came from the U.S. National Aeronautics and Space Administration (NASA) that the long-predicted global warming had apparently become reality. James E. Hansen, head of NASA's Goddard Institute for Space Studies, released findings from a study of global temperature records spanning the last century. Not only had there been

Units of measurement are metric unless common usage dictates otherwise.

a gradual long-term warming consistent with models of the greenhouse effect, but the four warmest years had all occurred in the eighties—1980, 1981, 1983, and 1987. It appeared then that 1988 would join them, and would become the hottest year on record.[1]

As if to lend import to NASA's findings, weather conditions in key parts of the world seemed to preview what life in a greenhouse world would be like. Temperatures in parts of central China soared to between 36 and 40 degrees Celsius (97 and 104 degrees Fahrenheit) on 10 consecutive days in July. For the hundreds of millions of Chinese who live in this densely populated region—which embraces Shanghai, Nanjing, and Wuhan—the heat wave was nothing less than frightful. Hospitals in Nanjing were overwhelmed by the number of heat stroke victims; temporary cots had to be set up in corridors and shaded areas. With daily highs climbing well above normal body temperature, hundreds of people died.[2]

Meanwhile, heat waves and drought

were also striking North America. Temperature records were set across the continent. Crop yields declined so sharply in the United States that grain production fell below domestic consumption, probably for the first time in history. Fortunately, grain reserves could easily fill this deficit as well as satisfy export commitments. But with reserves largely depleted, a drought in 1989 would slow U.S. grain exports to a trickle, send food prices soaring, and lead to a frantic scramble for grain among scores of importers.

Additional worrisome news came from NASA in March: the atmospheric ozone layer that protects earthly life from harmful ultraviolet radiation had begun to thin globally. Depletion was no longer confined to the polar regions. More than 100 scientists from seven countries had spent 16 months carefully analyzing ground-based and satellite measurements of atmospheric ozone. They found that from 1969 to 1986, ozone decreased between 1.7 percent and 3 percent in a heavily populated band of the northern hemisphere encompassing virtually all of continental United States and Europe. Wintertime ozone losses were even greater, ranging from 2.3 percent to 6.2 percent. Failure to adequately control emissions of ozone-depleting chemicals thus virtually assures a future of increased skin cancer rates, crop losses, and damage to marine life. (See Chapter 5.)[3]

Local and regional signs of environmental stress, some verging on the catastrophic, seemed commonplace in 1988. Early September found two thirds of Bangladesh under water, a direct result of heavy monsoon rains but also indirectly due to the disruption of the hydrological cycle in the Himalayan watershed because of progressive deforestation in recent decades. Flooding in Bangladesh has worsened measurably during the eighties. The 1988 flood, the worst in living memory, left 25 million of the country's 110 million people homeless, adding to the growing ranks of "environmental refugees." (See Chapter 4.)[4]

Alarming news about deforestation came from Brazil. Satellite data covering the 1987 dry season showed that the Amazon rain forest is being cleared far faster than previously thought. An astonishing 8 million hectares—an area about the size of Austria—were burned in 1987 alone, and burning during the 1988 dry season was expected to be even worse. This accelerated destruction is driving uncounted numbers of plant and animal species to extinction, adding to carbon dioxide–induced climate change, and threatening to disrupt the region's powerful hydrological cycle—which in turn could alter hemispheric and possibly even global climatic patterns. (See Chapter 2.)[5]

Perhaps the most distinguishing feature of 1988 was the extent to which environmental threats began to directly touch the emotions and lives of people. Like the mercury in their outdoor thermometers, Americans' concern for the environment seemed to rise to unprecedented heights during the summer. Within the span of a few weeks, they were bombarded by news of medical waste washing up on East Coast beaches, persistent drought searing crops throughout the agricultural heartland, fires raging through popular Yellowstone National Park, and health-threatening pollution levels in the air outside their homes.[6]

In Europe, concern about the environment escalated with the deaths of thousands of seals in north European waters, even though the role of pollution was later minimized. Pollution of the Adriatic Sea led to fish kills and an exodus of tourists from long stretches of the Italian coastline. Soviet officials banned swimming in the Baltic, Black, and Aral seas because of pollution-related health threats. West Africans sounded alarms over the dumping of toxic waste on their shores. And the human suffering caused by the flood disaster in Bangladesh went beyond most people's imaginations. The natural world, it seemed, was striking back.[7]

But what will become of this ground swell of concern arising from the events of 1988? Will it fade like the summer heat? Or will it translate into sufficient pressure to force policymakers to respond to the looming threats of which this year provided a sampling?

The environmental era now dawning is distinguished by problems truly global in scale. Even while countries grapple with the more localized problems of acid rain, toxic waste, and soil erosion, global threats of unprecedented proportions are now overlaid upon them. The immediate challenge is to translate a common vision of a world at risk into the international alliances and bold actions needed to safeguard the earth.

An effective response to the environmental threats now unfolding will require that humanity's perception of its relationship to the earth's natural systems cross a new threshold. During the eighties, a number of shifts occurred on the environmental front that led to major turnarounds on some important issues. They give cause for optimism in dealing with the larger threats because they show that major reversals are possible in a fairly short period of time. But they also engender concern because it often seems to take a crisis before people's perceptions change sufficiently to support an effective political response. With problems such as climate change and population growth, a continuation of that pattern means that much irreversible damage will be done before societies respond.

It often seems to take a crisis before perceptions change sufficiently to support an effective political response.

CROSSING PERCEPTUAL THRESHOLDS

Social change occurs when people alter the way they perceive some of the elements constituting their world. Spurred by a dramatic event, a charismatic leader, or a gradual awakening through education, people cross a "perceptual threshold" that forces them to see and judge some aspect of their world in a new light. These perceptual shifts often have a decidedly ethical component. Witness the turning of slavery from an implicit right to a moral abomination, or the subjugation of women from common practice to—at least in some parts of the world—a reprehensible condition.

The explosion at the Chernobyl nuclear reactor in the Soviet Ukraine in early April 1986 did what hundreds of studies assessing nuclear technology could never have done: it made the dangers of nuclear power real. Fresh vegetables were declared unfit for human consumption in northern Italy. Polish authorities launched an emergency effort to get iodine tablets administered to children. The livelihood of the Lapps in northern Scandinavia was threatened when reindeer upon which they depend became too contaminated with radiation to bring to market. In the Soviet Union itself, 100,000 people in the vicinity of the reactor were forced to abandon their homes.[8]

This single event shifted public attitudes so strongly against nuclear power that since then five countries have decided not to build more nuclear plants and two, Italy and Sweden, have decided to accelerate closings of existing plants. In the Soviet Union, at least five reactors have been canceled since the accident, and work has been suspended at several other sites.[9]

Rapid advances in recent years toward acid rain control in Europe stem in large part from the West Germans' sudden awakening to *waldsterben*, forest death. After a 1982 survey showed that trees in the fabled Black Forest and elsewhere were dying in large numbers—with suspected links to air pollution and acid rain—*waldsterben* rapidly emerged as a potent political and emotional issue. A poll taken during the summer of 1983 showed that West Germans were more concerned about the fate of their forests than about the Pershing missiles that were to be placed on their territory later that year.[10]

An environmental awakening has occurred in Eastern Europe and the Soviet Union.

Until that time, the nation had been firmly against cooperation toward stricter air pollution controls. Faced with such strong public concern, however, West German officials dramatically reversed their position in 1983. At a meeting of the U.N. Economic Commission for Europe (ECE) to discuss transboundary pollution, West Germany broke ranks and supported a Scandinavian proposal calling for each ECE member to cut sulfur dioxide emissions by 30 percent by 1993. Dissent from the United States, the United Kingdom, and others prevented the proposal's adoption. But it led to the formation of an

informal "30 percent club" made up of nations committed to this target, which in turn paved the way for the Protocol on the Reduction of Sulfur Emissions signed by 21 nations in Helsinki in 1985.[11]

By 1986, 10 countries had met or exceeded the 30-percent reduction goal —an astonishingly rapid achievement— and 4 had committed themselves to a 70-percent reduction. It is impossible to know how acid rain controls in Europe would have progressed had *waldsterben* not become such an emotional issue, especially in West Germany but also in other countries that discovered extensive damage to their woodlands. The spectre of dying forests clearly caused enough Europeans to cross a threshold of concern that made political action not only urgent, but unavoidable.[12]

Just since the mid-eighties, an environmental awakening has occurred in Eastern Europe and the Soviet Union. The Chernobyl accident and the spread of forest damage were precipitating factors, but the rising awareness seems to spring equally from concern about the deterioration of the region's air, drinking water, and soils.[13]

With the emergence of *glasnost*, this awakening has spurred much environmental activism. One western observer in the Soviet Union has compared the mood there with that in the United States in 1970, the year Earth Day was proclaimed. In Poland, there are now some 2,000 environmental organizations, most of them established since 1986. Freedom and Peace, among the most active of them, captures the fundamental nature of the growing concern with its statement: "Threatened with the ruin of the biosphere, pollution of air, water and soil, we realize that freedom should also be the possibility to live in non-devastated surroundings."[14]

Of course, perceptual shifts by themselves do not resolve problems. Additional pollution control measures are still needed in Europe, and the environmental awakening in Eastern Europe and the Soviet Union has led only to incipient action by governments. But such shifts are often prerequisites to effective responses, the sparks that ignite the processes of change.

In Western Europe, this evolution from perception to action may be hastened by the emergence of the so-called green political movement. With roots in West Germany in the late seventies, this movement now has official political parties in 16 countries and members of parliament (MPs) in 8. The European Parliament itself now includes Green Party members. In 1988, Sweden's Greens became the first new party to enter the parliament in 70 years, and Italy's less formal green parliamentary group became an important force in that nation's politics. In some countries, Green MPs are able to direct some public funds toward environmental research and into conferences and other events that raise the level of public awareness.[15]

Perceptual shifts of profound proportions are needed to respond adequately to global warming, to unchecked population growth, and to persistent poverty—arguably the greatest threats to environmental health and economic progress during the next decade and beyond. These problems are especially daunting because they involve deeply rooted patterns of behavior, beliefs, and values. And none can be alleviated through a simple action or technological fix. Environmental philosopher Lynn White hinted at the predicament more than two decades ago: "I personally doubt that disastrous ecologic backlash can be avoided simply by applying to our problems more science and more technology."[16]

Indeed, crossing the perceptual thresholds needed to respond to these problems launches humanity toward a new moral frontier. A growing sense of the world's interdependence and connectedness takes shape—the recognition, for example, that automobile use anywhere threatens climate stability everywhere, that persistent poverty and debt cast an economic shadow over industrial countries as well as those in the Third World. The old business of pursuing narrow economic and political self-interest falls away, anachronistic and plainly untenable. As historian Jeremy Brecher wrote in 1988, this "second ecological revolution . . . will have to say that preserving the conditions for human life is simply more important than increasing national power or private wealth."[17]

Without a strong sense that people favor the fundamental changes needed to respond to these problems, governments will not take the necessary actions. The immediate task, then, is for individuals everywhere to raise their understanding, concern, and voices to the point where political leaders are forced to respond. Scientists who not only convey the relevant facts but also articulate the consequences of political inaction will play a crucial role in this process of education and mobilization. So, too, will the media.

Will societies cross these new perceptual thresholds soon enough to avoid major ecological backlash? Though a major transformation of attitudes and priorities is still needed, there are a few glimmers of hope on the horizon.

Around the world, people concerned about direct threats to their health and livelihoods have banded together to take greater control over their destinies. Thousands of grassroots movements have arisen on virtually every continent in response to a host of injustices—including toxic contamination, industrial exploitation of forests, militarization's drain on resources, landlessness, and lack of access to basic water, sanitation, and health care services. (See Chapters 8 and 9.) These groups show that mobilization for change is possible; more important, perhaps, they form a critical part of the institutional foundation needed to do the work of sustainable development.

In Vietnam—a nation devastated by war, overpopulation, and poverty—there are unexpected signs of the kind of perceptual shifts that need to take place among national leaders. General Vo Nguyen Giap, the former commander-in-chief of the North Vietnamese Army and current vice president, is among the backers of a national plan calling for a large-scale family planning program and a massive reforestation effort—measures urgently needed to lift the country out of ecological and economic decline. General Giap has said, "The soldier comes to another front now, the environmental front. . . . Now I see that without environmental recovery, Vietnam cannot have economic recovery; the two are inseparable . . . . Today I fight for Vietnam's environment—and for peace."[18]

In several industrial countries, the urgency of climate change is beginning to hit home. The prime ministers of Canada and Norway have each publicly endorsed cutting carbon emissions by 20 percent by 2005. And in the United States, in the wake of the summer of 1988's record-breaking heat waves, three separate pieces of legislation to slow the pace of global warming were introduced in Congress. Few people could have imagined when 1988 began that climate change would rise so rapidly on the political agenda.[19]

Yet vast chasms separate glimmers of hope from effective responses. A committed, active, vocal public is essential to bring about the policy changes needed to safeguard the earth's environment. The difficult choices that lie ahead will challenge our social institutions and personal values as never before. It will help to remember that progress is an illusion if it destroys the conditions needed for life to thrive on earth.

THE THREAT OF CLIMATE CHANGE

When NASA scientist James Hansen announced at a Senate hearing during the intense June 1988 heat wave that "global warming has begun," he ignited a whirlwind of public concern that has yet to subside. The warming of the earth's climate is an environmental catastrophe on a new scale, with the potential to violently disrupt virtually every natural ecosystem and many of the structures and institutions that humanity has grown to depend on. Although climates have shifted only slightly so far, the world faces the prospect of vastly accelerated change in the decades ahead. Conditions essential to life as we know it are now at risk.[20]

The threat of climate change stems from the increasing concentrations of carbon dioxide (CO_2) and other "greenhouse gases" that hold heat in the lower atmosphere, allowing temperatures to rise. The burning of coal and of other carbon-based fuels such as oil and natural gas releases carbon as the basic product of the combustion, while the large-scale clearing of tropical forests adds additional carbon dioxide to the atmosphere. Just since 1958, when routine measurements began, the CO_2 concentration has gone from 315 parts per million to 352 parts per million—substantially above the highest concentrations experienced on earth in the past 160,000 years.[21]

Concentrations of other, more potent greenhouse gases—notably methane, nitrous oxide, and chlorofluorocarbons (CFCs)—are increasing even more rapidly. Based on current emission rates, they have as much potential as CO_2 to warm the atmosphere. While the carbon dioxide level has grown at a rate of 0.4 percent a year since 1958, these other gases are increasing at annual rates as high as 5 percent.[22]

Humanity added 5.5 billion tons of carbon to the atmosphere in 1988 through fossil fuel combustion and another 0.4 billion to 2.5 billion tons through deforestation. The United States is the largest contributor, but it may be passed soon by the Soviet Union and later by China. (See Figure 1-1.) While carbon emissions are growing slowly in the industrial countries that account for two thirds of the total, they are skyrocketing in the developing world. If recent worldwide consumption growth rates of about 3 percent per year continue, fossil fuels could contribute 10 billion tons of new carbon annually in the year 2010. Meanwhile, deforestation in the Amazon and perhaps other tropical regions appears to have accelerated to frighteningly rapid rates.[23]

Teams of British and American scientists have assembled series of global average temperatures going back 100 years. While experts still disagree about some of these numbers, the overall trend is clear. The global average temperature in the 1890s was 14.5 degrees Celsius, and by the 1980s it had climbed to 15.2 degrees. Temperatures leveled off between 1940 and 1970, but the accelerated rise during the eighties has more than offset this lull. As noted earlier, the five warmest years of the past century have all fallen in this decade.[24]

These trends appear to confirm the global circulation models that scientists use to assess the impact of greenhouse gases on the climate. NASA's Hansen, for example, is now 99 percent certain that the observed temperature increases reflect the impact of the greenhouse effect. Meanwhile, the upper atmosphere is becoming cooler while the lower atmosphere warms, and temperatures at higher latitudes are increasing faster than they are at the equator, just as the global warming models predict.[25]

The five warmest years of the past century have all fallen in this decade.

The limited warming that has occurred so far is important to scientists, but not threatening to society. Danger lies in the acceleration of climate change that appears imminent. Between 2030 and 2050, average temperatures could be 1.5–4.5 degrees Celsius (3–8 degrees Fahrenheit) higher than they have been in recent decades, or warmer than the earth has been for the past 2 million years. (See Figure 1–2.) This implies a warming that is 5 to 10 times as fast as that experienced during the past century.[26]

If the spurt in global temperatures that began about 1970 continues, droughts, heat waves, and other unusual weather may increase by the late nineties

Figure 1-1. Carbon Emissions from Fossil Fuels, 1950-87

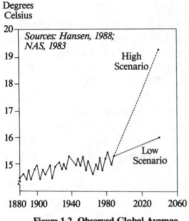

Figure 1-2. Observed Global Average
Temperatures, 1880-1987,
With Projections to 2040

to the point where even nonscientists will notice the climate is changing. Although there is no proof that the weather of 1988 is attributable to global warming, the extreme heat and dryness in areas such as central North America and China indicate what may be in store for the nineties and beyond. In the future, higher latitude and mid-continental regions in the United States and China are likely to experience greater temperature rises than the world as a whole. In these areas, stifling summer heat waves and devastating droughts may soon be commonplace.[27]

It is still argued by some that climate change will have positive as well as negative effects, and that it is a problem with which societies can readily cope. But this ignores the extraordinary rate of change that is now projected, and the impossibility of adjusting quickly enough. Scientists believe that the pace of climate change will soon overwhelm natural variability in the earth's climate. Indeed, it can be compared with nuclear war for its potential to disrupt a wide range of human and natural systems, complicating the task of managing economies and coping with other problems. Irrigation works, settlement patterns, and food

production would be tragically disrupted by a rapid warming.[28]

Trees are adapted to a narrow range of temperature and moisture levels, and cannot cope with rapid climate change. A temperature increase of 1 degree Celsius per decade in mid- to upper latitudes translates into a shift in vegetation zones of 60–100 miles northward. Terrestrial ecosystems cannot migrate that fast. Vast numbers of trees are likely to die, and new trees adapted to warmer temperatures are unlikely to be able to replace them rapidly. During such a disruption, huge areas of forest could die and, as they decay or burn, send large quantities of additional CO_2 into the atmosphere, accelerating the warming.[29]

Biological diversity, already being reduced by various human activities, may be one of the chief casualties of global warming. Massive destruction of forests, wetlands, and even the polar tundra could irrevocably destroy complex ecosystems that have existed for millennia. Indeed, various biological reserves created in the past decade to protect species diversity could become virtual death traps as wildlife attempt to survive in conditions for which they are poorly suited. Accelerated species extinction is an inevitable consequence of a rapid warming.[30]

Sea level rise is another threat. As ocean water warms, it will expand, and warming at the poles will melt parts of glaciers and ice caps. Studies conclude that a temperature rise of 3 degrees Celsius by 2050 would raise sea level by 50–100 centimeters. By the end of the next century, sea level may be up by as much as two meters.[31]

This would hurt most in the developing world, particularly in densely populated Asia, where rice is produced on low-lying river deltas and floodplains. Without heavy investments in dikes and seawalls to protect the rice fields from saltwater intrusion, such a rise would markedly reduce harvests. Large areas of wetlands that nourish the world's fisheries would also be destroyed.[32]

In Bangladesh, sea level rise and subsidence caused largely by human activities could flood up to 18 percent of the nation's land area by 2050, displacing more than 17 million people. In Egypt, where only 4 percent of the land area can be cultivated, food production could drop and 8.5 million people could be forced from their homes. In these already crowded countries, there is no place for these people to go and no alternative land available on which to grow crops. (See Chapter 4.)[33]

In the United States, a U.S. government–sponsored study has estimated the potential impacts of climate change on Cleveland, Miami, and New York. A few minor benefits are mentioned, such as lower snow removal budgets and winter heating bills, but the overall picture is bleak. In particular, many billions of dollars will likely have to be spent on improving already inadequate water supply systems, since demand will increase and supplies will be degraded as the climate changes.[34]

In New York, for example, salt water could move up the lower Hudson River while more-severe droughts limit the amount of water available from upstate watersheds. In Miami, most of which was once below sea level, even extensive diking will not preserve its porous freshwater aquifer. If global warming continues, Miami could one day be reclaimed by the sea. Meanwhile, air-conditioning costs are likely to soar.[35]

Global circulation models and the various studies that flow from them mainly forecast averages. But in the game of climate change, it is not the averages that kill, it is the extremes. Unexpected droughts, extraordinary heat waves, and devastating hurricanes are among the dangerous events likely to be more common in a warmer world, but their precise location and timing may never be entirely predictable. A handful of extreme storms could kill millions of people. In many developing countries, two or three droughts in a row could leave millions starving.[36]

When air pollution and solid waste disposal first commanded attention in the seventies, analysts were at least able to point to solutions to the problems and come up with 5- or 10-year action plans. One of the most disturbing things about global warming is that even as some of its implications are being discovered, it appears that substantial and damaging climate change is inevitable due to the enormous changes forced on the earth's atmosphere over the past century.

In the game of climate change, it is not the averages that kill, it is the extremes.

Climate change has so much momentum behind it now that it can only be slowed, not stopped. (See Chapter 10.) Future generations will have to cope with a warmer and ever-changing world, one in which major investments are required simply to maintain the status quo. Global warming will hurt rich and poor, North and South alike. But those most at risk are the almost 4 billion people who live in the Third World, many of whom already face declining living standards and who lack the resources to protect themselves from spreading deserts and rising sea levels.

Indeed, climate change, like no other issue, calls the whole notion of human progress into question. The benefits of newer technologies, more efficient economies, and improved political systems could be overwhelmed by uncontrolled global warming. Some warming is inevitable. But unless trends are reversed, tragic changes could occur in just the next two decades. The challenge is to act before it is too late—which means before the scientific evidence is conclusive. The longer society waits, the more radical and draconian the needed responses will be.

A LOSS OF FOOD SECURITY

As the eighties draw to a close, climate change is being added to an already long list of environmental stresses and resource scarcities that are undermining global food security. Soil erosion, desertification, the salting of irrigated lands, and a scarcity of new cropland and fresh water are combining to lower the growth in food output below that of population in dozens of developing countries. Partly as a result, the world now has far more hungry people than it did when the eighties began.[37]

A dramatic 2.6-fold increase in grain production between 1950 and 1984 raised per capita consumption by nearly 40 percent. But since then growth has stopped. In each of the past two years, world grain production has fallen sharply, marking the first steep back-to-back annual declines on record. A monsoon failure in India in 1987 and drought-reduced harvests in North America and China in 1988 explain only part of the reduction. In several populous countries, including China, India, Indonesia, and Mexico, little or no progress has been made in expanding grain production since 1984.[38]

Continuing rapid growth of world population during the last few years combined with the reduced harvests has led to a record fall in per capita output of grain, the food source that accounts for half of world caloric intake when consumed directly and a sizable part of the remainder when consumed indirectly as meat, milk, and eggs. Between 1986 and 1988, production per person fell 14 percent, dropping back to the level of 1970. (See Figure 1-3.) Roughly 11 percent was offset by using carryover stocks of grain; the remaining 3 percent translates into reduced food intake, largely because of higher world grain prices.[39]

This reversal in humanity's agricultural fortunes has occurred rather abruptly. For those accustomed to reading as recently as early 1988 of "a world awash in grain," the latest downturn in grain output may come as a surprise. Although not widely recognized at the time, the impressive growth in world production following the doubling of world grain prices in 1973 was achieved in part by plowing highly erodible land, and in part by drawing down water tables through overpumping for irrigation.

Farmers can overplow and overpump with impressive results in the short run, but for many the short run is drawing to a close. The result is a worldwide retrenchment in cultivated area and a dramatic slowdown in the spread of irrigation. As highly erodible cropland brought under the plow during the agri-

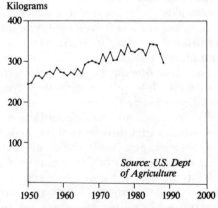

Kilograms

Source: U.S. Dept of Agriculture

Figure 1-3. World Grain Production Per Capita, 1950-88

cultural boom years of the seventies is taken out of cultivation, and as falling water tables in key food-producing countries force a reduction in irrigated area, the growth in world food output is slowing.[40]

In each of the past two years, world grain production has fallen sharply.

Evidence that environmental degradation in some regions is altering the food prospect and, in turn, the human prospect is unmistakable. In Africa, a deteriorating agricultural resource base, record population growth, and economic mismanagement lowered grain output per person throughout the seventies. During the eighties, mounting external debt reduced capital available for investment in agriculture, exacerbating the decline.[41]

The social effects of agricultural adversity are now becoming highly visible throughout the continent. In mid-1988, the World Bank reported that "both the proportion and the total number of Africans with deficient diets have climbed and will continue to rise unless special action is taken." The Bank went on to say that "barely a quarter of Africans are living in countries where food consumption was increasing in the 1980s, down considerably from about two-thirds in the 1970s."[42]

In Africa, the number of "food insecure" people, defined by the Bank as those not having enough food for normal health and physical activity, now totals over 100 million. Some 14.7 million Ethiopians, one third of the country, are undernourished. Nigeria is close behind, with 13.7 million undernourished people. The countries with 40 percent or more of their populations suffering from

chronic food insecurity are Chad, Mozambique, Somalia, and Uganda. (See Table 1–1.) The Bank summarized its findings by noting that "Africa's food situation is not only serious, it is deteriorating."[43]

The island of Madagascar, with a population of 11 million expanding by 3 percent per year, reveals in some detail how population growth and environmental deterioration are affecting people. As with the rest of Africa, per capita grain production peaked in 1967 and declined gradually until 1983, when the fall accelerated. Since then average grain consumption has fallen by nearly one fifth, pushing food intake below the survival level for many. Infant mortality, the most sensitive indicator of nutritional stress, rose from 75 to 133 per thousand between 1975 and 1985. Short of a mira-

Table 1-1. Food Insecurity in Selected African Countries, 1986

Country	Number of People	Share of Population
	(million)	(percent)
Ethiopia	14.7	34
Nigeria	13.7	13
Zaire	12.0	38
Tanzania	6.6	29
Kenya	6.2	29
Uganda	6.1	40
Mozambique	5.9	42
Algeria	4.1	18
Ghana	4.1	31
Sudan	3.4	15
Zambia	2.7	39
Mali	2.5	33
Chad	2.4	47
Morocco	2.4	11
Somalia	2.3	42

SOURCE: World Bank, *Report of the Task Force on Food Security in Africa* (Washington, D.C.: 1988); World Bank, *World Development Report 1988* (New York: Oxford University Press, 1988).

cle, the future of this country, with a birth rate among the world's highest and a rate of topsoil loss greater even than that of Ethiopia, is not bright.[44]

This deterioration is not limited to Africa. In Latin America, which exported more grain than North America did a mere half-century ago, per capita grain production has fallen 7 percent since reaching an all-time high in 1981. In its 1988 report "The Global State of Hunger and Malnutrition," the U.N.'s World Food Council reports that the share of malnourished preschoolers in Peru increased from 42 percent to 68 percent between 1980 and 1983. Infant deaths have risen in Brazil during the eighties. If recent trends in population growth, land degradation, and growth in external debt continue, Latin America's decline in food production per person will almost certainly continue into the nineties, increasing the number of hungry, malnourished people. The Council summarized its worldwide findings by noting that "earlier progress in fighting hunger, malnutrition and poverty has come to a halt or is being reversed in many parts of the world."[45]

When domestic food production is inadequate, the ability of countries to import becomes the key to food sufficiency. During the late eighties, low-income grain-deficit countries must contend not only with an increase in grain prices, but also in many cases with unmanageable external debt, which severely limits their expenditures on food imports. The World Bank nutrition survey of Africa just cited was based on data through 1986; since then, conditions have deteriorated further as world grain prices have climbed.[46]

The effect of higher grain prices on consumers is much greater in developing countries than in industrial ones. In the United States, for example, a $1 loaf of bread contains roughly 5¢ worth of wheat. If the price of wheat doubles, the price of the loaf would increase only to $1.05. In developing countries, however, where wheat is purchased in the market and ground into flour at home, a doubling of world grain prices translates into a doubling of prices to consumers. For those who already spend most of their income on food, such a rise can drive consumption below the survival level.[47]

For debt-ridden, food-deficit, low-income countries, higher world prices of wheat, rice, and corn mean lower consumption and more hunger. (See Table 1–2.) Higher corn prices will affect most directly corn-consuming countries in East Africa and Latin America. The rising price of rice will reduce caloric intake among the low-income populations of Asia, where 90 percent of the world's rice is consumed. The 1988 jump in the price of wheat, the principal grain used for food aid, will reduce the amount available from international development agencies.[48]

Already faced with a deteriorating food situation, the world is now confronted with climate change, an additional threat to food security. The

Table 1-2. World Grain Prices, July 1988, Compared With July 1987

Grain	July 1987	July 1988	Change
	(current dollars)		(percent)
Wheat (price per bushel)	2.85	4.07	+43
Rice (price per ton)	212	305	+44
Corn (price per bushel)	1.94	3.22	+66

SOURCE: International Monetary Fund, *International Financial Statistics* (Washington, D.C.: various months).

drought-damaged U.S. grain harvest in 1988, which fell below consumption for the first time in recent history, illustrates how global warming may affect agriculture over the longer term in the United States and elsewhere. With normal weather, the United States typically harvests more than 300 million tons of grain; Americans consume roughly 200 million tons and the rest is exported. Because this year's drought eliminated the share of harvest normally sold overseas, exports during the 1988–89 trade year will come entirely from reserves.[49]

As noted earlier, climate change will not affect all countries in the same way. The projected rise of 1.5–4.5 degrees Celsius (3–8 degrees Fahrenheit) is a global average, but temperatures are expected to increase much more in the middle and higher latitudes and more over land than over the oceans. They are projected to change little near the equator, while gains in the higher latitudes could easily be twice the anticipated global average. This uneven distribution will affect world agriculture disproportionately, since most food is produced in the middle and higher latitudes of the northern hemisphere.[50]

Though they remain sketchy, meteorological models suggest that two of the world's major food-producing regions—the North American agricultural heartland and a large area of central Asia—are likely to experience a decline in soil moisture during the summer growing season as a result of higher temperatures and increased evaporation. If the warming progresses as the models indicate, some of the land in the U.S. western Great Plains that now produces wheat would revert to rangeland. The western Corn Belt would become semiarid, with wheat or other drought-tolerant grains that yield 40 bushels per acre replacing corn that yields over 100 bushels.[51]

On the plus side, as temperatures increase the winter wheat belt might migrate northward, allowing winter strains that yield 40 bushels per acre to replace spring varieties yielding 30 bushels. A longer growing season would also permit a northward extension of spring wheat production into areas such as Canada's Alberta province, thus increasing that nation's cultivated area. On balance, though, higher temperatures and increased summer dryness will reduce the North American grain harvest, largely because of their negative impact on the all-important corn crop.

Drought, which afflicted most of the United States during the past summer, is essentially defined as dryness. For farmers, drought conditions can result from lower than normal rainfall, higher than normal temperatures, or both. When higher temperatures accompany below-normal rainfall, as they did during the summer of 1988, crop yields can fall precipitously. Extreme heat can also interfere with the pollination of crops. Corn pollination can easily be impaired by uncommonly high temperatures during the 10-day period when fertilization occurs, usually in July.[52]

A study from the National Center for Atmospheric Research in Boulder, Colorado, suggests that a rise in average temperatures will also increase the probability of extreme short-term heat waves. If these occur at critical times—such as the corn pollination period—they can have a much greater effect on crop yields than the relatively modest average temperature increase of a few degrees might indicate.[53]

This vulnerability of corn, which accounts for two thirds of the U.S. grain harvest and one eighth of the world's, can cause wide year-to-year swings in the world grain crop. An examination of U.S. corn yields since 1950 shows five sharply reduced harvests over the last 38 years. (See Figure 1–4.) The only pronounced drops before the eighties came

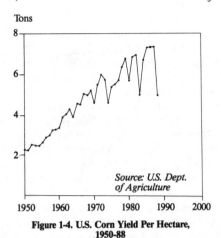

Figure 1-4. U.S. Corn Yield Per Hectare, 1950-88

in 1970, from an outbreak of corn blight, and in 1974, when a wet spring and late planting combined with an early frost to destroy a part of the crop before it matured.[54]

Three harvests since 1950 have been sharply reduced by drought, all in the eighties. Each drop has been worse than the last. Compared with the preceding year, the 1980 corn yield per hectare was down by 17 percent, that in 1983 was down by 28 percent, and that in 1988 by a staggering 34 percent.[55]

These three reduced harvests each occurred during one of the five warmest years globally of the last century. There is no way to conclusively link the drought-depressed U.S. harvests with the global warming, since annual weather variability is so much greater than the rise in average global temperatures measured during the eighties.[56]

Among other things, the prospect of climate change increases uncertainty over future harvests, making decisions more complicated for farmers and policymakers alike. For example, the 1989 U.S. grain crop could be a bin-buster, the largest ever harvested. With a normal harvest elsewhere in the world, this would permit at least a modest rebuilding of depleted grain reserves.

Judging by the historical record, the odds are against severe back-to-back droughts, but with the warming now apparently under way, hot dry summers will become more frequent. In the event of another disastrous drought, U.S. grain exports would drop dramatically. The world would face a food emergency for which there is no precedent in the decades since North America emerged as its breadbasket. There would be a desperate effort to corner available supplies as world grain prices soared to record levels. In such a situation, preventing starvation among the world's poor would require affluent countries to reduce the amount of grain fed to livestock.

Asian and African countries, in particular, would find it impossible to feed their people without North American grain. Many of the world's major cities—Leningrad, Cairo, Lagos, Caracas, and Tokyo, for example—depend largely on grain from the United States and Canada. In an integrated world food economy, all countries suffer the consequences of poor harvests.[57]

All available evidence indicates that the ranks of the hungry are expanding during the late eighties, reversing the trend of recent decades. Uncertainties and stresses from a changing climate are now being overlaid upon an already tightening food situation. In the absence of a major commitment by governments to slow population growth and strengthen agriculture, food insecurity and the social instability associated with it will preoccupy the political leaders of many countries during the nineties.

WORLD WITHOUT BORDERS

The global commons—the oceans, the atmosphere, and tropical forests—are now at risk. Ozone depletion, climate change, and oceanic pollution simply cannot be solved at the national level. Indeed, a world in which countries go their own way may not be worth living in. Whereas the seventies were marked by a series of national laws to address environmental problems, the nineties may well be marked by comparable initiatives at the international level.

One encouraging sign is that the North-South tensions that pervaded the United Nations and other international forums in the seventies have begun to ease. Industrial-country leaders recognize their interest in and responsibility for participating in sustainable development. And developing countries increasingly see their stake in environmental protection.

East-West differences are also being bridged. The Soviet Union has proposed a major strengthening of international institutions to deal with global problems. Addressing the U.N. General Assembly in September 1988, Soviet Foreign Minister Eduard Shevardnadze stated that "the dividing lines of the bipolar world are receding. The biosphere recognizes no division into blocs, alliances or systems. All share the same climatic system." Western leaders, still startled by the fading of Soviet intransigence, are daring to dream of a more unified world community. Protecting the biosphere is a new channel for the vast energies now directed to the cold war rivalry.[58]

Scientific cooperation is one aspect of environmental protection that has advanced in recent years. Most notable is the International Geosphere-Biosphere Program, also known as the Global Change Program. Established in 1986, it is intended to deepen understanding of the physical, chemical, and biological forces that affect the biosphere, using more extensive national monitoring, satellite reconnaissance, and advanced computer modeling. Although several countries are now actively participating in this program, funding commitments have lagged and need to be increased. Heightened awareness of these problems is likely to give the Global Change Program a boost.[59]

International environmental cooperation has come furthest in Western Europe, where a score of countries are squeezed into a small area and trade pollutants back and forth across their borders via winds and rivers. Much of the region's environmental regulation is now done under the auspices of the European Economic Community.

Protecting the biosphere is a new channel for the vast energies now directed to the cold war rivalry.

Production and trade of toxic substances in Western Europe is already regulated by the community. Automobile emission limits were also recently approved by the European Parliament, though further negotiations are required before their final shape is clear. Also, the European Commission is considering an environmental freedom-of-information proposal, ensuring public access to key environmental facts. When most of the remaining economic barriers in Western Europe are torn down in 1992, environmental cooperation will need to be strengthened.[60]

The world community as a whole has also moved forward in protecting the atmosphere. During the seventies, it became clear that air pollution was crossing borders and damaging forests. While countries are reluctant to make major investments to protect their neighbors' environments, all now have an interest in these kinds of agreements. Indeed, for Canadians and Scandinavians, imported air pollution has become a major foreign policy consideration. (See Chapter 8.)

In 1979, a U.N.-sponsored Convention on Long-Range Transboundary Air Pollution was agreed to by 35 countries in Eastern and Western Europe and North America. Its first concrete result was the Protocol on the Reduction of Sulfur Emissions, signed in 1985 by 21 nations. By 1986, as noted earlier, 10 nations had met the 30-percent reduction goal set for 1993, and 4 had committed to 70-percent cuts. A similar agreement to freeze nitrogen oxide emissions at 1987 levels was signed by 24 nations in 1988.[61]

In each of these agreements, scientific evidence sparked the process, but action was fueled by nations willing to make unilateral commitments. Concerned officials then grasped at the most readily available institution. Already, members of the Transboundary Air Pollution Convention are monitoring other pollutants with an eye to regulating them as well. However, without stricter enforcement and the participation of more countries, air pollution will continue to worsen.[62]

The world's oceans are another global commons needing international protection. The activities of one country can endanger the open ocean as well as the coastal ecosystems of other nations. Water pollution, ocean dumping of waste materials, and overfishing are among the threats.

On April 30, 1982, after 10 years of negotiations, the Convention on the Law of the Sea was signed by 119 nations, 35 of which have ratified it. Although 22 countries, including the Soviet Union and the United States, refused to sign, the Law of the Sea has already improved the way oceans are managed. It is in effect a constitution for the oceans, stating that the oceans are "the common heritage of mankind," ensuring free navigation and limiting actions that despoil the seas. It provides a framework for future international agreements to protect this global resource.[63]

Central to the Law of the Sea are the 200-mile exclusive economic zones created around coastal nations, giving them the legal authority and international obligation to manage their coastal resources effectively. These now encompass 40 percent of the world's ocean area, and have led, for example, to a cut in the Northwest Atlantic cod catch by long-range fleets of at least 90 percent. The Law of the Sea also calls for national laws that reduce ocean dumping. Additional, stricter regulations of pollution are needed if oceanic resources are to be protected from the bewildering profusion of new toxic chemicals. The next decade will likely see a continuation of the growing array of oceanic agreements, some connected to the Law of the Sea, and others independent.[64]

The international community also has a critical role to play in protecting the ozone layer. (See Chapter 5.) Although the United States and Scandinavian countries limited some uses of ozone-damaging chlorofluorocarbons as early as the mid-seventies, attempts to address the problem began in earnest in the eighties. As scientific evidence mounted, the United Nations Environment Programme led the effort to create the Vienna Convention for the Protection of the Ozone Layer, adopted in 1985 to provide a mechanism for CFC controls.[65]

Spurred by a dramatic annual thinning of the ozone over Antarctica, the United States led the push for CFC controls while the British and Japanese held back in favor of "economic caution." A middle position favored by West Germany and the Netherlands carried the day. In 1987, the Montreal Protocol was established and has now been signed by 35 countries. It freezes CFC production at 1986 levels and calls for a 50-percent cut by 1998 in industrial countries, but allows for some increases in the developing world. It has already become clear that this is not enough. The convention permits negotiations on stricter limits, preparations for which are being made.[66]

Climate change is fast becoming the next arena for international environmental agreement, and solutions to the problem may have to break new institutional ground. Indeed, if climate change is to be minimized, international action may have to precede rather than follow national actions. Already, business and political leaders are arguing against stringent national policies on the grounds that by themselves such actions would hardly make a difference. This is particularly true for small nations that feel impotent in the face of global changes over which they have only a tiny influence.

The first step is scientific cooperation. The International Council of Scientific Unions and the World Meteorological Organization are coordinating international research on climate change. At a November 1987 meeting in Bellagio, Italy, consensus was reached about the need for action. Policy discussions began in earnest in June 1988 at a world conference on The Changing Atmosphere: Implications for Global Security, held in Toronto. Sponsored by the Canadian government, the meeting included the prime ministers of Canada and Norway and the top environmental officials of other countries. The final statement said that carbon emissions should be reduced by 20 percent by 2005.[67]

If such goals are to be achieved, an international treaty will probably be needed. The Montreal Protocol and the Convention on Long-Range Transboundary Air Pollution provide useful models, but for a global warming treaty to be effective it must be far broader in scope and include additional nations.

Some have called for an international "Law of the Atmosphere" parallel to the Law of the Sea.[68]

Such a treaty must deal both with industrial countries that have caused much of the problem so far and developing ones whose use of energy is growing rapidly and adding to global warming. Developing countries argue convincingly that if they are going to vastly improve efficiency and reforest millions of hectares, they will need funding from richer nations.

If climate change is to be minimized, international action may have to precede rather than follow national actions.

At the U.N. General Assembly in the fall of 1988, a host of ministers and ambassadors drew attention to global warming and the need for the world community to address it. The Maltese Ambassador called for a major U.N. study on climate and the development of a global strategy. Cyprus suggested a special session on the environment, and the Soviet Union called for turning the U.N. Environment Programme into an Environmental Council that can take effective actions to ensure ecological security.[69]

As with other issues, unilateral commitments by individual countries may be the leadership spark needed to ignite international agreement. The governments of Canada, the Netherlands, and Norway are among those committed to international negotiations on global warming. The Soviet Union has expressed interest in it, and U.S. resistance is fading. Some have compared the scope of such negotiations to those of strategic arms talks. Indeed, similar approaches may have to be applied. For example, it may make sense to set up permanent negotiating teams in Geneva as a way to introduce and discuss approaches raised by various governments.[70]

The next step is to move beyond agreements on CFCs, the oceans, and climate change to a more comprehensive rescue plan for the global environment. Among the issues now ripe for discussion of new international conventions or protocols are the preservation of biodiversity, the slowing of deforestation, and perhaps even family planning. This will require a strengthening of international institutions and a willingness to give up unilateral authority in some areas. Today these institutions are often fragmented and ineffective in dealing with global problems. But just as national governments themselves first emerged as tentative and weak efforts to unite diverse tribes or city-states, so international institutions may one day become far more robust and central to the issues of our time.

The year 1988 was marked by a series of important steps in what Richard Gardner, professor of international law at Columbia University, has termed "practical internationalism." The United Nations played a central role in resolving major conflicts in the Middle East, Afghanistan, and southern Africa. (See Chapter 8.) In each case, the warring parties recognized that they had more to gain from peace than from further bloodshed. But the United Nations made the peace process work. In just recognition, U.N. Peacekeeping Forces were awarded the 1988 Nobel Peace Prize.[71]

A strengthening of the U.N. system, providing it with more reliable sources of revenue and clearer lines of authority, will be essential. Already, the world is moving in this direction. During 1988, both the Soviet Union and the United States began to settle large debts to the United Nations. And Japan has indicated a willingness to fund major new multilateral initiatives. At the same time, the United Nations has played a critical role in everything from the fight against AIDS (see Chapter 7) to the cease-fire in the Iran-Iraq war.[72]

Maurice Strong, the first head of the U.N. Environment Programme, has pointed out that the world faces the challenge of developing effective mechanisms for governance, or management, at the international level: "People have learned to enlarge the circles of their allegiance and their loyalty, as well as the institutions through which they are governed, from the family to the tribe to the village to the town to the city to the nation state. We are now called upon to make the next and final step, at least on this planet, to the global level."[73]

This does not mean an end to national governments. Just as people did not give up allegiance to family or town when nation-states were created, so national governments can exist within a strengthened world community. The solutions to many problems are close to home— often within a local government or grassroots organization. All these levels of human organization can continue and even thrive as international cooperation is expanded.

The era of superpower dominance of a bipolar world is rapidly fading, and perhaps with it the notion that one or two "great powers" can ever preside over the complex, multifaceted, problem-ridden world in which we now find ourselves. Looming threats to the world's climate and the undermining of other global commons may soon make the transition to stronger international institutions inevitable. As Prime Minister Brundtland of Norway stated at the 1988 Toronto Conference, "Now it is time to take a giant leap forward in the upgrading of civilization."[74]

2

Halting Land Degradation

Sandra Postel

Major droughts in Africa, China, India, and North America over the last four years have spotlighted an immutable reality for much of the world: despite a myriad of sophisticated technologies and scientific advances, humanity's welfare remains tightly linked to the land. Millions in these drought-stricken regions have watched their economic futures—or, in the worst cases, their chances for survival—fade. For the first time in more than a decade, global food security has come into question. (See Chapter 3.)

While these headline-making events ignite concern for a few weeks or months, the true tragedy goes unnoticed. Much of the world's food-producing land is being sapped insidiously of its productive potential through overuse, lack of care, or unwise treatment—a process scientists call "desertification." While the term conjures up images of the Sahara spreading beyond its bounds to engulf new territories, its most worrisome aspects are less dramatic. Desertification refers broadly to the impover-

ishment of the land by human activities. Perhaps a more appropriate term is land degradation, which in this chapter is used interchangeably with desertification.[1]

Each year, irreversible desertification claims an estimated 6 million hectares worldwide—a land area nearly twice the size of Belgium lost beyond practical hope of reclamation. An additional 20 million hectares annually become so impoverished that they are unprofitable to farm or graze. Most of the affected land, however, lies on the degradation continuum, somewhere between fully productive and hopelessly degraded. Unfortunately, much of it is sliding down the diminishing productivity side of the scale.[2]

Although the technologies to restore resilience and fertility to stressed lands exist, so far the political will does not. The majority of people affected are poor farmers and pastoralists living at society's margins and lacking a political voice. A lasting victory over land degradation will remain a distant dream without social and economic reforms that give rural people the security of tenure and access to resources they need to improve the land. And with degradation rooted in excessive human pressures, slowing population growth lies at the heart of any effective strategy.

Land degradation may be difficult to rally around and adopt as a cause. Yet its consequences—worsened droughts and floods, famine, declining living standards, and swelling numbers of environmental refugees—could not be more real or engender more emotion. A world of 5.1 billion people, growing by 86 million each year, cannot afford to be losing the productivity of its food base. Without good land, humanity quite literally has nothing to grow on.

LANDS AND PEOPLE AT RISK

More than a decade has passed since government representatives from around the world gathered at the United Nations Conference on Desertification. Held in 1977 in Nairobi, Kenya, the meeting followed on the heels of a devastating drought that struck much of western and north-central Africa from 1968 through 1973. It focused the world's attention for the first time on the problems and prospects of fragile lands.

Out of Nairobi came a Plan of Action to Combat Desertification, which recommended 28 measures that national, regional, and international institutions could take to halt land deterioration around the world. Sadly, the action plan never got off the ground, a victim of inadequate funding and lack of sustained commitment by governments. When severe drought and famine repeated themselves in Africa in 1983 and 1984, again bringing tragedy, Canadian

meteorologist F. Kenneth Hare remarked grimly: "It is alarming that ten years later . . . the news stories should be so familiar."[3]

Seven years after the Nairobi conference, the United Nations Environment Programme (UNEP) took a more careful look at the overall status and trends of desertification worldwide. This included sending a questionnaire to 91 countries with lands at risk. These data—incomplete, sketchy, and lacking in geographic detail though they are—remain the best available and are more than sufficient to grasp the severity of the problem.

According to UNEP's 1984 assessment, 4.5 billion hectares, or 35 percent of the earth's land surface, are threatened by desertification. Of this total—on which a fifth of humanity makes its living—three fourths has already been at least moderately degraded. (See Table 2–1.) Fully one third has already lost more than 25 percent of its productive potential.

What lies behind these numbers is a deteriorating relationship between people and the land that supports them (see Table 2–2), a situation all the more tragic because people themselves are not only degradation's victims but its unwitting agents. The four principal causes of land degradation—overgrazing on rangelands, overcultivation of croplands, waterlogging and salinization of irrigated lands, and deforestation—all stem from excessive human pressures or poor management of the land.

Rangelands and the animals that graze them play an important role in the global food supply. The 3 billion cattle, sheep, goats, and camels that roam the world's pastures can do something humans cannot: they convert lignocellulose—a main product of photosynthesis that is indigestible to humans—into meat and milk that provide the human population with high-quality protein. Shifts to livestock fed on grain or forage have diminished

Table 2-1. Status of Desertification in the World's Drylands, 1983–84[1]

Land-Use Category	Area at Least Moderately Degraded	Share of Category at Least Moderately Degraded	Area Annually Deteriorating to Level of Zero Net Economic Return
	(million hectares)	(percent)	(million hectares)
Rangelands	3,100	84	17.7
Rainfed Croplands	335	59	2.0
Irrigated Land	40	31	0.6
All Three Categories	3,475	77	20.3

[1]Drylands includes the arid, semiarid, and subhumid climatic zones.
SOURCES: United Nations Environment Programme, *General Assessment of Progress in the Implementation of the Plan of Action to Combat Desertification* (New York: United Nations, 1984); annual deterioration from H.E. Dregne, *Desertification of Arid Lands* (New York: Harwood Academic Publishers, 1983).

dependence on grazing animals in some regions. But in much of Africa and the Middle East, and in parts of India and Latin America, roaming ruminants still underpin subsistence economies and support millions of pastoralist families.[4]

Degradation on rangelands mainly takes the form of a deterioration in the quality and, eventually, the quantity of vegetation as a result of overgrazing. As the size of livestock herds surpasses the carrying capacity of perennial grasses on the range, less palatable annual grasses and shrubs move in. If overgrazing and trampling continue, plant cover of all types begins to diminish, leaving the land exposed to the ravages of wind and water. In the severest stages, the soil forms a crust as animal hooves trample nearly bare ground, and erosion accelerates. The formation of large gullies or sand dunes signals that desertification can claim another victory.[5]

Ironically, years of abundant rainfall—seemingly beneficial to pastoral peoples—can often sow the seeds of further degradation and hardship. During wetter periods the area suitable for grazing expands, leading pastoralists to increase the sizes of their herds as insurance against another drought. When the next

dry spell hits, the number of livestock exceeds what the reduced area of grass can sustain. The result is overgrazing and accelerated land degradation, a pattern most visible in Africa, where more than half the world's livestock-dependent people live.[6]

Livestock watering holes, a popular feature of international development projects, have contributed to rangeland desertification as well. Cattle cannot go more than three days without water, so digging water holes to sustain herds during dry seasons seems logical. But the concentration of livestock around the watering points leads to severe localized overgrazing, which gradually spreads outward from this central area. When drought strikes again, the animals rarely will die from thirst, but rather from lack of forage.[7]

For more than two decades, farmers in south-central Niger have lamented in Hausa to development workers that *kasar mu, ta gaji,* "the land is tired." Peasants in western parts of the country strike a more ominous chord in Zarma with *laabu, y bu,* "the land is dead." The phrases aptly depict land suffering from overcultivation, which now affects at least 335 million hectares of rainfed

Table 2-2. Observations of Land Degradation, Selected Countries and Regions

Country/Source	Observation
Mali Patricia A. Jacobberger, geologist, Smithsonian Institution, 1986	"On the Landsat maps, there is now—and there wasn't in 1976—a bright ring of soil around villages. Those areas are now 90% devoid of vegetation, the topsoil is gone, and the surface is disrupted and cracked."
Mauritania Sidy Gaye, *Ambio,* 1987	"There were only 43 sand-storms in the whole country between 1960 and 1970. The number increased tenfold in the following decade, and in . . . 1983 alone a record 240 sandstorms darkened the nation's skies."
Tunisia UNEP, 1987	"Rangelands have been overgrazed with three heads of cattle where only one could thrive . . . Two-thirds of the land area of Tunisia is being eaten away by desertification."
China *Beijing Review,* interview with Zhu Zhenda, Chinese Academy of Sciences, 1988	"Unless urgent measures are taken, desertification will erode an additional 75,300 square kilometers . . . by the year 2000, more than twice the area of Taiwan.'"
Indonesia Ronald Greenberg and M.L. Higgins, U.S. AID Jakarta, 1987	"Thirty-six watersheds . . . have critical erosion problems. . . . In Kalimantan, the silt load in streams has increased 33 fold in some logging areas."
Thailand D. Phantumvanit and K.S. Sathirathai, Thailand Development Research Board, 1988	"The pace of deforestation has been accelerating since the early 1900s, but it has moved into a higher gear since the 1960s . . . [Between 1961 and 1986,] Thailand lost about 45 percent of its forests."
Brazil Mac Margolis, interview with geologist Helio Penha, *Washington Post,* February 1988	"Every year, rains slash deeper into the bared soil, dumping tons of silt in waterways, causing rivers to overflow into the city's streets. Now 'people flee the drought in the Northeast only to die in floods in Rio'."

SOURCE: Worldwatch Institute, based on various sources.

cropland worldwide (excluding the humid regions), more than a third of the global total.[8]

Agricultural land left without vegetative cover or situated on steeply sloping hillsides is subject to the erosive power of wind and rainwater. An inch of soil takes anywhere from 200 to 1,000 years to form; under the most erosive conditions, that same soil can be swept off the land in just a few seasons. Erosion saps the land's productivity because most of the organic matter and nutrients are in the upper layers of soil. According to one estimate, about half the fertilizer applied to U.S. farmland each year is replacing soil nutrients lost through erosion. In addition, erosion degrades the soil's structure and diminishes its water-holding capacity. As a result, crops have less moisture available to them, which, especially in drier regions, is often erosion's most damaging effect.[9]

Only a handful of countries have attempted to estimate their rates of soil loss in any detail, so the magnitude of the problem worldwide is difficult to gauge in other than broad terms. (See Chapter 3.) One useful measure is the load of earth materials carried to the sea by rivers and streams. This figure totals at least 20.3 billion tons per year, which includes 15.3 billion tons of suspended sediment, 4 billion of dissolved material, and 1 billion of coarser bed load. Since this accounts only for material reaching the sea—and excludes, for instance, sediment trapped behind dams—it underestimates the total amount of soil lost from the land.[10]

A look at the geographic distribution of these sediment loads gives a quick sense of where severe erosion is taking place. (See Table 2-3.) A 1987 expedition of the internationally sponsored Ocean Drilling Program estimated that the Ganges and Brahmaputra rivers on the Indian subcontinent transport 3 billion tons of sediment to the Bay of Bengal each year, far more than any other river system. The sediment fan on the floor of the bay now spans 3 million square kilometers. Much of that sediment originates in the Himalayas, where

Table 2-3. Annual Sediment Load Transported to the Sea
by Major Rivers, Early Eighties

River System	Country/Region	Drainage Area	Annual Suspended Sediment Load
		(thousand square kilometers)	(million tons)
Ganges-Brahmaputra	South Asia	1,480	3,000
Huang He (Yellow)	China	770	1,080
Amazon	South America	6,150	900
Chang Jiang (Yangtze)	China	1,940	478
Irrawaddy	Burma	430	265
Magdalena	Colombia	240	220
Mississippi	United States	3,270	210
Orinoco	Venezuela	990	210

SOURCES: D.E. Walling, "Rainfall, Runoff and Erosion of the Land: A Global View," in K.J. Gregory, ed., *Energetics of Physical Environment* (New York: John Wiley & Sons, 1987); Ganges-Brahmaputra sediment load figure from Ocean Drilling Program, news release, Texas A&M University, College Station, September 4, 1987.

deforestation and cultivation of steep slopes in recent decades has added to millions of years of massive erosion from natural geologic activity.[11]

In China, the Huang He (Yellow River), with a drainage area half that of the Ganges-Brahmaputra system, carries more than a billion tons of sediment to the sea each year. About half of it comes from the Loess Plateau, in the Huang He's middle reaches, among the most water-eroded areas on earth. Deeply cut gullies and denuded hillsides span 430,-000 square kilometers, and erosion rates average some 65 tons per hectare annually.[12]

Today roughly one third of the world's food is grown on the 18 percent of cropland that is irrigated. Irrigated fields typically yield two to three times more than those watered only by rain, and, because crops are protected from the ravages of drought, provide a crucial degree of food security.[13]

Unfortunately, poor irrigation practices have degraded much of this valuable cropland. Over time, seepage from canals and overwatering of fields cause the underlying water table to rise. In the absence of adequate drainage, water eventually enters the root zone, damaging crops. Farmers belonging to a large irrigation project in the Indian state of Madhya Pradesh have referred to their once fertile fields as "wet deserts."[14]

In dry regions, salinization usually accompanies waterlogging as moisture near the surface evaporates, leaving behind a layer of salt that is toxic to plants. An aerial view of severely salinized fields can give the impression they are covered with snow. UNEP's assessment placed the irrigated area damaged by salinization at 40 million hectares.[15]

About half of the affected area is in India and Pakistan, but other regions suffering from salinization's effects include the Tigris and Euphrates basins in Syria and Iraq, California's San Joaquin Valley, the Colorado River basin, China's North Plain, and Soviet central Asia. In the Soviet republic of Turkmen, the government blamed salinization for a cotton harvest shortfall of one third in 1985. Meanwhile, another salinity threat has struck Soviet central Asia: because so much irrigation water is being siphoned off from the two major rivers flowing into the Aral Sea, the sea's surface area has shrunk by 40 percent since 1960 and its volume has dropped by two thirds. Winds picking up dried salt from the basin are now annually dumping some 43 million tons of it on more than 15 million hectares of cropland and pasture surrounding the shrinking sea.[16]

The last major cause of degradation—deforestation—cuts across all land use types. By accelerating soil erosion and reducing the soil's water-absorbing capacity, deforestation often accentuates the effects of overcultivation and overgrazing. Moreover, though forest clearing in humid regions was not included in UNEP's desertification assessment, in many cases it results in a net decline in the productivity of land. Most of the nutrients supporting moist tropical forests are held in the vegetation, so forest clearing removes them as well. Having lost its inherent fertility, the land cannot long support intensive agriculture. Large areas of pasture and cropland that replaced tropical forest in the Brazilian Amazon, for example, have been abandoned.

The U.N. Food and Agriculture Organization (FAO) estimates that each year 11.3 million hectares of tropical forest are lost through the combined action of land clearing for crop production, fuelwood gathering, and cattle ranching. Recent satellite data from Brazil, however, indicate that 8 million hectares of forest were cleared in 1987 in the Brazilian Amazon alone—strongly suggesting that the widely cited FAO figure is far too low. Some portion of deforested land goes into sustainable land uses—such as traditional shifting cultivation, which includes a fallow period that restores the land's fertility—but the bulk of it does not. In the tropics today, deforestation usually translates into land degradation.[17]

UNEARTHING DEGRADATION'S TRUE CAUSES

Desertification's direct causes—overgrazing, overcultivation, salinization, and deforestation—are easy to enumerate, but only by grappling with the complex web of conditions leading to these excessive pressures is there hope of stopping desertification's spread. Though they vary greatly from place to place, these underlying forces generally are rooted in population densities greater than the land can sustain and, more fundamentally, in social and economic inequities that push people into marginal environments and vulnerable livelihoods.

The number of people a given land area can support—what scientists call its carrying capacity—depends on climatic factors, the land's inherent productivity, the products it yields, and the methods used to increase its productivity. Though carrying capacity is difficult to measure accurately, few pieces of data are more crucial to wise development planning or tell more about the threat of desertification.

In response to mounting concern about environmental deterioration in West Africa, the World Bank set up a special working group led by Jean Eugene Gorse to study the problem in more detail. Gorse's group focused on a band of seven countries in what are known as the Sahelian and Sudanian zones: Burkina Faso, Chad, Gambia, Mali, Mauritania, Niger, and Senegal. In these countries, annual rainfall increases from north to south—from less than 200 millimeters (mm) in the northernmost zone to more than 800 mm in the southernmost—and so, consequently, does the carrying capacity of traditional farming and livestock practices. The study found that in two out of the five east-west trending zones, the rural population in 1980 had already exceeded that for which the land could sustainably provide sufficient food. Only in the southernmost band could the land withstand a substantial increase in human numbers.[18]

Even more important, wood resources emerged as the limiting factor in the carrying capacity of every zone in the region. Indeed, the 1980 population of all seven countries collectively exceeded the number of people the region's wood resources could support by 10.1 million. This finding is critical to development strategies because it means that efforts to raise the carrying capacity of the cropping and livestock systems will not increase the total population this land can sustain until more trees are planted, the efficiency of wood-burning is increased greatly, or some other means is found of meeting energy needs.[19]

Not surprisingly, this imbalance between what the land can sustainably yield and the numbers of people living on it has led to pervasive desertification. Virtually all the rangeland and an estimated 82 percent of the rainfed cropland in those same seven countries is already at least moderately degraded. Moreover, with a projected population in the year 2000 of 55 million—a 77-percent increase over the 1980 total—pressures on the land will increase markedly, and land productivity is bound to fall even further.[20]

Similarly, in India, growth in the human and animal populations, both of which have doubled since 1950, has outstripped the sustainable production levels of the nation's fuelwood and fodder resources. Estimated fuelwood and fodder demands in the early eighties exceeded available supplies by 70 and 23 percent, respectively. As a result, overgrazing and deforestation have led to extensive degradation. Out of an estimated 266 million hectares of potentially productive land, 94 million (35 percent) suffer varying degrees of degradation from water erosion, wind erosion, or salinization. Of the 75 million hectares of forestland, 40 million are degraded—30 million lacking tree cover and 10 million having only shrubs—and satellite data show that the nation continues to lose forests at the rate of 1.3 million hectares per year.[21]

In the Philippines, agrarian policy has promoted land resettlement rather than redistribution.

Next to population pressures, perhaps no other factors foster more degradation than the inequitable distribution of land and the absence of secure land tenure. In an agrarian society, keeping a disproportionate share of land in the hands of a few forces the poorer majority to compete for the limited area left, severely compromising their ability to manage sustainably what land they do have.

In the Philippines, for example, agrarian policy over the last several decades has promoted land resettlement rather than redistribution. The elite retained their holdings while landless peasants were encouraged to move to designated resettlement areas. One such area was in Palawan, the country's largest province. Incoming migrants cleared forest to grow crops, but the land could not long sustain production under the methods they used; weeds invaded, farmers abandoned their fields, and new lands were cleared.[22]

The government had made no provisions to protect the land rights of Palawan's indigenous communities, and so as migrant farmers moved in, the local farmers—who had developed sustainable agricultural practices—were forced to retreat to the interior hills. Their plots on the steep slopes yielded only half as much as their lowland fields had. As a result, fallow periods crucial to restoring the land's fertility were shortened from eight years to two, thereby exhausting the soil and further depressing yields.[23]

Similar scenarios have played out in numerous countries where striking inequities in land holdings compound population pressures. About 44 percent of South African blacks are forced to live in the "Bantu homelands," which have an average population density of 79 people per square kilometer compared with 15.5 people per square kilometer in the rest of the country. Much of the land set aside for the native people is not even arable, yet the majority of them are subsistence farmers. As John Hanks of the World Wide Fund for Nature says, "it is hardly surprising that these areas have some of the worst cases of overgrazing, deforestation, and soil erosion in the whole of the African continent."[24]

The flip side of the unequal distribution of land is lack of secure land tenure. Since land is often needed as collateral, farmers without titles to property have difficulty getting the loans they need to invest in their land's productivity, and as a result often abandon worn-out fields for less-degraded new land. Lack of secure tenure pervades much of the Third World. In Thailand, for example, only about 20 percent of all private land had title deeds as of 1985, and an estimated 500,000 farm families were landless.[25]

In many areas, these problems are aggravated by the denial of social and economic rights to women. In Africa, women grow 80 percent of the food their families eat, and, with their children's help, collect the water and wood their households need for cooking and heating. Yet despite their crucial role in the agrarian economy, women rarely have property rights or even access to their husbands' incomes. Extension services and training programs usually are directed toward men, even though it is the women who till the fields. Because women lack the resources needed to improve their farms' productivity, the land—and the families living on it—suffers.[26]

Unless existing land distribution patterns change, the number of smallholder and landless families in the developing world will grow by nearly 30 percent by the year 2000—to a total of 220 million households. Without access to secure property, credit, and extension services, these rural people will have no choice but to overuse the land and to farm areas that should not be cultivated.[27]

Finally, national land use policies foster degradation as well. For example, the governments of Brazil and Indonesia—supported by World Bank loans—have sponsored resettlement programs that encourage people to clear tropical forest to create new cropland, even though that land will only sustain cropping for a few years. During the mid-seventies, U.S. officials encouraged the plowing up of grassland to expand crop production in response to higher world grain prices, even though much of that land would experience soil erosion reminiscent of the Dust Bowl days. And numerous governments and development institutions have supported irrigation projects without adequate attention to drainage, even though the problem of salinization dates back at least to ancient Mesopotamia. Whether they reflect a profound igno-

rance of the land or simply a lack of concern for its long-term health, such misguided policies produce the same unfortunate result: more degraded land.[28]

DROUGHT, DESERTIFICATION, AND THE HYDROLOGICAL CYCLE

A natural phenomenon, droughts come and go with unpredictable regularity. They are the bane of a farmer's existence, for without sufficient water, agricultural land will bear only a meager harvest at best no matter how deep and fertile the topsoil, how high-yielding the variety of seed, or how well-tended the farmer's field. Human activities are now altering the hydrological cycle—on global, regional, and local scales—in ways that have profound implications for future food production and the long-term productivity of the land.

There now seems little doubt that global warming from the long-hypothesized "greenhouse effect" has begun. (See Chapter 1.) Since a warmer atmosphere will hold more moisture, average precipitation worldwide is expected to increase by 7 to 11 percent from the temperature rise associated with a doubling of preindustrial levels of atmospheric carbon dioxide. But higher evaporation rates and changing circulation patterns mean that some regions—including, possibly, the North American grain belt—will experience a reduction in soil moisture available for plant growth, if not an absolute reduction in rainfall. Models suggest that severe droughts, such as occurred in the North American heartland in 1988, could strike more frequently. If so, long-term average production and reliable crop output will de-

State of the World 1989

cline until adjustments in irrigation patterns and cropping systems—which will be enormously expensive and take decades to complete—are put in place.[29]

For good reason, climate change now commands higher priority in the halls of governments, in research institutes, and on the international environmental agenda. Far less attention, however, is being devoted to a less dramatic but equally serious change in the earth's physical condition: alterations in the hydrological cycle as a result of land degradation.

The Sahel had just gone through six dry years when Massachusetts Institute of Technology meteorologist J.G. Charney put forth the idea in 1975 that the removal of vegetation in dry regions could cause rainfall to diminish because of an increase in the albedo, the share of sunlight reflected back from the earth. Desert sands and bare rock, for example, have higher albedos than grassland, which in turn reflects more sunlight than a dense forest does. According to Charney's hypothesis, less of the sun's radiation is absorbed at the earth's surface as albedo increases, so surface temperatures drop. This in turn fosters greater subsidence, or sinking motion in the atmosphere. Since subsiding air is dry, rainfall would decline. The degraded area would feed on itself, becoming ever more desert-like.[30]

Tests of Charney's hypothesis using climate models generally confirmed it: large increases in albedo did indeed reduce rainfall. Less clear, however, was how smaller changes in reflectivity would affect rainfall and whether the patchy pattern of desertification could produce albedo changes sufficient to affect rainfall levels.

Another worrisome link surfaced from the modeling studies of J. Shukla and Y. Mintz. They examined the effects on rainfall of changes in evapotranspiration, the transfer of water vapor from the land surface to the atmosphere through evaporation or transpiration by plants. For evapotranspiration to occur, the soil must be sufficiently moist and vegetation must be present to bring that moisture into contact with the air. Presumably if evapotranspiration is an important source of atmospheric water vapor in a given locale, rainfall levels could decline if it diminishes. Shukla and Mintz found just that, although, as with Charney's study, their findings pertained to changes of a large magnitude and wide extent. Once again, land degradation—by diminishing the vegetative cover needed for evapotranspiration—was linked to climatic change.[31]

Meanwhile, meteorologist Sharon Nicholson was analyzing rainfall data from roughly 300 sites in some 20 countries of Africa. She calculated a long-term average from data covering 1901–74, and then calculated the annual percentage departures from that long-term average for 1901–84. Between 1967 and 1984, the region experienced 17 consecutive years of below-normal rainfall, by far the longest series of consecutive sub-par rains in the 84-year record. Annual rainfall in 1983 and 1984 fell more than 40 percent short of the long-term average. Interestingly, Nicholson also analyzed northern sub-Saharan rainfall levels according to three east-west trending zones and found that drought was most persistent in the northern, most arid band, where the albedo and low evapotranspiration feedbacks would be greatest.[32]

The global circulation models used in climate studies are composed of equations that mathematically describe the laws governing atmospheric motion. Such models allow scientists to examine how changes in certain parameters—such as albedo, soil moisture, or the carbon dioxide concentration—affect large-scale atmospheric circulation. Unfortunately, they are not sufficiently fine-tuned to predict changes for specific locations. Yet as meteorologist F. Kenneth Hare points out, plausible hypotheses exist "that blame the albedo and soil moisture feedbacks for the intensification of drought in Africa." While scientists cannot yet know whether dryness will persist, he says, "there are now many more climatologists who are prepared to say that desiccation will continue than there were at UNCOD [the U.N. Conference on Desertification] in 1977."[33]

Research in the Amazon basin of Brazil suggests that land degradation can alter the hydrological cycle in humid regions as well. Eneas Salati has studied the water budget of a 25-square-kilometer basin located 60 kilometers north of Manaus and found that streams carry away roughly 25 percent of rainfall, while transpiration by trees and plants returns to the atmosphere nearly 50 percent and evaporation the remaining 25 percent. Thus, fully three quarters of the rainwater falling in the basin returns as water vapor to the atmosphere.[34]

Salati points out that moisture-laden air from the Atlantic Ocean carried westward by the winds provides about half the water vapor leading to rainfall in the Amazon region. Evapotranspiration from the forest itself supplies the other half. Thus, water recycling by the Amazon vegetation plays a crucial role in sustaining rainfall levels, a role that increases in importance at greater distances from the Atlantic.[35]

Deforestation alters this hydrologic pattern. More rainfall runs off, and less gets recycled back to the atmosphere to generate new rainfall. It remains uncertain what amount of forest clearing might initiate significant rainfall declines, or if the crossing of some deforestation threshold could precipitate a sudden change. An estimated 12 percent of Amazonian rain forest in Brazil already has been cleared. Salati suspects,

though he cannot support this, that changes in the water budget may become noticeable when 20–30 percent of the region has been deforested, especially if most of the clearing occurs in the eastern Amazon, where rainfall recycling begins.[36]

Satellite data show clearly that deforestation in parts of the Amazon is accelerating. In the Brazilian state of Rondonia, for example, the area deforested has grown at an exponential rate between 1975 and 1985; 1 million hectares were cleared just between 1984 and 1985. If the exponential rate continues, half of the state's tropical forests will disappear by the early nineties, and all will be gone sometime around the turn of the century.[37]

As noted earlier, satellite data for the whole Brazilian Amazon show that 8 million hectares were cleared in 1987 alone, 5 to 6 million more than were thought to have been cleared annually in the early eighties.[38] If clearing continues at such a pace, Brazilians may face a multiple tragedy: the replacement of productive rain forest with cropland or grassland that loses its fertility and must be abandoned after several years, and reduced rainfall—not only in the Amazon basin itself, but, because the basin exports water vapor to the south, possibly in the agricultural lands of the central plateau.

Regardless of whether desertification and deforestation cause rainfall to diminish, hydrologic balance hinges on how the land and its vegetative cover are managed. When rainwater hits the land, it either immediately runs off into rivers and streams to head back to the sea, soaks into the subsurface to replenish soil moisture or groundwater supplies, or is evaporated or transpired back into the atmosphere. Land degradation shifts the proportion of rainfall following each of these paths. With less vegetative cover and with soils less able to absorb water, degraded land increases runoff and decreases infiltration into the subsurface. The resulting reduction in soil moisture and groundwater supplies worsens the effects of drought, while the increase in rapid runoff exacerbates flooding.

In India, scientists now blame deforestation and desertification for the worsening of droughts and floods.

What appear, then, to be consequences and signs of meteorological drought—withered crops, falling groundwater levels, and dry stream beds—can actually be caused as much or more by land degradation. Perhaps nowhere has this case been made more convincingly than in India, where a growing number of scientists now blame deforestation and desertification for the worsening of droughts and floods. Writes Jayanta Bandyopadhyay of the Research Foundation for Science, Technology and Natural Resource Policy in Dehra Dun, "With an amazing rapidity acute scarcity of water has grabbed the centre stage of India's national life . . . . State after state is trapped into an irreversible and worsening crisis of drought, desertification and consequent water scarcity, threatening plant, animal and human life."[39]

Water shortages plagued some 17,000 villages in the state of Uttar Pradesh in the sixties; by 1985, that figure had risen nearly fourfold, to 70,000. Similarly, in Madya Pradesh, more than 36,400 villages lacked sufficient water in 1980; in 1985, the number totaled more than 64,-500. And in Gujarat, the number of villages short of water tripled between 1979 and 1986, from roughly 3,840 to 12,250.[40]

Michael Mortimore of Bayero University in Nigeria has studied villagers' re-

sponses to drought and famine in parts of the northern states of Kano and Borno. He finds that their survival strategies lead inevitably to further degradation of the land, diminishing their chances for complete recovery. When drought claims large portions of their livestock and crops, for example, they may turn to cutting and selling more firewood, construction materials, and other wood products, thereby increasing pressures on local woodlands. To compensate for lower yields, they may also shorten fallow periods and cultivate additional marginal land. Their reduced animal herds supply less manure, leading to a drop in the fertility of their fields.[41]

When drought ends, the villagers thus begin their recovery from a severely compromised position: more highly degraded fields and woodlands, not to mention greater poverty. As Mortimore says, "By a set of actions—rational in themselves—the overall productivity of the system deteriorates in a series of irreversible steps linked with the occurrence of droughts. It is only necessary for us to add population growth—as an independent variable—to complete this scenario of a structurally unstable system."[42]

Drought and degradation reinforce each other by preventing land from recovering from stress. Whereas healthy land will bounce back to its former productivity after a drought, degraded and abused land frequently will not. For much of the Third World, especially parts of Africa and India, a return to "normal" rainfall levels may not mean a return to past levels of productivity. And if land degradation actually causes rainfall to diminish, a cycle could be set in motion that leads to long-term economic and environmental decline—and to even greater hunger and human suffering than witnessed in Africa and India during the eighties.

REGAINING LAND PRODUCTIVITY

A search for solutions to halting desertification's spread turns up no quick fixes. With the causes tied to varied mixes of physical, social, and economic conditions, the remedies must be diverse and tailored to the problems and needs of particular locales. But here and there —in villages, grassroots organizations, research institutes, experiment stations, development agencies, and government bureaus—technologies and policies geared to restoring the land are being devised, tried, and shown to have promise.

Since much degradation stems from the extension of cropping or grazing onto marginal lands that cannot sustain those activities, changes in the way land is used and managed lie at the heart of rehabilitation efforts. In some cases, degrading lands can simply be removed from production and allowed to recover. The U.S. government has done just this in setting up a Conservation Reserve and calling for 16 million hectares (40 million acres) of highly erodible cropland to be planted in grass or trees by 1990. Farmers get compensation from the government for their lost production, and have already placed an estimated 12 million hectares into the reserve under 10-year contracts. (See Chapter 3.) Three fourths of the way to its 1990 goal, the program has slashed the national annual erosion rate by more than 800 million tons—nearly one third of the excessive soil losses from U.S. cropland before the program began.[43]

A creative initiative, the Conservation Reserve works in large part because a price-depressing surplus of crops made the removal of land from production attractive to farmers and the government alike. Removing the most erodible, marginal land only makes good sense. But in most Third World regions threatened with desertification, the struggle to keep food production increasing apace with population growth and the swelling numbers of land-hungry peasants makes shifting a large portion of cropland out of production almost unthinkable.

In a few pockets of the developing world, however, land is being restored in ways that both conserve the resource base and improve people's living standards. These efforts take various forms, but center around measures that concentrate production on the most fertile, least erodible land, that stabilize soils on sloping and other marginal land, and that reduce rural people's vulnerability to crop failure, often by diversifying income-generating options at the village level.

One such effort is under way in China's Loess Plateau, the highly eroded area spanning some 60 million hectares around the middle reaches of the Huang He. Because of the constant threat that the silt-laden river will flood, the central government has supported efforts to control erosion on the plateau for several decades. Planting of trees and grass and the construction of terraces on sloping land have helped stabilize soils on some 10 million hectares, nearly one quarter of the area suffering from erosion.[44]

During the past decade, the Chinese government's erosion control strategy has turned to sustainable land use systems that improve the livelihoods of the region's rural inhabitants. In 1979, with support from the United Nations Development Programme, an experiment station was established in Mizhi County in northern Shaanxi Province, a drought-prone, highly gullied area, where more than 60 percent of the land slopes at angles of 25 degrees or greater. Scientists developed a plan aimed at intensifying crop production on a smaller cropland area, planting much of the sloping land in trees or grass, and developing animal husbandry as an added source of income for the villagers.[45]

In 1984, armed with promising results from pilot experiments, the government sought assistance from FAO's World Food Programme (WFP) to replicate the strategy in a portion of Mizhi County encompassing 105,000 people and 241 villages. WFP provides food as an incentive for farmers to do the work of land reclamation and as compensation for the cropland converted to trees or grass.[46]

Quanjiagou, one of the villages in the project, gives a visitor who has traversed hundreds of kilometers of the degraded Loess Plateau an overwhelming sense of a land transformed. Earthen dams built across the deep gullies have captured topsoil eroding off the hillsides, creating flat, fertile fields where farmers have planted corn, potatoes, and other vegetables. Terraces allow cropping with minimal erosion on a portion of the slopes, while cash crop trees, such as apple, and a leguminous shrub good for fuel and fodder stabilize the remaining sloping land. Between 1979 and 1986, the area planted in crops was halved, but total crop production increased 17 per-

cent—an amazing 134-percent gain in productivity. (See Table 2–4.) With the added value from tree products and animal husbandry, per capita income in the village has more than doubled.[47]

Average costs of these efforts, including the value of grain supplied by WFP, total about $162 per hectare if the villagers' labor is valued monetarily, $54 per hectare if it is not. While this sum is large relative to per capita income, the investment is modest compared with many other development projects, such as establishing fuelwood plantations or expanding irrigation, which often cost upwards of $1,000 per hectare.[48]

In the drought-plagued, degraded highlands of Ethiopia, similar food-for-work projects are under way in some 44 catchments. Like efforts on the Loess Plateau, they are aimed at integrating conservation and development to both rehabilitate the land and boost crop production. A key feature of the Ethiopian efforts is simple structures called bunds, walls of rock or earth constructed across hillsides to catch soil washing down the slope. Soil builds up behind the bund, forming a terrace that both diminishes erosion and enhances water infiltration.

Table 2-4. China: Effects of Land Rehabilitation Strategy in Quanjiagou, Mizhi County, 1979–86

Effects	1979	1986	Change
Land Use	(hectares)		(percent)
Cropland	234	117	− 50
Trees	60	111	+ 85
Pasture	16	83	+419
	(tons)		(percent)
Crop Production	250	293	+ 17
	(yuan[1])		(percent)
Per Capita Income	127	313	+146

[1]As of mid-November 1988, 1 yuan exchanged for U.S. 27¢.
SOURCE: Shaanxi Control Institute of the Loess Plateau, "Brief Introduction on the Comprehensive Control in Quanjiagou Experimental Watershed," unpublished paper, Shaanxi Province, China, August 1987.

Between 1976 and 1985, through projects sponsored by the United Nations and various foreign aid agencies, Ethiopian farmers built 600,000 kilometers of bunds and about 470,000 kilometers of terraces for reforestation of steep slopes. Though impressive, these efforts are only a start: just 6 percent of the threatened highlands are now protected.[49]

No matter how creative a strategy, land rehabilitation hinges on a set of effective technologies that will be adopted. By working in partnership with villagers, scientists and development workers come to know their needs, priorities, and cultural practices, and can promote appropriate technologies. Soil scientist Rattan Lal makes the basic but crucial observation that "the subsistence farmer who risks famine would consider a successful technology to be the one that produces some yield in the worst year rather than the one that produces a high yield in the best."[50]

Simple techniques of soil and water conservation that add nutrients and moisture to the land form the core of promising rehabilitation efforts. Work at the International Institute of Tropical Agriculture in Ibadan, Nigeria, has shown, for example, that applying a mulch of crop residues at rates of six tons per hectare can provide nearly complete erosion control on slopes of up to 15 percent, allowing sustainable cropping of such land. The mulch protects the soil from the impact of raindrops, increases rainfall infiltration, conserves soil moisture, and improves soil structure, all helping to boost yields. In field trials, a mulch of six tons per hectare has led to yield increases over nonmulched plots of 83 percent for cowpeas, 73 percent for cassava, 33 percent for soybeans, and 23 percent for maize.[51]

Many subsistence farmers are aware of the benefits of mulching, but usually do not have sufficient plant residues to apply to their fields at the needed rates. One strategy that remedies this is alley cropping—an agroforestry design in which food crops are planted in alleys between hedgerows of trees or shrubs. The hedgerow trimmings provide a good mulch for the crop, besides helping meet other needs such as fodder for animals and fuelwood for heating and cooking. Planting the hedges along the contours of sloping land reduces rainfall runoff and soil erosion. Even though the hedgerows take up land, crop yields per hectare suffer little if at all, and sometimes even increase.[52]

Nitrogen-fixing trees, including some species of acacia, gliricidia, and leucaena, are especially useful for agroforestry since they help improve soil fertility and maintain productivity. Sudanese farmers who leave native *Acacia senegal* trees on their cropland can grow millet continuously for 15–20 years, compared with 3–5 years if they remove the trees. Similarly, research in Senegal has shown that an integrated crop-livestock-tree system, using *Acacia albida*, could sustainably support several times more people per hectare than the average for the region. This acacia drops its leaves during the rainy season, adding nitrogen and organic matter to the soil; in the dry season, it produces pods good for fodder and leaves that offer shade to livestock whose dung, in turn, enhances soil fertility.[53]

Another promising prospect for fighting land degradation is a densely tufted, deep-rooted plant called vetiver grass. Native to India and known there as *khus*, vetiver grass offers a simple, inexpensive alternative to the construction of bunds and earthen walls to slow sheet erosion on sloping cropland. It can be established for between 1 and 10 percent of the cost of these other measures, and it requires no maintenance. Vetiver seems to survive in all climates, and has done well even during the last four years of drought in India. Since the most commonly used species (*Vetiveria zizanioides*) propogates only by root division, there is no danger of it spreading out of control.[54]

Vetiver grass forms a vegetative barrier that slows runoff, allowing rainfall to spread out and seep into the field.

When planted to form continuous hedges along the contours of a hillside, vetiver grass forms a vegetative barrier that slows runoff, allowing rainfall to spread out and seep into the field, and traps sediment behind it, forming a natural terrace. Farmers need only give up a 50-centimeter strip of their cropland for each contour hedge of vetiver, and the resulting soil and water conservation gains far outweigh the small amount of land lost from production. Yields typically increase at least 50 percent over those from traditional cultivation methods.[55]

Land restoration also requires incentives that motivate rural people to build terraces, plant trees, or do whatever needs to be done and—equally important—to maintain what they put in place. Without such incentives, governments and aid organizations face the prospect of footing the bill for land rehabilitation efforts everywhere they are needed—clearly, an impossible task.

Recent economic reforms in China, for example, give farmers the security in land tenure and fair prices needed to encourage improvements in the land. Under the "responsibility system," farmers can sell on the free market whatever they produce above their quota to the state. Although the government still owns the land, families can enter into long-term contracts to

use it, and in many cases this right-of-use is inheritable. In Mizhi County, each household's allocation of cropland remains valid for 15 years. Tenure for pasture and wooded land ranges from 30 to 50 years, and can often be passed on to children.[56]

In Ethiopia, on the other hand, the government owns the land and gives Peasant Associations the responsibility of allocating it to farm families for their use. Since the Peasant Associations can redistribute the land, farmers using any given plot have no guarantee that they will benefit from any long-term improvements they make. As in many countries, a long-standing policy of keeping food prices low to appease urban dwellers has further discouraged farmers from investing in land productivity. A promising step was taken in mid-1988, however, when plans were announced to begin raising prices in certain regions for the portion of crops that farmers must sell to the government.[57]

Unfortunately, successes with rangeland rehabilitation form a rather short and unconvincing list. Restoring the naturally fluctuating range resource—given periodic drought, shifting numbers of range animals, and the fact that mobility is central to nomadic pastoralists' survival—presents formidable challenges. Yet a few promising efforts dot the landscape. In northern Nigeria, researchers at the International Livestock Center for Africa (ILCA) are experimenting with "fodder banks," reserves of nitrogen-fixing crops that can provide nutritious feed for livestock during the dry season. Other efforts focus on redistributing livestock to even out pressures on the range. For example, ILCA is helping Ethiopian pastoralists to dig more ponds that retain water for several months into the dry season, thereby hoping to reduce localized overgrazing.[58]

Perhaps the clearest success in rangeland restoration springs from the revival of the ancient "Hema" system of cooperative management in Syria. Cooperatives are established that each have sole grazing rights to a demarcated area of range. Families in the cooperative are then granted a license to graze a certain number of sheep within that area. By reducing overgrazing, the system has enabled the revegetation of 7 million hectares of rangeland.[59]

Much less irrigated cropland than rainfed land suffers from degradation, but the cost of this degradation is great, both because of irrigated land's high production potential and because of the large investments that have gone into it. An expensive and daunting task, rehabilitation of salinized land has not received the attention it deserves. Pakistan, among the countries most affected, has perhaps tried hardest to tackle it, but has achieved only mixed results.

In 1960 the government committed itself to draining salt-affected lands by installing vertical tube wells. Two decades and over 12,000 tube wells later, the area reclaimed still fell far short of the target. Although the technology had proved effective, the public programs had actually reclaimed less land than the combined effects of private tube wells and an improved water supply. The Sixth Five Year Plan, 1983 to 1988, allocated an astonishing 43 percent of the total water budget to drainage activities, and established credits and subsidies to further encourage private development of tube wells.[60]

In Egypt, a drainage system covering only a small portion of the Nile Delta Valley has been estimated to cost $1 billion. Such high sums partly explain why governments tend to ignore the problem, and why preventing salinization in the first place—by increasing irrigation efficiency and providing for adequate drainage when irrigation systems are built—is crucial.[61]

JOINING THE BATTLE

Why, more than a decade after a global goal was set to stop desertification by the year 2000, are we losing more trees, more topsoil, and more grazing land than ever before? The easy answers are that governments fail to grasp the severity of the threat, lack the political will to give it priority, and devote insufficient financial resources to combat it. But a more fundamental reason may lie in the very nature of "desertification control" itself. It crosses all traditional disciplinary and bureaucratic boundaries, including agriculture, forestry, pastoralism, and water management. Lasting solutions are rooted as much in social and economic reforms as in effective technologies. Telescoping desertification control into a single program or plan of action defies the reality that it is inseparable from the broader notion of sustainable development.

All the elements needed to reverse land degradation exist, but they have not been joined effectively in the battle or given the resources needed to mount an adequate fight. In the United Nations Environment Programme and its Executive Director, Mostafa Tolba, desertification control has a strategic headquarters and a strong, committed leader. But the amount of funding mobilized for desertification control over the last decade has fallen far short of needs. Harold Dregne estimates that an average of $170 million per year was spent by donor agencies on field-level desertification control between 1978 and 1983, compared with an estimated $1.8 billion of annual expenditures needed to combat desertification adequately. UNEP places investment needs at $4.5 billion per year to bring desertification under control within 20 years. Several countries have developed the national plans of action called for by the 1977 Nairobi conference, but only three—Burkina

Faso, Mali, and Tunisia—have apparently drummed up sufficient support to begin successfully implementing them. The United Nations Sudano-Sahelian Office intends to push implementation of four existing plans before the end of 1989 in this northern part of Africa.[62]

While this top-down approach proceeds at a glacial pace with few measurable gains, efforts at the village level have produced numerous, albeit small successes. (See also Chapter 9.) On the island of Cebu in the Philippines, for example, local farmers have been working with U.S.-based World Neighbors since 1982 to stem soil erosion on the steep slopes they cultivate. Initially, the World Neighbors project director led the seminars on contouring and other techniques; later, villagers familiar with the methods took over the presentations. Two years into the project, 74 farmers were participating and 25 kilometers of erosion control structures had been built. Three new sites were added by the end of 1987, and project workers now expect 750 farmers to adopt the conservation techniques.[63]

Efforts at the village level have produced numerous, albeit small successes.

In western Kenya, 540 different local organizations—mostly women's groups and primary schools—are working with the U.S.-based organization CARE to promote reforestation. CARE provides the materials needed to establish nurseries, as well as training and extension services, but local people do the planting. Each group plants between 5,000 and 10,000 seedlings annually, collectively amounting to nearly a third of the plantings the government estimates are needed.[64]

The greatest hope of reversing land degradation lies in marrying stepped-up international support and technical guidance with the commitment and experience of organizations operating at the local level. Although that presents an onerous set of institutional challenges, there are some promising signs.

Recognizing that community-based initiatives have higher success rates and more lasting impacts than "top-down" projects, UNEP is strengthening its cooperation with nongovernmental organizations (NGOs). The agency currently supports several grassroots projects through the Nairobi-based African NGOs Environmental Network, and has also helped launch the Deforestation and Desertification Control NGO Network in the Asia-Pacific region. A similar network is being established for Latin America. In addition, UNEP has provided $35,000 to bolster tree planting efforts in southern India through the Millions of Trees Club, a grassroots group that has set up people's nurseries and training centers for reforestation. During the two years of UNEP's support, the number of nurseries grew from 20 to 45, and from them more than 2 million trees and shrubs were planted.[65]

Another promising sign emerged in December 1985, when representatives from 41 African governments, regional organizations, and NGOs gathered in Cairo for the first African Ministerial Conference on the Environment. The conference's prime objective was developing a cooperative program aimed at arresting environmental degradation on the continent and helping Africans achieve food and energy self-sufficiency. Toward that end, a Cairo Plan was set forth that called for two sets of pilot projects.[66]

The first involves selecting three villages in different ecological zones in each of 50 African countries and implementing ecologically based development schemes in each. The second focuses on rehabilitating rangelands, and calls for one pilot project in each of 30 countries designed to produce fodder from small plots irrigated by animal-powered water pumps. The goal is to produce enough fodder to carry village herds through the dry season so that degraded rangelands have a chance to recover. It is hoped that through these 180 demonstration projects, which will involve working closely with NGOs and villagers, successful and replicable strategies will emerge.[67]

Funding for the Cairo Plan is to come from African governments themselves as well as from international donor agencies. UNEP, which is helping coordinate the effort, is currently working to round up support. So far, about 5 projects have received funding, and up to 20 others are in the pipeline.[68]

Bilateral donor agencies also have an important role to play in stimulating action at the local level. By funneling more money through NGOs rather than national government agencies, they can often ensure more bang for the development buck. The U.S. Agency for International Development (AID), for example, sponsors a $27-million Agroforestry Outreach Project in Haiti, which is administered through three private voluntary organizations. Operation Double Harvest produces and distributes seedlings and manages demonstration tree farms. CARE provides agroforestry training and extension services to farmers in the severely degraded northwestern region. And the Pan American Development Foundation works with more than 120 Haitian voluntary groups, many of them church-related, by training "promoters" to help farmers plant and care for trees on their farms and to report back on which strategies are proving successful.[69]

So far, some 130,000 farmers have planted more than 35 million trees, not only conserving soils and boosting crop yields, but helping meet their needs for fuel and fodder. While initially the project paid farmers to plant and care for the seedlings, the benefits of agroforestry soon rendered the payments unnecessary. Indeed, farmers' demand for seedlings currently exceeds what the nurseries can provide. Project officials hope that, having tapped into and strengthened existing networks at the local level, the reforestation effort will continue long after the project money is spent.[70]

Building institutional bridges between research organizations and farmers' fields is also crucial in the battle against land degradation. Technologies perfected on experimental research plots often need adapting to suit the needs and conditions of small farmers. The Tropical Agricultural Research and Training Center (CATIE, from the Spanish), located in Turrialba, Costa Rica, serves just such a role for its six Central American and Caribbean members: Costa Rica, the Dominican Republic, Guatemala, Honduras, Nicaragua, and Panama.[71]

CATIE's activities focus on developing integrated crop, livestock, and forest production systems suited to subsistence farming in the tropics. David Joslyn of AID, which provides 65 percent of CATIE's $13-million annual budget, knows of no other institution like it: "In both training and research, the organization accomplishes what the small countries of Central America could never accomplish alone."[72]

Without adequate incentives for small farmers to invest in their land, the technologies developed at research institutes and the land use strategies tested through aid projects will not spread widely enough to make more than a dent in desertification. As noted earlier, reforming land ownership and tenure policies and providing access to credit for smallholders is vital to the reversal of land degradation. Special emphasis needs to be placed on the status of women—especially in Africa, where the disparity between the work women do and the rights they have is greatest.

Of the multilateral development organizations, the International Fund for Agricultural Development (IFAD) is heads above the others in incorporating these needs into its projects more thoroughly. This decade-old U.N. agency has now carried out about 190 projects, and in the words of IFAD president Idriss Jazairy, they are "people-oriented" and built upon the philosophy that development involves the "liberation of [people's] creative potential."[73]

An IFAD project in Kenya, for instance, operates through women's savings clubs and other community groups to enhance women's access to credit, farm supplies, and extension services. Another, in The Gambia, works to uphold women's traditional cultivation rights under a new land distribution scheme and establishes day-care centers for children of women whose workloads have increased with the introduction of double-cropping. While the provision of child-care services may seem far removed from desertification control, freeing women to do the work of raising land productivity could in fact be an essential first step.[74]

Expanded research into crop varieties and production systems appropriate for the lands and people at risk from desertification is also crucial. With the high-yielding, Green Revolution package of technologies having captured the research limelight over the last several decades, efforts to improve the productivity of subsistence farming are just beginning to get the attention they deserve. Research on cowpeas, for example, an important leguminous crop in Africa, has led to varieties harvestable in 50–60 days instead of 90–100. That paves the way for double- or even triple-cropping in some regions, which would reduce pressures to extend cultivation to marginal lands. A new drought-tolerant sorghum has yielded double or triple that of traditional varieties in the Sudan. By boosting per-hectare production, its spread among smallholders also would allow some erodible lands that would otherwise be cultivated to be planted in soil-stabilizing tree or fodder crops.[75]

Finally, with much degradation stemming from excessive human pressures on the land, reversing it will require a dramatic slowing of population growth. If current growth rates persist, Africa's worn-out lands will need to support an additional 263 million people by the year 2000, roughly equivalent to adding two more Nigerias. India will grow by nearly 200 million people, or 24 percent, and the Philippines—with the fastest growth rate in Southeast Asia—by more than a third. No matter how much funding comes forth, or how fast effective technologies spread, or how diligently governments implement land reforms, a lasting victory over land degradation will remain out of reach until population pressures ease.[76]

3

Reexamining the World Food Prospect

Lester R. Brown

At the start of the 1987 harvest, world grain stocks totaled a record 459 million tons, enough to feed the world for 101 days. When the 1989 harvest begins, the "carryover" stocks will likely drop to 54 days of consumption, lower even than the 57 days at the beginning of 1973, when grain prices doubled. During a brief two years, world reserves of grain—which account for half of all human caloric intake when consumed directly and part of the remainder in the form of meat, milk, cheese, butter, and eggs—will have plummeted from the highest level ever to the lowest since the years immediately following World War II.[1]

Stocks have declined precipitously because food demand has continued its population-driven rise while production has fallen at a record rate. In 1987, a monsoon failure in India contributed to an 85-million-ton drop in world output.

An expanded version of this chapter appeared as Worldwatch Paper 85, *The Changing World Food Prospect: The Nineties and Beyond.*

In 1988, drought-reduced harvests in the United States, Canada, and China reduced world grain output a further 76 million tons.[2]

The drought that afflicted the United States in 1988 is by many criteria the most severe on record—so severe that domestic grain production has fallen below consumption for perhaps the first time ever. North America, which supplies most of the world's wheat and feed-grain exports, is able to maintain exports during the 1988/89 trade year only by selling its carryover stocks. A severe drought in 1989 will reduce exports to a trickle, creating a world food emergency.[3]

The central question raised by this overnight depletion of world grain reserves is, What are the odds that North America will experience another severe drought in 1989? Are the three drought-reduced harvests of 1980, 1983, and 1988 simply reruns of the types of droughts that occurred in the thirties, or do they foreshadow an agricultural future in a world where summers in midcontinental North America will be far hotter? No one knows.

Drought can be caused by below-normal rainfall, by above-normal temperatures (which increase evaporation), or both, as was the case in 1988. Record-high temperatures in key U.S. agricultural areas during the summer of 1988 contributed to the reduced harvest. This unprecedented summer cannot be conclusively linked to the long-projected global warming, but both the reduced rainfall and the higher temperatures in the North American agricultural heartland are consistent with projected changes in climate associated with the buildup of greenhouse gases. Many meteorologists believe it is likely that the warming is now under way. If so, droughts and heat waves will occur with increasing frequency, making it more difficult to rebuild stocks once they are depleted. (See Chapter 1.)[4]

The future of agriculture is being shaped increasingly by environmental trends and resource constraints.

In addition to the drought-reduced harvests, the growth of world food production appears to be losing momentum. Between 1950 and 1984, world grain output climbed from 624 million tons to 1,645 million tons, a prodigious 2.6-fold gain that raised per capita grain production by 40 percent. Since then, output per person has declined each year, falling 14 percent over the last four years. In part, this fall measures the unsustainable use of soil and water.[5]

No one knows what share of world food output is unsustainable, but some idea of its scale can be gleaned by looking at U.S. agriculture. Under the Conservation Reserve Program, the U.S. De-

partment of Agriculture (USDA) is taking 11 percent of the country's cropland out of production, converting it to grassland or woodland, because it is too erodible to sustain continuous cropping. Irrigated area has shrunk 7 percent since 1978. Even so, water tables are still falling by six inches to four feet per year beneath one fourth of U.S. irrigated cropland, suggesting that further shrinkage is in prospect.[6]

If the estimated 57 million tons of U.S. grain output—roughly one sixth of the total—produced with this unsustainable use of soil and water is subtracted from world output, the surpluses of the eighties disappear. More seriously, subtracting unsustainable output for the United States alone from world food production puts sustainable world production below consumption.[7]

Depressed farm prices during the eighties have clearly slowed investment in agriculture, but other forces are shaping the world food prospect. For instance, the backlog of unused agricultural technologies that farmers can draw upon in some countries is dwindling, making it more difficult for them to maintain the rapid output growth of recent decades.

But beyond these economic and technological influences, the future of agriculture is being shaped increasingly by environmental trends and resource constraints. Prominent among these are the continual loss of topsoil from croplands, the conversion of cropland to nonfarm uses, the waterlogging and salting of irrigation systems, falling water tables, the diversion of irrigation water to nonfarm uses, and now the possible adverse effects of climate change.

In addition, demographic trends are making it ever more difficult to achieve a satisfactory balance between food and people. The annual addition to world population, estimated at 86 million in 1988, is projected to exceed 90 million in the early nineties. By the end of the decade, there will be nearly a billion more people to feed. In the two regions with the fastest population growth, Africa and Latin America, per capita grain production is falling. If action is not taken soon to reverse these declines, hunger and malnutrition will spread, and eventually food consumption for more people will fall below the survival level.[8]

PRODUCTION TRENDS

The enormous growth in world grain output between 1950 and 1984 has no precedent. Never before had the world witnessed such an increase in food production within one generation. But can this rapid growth be restored and sustained indefinitely?

The last four years may help answer these questions. After increasing only slightly in 1985 and 1986, global grain production fell sharply in 1987 and again in 1988. (See Figure 3–1.) As noted earlier, in per capita terms it has fallen each year since 1984.[9]

The overall loss of momentum in

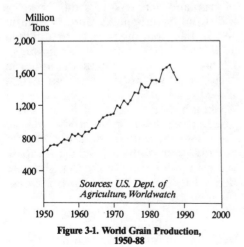

Million
Tons

Sources: U.S. Dept. of Agriculture, Worldwatch

1950   1960   1970   1980   1990   2000

Figure 3-1. World Grain Production, 1950-88

world grain output, exacerbated by the monsoon failure in India in 1987, the North American and Chinese droughts in 1988, and large areas of cropland idled under U.S. commodity supply management programs in both years, has depressed the world grain harvest by nearly 10 percent in two years. Record back-to-back declines have interrupted nearly four decades of steady growth in world grain output, one of the most predictable of global economic trends since World War II.

During the mid-eighties, grain production plateaued in some of the world's most populous countries, including India, Indonesia, Mexico, and China. India more than tripled its wheat harvest between 1965, when the Green Revolution was launched, and 1983, sharply boosting total grain output. Since then, grain production has not increased there at all.[10]

Indonesia doubled its grain harvest, consisting almost entirely of rice, between 1970 and 1984, but output has since leveled off. Indonesia's resettlement program, designed to alleviate land hunger by moving people from densely populated Java to the outer islands, has been widely judged a failure and has nearly halted. In contrast to Java's rich soils, those of the outer islands typically deteriorate, and rather quickly, once the dense rain forest is cleared for farming.[11]

Mexico, where the Green Revolution originated, boosted its grain harvest fourfold between 1950 and 1984. There, too, production has stagnated, largely because the area in grain has declined one tenth during the eighties. This shrinkage, as degraded cropland is abandoned and as some areas are converted to nonfarm uses, is offsetting the gains in yield per hectare.[12]

China may illustrate the leveling off most dramatically. The economic reforms that quickly led to exploitation of a large backlog of unused technologies boosted grain production by nearly half between 1976 and 1984, an impressive achievement by any standard. Since then, China's output has actually fallen slightly. Beijing's official goal early in 1988 was to regain the record level of 1984. Notwithstanding an increase in grain procurement prices for the 1988 crop, China's efforts to regain the 1984 harvest level failed for the fourth consecutive year.[13]

The food prospect for China is of special concern, not merely because it is the world's largest consumer, but because its planners may be greatly overestimating future gains in production. They project a 130-million-ton increase in grain production by the end of the century, or roughly a third, but is this really feasible? The recent experience of three other countries in East Asia with similar population/land ratios, and that have undergone rapid industrial development comparable to that now under way in China, calls this goal into question.[14]

In Japan, Taiwan, and South Korea, grain production has been declining for many years. In each of the three, the historical peak came during the 11-year span between 1967 and 1978. From their respective peaks, production has declined more than one fourth in Japan, by one fifth in Taiwan, and by one sixth in South Korea.[15]

The reasons for these common trends are clear. With a small area of cropland per person, it becomes difficult to boost output per worker in agriculture as fast as in industry. The rapid rise in labor productivity and income in the industrial sector pulls workers out of agriculture. As a result, the area multiple-cropped—growing more than one crop per year in one field—begins to decline. In addition to siphoning labor out of agriculture, the nonfarm sector also draws land away from farmers. Record rates of industrialization lead to rapid growth in land used for the construction of factories, ware-

houses, access roads, and, as affluence rises, new housing. In each of these East Asian countries, the decline in grain area was followed in a matter of years by a decline in grain production.

For densely populated countries that are industrializing rapidly, the comparative advantage lies in industry, not in agriculture. As a result, these three countries have greatly increased their grain imports over the last decade or two—an obviously sensible policy. Although all three are largely self-sufficient in rice, they import most of their wheat and nearly all of their feedgrains. In 1987, imports accounted for 71 percent of Japan's grain consumption, 72 percent of Taiwan's, and 59 percent of South Korea's.[16]

Eastern Europe and the Soviet Union are slowly reducing their dependence on outside grain.

The experience of these three countries may explain why China is now having such difficulty boosting grain production. Like its neighbors, China is densely populated and has a small area of cropland per person, a rapid rate of industrial development, and a nonfarm sector that is pulling both labor and land away from agriculture. In addition, in China's water-scarce north, the nonfarm sector is diverting water from irrigation.[17]

China's grain area peaked in 1976, just 12 years before grain production did the same. With grain yield per hectare already four fifths of that in Japan, achieving the yield increases that are needed to reach the one-third increase planned by the year 2000 will not be easy.[18]

In 1988, China imported 5 percent of its grain, roughly 15 million tons. If the nation's efforts to expand output are no more successful than those of its three smaller neighbors, it might be importing a steadily growing share of its food during the nineties. If China were to import 15 percent of its needs by 1995, the amount would total 45 million tons— more than the 28 million tons now bought by Japan and the 24 million tons by the Soviet Union, the world's leading grain importers.[19]

Perhaps the best indicator of long-term shifts in food production relative to demand can be seen in the changing geographic pattern of world grain trade. (See Table 3–1.) In 1950, most of the grain in international trade flowed from North America to grain-deficit Western Europe. The rest of the world was essentially self-sufficient. That has changed dramatically in recent decades. Since mid-century, North America has increased its grain exports more than five-fold, from 23 million to 119 million tons, emerging as the world's breadbasket.

Latin America became a grain-deficit region in the seventies, with net imports of roughly 11 million tons by 1988. Despite a vast land area, Brazil now regularly imports both wheat and feedgrains. These imports plus those of Mexico, with its growing food deficit, and of several smaller countries more than offset exports from Argentina.[20]

Africa, a largely agrarian continent beset by environmental deterioration and a record population increase, has become heavily dependent on imported grain as it tries to offset a two-decade decline in per capita production. The northern tier of countries—Egypt, Libya, Tunisia, Algeria, and Morocco— now bring in half the grain they consume. Even with continental imports of an estimated 28 million tons in 1988, millions of people in sub-Saharan Africa were left hungry and malnourished, some on the verge of starvation.[21]

The combination of a small and shrinking cropland area per person and rising prosperity in many countries has made Asia the leading food-importing region. Its purchases surpassed those of Europe during the mid-sixties, and all indications are that they will continue to rise during the nineties and beyond.

Eastern Europe and the Soviet Union, which were importing at record levels in the late seventies and early eighties, are slowly reducing their dependence on outside grain. Whether they reach self-sufficiency will depend heavily on the success of Soviet agricultural reforms.

Western Europe is perhaps the most interesting regional story. In the early eighties, it ended two centuries of dependence on imported grain, a dependence that began with the industrial revolution and the exchange of manu-

Table 3-1. The Changing Pattern of World Grain Trade, 1950–88[1]

Region	1950	1960	1970	1980	1988[2]
	(million metric tons)				
North America	+23	+39	+56	+131	+119
Latin America	+ 1	0	+ 4	− 10	− 11
Western Europe	−22	−25	−30	− 16	+ 22
E. Eur. and Soviet Union	0	0	0	− 46	− 27
Africa	0	− 2	− 5	− 15	− 28
Asia	− 6	−17	−37	− 63	− 89
Australia and New Zeal.	+ 3	+ 6	+12	+ 19	+ 14

[1]Plus sign indicates net exports; minus sign, net imports. [2]Preliminary.
SOURCES: U.N. Food and Agriculture Organization, *Production Yearbook* (Rome: various years); U.S. Department of Agriculture, Foreign Agricultural Service, *World Rice Reference Tables* and *World Wheat and Coarse Grains Reference Tables* (unpublished printouts) (Washington, D.C.: June 1988).

factured goods for food and raw materials with the rest of the world. Steadily advancing farm technologies, farm support prices well above the world market level, and a population growth rate that is approaching zero have combined to push the region's net exports above those of Australia. Although West European farmers could face some reductions in support prices as the costs of maintaining current levels soar, they still may be able to sell more grain abroad than Australia, which with its semiarid climate will find it difficult to increase exports substantially.

Until recently, expanding food production was largely an economic concern, a matter of formulating agricultural price policies that would stimulate investment. Today, rises in commodity support prices in some countries may simply result in the plowing of highly erodible land or the installation of more irrigation pumps where water tables are already falling. Given the soil and water constraints now facing farmers, the slower growth in food output of recent years is not surprising.

THE CROPLAND BASE

From the beginning of agriculture until the mid-twentieth century, most of the growth in world food output came from expanding the cultivated area. Since 1950, a combination of the diminishing fertility of new land to plow and the availability of new technologies shifted the emphasis from plowing new land to raising land productivity. Roughly four fifths of the growth in world food output since mid-century has come from this source.[22]

The world grain area increased some 24 percent between 1950 and 1981, when it reached an all-time high. (See

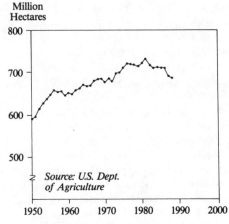

Figure 3-2. World Harvested Area of Grain, 1950-88

Figure 3–2.) Since then, it has fallen some 7 percent. That the world's cropland area would expand when the world demand for food was growing rapidly is not surprising. What is surprising—and worrying—is the recent decline. This is due partly to the abandonment of eroded land, as in the Soviet Union; partly to the systematic retirement of such land under conservation programs, as in the United States; and partly to growing competition from nonfarm sources, a trend most evident in densely populated Asia.[23]

From mid-century until 1981, two major surges in the world grain area occurred. The first came in the early fifties, when the Soviets embarked on the Virgin Lands project. Between 1951 and 1956, they added some 40 million hectares to their cropland base, accounting for most of the steep growth in the world grain area.[24]

The second surge began when world grain prices doubled between 1972 and 1973. Farmers throughout the world responded to record prices by plowing more land. In the United States, they not only returned idled cropland to use, they also plowed millions of acres of highly erodible land. Between 1972 and 1976, the U.S. area in grain climbed some 24 percent. But soil erosion increased as well. By 1977, American farmers were losing an estimated six tons of soil for every ton of grain they produced.[25]

Meanwhile the Soviet Union, embarrassed by its 1972 crop failure, expanded its area in grain some 7 percent. By 1977, it had reached a record high. But erosion of soil by both wind and water also increased. Although detailed data on soil loss are not available, papers published by the Soil Erosion Laboratory at the University of Moscow indicated severe and worsening erosion.[26]

In early 1982, Mikhail Gorbachev, then only a Politburo member, urged planners to heed the advice of soil scientists and adopt measures to limit erosion. But in the face of pressures to reduce food imports—then the world's largest—the scientists often were ignored and responsible management practices cast aside.[27]

Soil erosion is making future production gains more difficult in China as well. The Yellow River Conservancy Commission reported in 1980 that the Huang He, or Yellow River, was depositing 1.2 billion tons of soil in the ocean each year. At the Mauna Loa observatory in Hawaii, scientists taking air samples can tell when spring plowing starts in China by the surge of dust carried eastward by prevailing winds.[28]

Perhaps the grimmest soil erosion report came in a 1978 dispatch from the U.S. embassy in Addis Ababa, stating that an estimated 1 billion tons of topsoil were washing down from Ethiopia's highlands each year. The result for that country has become well known: recurrent famine, a window on the future of other developing countries that are failing to control soil loss.[29]

The use of land for building is also shrinking the cropland area. In China, one result of the past decade's welcome prosperity is that literally millions of villagers are either expanding their existing dwellings or building new ones. And an industrial sector expanding at more than 12 percent annually since 1980 means the construction of thousands of new factories. Since most of China's 1.1 billion people are concentrated in its rich farming regions, new homes and factories are often built on cropland. This loss of agricultural land combined with the shifts to more profitable crops has reduced the grain-growing area in China 9 percent since 1976.[30]

Throughout the Third World, mounting population pressures continue to push farmers onto lands too steeply sloping to sustain cultivation and semi-arid lands too dry to be protected from the winds when plowed. As erosion continues, land gradually loses its inherent productivity, threatening the livelihood of those who depend on it.

Continual overuse of biological systems can set in motion changes that become self-reinforcing.

During the eighties, the results of this process became clear. Researchers now realize that continual overuse of biological systems can set in motion changes that become self-reinforcing. World Bank ecologist Kenneth Newcombe has described how complex systems unravel through several stages, each of which hastens the onset of the next. His model, drawn from the experience of Ethiopia, shows how a decline in biological productivity can be triggered by a loss of tree cover.[31]

All too often, this starts when the firewood demands of growing populations begin to exceed the sustainable yield of local forests. As the woodlands recede from the towns, firewood becomes scarce. At this point, villagers

start using crop residues and animal
dung for cooking. This interrupts two
important cycles, depriving the land of
nutrients and also of the organic matter
essential to maintaining a productive
soil structure. As protective vegetation
disappears and as soils become more
compact, more rainfall runs off, soil erosion accelerates, less water is absorbed
by the soil, and the soil moisture
needed for healthy crops diminishes.
Water tables begin to fall. Over time,
wells go dry. Eventually, not enough
soil is left to support even subsistence-
level agriculture. At this point, villagers
become environmental refugees, head-
ing for the nearest city or relief camp.
(See Chapter 4.)

Official recognition of this cycle of
land degradation and its consequences
is emerging in India. Agronomists there
estimated that their country, with the
same cropland area as the United States,
was losing some 5 billion tons of topsoil
each year as of 1975, compared with a
U.S. loss of just over 3 billion tons. In
1985, Prime Minister Rajiv Gandhi set
up a National Wastelands Development
Board; its aim is to transform 5 million
hectares of degraded land every year
into fuelwood and fodder plantations.[32]

This grim process of eroding soils is
leading the world into a period of agricultural retrenchment. Even ignoring
the cropland idled under U.S. commodity programs, the world area in grain has
declined steadily since reaching the historical high in 1981. The United States is
in the midst of a five-year program to
convert at least 40 million acres (16 million hectares) of highly erodible cropland—11 percent of its total cropland
—to grassland or woodland before it
becomes wasteland. (See Table 3-2.)[33]

In contrast, the Soviet Union does not
have a program for converting highly
erodible land to less-intensive, sustainable uses. As a consequence, each year
since 1977 it has abandoned roughly a
million hectares of cropland, leading to

a 13-percent shrinkage in grain area.
Abandonment on this scale suggests that
inherent fertility may be falling on a far
larger area, helping explain why the
Soviets now lead the world in fertilizer
use while still ranking a distant third in
grain production after the United States
and China.[34]

In some developing countries, cropland degradation from erosion is leading
to the wholesale abandonment not only
of cropland, but of entire villages.
Across the southern fringe of the Sahara
Desert, thousands of villages and their
surrounding farmlands are surrendering
to the sand. Declining rainfall and desertification are forcing the agricultural
frontier to retreat southward across a
broad band of Africa, from Mauritania in
the west to the Sudan in the east.[35]

As the eighties draw to a close, such

**Table 3-2. United States: Sign-Up for
Conservation Reserve Program, March
1986–July/August 1988**

Sign-up Period	Area Signed Up	Average Annual Rental Rate Per Hectare
	(million hectares)	(dollars)
March 1986	0.30	104
May 1986	1.12	109
August 1986	1.90	116
February 1987	3.84	126
July 1987	2.14	119
February 1988	1.38	119
July/August 1988	1.05	121
Total	11.73	120

SOURCES: U.S. Department of Agriculture (USDA), Economic Research Service (ERS), *Agricultural Resources: Cropland, Water, and Conservation Situation and Outlook Report* (Washington, D.C.: September 1987); "Sixth CRP Signup Adds 3.4 Million Acres," *Agricultural Outlook*, August 1988; data for July/August 1988 are preliminary Worldwatch estimates based on Tim Osborn, USDA, ERS, private communication, November 1, 1988.

data as are available indicate that soil erosion is slowly reducing the inherent productivity of up to one third of the world's cropland, though increased use of chemical fertilizers is temporarily masking this deterioration. Worldwide, an estimated 25 billion tons of topsoil is being lost from cropland each year, roughly the amount that covers Australia's wheat lands.[36]

WATER FOR IRRIGATION

The spread of irrigation from its initiation in the Middle East several thousand years ago has been dramatic, as detailed in *State of the World 1987*. At the start of this century, the world total stood at some 40 million hectares. By 1950, it had reached 94 million hectares; by 1980, 249 million hectares. After 1980, however, growth slowed dramatically, expanding by an estimated 8 million hectares since then. (See Figure 3–3.)[37]

Irrigation often holds the key to cropping intensity, especially in monsoonal climates, where the wet season is followed by several months with little or no rain. Where temperatures permit year-

round cropping, as they often do where monsoons prevail, irrigation allows the production of two, three, or even more crops per year.

China and India lead the world in irrigated land. In China, this agricultural practice grew impressively between 1950 and 1980, increasing from scarcely 20 million hectares in 1950 to some 48 million by 1980. The growth facilitated an increase in multiple cropping, from an average of 1.3 crops per hectare in 1950 to 1.5 in 1980.[38]

India's net irrigated area in 1950 was almost exactly the same as China's. Though growth has been less rapid, the total nonetheless reached some 39 million hectares as of 1980. The most rapid growth has occurred since the mid-sixties, following the introduction of high-yielding wheat and rice varieties that were both more responsive to the use of water and more exacting in their demands. This enhanced profitability stimulated widespread investments by small farmers in wells of their own so they could more fully exploit the yield potential of the new varieties.[39]

The United States and the Soviet Union rank third and fourth, respectively, in irrigated area. Growth in U.S. irrigated area from 1950 to 1980 was concentrated in the southern Great Plains. Soviet irrigated area grew steadily during the same period. With some 18 million hectares already under irrigation in 1983, the government planned to add over 600,000 hectares a year during the mid-eighties. The Soviets look to irrigation not only to help boost food production but also to minimize the wide swings in crop output that result from highly variable rainfall.[40]

Unfortunately, not all of the irrigation expansion during the preceding three decades is sustainable. Some, as in the U.S. southern Great Plains, is based on the use of fossil water, which will eventually be depleted. In other parts of the

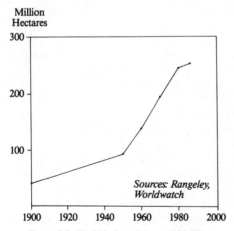

Figure 3-3. World Irrigated Area, 1900-85

United States and in other countries, some irrigation growth has resulted in the drawing down of water tables as pumping exceeds aquifer recharge. In addition, the water available for irrigation is being reduced in still other areas by the growing water demands of industries and cities.[41]

In recent years, the world's two leading food producers—the United States and China—have experienced unplanned declines in irrigated area. The U.S. irrigated area, which peaked in 1978, has fallen some 7 percent since then, reversing several decades of growth. (See Figure 3–4.) In addition to falling water tables, depressed commodity prices and rising pumping costs have contributed to the shrinkage.[42]

Further declines are in prospect. In 1986, USDA reported that more than one fourth of the 21 million hectares of irrigated cropland was being watered by pulling down water tables, with the drop ranging from six inches to four feet per year. They were falling either because the pumping exceeded the rate of aquifer recharge or because the water was from the largely nonrenewable Ogallala Aquifer. Although water mining is an option in the short run, in the long run withdrawals cannot exceed aquifer recharge.[43]

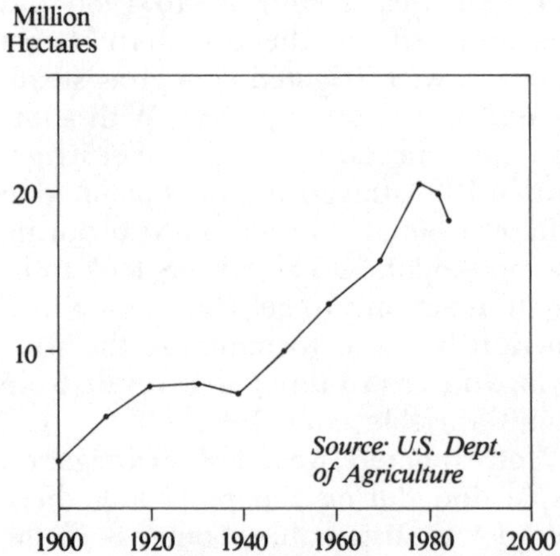

In China, where the expansion also peaked in 1978, irrigated area had shrunk 2 percent by 1987. Under parts of the North China Plain in the region surrounding Beijing and Tianjin, the water table is dropping by one to two meters per year. Industrial, residential, and agricultural users compete for dwindling supplies of fresh water. Deterioration in some community irrigation systems is also evident due to neglect arising from the shift to family-centered farming.[44]

Overpumping is evident in India as well. Although no groundwater study comparable to the USDA survey has been done, several states have reported that water tables are falling and that wells are going dry. In Tamil Nadu, on India's eastern coast, the water table in some areas fell 25–30 meters during the seventies. In Maharashtra, on the west coast, competition is growing between large-scale producers of commercial crops, such as sugarcane, and local villagers who are producing food staples for their own consumption. As commercial growers invest in deeper wells, they lower the water table, and the shallow, hand-dug wells of the villagers go dry. Thousands of Indian villages now rely on tank trucks for their drinking water. Notwithstanding widespread water shortages in some states, there is still a large potential for irrigation expansion in parts of India, such as in the water-rich Gangetic Plain.[45]

In the Soviet Union, the excessive use of water for irrigation takes the form of diminished river flows rather than falling water tables. A good part of the nation's irrigated cropland is in central Asia, and much of it is watered by the Syr-Darya and Amu-Darya, the two great rivers of the region. Irrigation diversions from these rivers have greatly reduced their

Million
Hectares

Source: U.S. Dept. of Agriculture

Figure 3-4. Irrigated Land in the United States, 1900-84

flow into the landlocked Aral Sea. As a result, the sea's water level has fallen some 12 meters since heavy river diversions got under way some two decades ago.[46]

Since 1960, the area covered by the Aral Sea has shrunk by 40 percent. Muynak, once a port city and major fish-processing center, is now nearly 50 kilometers from the shore. Soviet scientists fear a major ecological catastrophe is unfolding as the sea slowly disappears. The dry bottom is now becoming desert, the site of sandstorms that may drop on the surrounding fields up to half a ton per hectare of a sand-salt mix—damaging the very crops that water once destined for the sea is used to grow.[47]

The Soviet Union's prospects for future irrigation expansion are limited. Two years ago, the government abandoned its ambitious plan to divert southward into central Asia the Siberian rivers that flow into the Arctic Ocean. Although investment in irrigation continues, the prospective net gains are modest ones.[48]

Apart from the growing scarcity of fresh water, the productivity of perhaps one third of the world's irrigated land is being adversely affected by severe waterlogging and salting. (See also Chapter 2.) Like soil erosion, this process at first gradually reduces land productivity and eventually leads to abandonment.

If underground drainage of irrigated land is not adequate, percolation from river water diverted onto farmland gradually accumulates and over time slowly raises the water table until it moves to within a few feet of the surface. As a result, deep-rooted crops begin to suffer. As the water table continues to rise, it begins evaporating through the remaining inches of soil into the atmosphere, leaving salt on the surface and reducing the land's productivity.

With all natural water containing a certain amount of salt, the buildup of this natural compound is a common threat to the sustainability of irrigated agriculture. As long as the hydrodynamics of the irrigation system provide sufficient flushing, salt does not accumulate in the surface soil. But in many semiarid and arid regions, this is not the case.

The productivity of one third of irrigated land is being adversely affected by severe waterlogging and salting.

Worldwide, the prospects for major gains in irrigated area are not good. To be sure, India's irrigated area is projected to expand steadily in the years ahead, and the Soviet Union's continuing investments will lead to some modest increases. In several of the smaller countries of Asia, such as Thailand and the Philippines, naturally flooded riceland is being converted to irrigated riceland, a shift that permits farmers to raise yields dramatically. At least some developing countries on each continent are planning new additions to their irrigated land. As food prices go up, investment in irrigation will also rise. But as noted earlier, irrigated area in the United States and China has declined in recent years and may well drop further.[49]

On balance, it now seems unlikely that the world will be able to reestablish a trend of rapid, sustained gains in irrigated area of the sort that characterized the period from 1950 to 1980. In retrospect, this three-decade growth era will probably be seen as unique. To the extent that the irrigated area expands in the future, it may depend as much on gains in water-use efficiency as on new supplies.[50]

LAND PRODUCTIVITY POTENTIAL

The ancients calculated yield as the ratio of grain harvested to that sown. For them, the scarce resource was the seed grain itself. In the late twentieth century, land is becoming the constraint. The key to meeting future needs is raising land productivity.

With little opportunity to add productive land to the world's cultivated area, the food prospect in the nineties is directly tied to the potential for raising land productivity. Between 1950 and 1984, farmers more than doubled the output of their cropland. World grain yield per hectare increased from 1.1 tons to 2.3 tons, a remarkable feat. (See Figure 3–5.)[51]

Since 1984, however, grain yields have changed little. One reason is undoubtedly the depressed level of farm prices during this period, which has discouraged both short-term investment in inputs, such as fertilizer, and longer-term investments in land improvement. The monsoon failure in India in 1987 and the droughts in North America and China in 1988 also lowered the global average yield. If grain prices increase,

however, yields should resume their long-term rise.[52]

By far the most important source of rising grain yields in recent decades has been the growth in fertilizer use. From 1950 through 1984, world fertilizer use moved higher each year, with only occasional interruption. It increased during this time from 14 million to 125 million tons, a gain of more than 11 percent per year. Between 1984 and 1988, however, usage went from 125 million to 135 million tons, an annual rise of less than 2 percent. The trend has become somewhat erratic as agricultural commodity prices have weakened, Third World debt has soared, the yield response to fertilizer use has diminished, and many financially pressed governments have reduced fertilizer subsidies.[53]

In per capita terms, world fertilizer use quintupled between 1950 and 1984, going from 5 kilograms to 26 and offsetting a one-third decline in grain area per person. (See Figure 3–6.) As land becomes scarce, farmers rely more on additional fertilizer to expand output, in effect substituting energy in the form of fertilizer for land in the production process.[54]

The bulk of this impressive increase in world fertilizer use during the fifties and most of the sixties occurred in the industrial world. But the practice spread in Asia as Green Revolution varieties of wheat and rice were widely introduced. In China, chemical fertilizers were not widely used until 1960, when it became clear that organic fertilizers were not going to be able to produce enough food for the country's growing population. Usage more than doubled between 1976 and 1981—the steepest increase ever in a major food-producing country—although organic fertilizer continues to be a major source of plant nutrients in China.[55]

Some sense of the potential for raising land productivity worldwide can be

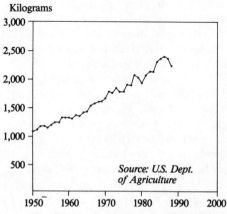

Figure 3-5. World Grain Yield Per Hectare, 1950-88

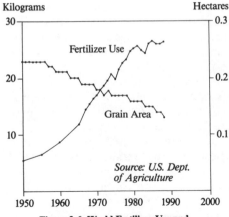

Kilograms — Hectares

Fertilizer Use

Grain Area

Source: U.S. Dept. of Agriculture

1950   1960   1970   1980   1990   2000

Figure 3-6. World Fertilizer Use and Grain Area Per Capita, 1950-88

gleaned from looking at yield trends for wheat, rice, and corn in countries with the highest yield levels—for example, rice in Japan, corn in the United States, and wheat in the United Kingdom. In 1950, crop yields in these countries were essentially the same, at about 2.25 tons per hectare. Over time, the Japanese rice yield increased slowly, reaching 4 tons per hectare in the mid-seventies. Since then, it has increased relatively little, even though the government support price is far above the world market price.[56]

A similar trend exists in other high-technology rice-producing countries, such as South Korea, Taiwan, and Italy. In each case, once rice yields pass 4 tons per hectare, they rise quite slowly or even level off, suggesting that dramatically surpassing this level may await new technological advances. Agricultural economists Duane Chapman and Randy Barker of Cornell point out that "the genetic yield potential of rice has not increased significantly since the release of the high yielding varieties in 1966." In effect, the highest yielding rice varieties available to Asian farmers in 1989 were released 23 years ago.[57]

With both corn and wheat, yields have

gone much higher. Corn yields in the United States, for example, have exceeded 7 tons per hectare (112 bushels per acre) in good crop years. Likewise, wheat in the United Kingdom has ranged between 6 and 7 or more tons per hectare in recent years.[58]

At this point, no one knows how far yields can profitably be raised. Eventually, growth in yield per hectare, like the growth of any other biological process in a finite environment, will conform to the S-shaped growth curve. What is not clear is how close output in the higher-yield countries is to the upper inflection point on this curve, where the rise will slow markedly and begin to level off.

The systematic application of science to agriculture and the increasing investment of energy in agricultural inputs and processes has permitted a regular yearly increase in yields for more than a generation, making it difficult to imagine a situation where yields will not continue their steady rise. Nonetheless, some analysts are becoming concerned about the potential for indefinitely raising yields, a concern heightened by the limited potential for finding new cropland.

Robert Herdt, senior economist at the Rockefeller Foundation, anticipates a slowdown in grain production growth in the developing countries. He observes that "in the next five to ten years there is little potential for further rapid spread of existing semi-dwarf varieties that provided the breakthrough in developing-country wheat and rice production in the mid-1960s. Likewise, it appears that there is little scope for increasing the rates of fertilizer [application] on those varieties much above their mid-1980s levels."[59]

In some farming communities crop yields on the best farms now approach those on experimental plots. It is unrealistic, however, to expect yields on farms actually to reach these high levels. Such plots are used to determine the maximum physical response to an input, such as fertilizer. Farmers, on the other hand, are concerned with the maximum profit response. Scientists working on experimental plots can increase fertilizer use until there is no more response. Farmers must stop when the value of the additional yield no longer covers the cost of the extra fertilizer.

Similarly, scientists on experimental plots can plant during the period that will produce maximum yields. Farmers, who must deal with such real-world constraints as multiple-cropping and the demands on their time imposed by other crops, often cannot plant during this narrow time window.

Rising grain yield per hectare must eventually give way to physical constraints. With cereal yields, the ultimate limit may be photosynthetic efficiency. Where the best farmers supply all the nutrients and water that advanced varieties can use, cereal yields may now be approaching this limit.

Biotechnology is a timely addition to the scientist's tool kit, but it does not promise dramatic production gains.

Evidence that photosynthetic constraints may be emerging can be seen in the diminishing returns on fertilizer use. Whereas 20 years ago the application of each additional ton of fertilizer in the U.S. Corn Belt added 15 to 20 tons to the world grain harvest, today it may add only 5 to 10 tons. In analyzing recent agricultural trends in Indonesia, Chapman and Barker note that "while one kilogram of fertilizer nutrients probably led to a yield increase of 10 kilograms of unmilled rice in 1972, this ratio has fallen to about one to five at present." This, combined with depressed farm prices, helps explain why growth in world fertilizer use has slowed in recent years, and why it has actually declined in some countries, including the United States.[60]

Hybrid wheats and rices have been available for many years but, except for hybrid rice in China, their widespread use awaits far higher grain prices. And since yields of the more productive wheat and rice strains now in use are much closer to the photosynthetic limit than were those of corn when hybrids were introduced 50 years ago, the potential for raising output is comparatively modest.

Other possibilities for boosting yield lie in breeding cereals more tolerant of salt, drought, and heat. In a world growing warmer, gains from this source will loom far larger than they do today.

Contrary to popular belief, biotechnology is not an agricultural panacea that will end hunger. For instance, the widely discussed development of nitrogen-fixing cereals, which biotechnological techniques could facilitate, would reduce the need for fertilizer but would also likely lower yields, since some of the plant's metabolic energy is diverted to fixing nitrogen rather than producing seed. Biotechnology is a timely addition to the scientist's tool kit, one that will speed the pace and the potential return on investment in agricultural research, but it does not promise dramatic production gains. The contribution of this research tool, like all the others that scientists use, is ultimately constrained by the limits of photosynthetic efficiency.

Unfortunately, no identifiable technologies are waiting in the wings that will lead to the quantum jumps in world food output such as those associated with the spread of hybrid corn, the ninefold increase in fertilizer use between 1950 and 1984, the near-tripling of irrigated area during the same period, or the relatively recent spread of the high-yielding dwarf wheats and rices in developing countries. The contribution of these technologies is diminishing in some situations and no major new technologies are emerging to take their place.

Although countries where yields are already quite high are finding it difficult to maintain a rapid rise, those where yields are low can tap existing technologies to boost their output. For example, Japan may not be much more successful in raising rice yields in the nineties than it has been in the late eighties, but India, where rice yields are less than half those of Japan, still has a large unrealized potential.[61]

FOOD SECURITY TRENDS

The two most useful global indicators of food security are per capita grain production and carryover stocks of grain—the amount in the bin when the new harvest begins. The trend in per capita production gives a sense of whether overall food availability is improving or deteriorating. Changes in carryover stocks indicate whether production is exceeding consumption or falling short of it.

World grain production increased substantially faster than population from 1950 through 1984, boosting per capita output from 246 to 345 kilograms. This 40-percent increase led to impressive improvement in diets in many countries, boosting consumption of livestock products. Per capita output declined slightly in 1985 and 1986 before dropping sharply in 1987 and again in 1988. Between 1984 and 1988, grain production per person fell from an all-time high of 345 kilograms to 296 kilograms.[62]

The decline in total grain production in 1988—largely the result of the droughts in North America and China—completed the largest two-year drop on record. The accompanying 14-percent fall in per capita production since 1984 brought this indicator back to the levels of the mid-seventies. Record grain reserves permitted a drawdown of stocks to offset most of the decline, limiting the drop in consumption per person to 3 percent.[63]

This look at global changes in per capita production, however, obscures wide differences in regional trends. The principal determinant of whether food production per person is rising or declining in this case is the differential rate of population growth. For example, while per capita production in Western Europe was climbing rapidly, that in Africa peaked in 1967 and has declined some 27 percent since then. These two regions illustrate the extremes.[64]

Unfortunately, Latin America has joined Africa during the eighties as the second region to experience a decline in food production per person. Since 1981, the year before the debt crisis began, the region's output per person has fallen by roughly one tenth, expanding the region's grain deficit.[65]

As total grain production has declined during the last two years, so too have stocks. World carryover stocks reached an all-time high at the beginning of 1987 of 459 million tons, enough to feed the world for 101 days. During 1987, stocks dropped to 402 million tons. In 1988, world consumption is likely to exceed production by a staggering 152 million tons. (See Table 3–3.) Unless the mid-year USDA world grain consumption estimate of 1,673 million tons is reduced by rising prices, year-end stocks are expected to fall to roughly 250 million tons. This amounts to 54 days of consumption, less than the 57-day supply at

State of the World 1989

Table 3-3. World Grain Production, Use, and Carryover Stocks, 1961–88

Year	Production	Consumption	Carryover Stocks Quantity	Carryover Stocks Consumption Equivalent
	(million metric tons)			(days)
1961	813	835	185	81
1965	917	952	159	61
1970	1,096	1,130	198	64
1971	1,194	1,169	223	70
1972	1,155	1,192	186	57
1973	1,271	1,259	198	57
1974	1,219	1,213	203	61
1975	1,250	1,229	221	66
1976	1,363	1,303	281	79
1977	1,337	1,338	279	76
1978	1,467	1,418	328	84
1979	1,428	1,440	315	80
1980	1,447	1,475	286	71
1981	1,497	1,476	307	76
1982	1,548	1,500	355	86
1983	1,485	1,537	303	72
1984	1,645	1,585	363	84
1985	1,661	1,594	430	98
1986	1,682	1,653	459	101
1987	1,597	1,653	402	89
1988	1,521	1,673	250	54

SOURCES: 1961–87, U.S. Department of Agriculture, Foreign Agricultural Service, *World Grain Situation and Outlook,* Washington, D.C., July 1988; 1988, Worldwatch Institute.

the end of 1972, when world grain prices doubled.[66]

At this low level, carryover stocks amount to little more than "pipeline" supplies. Substantial quantities of grain are required to keep the trucks and barges between producer and consumer filled. The supply lines from the United States, which holds a disproportionately large share of global carryover stocks in order to assure regular supplies to its customers, often stretch halfway around the world.

In addition to its carryover stocks, the world has a second line of defense

against food shortages—the cropland idled under U.S. commodity programs. In 1988, some 20 million hectares (50 million acres) were idled under farm programs designed to maintain price stability. (See Table 3–4.) Virtually all this land can be returned to production within a year if the USDA decides it is needed.

Amounting to roughly 2 percent of the world cropland area, this reserve can help boost production now that stocks are depleted. Given the precariously low level of carryover stocks, prudence argues for bringing this land back into

Table 3-4. United States: Cropland Idled Under Commodity Programs, 1965–88

Year	Land Area
	(million hectares)
1965	17.4
1966	19.3
1967	10.2
1968	14.5
1969	20.3
1970	21.5
1971	13.7
1972	23.8
1973	6.8
1974	0.0
1975	0.0
1976	0.0
1977	0.0
1978	7.4
1979	5.3
1980	0.0
1981	0.0
1982	4.5
1983	31.5
1984	10.9
1985	12.5
1986	17.5
1987	21.7
1988	20.1

SOURCE: Brad Karmen, U.S. Department of Agriculture, private communication, June 24, 1988.

production in 1989. However, the 12 million hectares of highly erodible cropland that has been planted to grass or trees since early 1986 under the Conservation Reserve Program should not be disturbed.[67]

The overwhelming dependence on North America, where agricultural output in both the United States and Canada is affected by the same climatic cycle, introduces a special dimension of food insecurity. A drought in the United States is invariably accompanied by one in Canada. In 1988, when the U.S. grain harvest was down 29 percent, that of Canada was reduced by 33 percent. With the United States and Canada controlling a larger share of grain exports than the Middle East does of oil, this is an issue of concern to food-importing countries everywhere.[68]

The risk of such overwhelming dependence on one region is obvious. During the eighties, North American grain exports have averaged around 110 million tons per year. Even at this level, some U.S. cropland has been idled during most of the decade.

As stocks have dropped, higher prices and scarce supplies increasingly pose a serious threat to those food-importing countries with low incomes. When carryover stocks hit 57 days at the end of 1972, the United States returned its idled cropland to use. Four years passed, however, before world grain reserves were rebuilt and food-importing countries could again breathe easily.

Thus, the devastated grain crop in North America in 1988 is sobering news for the more than 100 countries that depend on imports from the North American breadbasket. For the poorer food-deficit countries, many with external debts that are already unmanageable, maintaining needed imports in the face of sharp price rises may not be possible. For people living in these countries, the road to the next harvest could be a long one.

In the drought-stricken year of 1988, the U.S. grain harvest fell below domestic consumption, probably for the first time in history. (See Table 3–5.) With a harvest of 196 million tons and an estimated consumption of 206 million tons, there was no surplus for export from the 1988 crop. Export demands until the 1989 harvest begins are being

Table 3-5. United States: Grain Production, Consumption, and Exportable Surplus by Crop Year, 1980–88

Year	Production	Consumption	Exportable Surplus from Current Crop[1]
		(million metric tons)	
1980	268	171	+ 97
1981	328	179	+ 149
1982	331	194	+ 137
1983	206	182	+ 24
1984	313	197	+ 116
1985	345	201	+ 144
1986	314	217	+ 97
1987	277	215	+ 62
1988	196	206	− 10

[1]Does not include carryover stocks.
SOURCE: USDA, Foreign Agricultural Service, *World Grain Situation and Outlook,* Washington, D.C., October and November 1988.

met almost entirely by drawing down stocks. If those had not been available, the 10-million-ton shortfall would also have forced a reduction in domestic consumption, or the importation of grain if it were available.

What will happen if there is a severe drought in 1989? Historically, the odds against severe back-to-back droughts have been rather high. But with global warming now apparently under way, the frequency of hot, dry summers is increasing. In the event of even a moderate drought in North America, world food prices would soar. A severe drought would cause a global food emergency.

In sum, overall food security is being threatened by two trends. One is the loss of momentum in the growth in output, a loss that is particularly noticeable in major developing countries, such as China, India, Indonesia, and Mexico.

The second trend is the warming of the planet. The areas that are likely to experience higher temperatures and lower rainfall include some of the earth's key food-producing regions, such as midcontinental North America. The world's farmers—already struggling to keep up with the record year-to-year growth in population—are facing the nineties with a great deal of uncertainty about how quickly the warming will progress and how it will affect their production.

Meeting adequate food needs during the nineties and beyond will require far more of the attention of political leaders, particularly those in the Third World, than ever before. (See Chapter 10.) Unless national governments are prepared to wage the war against hunger on a much broader front, it may not be possible to arrest the decline in per capita food production that is now undermining the future of so many people.

4

Abandoning Homelands

Jodi L. Jacobson

More than two years after an explosion at a nuclear reactor in the Ukraine spewed clouds of radiation from Kiev to Krakow, Soviet officials have announced plans to demolish the adjacent town of Chernobyl. This death warrant extinguished any hope of returning home for the city's 10,000 former residents. Because the world's worst nuclear disaster has permanently contaminated their town, they will be forced to settle elsewhere.[1]

These people are refugees, though ·not by any standard definition. According to widely accepted doctrine, refugees are people who decide to seek asylum out of fear of political, racial, or religious persecution, or who leave their homes because of war or civil strife. This conventional notion, however, leaves out a new and growing class—environmental refugees.

Throughout the world, vast areas are becoming unfit for human habitation. These lands are being despoiled either through long-term environmental degradation or by brief but catastrophic events. Unsustainable land use practices,

An expanded version of this chapter appeared as Worldwatch Paper 86, *Environmental Refugees: A Yardstick of Habitability*.

for example, have reduced the ability of ecosystems to support life throughout the Third World. At the same time, high-risk technologies have sometimes resulted in accidents, such as the Chernobyl explosion, that leave whole regions uninhabitable for extended periods. Moreover, the expected rise in sea level because of global warming threatens to reduce the planet's habitable area on a grand scale.

The growing number of people fleeing from environmental decline adds a new dimension to an already controversial global refugee problem. The number needing protection and assistance under traditional refugee classifications, now more than 13 million, mounts daily due to wars and insurrections, despotic governments, and deteriorating economic conditions, particularly in the Third World. Meanwhile, nations that have been traditional havens are increasingly trying to restrict this form of immigration.[2]

Most governments do not recognize environmental decline as a legitimate cause of refugee movements. Neither the U.S. State Department nor the U.N. High Commissioner for Refugees, for example, collects data on this problem.

Yet the number of environmental refugees—estimated to be at least 10 million—rivals that of officially recognized categories and is sure to overtake them.[3]

Judging by what people will put up with before they move away from an environmental hazard, society's standards concerning habitability are fairly lax. People are willing to tolerate a broad range of threats to health and longevity. Witness the fact that, throughout the world, densely populated cities plagued by air and water pollution are the rule rather than the exception. And in many countries, millions have built homes in areas prone to avalanches and floods.

For every environmental refugee, then, there are thousands more whose lives are compromised every day by unhealthy or hazardous conditions. Because migration is a last resort—when conditions become so poor that life itself is in imminent danger—the rising number of environmental refugees should be seen as an important indicator of the extent and severity of worldwide environmental deterioration.

In Search of Fertile Soils

In his landmark historical novel *The Grapes of Wrath,* John Steinbeck chronicled the economic and environmental disintegration of American farms in the Great Plains during the thirties. During that period, small farmers caught in the vise of poverty and debt took to planting crops from fencerow to fencerow to survive. Failed harvests and subsequent foreclosures rent the fabric of rural society, sending thousands of families westward in search of a livelihood. Most of these former landowners and sharecroppers became migrant workers.[4]

Though Steinbeck never used the term, his "Okies" were environmental refugees. To be sure, the depression had a strong impact on U.S. agriculture. But it was the severely degraded environment dubbed the Dust Bowl that ultimately forced farmers from their land. Unsustainable farming practices had impoverished soils and made them more vulnerable to erosion by wind and rain. As the drought that became a hallmark of that decade deepened, rural people's economic margin of safety vanished along with their topsoil.

Today, this story is repeating itself in many parts of the world. Agricultural lands are degrading on every continent. This deterioration is most acute and its impact is greatest in those developing countries where the majority of the people are farmers. Soil erosion may cost Canada some $1 billion annually in reduced yields, but Canadians do not starve. By contrast, sharply deteriorating land resources in Africa imperil the lives of millions.[5]

Land degradation is most often associated with poverty. Indeed, the two form a vicious circle. Throughout the Third World, subsistence farmers eke out a living on land depleted of nutrients, stripped of topsoil, and no longer able to withstand natural stresses such as drought or heavy rain.

These cultivators are, in a sense, victims of circumstance. Though the gross domestic product of most developing countries is dominated by farm goods, few invest in the agricultural sector beyond their support of cash crops for export. The low, government-regulated prices, inadequate credit and extension services, and inequitable land tenure characteristic of many developing countries have kept small landholders from increasing productivity in a sustainable manner. Eventually their land is depleted beyond restoration. Once this stage is reached, people are forced to move.

Pressed by growing families and deepening poverty, farmers make decisions to increase productivity that, in the long run, prove environmentally and economically disastrous. Cultivating land that should be fallowed, dividing already small plots among family members, bearing numerous children to help with farm chores, cutting ever-scarcer trees for fuel and fodder are all practices that, while they may ensure a meager harvest for tomorrow, make certain that famine is inevitable.

Mass migrations have become the enduring symbol of hunger. In Ethiopia, relief workers watch the movements of villagers toward food distribution centers as one indicator of conditions in the rural areas. In the country's northern region, "stone deserts" have replaced nearly 4 million hectares of once-fertile farmland. In June 1988, the U.S. embassy in Addis Ababa reported that about 1 million people in the highlands were about to move unexpectedly due to famine conditions. Soil erosion and rapid loss of productivity ensure that the next drought will create a new wave of environmental refugees.[6]

Many fleeing land degradation are not classified as environmental refugees because they simply move on to cultivate increasingly marginal lands. In Africa, thousands end up in the relief camps that are now regular fixtures on that continent. Others move to urban areas: the massive shift to cities that has occurred in the Third World since mid-century is due in large part to the complex of factors underlying land degradation.

"Throughout the Third World, land degradation has been the main factor in the migration of subsistence farmers into the slums and shantytowns of major cities, producing desperate populations vulnerable to disease and natural disasters and prone to participate in crime and civil strife," according to the United Nations Environment Programme (UNEP). "Such exodus . . . exacerbate[s] the already dire urban problems. . . . And, at the same time, it has delayed efforts to rehabilitate and develop rural areas—through the lack of manpower and the increased negligence of land."[7]

Mass migrations have become the enduring symbol of hunger.

Desertification, the most severe form of land degradation, is most acute in the arid and semiarid regions. (See Chapter 2.) A UNEP survey estimated that 4.5 billion hectares around the world—fully 35 percent of the earth's land surface—are in various stages of desertification. More than 850 million people live in these areas; many risk having their homes and livelihoods foreclosed by land degradation.[8]

About 135 million people inhabit areas undergoing severe desertification. Soil scientist Harold Dregne of Texas Tech University notes that "50 million . . . have already experienced a major loss in their ability to support themselves. [Furthermore] an unknown percentage of that 50 million will have to abandon their agricultural way of life and join the overcrowded cities to seek relief."[9]

Africa, a land where poor soils and variable rainfall pose a harsh climate for agriculture, has spawned the most environmental refugees. Most come from the Sahel, a belt that spans several agroecological zones and stretches west to east across some nine countries from Mauritania and Senegal on into the Sudan. Desertification is accelerating in the Sahel, the world's largest area to be threatened by the wholesale loss of arable land. As the region's habitability declines, the movement of people increases: in the last 20 years, the area's urban population has quadrupled.[10]

Two major droughts have occurred in the Sahel over the past two decades. In the first, from 1968 to 1973, between 100,000 and 250,000 people who waited too long to migrate died. To escape this fate, many Sahelians moved south and west to coastal African nations. Whole villages were abandoned as the movement across and within borders got under way. The flux of environmental refugees was the largest ever witnessed: more than 250,000 people in Mauritania, 20 percent of its population, joined the already growing ranks of destitute farmers in the country's towns. Nearly 1 million environmental refugees in Burkina Faso (then Upper Volta), a sixth of the country's population, migrated to cities.[11]

By 1974 there were 200,000 people in Niger completely dependent on food distribution in towns and camps. In Mali, 250,000, or 5 percent of the population, were totally aid-dependent. Côte d'Ivoire, with a relatively stable and developed economy, became the principal destination for many refugees from the growing desert.[12]

Years of lower-than-average rainfall persisted throughout the seventies and eighties, leading up to the second drought. By early 1984, more than 150 million people in 24 western, eastern, and southern African countries were on the brink of starvation. By March 1985, the drought had forced an estimated 10 million people to abandon their homes in search of food.[13]

In just five countries—Burkina Faso, Chad, Mali, Mauritania, and Niger—more than 2 million people were displaced during this second drought. (See Table 4–1.) Some 3 million, half of Niger's population, were affected by drought during 1983. There, Fulani and Tuareg pastoralists became paupers as two thirds of their herds died. By

Table 4-1. Displaced Population in Selected African Countries, September 1985

Country	People Displaced	Share of Population
	(number)	(percent)
Burkina Faso	222,000	3
Chad	500,000	11
Mali	200,000	3
Mauritania	190,000	12
Niger	1,000,000	16

SOURCES: U.N. Office of Emergency Operations in Africa, *Status Report on the Emergency Situation in Africa as of 1 September 1985* (New York: United Nations, 1985).

June 1985, some 400,000 nomads had moved to the cities. The population of Mauritania's capital, Nouakchott, swelled to four times its original size as desert swept the countryside. Its ancient cities of Chinguetti, Tichitt, Oualata, and Ouadane are now under constant siege from glacier-like waves of sand. Mauritania's only major roadway, optimistically christened the "Highway of Hope," has become hopelessly impassable.[14]

Changes in land use since colonial times that have undermined the partnership between people and land are among the causes of the Sahel's decline. Both human and livestock populations have increased dramatically. One result has been a growing competition between farmers and livestock herders for scarce land. In the state of Borno in Nigeria, a stable agricultural balance had held for centuries due to complementary land use patterns developed by the Hausa planters and the itinerant cattle-herders, the Fulani. But a breakdown in land stewardship, combined with the region's droughts, has reduced productivity and heightened tensions between the groups. In many cases, the herders have had to migrate.[15]

Pastoralists, politically less powerful

than their agrarian counterparts, often lose out in the struggle for land and are faced with the choice of grazing their herds on smaller patches or becoming settled farmers themselves. Long accustomed to wandering the continent's arid and semiarid lands in an ecologically balanced if somewhat tenuous partnership with nature, many of the great pastoral tribes, like the Fulani and the Tuareg, have been forced by government policy and land degradation to adopt a more sedentary life-style.

Governments throughout the Sahel encourage the establishment of cash-crop plantations and settled agriculture in rangelands for a host of economic and political reasons. But these types of farming, less ecologically appropriate than pastoralism in arid lands, reduce fallow periods and intensify degradation on land that is far too fragile for sustained cultivation. Not only have these policies further diminished the nomads' domain, but their increased conversion to sedentary farming concentrates large numbers of people and livestock around oases that in the past were visited only on a seasonal basis. (See Chapter 2.) Refugees from land degradation today, former nomads like the Tuaregs are sure to be on the move again within the next decade or so due to the declining habitability of the ecosystems they are crowding into.

Land degradation is also undermining habitability north of the Sahel. Larger human and cattle populations have exceeded the carrying capacity of arid lands in Algeria, Egypt, Libya, Morocco, and Tunisia. In Algeria, for example, desertification has begun to undercut the economy. UNEP notes that north of the Saharan Atlas mountains "some large settlements and cultivated lands are threatened by shifting sand dunes and sand drift." In Morocco, high population densities on arid lands are leading

to desertification. Irrigation canals, roads, and oases are threatened by drifting sand and shifting dunes.[16]

In the southern part of the continent, deforestation, soil erosion, and the depletion of water supplies have driven tens of thousands of environmental refugees from their farmlands to other rural areas, into towns and cities, or into relief camps. In Botswana, for example, boreholes have been drilled in many parts of the country to supply the water needs of cattle herds that have multiplied in part due to government incentives to export beef. Water tables are now dropping steadily as a result, forcing herders to migrate or give up their stock.[17]

What seems to be self-reinforcing drought conditions have also taken hold in India. Between 1978 and 1983, western Rajasthan and parts of eastern India were gripped by serious drought. Thousands of farmers whose crops had failed for years on end began moving out of these areas by mid-1983 to neighboring Haryana and Madhya Pradesh. Many moved to the huge coastal city of Madras, where the influx caused lines for such basic commodities as water.[18]

Mauritania's ancient cities of Chinguetti and Oudane are now under siege from glacier-like waves of sand.

In Latin America and the Caribbean, land degradation results from the combination of highly inequitable land distribution and rapidly growing populations. Latin America is home to some of the world's biggest cities in large part because of migration from rural areas. Millions of poverty-stricken farmers facing decades of agricultural neglect and land degradation throughout the mountains and the plains of South America fill the urban shantytowns of São Paulo, Rio de Janeiro, Mexico City, Lima, and La Paz. In many countries, particularly in Central America, the response to enduring poverty and environmental decline has been civil war and migration, often illegal, to the United States.[19]

Haiti, already the poorest country in the western hemisphere, also has the fastest-growing population. One third of the nation's land, exhausted by decades of deforestation and poor husbandry, is now virtually useless, and about 40 percent of the population is malnourished. More than half the land is held by less than 4 percent of the planters. The average holding for a peasant farmer is less than an acre. When food production per person began to decline in the fifties, farmers started adding to their incomes by selling charcoal. As trees vanished, so did the topsoil, further reducing food production and increasing reliance on charcoal for income. A combination of political repression, economic decline, and environmental devastation has pushed an estimated 1 million refugees—one sixth of Haiti's population— out of the country over the past decade.[20]

Agriculture is the backbone of developing economies. Yet throughout the Third World, farmers have been forced by financial and population pressures to adopt shortcut methods that are leading to long-term land degradation. By interfering with important natural cycles and overusing fragile, barely stable ecosystems, they are creating a self-reinforcing cycle of land deterioration. When the countryside is no longer able to produce a crop, the farmers along with the rest of the rural populace are forced to move on. Whether they end up in cities, in relief camps, or on other marginal lands, these people constitute a growing class of environmental refugees.

UNNATURAL DISASTERS

When an earthquake in Colombia or a flood in India causes hundreds of deaths and leaves thousands homeless, society accepts these losses as unfortunate accidents of fate. But more people are being killed or displaced by avalanches, cyclones, earthquakes, and floods than ever before, and close examination of the environmental backdrop against which these events occur suggests a strong human component. These disasters are second only to land degradation as a factor in the growing number of environmental refugees.

"Unnatural disasters"—normal events whose effects are exacerbated by human activities—are on the rise. Human pressures on forests, soils, and land have rendered ecosystems less resilient, less able to cope with natural fluctuations. Ultimately, they collapse under otherwise normal stresses, creating and magnifying disasters such as landslides and floods.

At the same time, competition for land and natural resources is driving more people to live in these marginal, disaster-prone areas, leaving them more vulnerable to natural forces. Hence, millions of Bangladeshis live on *chars*, bars of silt and sand in the middle of the Bengal delta, some of which are washed away each year by ocean tides and monsoon floods. Millions of Nepalis live in the areas most likely to be hit by earthquakes. And thousands of slum dwellers in the cities of Latin America perch on deforested hillsides prone to mudslides in heavy rain.

Human-induced changes in the environment can turn a normal event into a catastrophe. The deterioration of major watersheds in many developing countries, for example, increases the number of devastating floods. A 1988 flood in Bangladesh came on the heels of heavy monsoon rains in the Himalayan watershed of the Ganges river system. In addition to an astounding 25 million left homeless, at least 1,200 people died and hundreds of thousands more contracted diseases as a result of contaminated food and water supplies.[21]

Bangladesh, with its per capita income of $160 ranking it among the world's poorest, is one of the most densely populated nations. More than 110 million people—almost half the population of the United States—are packed into a country about the size of Wisconsin. The nation sits on a vast, low-lying island of silt that makes up the world's largest river delta.[22]

Bangladeshis are accustomed to having water overflow the banks of their mighty rivers. Each year, monsoon rains quench the thirsty Indian subcontinent, shedding moisture essential for crops. Water accumulated in the Himalayan ranges of Bhutan, India, Nepal, and Tibet runs through the Ganges and two other large rivers, the Brahmaputra and the Meghna, into Bangladesh, supplying all but 10 percent of the country's water.[23]

This water is critical to Bangladesh's agricultural output: rice farmers, for example, depend on moderate annual floods for a successful harvest. And the silt carried by rivers and streams into the delta region helps maintain soil fertility. In moderation, these natural commodities are essential to Bangladesh; in excess, they can be disastrous.

But up in the Himalayan watershed, where agrarian people depend on wood for fuel, a large and rapidly expanding rural population has been outstripping the carrying capacity of the environment. Deforestation, overgrazing, and unsustainable farming practices have diminished the soil's ability to absorb water. Available data, though not comprehensive, suggest that from half to three fourths of the middle mountain

ranges in Nepal and India have been deforested in the last four decades.[24]

In the past, truly massive floods hit Bangladesh only once every 50 years or so. But since mid-century the number of large-scale floods has markedly increased. The country was heavily inundated on average once every four years through the seventies. After a flood in 1974, an estimated 300,000 people died in a famine that led to the overthrow of the country's founder, Sheik Mujibur Rahman. Since 1980, several "50-year" floods have occurred, each worse than the last.[25]

Similarly, degradation of the Nile watershed contributed to flooding in the Sudan in 1988. The headwaters of the Blue Nile are in the highlands of Ethiopia, where a rich and diverse agriculture developed thousands of years ago. Today, the highlands constitute 90 percent of the arable land, supporting 88 percent of the country's population and 60 percent of its livestock. But deforestation and poor soil husbandry, coupled with rapid population growth, have undermined the nation's agricultural base.[26]

Thousands of slum dwellers in Latin America perch on deforested hillsides prone to mudslides in heavy rain.

Because land degradation has disrupted the hydrological cycle, in which water is recycled to and from the atmosphere through soil absorption and plant transpiration, the entire region is considerably drier than in the past. Extensive floods are not normally a feature of the region downstream of the highlands, but in 1988 an exceptionally heavy rainfall, together with the watershed's reduced holding capacity, allowed a torrent to wreak havoc on the Sudanese plain below. Khartoum was ravaged by the deepest flooding to strike the Sudan in this century, and some 1.5 million people were left homeless.[27]

Some "natural" tragedies are the result of development strategies that blatantly disregard their impact on the environment. In 1983, a cyclone in the Philippines that normally might have caused fewer than 100 fatalities killed thousands. Floods caused by the tropical storm were far more numerous and severe than in the past. "Villages built in places where flooding had not been a problem before are having to deal with patterns of water runoff that have been radically changed by the lumbering and mining operations which have spread unchecked," writes Debora MacKenzie in the *New Scientist.* "Slag heaps from mines have been thrown up in valleys, sometimes completely rerouting rivers, and whole forests have disappeared."[28]

Deforestation of mountains and hills that ring cities in the developing world has led to an increasing number of mudslides in urban shantytowns. In September 1987, more than 500 people were killed in a cascade of mud and rocks in Medellín, Colombia, after torrential rains had soaked the Andes for a week. Only half the population of Villa Tina, an impoverished suburb of Medellín, survived the catastrophe.[29]

Five months later a similar disaster hit the shantytowns of Rio de Janeiro. Eighteen inches of rain fell on the city over three weeks, destabilizing the mountainsides once forested by soil-grabbing trees but now blanketed with huts of scrap wood, adobe, and sheet metal. Nearly 300 people died, 1,000 were injured, and more than 18,000 were left homeless. Mac Margolis of the *Washington Post* noted that although this was the worst such storm since 1966, "Lately . . . even modest rains have proven deadly . . . render[ing] this sophisticated

metropolis a hostage to the elements."[30]

These "unnatural disasters" are largely a product of the same kind of land degradation discussed in the previous section, in which financial and population pressures force both farmers and urban dwellers onto marginal lands that soon lose their stability. But in this case the land degradation—while devastating in itself and also to be feared because it is self-reinforcing—inhibits the ability of ecosystems to roll with nature's punches. The result has been that the rare has become commonplace, the extremes of weather that have been endured and survived through the millennia are increasingly turning into full-fledged catastrophes on an unprecedented scale.

A TOXIC HOME

Although Guy Reynolds and his wife moved to Springfield, Vermont, in a mobile home, they arrived with the intention of staying put. But the Reynolds family and 59 other residents of the mobile-home park in which they live have been forced to evacuate. In July 1988, the U.S. Environmental Protection Agency (EPA) ordered their relocation when it determined that the park was atop a landfill containing toxic chemicals. The Reynolds family and their neighbors are among a small but growing number of refugees from land poisoned by hazardous wastes. Once confined to industrial countries, the inherent conflict between disposal of toxic wastes and human habitation is spreading around the world.[31]

Chemical contamination can be sudden—the result of a rail accident, for instance. Or it can result from the insidious penetration of toxics into the atmosphere, the food chain, or water supplies. Although toxic wastes pose a pervasive threat to the environment, until recently few countries had laws regulating their disposal. As a result, many companies found it easier and cheaper to discard their wastes into landfills, waterways, or the atmosphere. The disposal of chemical wastes in landfills over the past several decades has created enormous problems for communities throughout the world now faced with the choice of expensive cleanups or contamination of their environment by leaking toxics.

In the United States, dumping wastes into landfills that were later topped off and used for other purposes, such as housing developments, became commonplace. Today, thousands of toxic waste sites are festering sores in towns and cities throughout the country, and a battle continues over the hazards they represent and who should bear the responsibility for cleaning them up. In some cases, people remain in their homes, accepting higher risks to health because they are unable to sell their property and cannot otherwise afford to move. In other cases, toxic contamination is so bad that whole communities become ghost towns virtually overnight.

Love Canal was one such community. Beginning in 1920, a partially completed channel between the upper and lower Niagara Rivers in upstate New York came into use as a municipal and chemical waste dump. In 1953, the channel was filled in, and homes and schools were subsequently built on and around the site. Over time, chemicals buried in the canal began to surface, and residents often complained of strange odors and substances. In 1976, a consultant discovered toxic chemical residues in the air and sump pumps of a good percentage of homes bordering the canal. High levels of carcinogenic polychlorinated biphenyls (PCBs) were found in the storm sewer system.[32]

Not until 1978 did the New York State Department of Health—based on evidence of a high incidence of reproductive problems among women and high levels of chemical contamination in homes, the soil, and air—order the evacuation of pregnant women and of children under the age of two from 239 homes. Eventually, all but 86 of the 900 families living in Love Canal were evacuated. Purchasing the homes of the former residents cost the federal government $20 million. Another $200 million is being spent to clean up the area.[33]

In the United States, thousand of toxic waste sites are festering sores in towns and cities.

Love Canal proved to be just the first of many. Thousands of other sites across the country are contaminated by both legally and illegally dumped wastes. Realizing that both government and industry would have to share the burden of the cleanup, the U.S. Congress enacted the Superfund program in 1980.[34]

Since then, 1,390 families in 42 communities across the United States have been relocated with Superfund money. In 1983, Times Beach, Missouri, a suburb of St. Louis with a population of 2,400, was abandoned and disincorporated as a result of the careless spraying on city streets of oil laced with highly toxic dioxin. A combination of federal and state funds helped relocate families from Globe, Arizona, and Centralia, Pennsylvania, in the same year.[35]

Because relocation is less costly and simpler than detoxifying contaminated sites—not to mention a faster way of protecting people—the U.S. government has increasingly used this option to deal with the toxic waste problem. Since

1985 this class of environmental refugees has more than doubled.[36]

Some who would flee remain in hazardous areas because of financial circumstances. About a fifth of the petrochemical production in the United States is concentrated along the 85-mile stretch of the Mississippi River that winds from Baton Rouge to New Orleans, Louisiana. Local economies are primarily dependent on the jobs and income offered by the 135 chemical plants and seven oil refineries that line this corridor. But the region absorbs more toxic substances annually than do most entire states, including such dangerous substances as vinyl chloride, a carcinogen and suspected embryotoxin.[37]

The Polish government recently declared Bogomice and four other villages "unfit for human habitation."

According to the *Washington Post,* "the air, ground, and water along this corridor are so full of carcinogens, mutagens, and embryotoxins that an environmental health specialist defined living [there] as 'a massive human experiment,' the state attorney general called the pollution 'a modern form of barbarism,' and a chemical union leader now refers to it as 'the national sacrifice zone.'" Several towns in the corridor exhibit uncommonly high rates of cancer and miscarriages.[38]

Because most of these compounds represent creeping rather than sudden dangers to health, and because little research has been undertaken to separate out the contribution of toxic chemicals from other health threats, government protection or assistance for relocation does not extend to residents of Louisiana's chemical corridor. Indeed, public policies—such as lax controls on pollut-

ers—have encouraged the growth of this industry. As a result, hundreds of thousands of people remain subject to the dangers of toxic poisoning and disease in an area that is barely inhabitable.

Urban residents around the world have long tacitly accepted the reality of living with higher levels of pollution in their immediate environment, particularly in the air they breathe. Automobiles, power plants, and industrial plants are the biggest contributors to air pollution. Where pollution control technology is unavailable or regulations are unenforced, as in Eastern Europe and the Soviet Union, regions where the postwar rush to industrialize was given precedence over environmental protection, emissions have made atmospheric pollution so bad that whole regions are virtually uninhabitable.

Pollution poses grave threats to agriculture and human health throughout Eastern Europe. The Polish government, for example, recently declared Bogomice and four other villages "unfit for human habitation" due to the extremely high levels of heavy metals in the air and soil deposited by emissions from nearby copper-smelting plants. The government is encouraging villagers from this region to resettle elsewhere by offering compensation.[39]

Likewise, in the Soviet Union the quality of air, soil, water, and forest resources is in rapid decline. Fyodor Morgun, head of the country's Environmental Protection Committee, declared recently that degradation from industrial waste has reached the proportions of "a Chernobyl-like catastrophe." Problems are particularly acute in the Ural Mountains, a region of heavy industry. In December 1987, *Pravda* stated that the industrial city of Ufa, with a population of nearly 1 million, had become "unfit for human habitation."[40]

Sudden accidents, such as a rail crash, fire, or explosion, can instantaneously confer upon thousands of people the status of environmental refugee. In the 19 years leading up to 1978, seven major chemical accidents worldwide killed 739 people, injured 2,647, and forced 18,-230 from their homes. All but one occurred in industrial countries. Since then, the number and severity of toxic disasters has increased, with more of these in the Third World. In the eight years following 1978, there were 13 major chemical accidents. The numbers tell the tragedy: 3,930 dead; 4,848 injured; and nearly 1 million evacuated.[41]

Among the worst examples of an accident in the industrial world was the 1976 explosion at a small chemical plant in Seveso, Italy, that sent a cloud of smoke and highly toxic dioxin particles wafting over the countryside. Eight hundred people were evacuated from their homes for more than a year; although many have returned, questions about their health linger. Incomplete data suggest an elevated rate of birth defects in the two years following the explosion. Whether the accident will result in a higher incidence of cancers with long latency periods will only be known over time.[42]

Higher wage costs and tighter controls on production and disposal of hazardous chemical materials in industrial nations, along with the development of a global market for chemical products, have sent some multinational firms scurrying to build plants in developing nations. Experience shows that such investments can be a mixed blessing. Although they gain some jobs and revenue from the chemical industry, most developing countries have neither laws controlling toxic chemicals nor the technical and institutional capacity to put them into force. The general lack of controls makes incidents of contamination more likely.[43]

The toxic leak in 1984 at Bhopal, India, was perhaps the worst example of this trend. A Union Carbide pesticide plant accidentally released a cloud of deadly methyl isocyante over the town, killing about 2,500 and sending more than 200,000 fleeing for their lives. As many as 100,000 people are still suffering side effects, such as blurred vision, disabling lung diseases, intestinal bleeding, and neurological and psychological disorders. Bhopal, less a case of permanently reduced environmental habitability, is certainly evidence of the dangers inherent in many of the industrial and development choices being made today.[44]

Nuclear reactor accidents have the most pervasive and long-lasting consequences of any industrial catastrophe. The April 1986 explosion and fire at Chernobyl in the Soviet Union caused a partial meltdown of the plant's reactor core. More than seven tons of radioactive material were hurled into the atmosphere, eventually contaminating land, food, and water throughout much of Europe. Twenty-eight people died from acute radiation poisoning within 75 days of the accident, while another 300 were treated for serious radiation exposure. More than 100,000 people were evacuated from their homes, and up to 2,500 square kilometers became uninhabitable.[45]

Chernobyl was the worst reactor accident in history and will not easily be forgotten. But the fact remains that an even more serious disaster could occur at any time at a reactor in a densely populated area. A Chernobyl-like accident at the Indian Point plant in the New York metropolitan region could require the permanent evacuation of more than 1 million people. Assessing the risks inherent in using nuclear power under the most optimistic conditions, nuclear analysts have determined that with 500 nuclear plants in operation, there would be one core-damaging accident every 20 years, based on one accident for every 10,000 years of reactor operation. But the Three Mile Island accident in the United States occurred after only 1,500 years of worldwide reactor operation, and Chernobyl occurred after another 1,900 years.[46]

The rapidly growing volume of hazardous waste in industrialized nations, coupled with high disposal costs, has led some companies to export their industrial residues to the Third World, threatening a new wave of chemical illnesses and refugees. It costs from $250 to $350 per ton to dispose of hazardous municipal and industrial wastes in the United States, for example, but some developing countries will accept such wastes for as little as $40 per ton.[47]

Local conditions and lack of monitoring or waste treatment means that a large proportion of these imported wastes will end up in the local environment. Frequent rains and poor soils in tropical areas hasten the migration of chemical wastes into groundwater supplies.

Thousands of tons of U.S. and European wastes have already been shipped to Africa and the Middle East. Some 3,800 tons of toxic waste from Italy dumped in the small Nigerian port town of Koko in five shipments between 1987 and 1988 contained at least 150 tons of PCBs—the chemical that put Love Canal on the map. The contamination was the result of an illegal deal between an Italian waste contractor and several corrupt Nigerian government officials. Residents of Koko complained that the odors given off by the leaking sacks and containers of waste made them ill. The government plans to evacuate the 5,000 residents. The Italian government has since accepted responsibility for reclaiming and destroying the wastes but, as of early December 1988, a ship laden with the toxics from Koko had yet to find a port that would accept the hazardous chemicals.[48]

Similarly, waste shipped from Italy to Lebanon in May 1988 will be reclaimed by Italy and incinerated aboard a ship in the middle of the Pacific. More than 2,400 tons of toxic chemicals found their way to Beirut in a transaction involving both Lebanese and European merchants, without government supervision. Lebanon's health minister recognized the threat immediately: these wastes are "poisonous and harmful to man and the environment," he said. Other countries, such as Benin, the Congo, and Guinea-Bissau, are reconsidering plans to accept large quantities of waste from the United States and Europe in the wake of an international outcry against dumping. The Congo, for example, recently canceled a contract to accept 20,000–50,000 tons of pesticide residue and sludge waste a month from a firm in New Jersey.[49]

Growing recognition and control of hazardous waste disposal may make the world a safer place to live—for a while. Two international treaties that would curtail trade in hazardous exports are being negotiated, and individual countries and regions are beginning to take action on their own. In May 1988, the Organization of African Unity passed a resolution condemning the practice of accepting toxic chemicals from the industrial world, and various of its member states are taking action to implement the declaration. The same month, the European Parliament urged its governments to adopt national legislation that would ensure recipient countries can handle the wastes. In the United States, two bills introduced in Congress would restrict the export of hazardous substances. Despite these laudable efforts, little has been done to reduce at the source the large volumes of toxic substances produced by industrial activity.[50]

THE THREAT OF INUNDATION

Around the world, the Dutch are perhaps best known for their achievements in water engineering. And well they should be: without the carefully maintained stretches of dikes (400 kilometers long) and sand dunes (200 kilometers) built by Holland's engineers to hold back the sea, more than half the country would be uninhabitable. Currently, 8 million people make their homes and livelihoods on this reclaimed delta, a region of unquestioned social and economic importance. The stakes in protecting it, however, are certain to mount. Rising sea levels promise to test even the Dutch capabilities in water management.[51]

Among the various environmental problems that cause the displacement of people from their homes, none rivals the potential effects of sea level rise as a result of human-induced changes in the earth's climate. A one-meter rise in ocean levels worldwide, for example, may result in the creation of 50 million environmental refugees from various countries—more than triple the number in all recognized refugee categories today.

Most scientists agree that a global warming is under way, caused by the accumulation of "greenhouse gases" due primarily to fossil fuel use in industrial countries. The uncertainties lie in just how much higher the earth's average temperature will go, and how quickly the increase will take place. Recent estimates predict that a global temperature increase of 1.5–4.5 degrees Celsius (3–8 degrees Fahrenheit) can be expected as early as 2030, rising to as much as 5 degrees by 2100. (See Chapter 1.)[52]

If correct, this would precipitate a rise in sea level of 1.4–2.2 meters by the end of next century. (By comparison, global sea level rise has probably not exceeded 15 centimeters over the past century.) Such an increase will affect people and infrastructure around the globe, but developing countries stand to suffer the most immediate and dramatic impacts.[53]

President Maumoon Abdul Gayoom of the Maldives has put the problem bluntly: "The predicted effects of the change are unnerving: There will be significant shoreline movement and loss of land. A higher mean sea level would inevitably . . . increase frequency of inundation and exacerbate flood damage. It would inundate fertile deltas, causing loss of productive agricultural land and vegetation, and increase saline encroachment into aquifers, rivers and estuaries. The increased costs of reconstruction, rehabilitation and strengthening of coastal defence systems could turn out to be crippling for most affected countries."[54]

Some climatologists now estimate that the rate of sea level rise will accelerate after 2050, reaching 2–3 centimeters a year. But actual sea level rise will be much higher in some regions than others because of obvious differences like land elevation and less obvious differences in geological processes such as tectonic uplift (natural shifts in the earth's crust) or subsidence in coastal areas. Subsidence is a key issue in the case of river deltas.[55]

Under natural conditions, deltas are in a state of dynamic equilibrium, forming and breaking down in a continuous pattern of accretion and subsidence. The Mississippi River delta in the United States, for example, was built up by sediments deposited during floods and laid down by the river on its way to the sea. Over time, these sediments accumulate. But regional and local tectonic effects, along with compaction, cause the land created to subside. Local subsidence alone can translate into a water level rise as great as 10 centimeters per year. Relative rates of sea level rise, then, depend on the sum of global sea level rise and local subsidence.[56]

Subsidence is likely to accelerate where subterranean stores of water or oil are tapped. In Bangkok, Thailand, local subsidence has reached 13 centimeters per year due to a drop in the water table caused by excessive withdrawals of groundwater over the past three decades. Moreover, channeling, diverting, or damming rivers can greatly reduce the amount of sediment that reaches a delta. When this happens, as it has on the Mississippi and the Nile, sediment accumulation will not offset subsidence, resulting in heavier shoreline erosion and an increase in water levels.[57]

Low-lying delta regions, important from both an ecological and social standpoint, will be among the first land areas lost to inundation under even slight rises in sea level. Fertile deltas are important sources of food and other products. Of the world's major deltas, several, including the Bengal and Nile, are also densely populated. As a result, these regions will be the single greatest source of refugees from sea level rise. A recent study by researchers at Woods Hole Oceanographic Institute in Massachusetts showed the combined effects of sea level rise and subsidence on Bangladesh and Egypt, where the homes and livelihoods of some 46 million people are potentially threatened.[58]

The researchers developed three possible scenarios under two estimates of sea level rise: a minimum of 13 centimeters by 2050 and 28 centimeters by 2100, and a maximum of 79 centimeters by 2050 and 217 centimeters by 2100. The "best case" scenario assumes the minimum rise in global sea level and a delta region in equilibrium. The second scenario, called the "worst case," assumes the maximum rate of sea level rise and the complete damming or diversion of the river system draining into the delta.

In this case, the rate of natural subsidence must then be added to the absolute rise in sea level. The third scenario is accurately referred to as the "really worst case." It assumes that excessive groundwater pumping from irrigation and other uses accelerates natural subsidence.

Low-lying delta regions will be among the first land areas lost to inundation under rises in sea level.

To calculate the economic implications of these three cases on both Egypt and Bangladesh, the researchers assumed present-day conditions, such as the estimated share of total population now living in areas that would be inundated and the share of economic activity that is derived from them. Continued settlement and population growth in these areas will of course translate into even more future environmental refugees.

The Bengal Delta, resting at the confluence of the Ganges, Brahmaputra, and Meghna rivers, is the world's largest such coastal plain and constitutes about 80 percent of the country's total area (the other one fifth is water). As a result, the region's inhabitants are subject to annual floods both from the rivers and from ocean storm surges.

Just how severely sea level rise will affect Bangladesh depends in part on the pace at which damming and channeling of rivers proceeds and the rate of groundwater withdrawal. Although annual flooding is severe and can damage up to one third of the crops grown on the flood plains, large areas of the delta region suffer rain deficits for the rest of the year, thus creating a large incentive to divert river water for agriculture.

Table 4-2. Effects of Sea Level Rise on the Bengal and Nile River Deltas Under Two Scenarios

	Sea Level Rise					Gross National Product Lost
	Global Sea Level Rise	Local Land Subsidence	Local Sea Level Rise	Habitable Land Lost	Population Displaced	
	(centimeters)			(percent)		
Bangladesh in 2050						
Worst Case[1]	79	65	144	16	13	10
Really Worst Case[2]	79	130	209	18	15	13
Bangladesh in 2100						
Worst Case[1]	217	115	332	26	27	22
Really Worst Case[2]	217	230	447	34	35	31
Egypt in 2050						
Worst Case[1]	79	22	101	15	14	14
Really Worst Case[2]	79	65	144	19	16	16
Egypt in 2100						
Worst Case[1]	217	40	257	21	19	19
Really Worst Case[2]	217	115	332	26	24	24

[1]Assumes complete damming or diversion of river system draining into delta. [2]Assumes excessive groundwater pumping accelerates natural subsidence.
SOURCE: John D. Milliman et al., "Environmental and Economic Impact of Rising Sea Level and Subsiding Deltas: The Nile and Bengal Examples," Woods Hole Oceanographic Institute, Woods Hole, Mass., unpublished paper, 1988.

Such diversions would have a severe impact on the amount of sediment available to offset natural subsidence.

On the basis of the limited data available, the Woods Hole researchers have concluded that the increasing withdrawal of groundwater in Bangladesh is affecting subsidence rates. Between 1978 and 1985, the number of wells drilled in the country increased at least sixfold; more than 100,000 shallow tubewells and 20,000 deeper ones were counted. Sediment samples suggest that groundwater withdrawal may have raised subsidence to at least twice the natural rate.

Half the country lies at elevations of less than five meters. Loss of land under the 13-centimeter rise in the best case scenario would be minimal by 2050—less than 1 percent of the country's total. In the 144-centimeter rise assumed in the worst case, however, 16 percent of the nation's land would be lost. And in the really worst case, local sea level rise would be 209 centimeters and 18 percent of the habitable land would be under water. (See Table 4–2.) As a result, more than 17 million people would become environmental refugees.

By the year 2100, the really worst case scenario shows that 35 percent of the nation's population—some 38 million people—would be forced to relocate. The economic effects would be devastating. Because nearly a third of Bangladesh's gross national product is realized within the land area that could be lost, an already poor country would have to accommodate its people on a far smaller economic base.[59]

The combined effects of warmer climates and higher seas will make tropical storms more frequent and more destructive, raising the toll in lives and further decreasing the habitability of coastal areas. Cyclones originating in the Bay of Bengal before and after the rainy season already devastate the southern part of Bangladesh on a regular basis. On average, 1.5 severe cyclones now hit the country each year. Storm surges as much as six meters higher than normal can reach as far as 200 kilometers inland. Total property loss from storms in the region between 1945 and 1975 has been estimated at $7 billion, and some 300,000 lives were lost in 1970 when surge waters covered an estimated 35 percent of Bangladesh. The impact of stronger and more frequent storms on this densely populated country is unthinkable.

Bangladesh as it is known today may virtually cease to exist.

Where will those displaced by rising seas go? Moving farther inland, millions of environmental refugees will have to compete with the local populace for scarce food, water, and land, perhaps spurring regional clashes. Moreover, existing tensions between Bangladesh and its large neighbor to the west, India, are likely to heighten as the certain influx of environmental refugees from the former rises. Eventually, the combination of rising seas, harsher storms, and degradation of the Bengal delta may wreak so much damage that Bangladesh as it is known today may virtually cease to exist.

Egypt's habitable area is even more densely populated than Bangladesh. By and large, Egypt is desert: less than 4 percent of the country's land is cultivated and settled, supporting a population of 1,800 people per square kilometer. The Nile River and its delta, accounting for nearly all the country's productive land, is Egypt's economic lifeline.

Damming has virtually reduced the Nile's contribution of sediment and fresh water to the Mediterranean to a trickle. The Woods Hole study points out that because the Nile has been dammed, only the "worst" and "really worst" cases are relevant for Egypt, since most of the sediment that would offset subsidence of the delta is trapped upstream. Consequently, sea level rise would range between 101 and 144 centimeters by 2050, rendering up to 19 percent of Egypt's already scarce habitable land unlivable.

If the higher increment were realized, more than 8.5 million people would be forced to relinquish their homes to the sea and Egypt would lose 16 percent of its gross national product. By 2100, sea level rise would range between 257 and 332 centimeters, inundating up to 26 percent of habitable land and affecting an equal portion—24 percent—of both population and domestic economic output. Several shallow, brackish lakes along the coast, accounting for half the nation's fish catch, would also be endangered.[60]

Although neither Bangladesh nor Egypt is likely to markedly influence global emissions of greenhouse gases or sea level rise, they each wield considerable control over local sea levels. Development policies chosen in the near future will determine the rates of degradation and subsidence of these respective deltas.

In 2100, cartographers will likely be drawing maps with new coastlines for many countries as a result of sea level rise. They may also make an important deletion: by that year, if current projections are borne out, the Maldives may have been swallowed up by the sea. This small nation, a series of 1,190 islands in atolls, is nowhere higher in elevation than two meters. A mean sea level rise of equal height would submerge the entire country. With a one-meter rise, well within the expected increment of the next century, a storm surge would, in the words of President Gayoom, be "catastrophic and possibly fatal." Other such endangered areas include the Pacific islands of Kiribati, Tuvalu, and the Marshall Islands.[61]

Industrial nations, heavily reliant on the burning of fossil fuels over the past century, must assume the primary responsibility for global warming and its consequences. And while they are in a far better financial position than developing countries to undertake the remedial technological measures necessary to save coastal areas and inhabited land (thereby mitigating the problem of environmental refugees), these actions will cost them dearly. The Dutch spent tens of billions of dollars over the past three decades building dikes and pumping systems to hold back the sea. They will have to spend at least $5 billion more by 2040 simply maintaining this system to save their delta region as sea levels rise. Large though these expenditures are, they are trivial compared with what the United States, with more than 19,000 kilometers of coastline, will have to spend to protect its territorial integrity.[62]

A YARDSTICK OF HABITABILITY

On every continent, the living patterns of people are at odds with natural systems. In industrial countries, consump-

tion patterns and industrial policies that ignore environmental limits have fouled the planet with everything from toxic wastes to greenhouse gases. In the Third World, population growth, poverty, and ill-conceived development policies are the root cause of environmental degradation. The large and growing number of refugees worldwide that has resulted from these trends is living evidence of a continuing decline in the earth's habitability.

Environmental refugees have become the single largest class of displaced persons in the world. They fall into three broad categories: those displaced temporarily because of a local disruption such as an avalanche or earthquake; those who migrate because environmental degradation has undermined their livelihood or poses unacceptable risks to health; and those who resettle because land degradation has resulted in desertification or because of other permanent and untenable changes in their habitat. Although precise numbers are hard to fix due to lack of data, it appears that this last group—the permanently displaced—is both the largest and the fastest growing. Until sea level rise overtakes it, land degradation will remain the single most important cause of environmental refugees. As it occurs in stages, moving from moderate to severe desertification, it produces refugees in both the second and third categories.

Current trends are likely to worsen over the next few decades unless society acts to combat the problems underscored by the creation of environmental refugees. More and more land will be rendered unproductive or uninhabitable, whether through desertification, toxic pollution, or unnatural disasters. By the middle of the next century, the combined number of environmental refugees from all these and the inevitable rise in sea level because of global warming will probably exceed the number of refugees today from all other causes by a factor of six.

The vision of tens of millions of persons forced to abandon their homelands is a frightening prospect, one without precedent and likely to rival most past and current wars in its impact on humanity. The growing number of environmental refugees today is already a rough indicator of the severity of global environmental decline. This yardstick may be imprecise but its message could not be clearer.

5

Protecting the Ozone Layer

Cynthia Pollock Shea

When British scientists reported in 1985 that a hole in the ozone layer over Antarctica had been occurring each spring since 1979, the news came as a complete surprise. Although the theory that a group of widely used chemicals called chlorofluorocarbons (CFCs) would someday erode upper atmospheric ozone had been advanced in the mid-seventies, none of the models had predicted that the thinning would first be evident over the South Pole—nor that it would be so severe. Scientists were baffled: What was threatening this key life-support system? And how many other surprises lay in store?[1]

Ozone, the three-atom form of oxygen, is the only gas in the atmosphere that prevents harmful solar ultraviolet radiation from reaching the surface of the earth. Most of it is found at altitudes of between 12 and 25 kilometers, but even there, at its greatest concentration,

it is present at only a few parts per million. Sunlight-triggered chemical reactions constantly replenish ozone above the tropics and global air circulation transports some of it to the poles.

By the Antarctic spring of 1987, the average ozone concentration over the South Pole was down 50 percent. In isolated spots it had essentially disappeared. Although the depletion was alarming, many were convinced that the thinning was seasonal and unique to Antarctica, a phenomenon attributable to altered atmospheric chemistry and to perplexing polar air circulation.[2]

A scientific report issued in March 1988 shattered this view: more than 100 international experts reported that the ozone layer around the entire globe was eroding much faster than any model had predicted. Between 1969 and 1986, the average global concentration of ozone in the stratosphere had fallen by approximately 2 percent. The magnitude of the decline varied by latitude and by season, with the most heavily populated regions of Europe, North America, and the So-

An expanded version of this chapter appeared as Worldwatch Paper 87, *Protecting Life on Earth: Steps to Save the Ozone Layer.*

viet Union suffering a year-round depletion of 3 percent and a winter loss of 4.7 percent.[3]

As ozone diminishes in the upper atmosphere, the earth receives more ultraviolet radiation, which promotes skin cancers and cataracts and depresses human immune systems. Reduced crop yields, depleted marine fisheries, materials damage, and increased smog are also attributable to higher levels of radiation. The phenomenon is global and will affect the well-being of every person in the world.

In 1984 the ozone hole was larger than the United States and taller than Mount Everest.

Compounds containing chlorine and bromine, which are released from industrial processes and products and then move slowly into the upper atmosphere, are considered the primary culprits. Most of the chlorine comes from CFCs; the bromine originates from halons used in fire extinguishers. Spurred to action by the ozone hole over Antarctica, 35 countries have signed an international agreement—the Montreal Protocol—aimed at halving most CFC emissions by 1998 and freezing halon emissions by 1992. Although an impressive diplomatic achievement and an important first step, the agreement is so riddled with loopholes that its objectives will not be met. Furthermore, scientific findings subsequent to the negotiations reveal that even if the treaty's goals were met, significant further deterioration of the ozone layer would still occur. The fact that CFCs and halons are also "greenhouse gases" and that global warming may already be under way (see Chapter 1) strengthens the need to further control and eliminate emissions.[4]

The fundamental links between CFCs, halons, and ozone depletion are no longer in doubt. Currently available control technologies and stricter standards governing equipment operation and maintenance could reduce CFC and halon emissions by some 90 percent. But effective government policies and industry practices to limit and ultimately phase out chlorine and bromine emissions have yet to be formulated. Encouraging steps have been taken by some countries, particularly in Scandinavia, and by some corporations. But just as the effects of ozone depletion will be felt worldwide, a lasting remedy to the problem must also be global.

THE OZONE DEPLETION PUZZLE

In 1985, a team led by Joseph Farman, of the British Antarctic Survey, startled the world by reporting a 40-percent loss in the springtime ozone layer over Antarctica. Using equipment developed in the twenties, the team discovered the lowest concentration of ozone ever recorded on earth. Although Sherwood Rowland and Mario Molina of the University of California at Irvine had predicted a decline in global ozone back in 1974, the international scientific community was skeptical; why hadn't state-of-the-art monitoring devices aboard sophisticated satellites detected the drop?[5]

Closer examination revealed that satellite sensors had in fact recorded the decline, and even flagged the lowest values, but that scientists had fallen behind in processing the voluminous data. Indeed, computer archives showed that in 1984 the previously undetected ozone hole was larger than the United States and taller than Mount Everest.[6]

Faced with evidence of a phenomenon that had not been predicted by atmospheric models, scientists scurried to explain the cause and to determine if more widespread depletion, outside of Antarctica, was likely. Numerous theories based on both chemical and natural causes were put forth. A reassessment of satellite and terrestrial data was planned, along with ground- and air-based expeditions to the continent.

Scientists on the first Antarctic expedition arrived in late August 1986, hoping to determine quickly whether the ozone hole was caused by natural forces or by manufactured chemicals. The secret was not easily revealed. Several experiments cast doubt on the theories that blamed solar cycles and the upward movement of tropospheric air, but tests to confirm chemical destruction theories were inconclusive. Team leader Susan Solomon carefully summed up the findings, "Based on the existing theories, chlorine is the only one we can't rule out . . . .We believe that a chemical mechanism is fundamentally responsible for the hole."[7]

Another, much larger expedition composed of 150 scientists and support personnel representing 19 organizations and four nations was planned for 1987. Based in Punta Arenas, Chile, the NOZE II (National Ozone Expedition) team conducted satellite, aircraft, balloon, and ground measurements. Satellite data, available within 24 hours, helped researchers direct two specially retrofitted planes into the center of the hole.[8]

Monitoring equipment detected that the average ozone concentration in a hole twice as large as the United States dropped by nearly half from August 15 to October 7. In some areas within the hole, ozone had vanished completely. The scientists attributed the decline to a combination of factors: unique meteorological conditions present in Antarctica, the presence of polar stratospheric clouds, low concentrations of nitrogen oxides, and, most important, high concentrations of active chlorine.

The pieces of the puzzle started to fall into place. During the long, sunless Antarctic winter (from about March to August), air over the continent becomes isolated in a swirling polar vortex that causes temperatures to drop below minus 90 degrees Celsius. This is cold enough for the scarce water vapor in the dry upper atmosphere to freeze, forming polar stratospheric clouds. Chemical reactions on the ice crystals convert chlorine from nonreactive forms such as hydrogen chloride and chlorine nitrate into molecules that are very sensitive to sunlight. In addition, gaseous nitrogen oxides able to inactivate chlorine are transformed into frozen, and therefore nonreactive, nitric acid.[9]

The first spring sunlight releases the chlorine, and the virulent ozone-destroying chain reaction proceeds unimpeded for five or six weeks. The reactions transform two molecules of ozone into three molecules of ordinary oxygen, and the chlorine survives unscathed, ready to attack more ozone. Experiments conducted by James Anderson and his colleagues at Harvard University found that chlorine monoxide levels in the most disturbed regions of the hole were up to 500 times higher than normal. Throughout the hole, as chlorine monoxide increased, ozone concentrations decreased. (See Figure 5–1.)[10]

Diminished ozone in the vortex means that less incoming solar radiation is absorbed, thereby perpetuating lower temperatures and the vortex itself. In 1987, the vortex did not break down until early December, a month later than usual. In addition, the hole was some 8 degrees Celsius colder at an altitude of 15 kilometers than it was in 1979. Polar stratospheric clouds were more pervasive and persistent. In essence, the ozone hole was feeding on itself.[11]

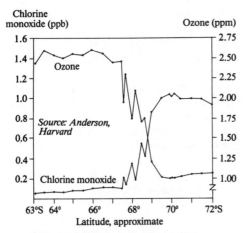

Figure 5-1. Atmospheric Concentration of Chlorine Monoxide and Ozone by Latitude, Southern Hemisphere, 1987

The phenomenon of global warming paradoxically encourages the process. Higher concentrations of greenhouse gases (including CFCs, which contribute about 15–20 percent of the total) are thought to be responsible for an increase in the earth's surface temperature and a decrease in the temperature of the stratosphere. Methane, one of the primary greenhouse gases, is a significant source of stratospheric water vapor. Colder temperatures and increased moisture both facilitate the formation of stratospheric clouds.[12]

Since the ozone hole cannot get much deeper, some fear it may spread outward, encompassing larger areas of Argentina and Chile and expanding above portions of Australia, Brazil, New Zealand, and Uruguay. These areas may also suffer when the vortex breaks up and its ozone-depleted air diffuses throughout the lower southern hemisphere. In December 1987, three out of five Australian ozone-monitoring stations observed a sharp drop in ozone. The abnormally low values persisted for three weeks over Melbourne, resulting in the lowest December mean ozone levels on record. Roger Atkinson of the the Australian Bu-

reau of Meteorology wonders if "it's possible that this is the first sign of depletion extending over Australia."[13]

While many of the meteorological and chemical conditions conducive to ozone depletion are unique to Antarctica, ground-based research in Greenland in the winter of 1988 found elevated chlorine concentrations and depressed ozone levels over the Arctic as well. Although a strong vortex does not develop there and temperatures are not as low, polar stratospheric clouds do form.[14]

To find out more about the atmospheric chemistry of the Arctic, the U.S. National Aeronautics and Space Administration (NASA) sent teams to Stavanger, Norway, and Ellesmere Island, Canada, in early 1989. Instruments on the ground analyzed the chemical components of the atmosphere, while similar instruments aboard specially equipped planes sampled the air in the ice clouds, and equipment aboard the Nimbus-7 satellite examined reflected sunlight. Ground-based measurements were to be gathered simultaneously by the Danes in Greenland and by the Soviets over their northernmost territories. The Soviet Union also planned to make aircraft observations at about the same time.[15]

The importance of cloud surface chemistry in the destruction of ozone was not realized until 1986. Now its role is viewed as fundamental, and some scientists postulate that sulfate chemical surfaces may host the same catalytic chlorine reactions that occur over Antarctica. Sulfate aerosols from volcanoes and biological processes are present in the atmosphere at all latitudes, at heights of 15 to 22 kilometers. They are especially prevalent over the most densely populated areas of the northern hemisphere, perhaps indicating the involvement of sulfur emissions from human activities. If these chemicals are capable of hosting the same catalytic reactions, global ozone depletion may accelerate even more rapidly than anticipated.[16]

A greater understanding of and consensus about ozone depletion was made possible by the release of the NASA Ozone Trends Panel report on March 15, 1988. More than 100 scientists from 10 countries spent 16 months reviewing the published literature and performing a critical reanalysis and interpretation of nearly all ground-based and satellite-derived ozone data. Their purpose: to eliminate any errors caused by improperly calibrated instruments.[17]

Ozone losses were documented around the globe, not just at the poles; the blame, particularly for the Antarctic ozone hole, was firmly placed on chlorofluorocarbons. The panel reported that between 30 and 60 degrees north, where most of the world's people live, total-column ozone had decreased by 1.7–3.0 percent between 1969 and 1986. Further, "ozone decreases were most pronounced in winter, ranging from 2.3–6.2 percent (depending on latitude), and those winter changes were higher than predicted by atmospheric models."[18]

Because monitoring stations are not as prevalent in the southern hemisphere, the panel cautioned that data for regions south of 30 degrees north were not as reliable, nor could seasonal variations be accurately determined. The report further stated that while the problem was worst over Antarctica during the spring, "ozone appears to have decreased since 1979 by 5 percent or more at all latitudes south of 60 degrees south throughout the year." The hole alone covers approximately 10 percent of the southern hemisphere.[19]

The report's findings startled policymakers, industry representatives, and researchers around the world. Prior to March 15, the phenomenon of global ozone depletion and the role of CFCs had been hotly contested. Within a matter of weeks the report's conclusions were widely accepted, and public debate on the issue was building to a new fever pitch. Suddenly, ozone depletion was real, no longer just a theory, and people around the globe knew just how bad the problem overhead had become.

Ozone losses were documented around the globe, not just at the poles.

Scientists were alarmed not only by the documented damage to the ozone layer, but by the inadequacy of their models to predict it. Ozone depletion is occurring far more rapidly and in a different pattern than had been forecast. Projections of the amount and location of future ozone depletion are still highly uncertain. Although the fundamental mechanisms of ozone depletion are generally understood, the quantitative effect of cloud surface chemistry, the rate of various chemical reactions, and the specific chemical pathways are still in doubt. According to Sherwood Rowland, one of the first to sound a warning, policy decisions now and for at least another decade must be made without good quantitative guidelines of what the future holds.[20]

EFFECTS OF ULTRAVIOLET RADIATION

Tanned, wrinkled, and leathered skin, certain eye disorders, and brittle plastics are all caused by ultraviolet (UV) radiation that reaches the earth's surface. At present, ozone absorbs much of the ultraviolet radiation that the sun emits in wavelengths harmful to humans, animals, and plants. (The most biologically damaging wavelengths occur within the 290–320 nanometer band, referred to as UV-B.) But, according to uncertain projections from computer models, erosion of the protective ozone shield could result in 5 to 20 percent more ultraviolet radiation reaching populated areas within the next 40 years—most of it in the UV-B band.[21]

In light of the findings of the NASA Ozone Trends Panel, the U.S. Environmental Protection Agency (EPA) damage projections cited in this section are conservative. Although the EPA ranges are based on current control strategies, they assume ozone depletion levels of 1.2–6.2 percent. Yet, all areas of the globe have already suffered depletion beyond this lower bound. At extreme latitudes, depletion has exceeded EPA's most realistic upper bound. Although these damage estimates are the best currently available, it is prudent to consider them on the low side.[22]

Globally, skin cancer incidence among Caucasians is already on the rise, largely because of more outdoor activity, but it is expected to increase alarmingly in the presence of more UV-B. Some 600,000 new cases of squamous and basal cell carcinoma—the two most common but rarely fatal skin cancer types—are reported each year in the United States alone. Worldwide, the number of cases is at least three times as high. The incidence is closely tied to cumulative exposure to ultraviolet radiation.[23]

Each 1-percent drop in ozone is projected to result in 4–6 percent more cases of these types of skin cancer. Ozone depletion is expected to cause 3 million to 15 million new cases in Americans born before 2075; some 52,000 to 252,000 of those patients are likely to die from the disease. Most at risk are those with light coloring who live nearest the equator. Also particularly susceptible are Argentinians, Australians, Chileans, and New Zealanders who live in areas under the springtime reach of the Antarctic hole. Members of the U.S. National Science Foundation are working with colleagues in Argentina and Chile to measure the increased amount of incoming UV radiation.[24]

Melanoma, a more deadly form of skin cancer, already attacks 26,000 Americans annually and results in 8,000 deaths. Melanoma represents only 4 percent of all skin cancers, but is responsible for 65 percent of all skin cancer deaths. Although the tie between melanoma and increased UV-B levels is less clear, EPA estimates that ozone depletion will lead to an additional 31,000 to 126,000 cases among U.S. whites born before 2075, resulting in an additional 7,000 to 30,000 fatalities.[25]

Melanoma incidence and mortality are already rising in all Caucasian populations studied. In Australia, melanoma deaths have risen fivefold over the past 50 years. In the United States, the number of cases has increased 83 percent over the past seven years. In other countries, the incidence is increasing at 3–7 percent annually. Unlike basal and squamous cell carcinoma, melanoma appears to be associated with acute UV radiation exposure, such as severe sunburns.[26]

Under the same EPA scenarios, from 555,000 to 2.8 million Americans born before 2075 will suffer from cataracts who would not have otherwise. Victims will also be striken earlier in life, making treatment more difficult. Cataracts, a clouding of the lens that blurs vision, can be removed in a relatively simple operation, but if left untreated can result in blindness. The surgical procedure is performed routinely in industrial countries, but victims in the developing world are less likely to have access to, or funds for, the operation.[27]

Medical researchers also fear that UV-B depresses the human immune system, lowering the body's resistance to attacking organisms, making it less able to fight the development of tumors, and rendering it more prone to infectious diseases, such as herpes. The response may even decrease the effectiveness of some inoculation programs, such as those for diphtheria and tuberculosis. Instead of building an immune response to the antigen, the patient might develop a full-fledged case of the disease. In developing countries, particularly those near the equator that are exposed to higher UV-B levels, parasitic infections could become more common.[28]

Unlike skin cancer, which predominantly affects whites, a lowered immune response is likely to affect everyone. Individuals already immunosuppressed, such as transplant patients or those with AIDS, could be at greater risk due to additive effects. Although the extent of immunosuppression cannot yet be quantified, some evidence suggests it could be induced with much lower doses of UV radiation than those required to cause cancer. This may mean that doses too low to cause a sunburn could lower the body's resistance to disease. An Australian study has already measured immunological effects in sunbathers.[29]

Terrestrial and aquatic ecosystems are also affected. Screenings of more than 200 different plant species, most of them crops, found that 70 percent were sensitive to UV-B. Increased exposure to radiation may decrease photosynthesis, water use efficiency, yield, and leaf area. Soybeans, a versatile and protein-rich crop, are particularly susceptible. Alan Teramura, at the University of Maryland, discovered that a simulated ozone loss of 25 percent reduced the yield of one important soybean species by as much as 25 percent. He also found that plant sensitivity to UV-B increased as the phosphorus level in the soil increased, indicating that heavily fertilized agricultural areas may be the most vulnerable.[30]

Botanists are worried because although plants can be bred for many traits, including UV radiation tolerance, rapid ozone depletion could overwhelm the capacity to evolve protective mechanisms. As a consequence, those varieties most resistant to the radiation would be the ones to thrive, not necessarily those with the greatest economic value or nutritive content. So far, only 4 of the 10 major terrestrial ecosystem types have been examined; tropical forests, rangelands, and wetlands have yet to be studied.[31]

Increased exposure to radiation may decrease photosynthesis.

Aquatic ecosystems may be the most threatened of all. Phytoplankton, the one-celled microscopic organisms that engage in photosynthesis while drifting on the ocean's surface, are the backbone of the marine food web. Because they require sunlight, already the limiting growth factor in high-latitude ocean areas, they cannot escape incoming ultraviolet radiation and continue to thrive. Yet if they remain at the water's surface, studies show that a 25-percent reduction in ozone would decrease their productivity by about 35 percent.[32]

Experiments with marine diatoms, a minute algae, show reductions in biomass, protein, and chlorophyll at UV-B levels corresponding to ozone reductions of 5 to 15 percent. A significant destruction of phytoplankton and its subsequent decomposition could even raise carbon dioxide levels, speeding the warming of the atmosphere.[33]

Zooplankton and the larvae of several important fish species will be doubly strained: they too live on the water's surface and their sole food supply, phytoplankton, will be scarcer. Preliminary studies indicate that sunlight is essential to the larval stage of growth, yet there is no adaption or flight mechanism to respond to increased UV radiation. For some shellfish species, a 10-percent decrease in ozone could result in up to an 18-percent increase in the number of abnormal larvae. A study of anchovies calculated that 8 percent of the annual larvae population would be killed off by a 9-percent decrease in ozone.[34]

Commercial fish populations already threatened by overfishing may have more difficulty rebuilding due to effects of increased UV-B. Most worrisome to many marine biologists is how the species composition of ocean environments will change. Some species will undoubtedly be more vulnerable to increased UV radiation than others and the changes are likely to be dramatic. Exposure resulting from ozone loss of 10 percent corresponds to moving 30 degrees closer to the equator—like moving New York City to Caracas, Venezuela. Ultimately, entire ecosystems may become more unstable and less flexible.

Increased UV-B levels also affect synthetic materials. Plastics are especially vulnerable. Studies conducted for EPA estimated that without added chemical stabilizers, the cumulative damage to just one polymer, polyvinyl chloride, could reach $4.7 billion by 2075 in the United States alone.[35]

Ozone, the same compound that acts as a protective shield in the stratosphere, is a noxious pollutant at ground level. Ironically, destruction of the upper ozone could augment the damage done by the lower. As more UV radiation reaches the earth's surface, the photochemical process that creates smog will accelerate.

Studies show that ground-level ozone, the main component of smog, retards crop and tree growth, limits visibility, and impairs lung functions. Recent research indicates that the biological risks are higher than previously believed.

Most economically valuable plant species are affected, including cotton, soybeans, corn, and wheat; the first two are especially sensitive. A Resources for The Future study found that reducing rural ozone levels by 10 percent in the United States would have resulted in a $700-million gain in 1986.[36]

Animal studies suggest that chronic exposure to ozone causes permanent damage to and premature aging of the lungs. It also impairs that organ's ability to fight off bacterial infections and to clear out toxic particles. Doctors now warn that everyone, not just people with impaired respiratory functions, is threatened.[37]

More than 60 U.S. cities still do not meet air quality regulations issued during the seventies; air quality is similarly poor in Western Europe, and often worse in the urban areas of developing countries. The problem is exacerbated by the fact that ground-level ozone is a greenhouse gas and that the warmer temperatures induced by the greenhouse effect will result in even greater formation of ozone-containing smog. In addition, stratospheric ozone decline is predicted to increase tropospheric amounts of hydrogen peroxide, an acid rain precursor.[38]

Most of the research to date on the effects of increased ultraviolet radiation has been conducted by U.S. government agencies. Annual funding has recently been boosted to some $15–20 million, but there are still many unanswered questions. Ironically, the most uncertainty surrounds the effects of increased UV-B on the immune system and on aquatic and plant life, where we have the greatest potential to harm our health and food supplies. West Germany also has an extensive UV-B effects program, financed by the Ministry of Research and Technology. Joint programs under the auspices of the European Community are to commence shortly.[39]

Despite the many uncertainties regarding future ozone depletion levels, the incremental amount of UV-B that will reach the earth's surface, and overall biological effects of these changes, one point is certain: the risks to aquatic and terrestial ecosystems and to human health are enormous. The overwhelming conclusion of EPA studies is that "the benefits of limiting future CFC/Halon use far outweigh the increased costs these regulations would impose on the economy." In the United States alone, the present value of the benefits of controlling emissions through the year 2075 is estimated at $6 trillion—some 240 times greater than the costs.[40]

CHEMICAL WONDERS, ATMOSPHERIC VILLAINS

Chlorofluorocarbons are remarkable chemicals. They are neither toxic nor flammable at ground level, as demonstrated by their discoverer Thomas Midgley, Jr., in 1930 when he inhaled vapors from a beaker of clear liquid and then exhaled to extinguish a candle. A safe chemical that was inexpensive to produce was exactly what the refrigeration industry was looking for, and CFCs soon became a universal coolant, marketed by E.I. du Pont de Nemours & Company under the trademark Freon. (In chemical shorthand, it is referred to as CFC-12.) International production soared, rising from 545 tons in 1931 to 20,000 tons in 1945.[41]

Another use for the chemical, as a blowing agent in rigid insulation foams, was discovered in the late forties. In this application, liquid CFC-12 is vaporized into a gas that forms lightweight, closed cell bubbles that are poor conductors of both heat and cold. Consumers referred to the product as Styrofoam, the Dow Chemical Company trademark. From 1945 to 1950, total production of CFCs doubled.[42]

Over the ensuing years, new chemical formulations were discovered, and the versatility of the various CFCs seemed almost endless. CFC-11 and CFC-12 were first used as aerosol propellants during World War II in the fight against malaria. In the postwar economy, they were employed in aerosol products ranging from hairspray and deodorant to furniture polish. By the late fifties, a combination of the blowing agents CFC-11 and carbon dioxide was used to make softer furniture cushions, carpet padding, and automobile seats.

Many social and technological developments in recent decades were assisted, at least in part, by the availability of CFCs. Huge chillers made it possible to build and cool shopping malls, sports arenas, and high-rise office buildings. Air conditioning brought comfort, business, and new residents to regions with warm climates. Automobile air conditioners, now installed in 80 percent of the cars sold in the United States, put the nation on wheels for summer vacations. And healthier, more interesting diets are now available because three fourths of the food eaten in the United States is refrigerated at some point in the production and distribution chain.[43]

Even the computer revolution was aided by CFCs. As microchips and other components of electronic equipment became smaller and more sophisticated, the need to remove the smallest contaminants became critical. CFC-113 is used as a solvent to remove glue, grease, and soldering residues and to leave a clean, dry surface. And, as is the case with so many of the CFCs, the chemical is versatile enough to be used on metals and plastics and to dry-clean clothes, largely replacing more-toxic chlorinated solvents. CFC-113 is now the fastest growing of the CFC family, and world-wide production exceeds 160,000 tons per year.[44]

Following the energy crises of the seventies, industrial, commercial, and residential customers looked for new ways to trim their heating and electric bills. Demand for rigid foam insulation, some types blown with CFC-11 and others with CFC-12, soared. In 1985, rigid foam accounted for two thirds of the insulation put into new U.S. commercial buildings, half the insulation in new single-family houses, and one third of the home re-insulation market. Appliance manufacturers also set to work—and are now required by U.S. law—to boost the energy efficiency of their products. Today, the foam walls of a household refrigerator contain five times as much CFC (one kilogram) as is used for refrigerant.[45]

An industry-sponsored group, the Alliance for Responsible CFC Policy, pegs the market value of CFCs produced in the United States at $750 million annually, the value of goods and services directly dependent on the chemicals at $28 billion, and the end-use value of installed equipment and products at $135 billion. Products that currently depend on the chemicals are ubiquitous: the United States alone has 85 million household refrigerators and 60 million auto air conditioners. In addition, billions of foam packaging containers are produced each year to keep fast foods hot, eggs cushioned, and meats displayed.[46]

Around the world, aerosols are still the largest user of CFCs, accounting for 25 percent of the total. (See Table 5–1.) Rigid foam and solvent applications, the fastest growing uses for CFCs, are tied for second place. In 1987, global CFC production (excluding China, the Soviet Union, and the Eastern bloc) surpassed the peak set in 1974, and came close to 1 million tons. Combined production of

CFC-11 and CFC-12 accounts for at least three quarters of this total. Only some two dozen firms produce CFCs, but production data are scarce and not totally reliable. Companies claim that such numbers are proprietary and that having them publicly available would put the manufacturers at a competitive disadvantage. Unfortunately, attempts to analyze and regulate markets are thwarted by lack of information.[47]

Total per capita use of the three most common CFCs is highest in the United States—at 1.2 kilograms—but Europe and Japan are not far behind. In most of the rest of the world, consumption rates are far lower. Indeed, Americans use six times the global average. Consumption patterns also differ by region. Aerosols account for 37 percent of European CFC use; mobile air-conditioning and other refrigeration constitute 39 percent of use in the United States; and solvents, primarily for the electronics industry, constitute 39 percent of Japanese CFC use.[48]

From 1931 through 1986, virtually all the CFC-11 and CFC-12 produced was

Table 5-1. Global CFC Use, by Category, 1985

Use	Share of Total
	(percent)
Aerosols	25
Rigid Foam Insulation	19
Solvents	19
Air Conditioning	12
Refrigerants	8
Flexible Foam	7
Other	10
Total	100

SOURCE: Daniel F. Kohler et al., *Projections of Consumption of Products Using Chlorofluorocarbons in Developing Countries* (Santa Monica, Calif.: Rand Corporation, 1987).

sold to customers in the northern hemisphere. Since raw chemicals and products made with and containing CFCs were then exported, in part to developing countries, final usage was not quite as lopsided, and the Third World accounted for 16 percent of global CFC consumption in 1986. (See Table 5–2.) As populations, incomes, and the manufacturing base grow in developing countries, CFC use there is projected to rise.[49]

Unlike most chemicals, CFCs are not broken down in the troposhere, the layer of air surrounding the earth. Instead, they waft slowly upward and after six to eight years reach the upper layer of the atmosphere, the stratosphere. Once there, the chemicals can survive for up to 100 years. When they are broken down, each chlorine atom released is capable of destroying tens of thousands of ozone molecules before it eventually gets washed out of the atmosphere.

Halons are also inert at ground level. They contain bromine, a more effective ozone destroyer than chlorine, and are long-lived in the atmosphere. Halons

Table 5-2. Global CFC Use, by Region, 1986

Region	Share of Total
	(percent)
United States	29
Other Industrial Countries[1]	41
Soviet Union, Eastern Bloc	14
Other Developing Countries	14
China and India	2

[1]European Community accounts for more than half, followed by Japan, Canada, Australia, and others.
SOURCE: "The Ozone Treaty: A Triumph for All," *Update from State*, May/June 1988.

are used for fighting fires: halon 1211 is employed in handheld extinguishers and halon 1301 is used in total flooding systems designed for enclosed areas with valuable contents, such as computer rooms, telephone exchanges, museums, and bank storage vaults.

The latest ozone measurements reflect only the response to gases released through the early eighties.

Halons were developed by the U.S. Army Corps of Engineers at the end of World War II as a way to fight fires in tanks and armored personnel carriers. Because they are nontoxic and can be applied directly to sensitive equipment without causing damage or leaving a residue, they have become the favored chemical for fighting fires. Demand quadrupled between 1973 and 1984 and is still growing at a rate of 15 percent annually.[50]

Alarming though the latest ozone measurements are, they reflect only the response to gases released through the early eighties; gases now rising through the lower atmosphere will take six to eight years to reach the stratosphere. An additional 2 million tons of substances containing chlorine and bromine are trapped in insulation foams, appliances, and fire-fighting equipment.[51]

Chlorine concentrations in the upper atmosphere have grown from 0.6 to 2.7 parts per billion in the past 25 years. Under even the most optimistic regulatory scenarios, they are expected to triple by 2075. Bromine concentrations are projected to grow considerably faster— exhibiting a tenfold increase from their current 1 part per trillion level despite an anticipated freeze on consumption.[52]

CFCs and halons are insidiously and

inexorably destroying the planet's protective ozone shield. Biological systems around the globe will soon start to suffer adverse effects, but the real losers will be future generations who inherit an impoverished environment and wonder at the folly of their ancestors.

REDUCING EMISSIONS

Determining the largest sources of potential ozone depletion is the first step toward curbing emissions. To do this requires knowing how much of each ozone-depleting chemical is currently used, its emissions profile, and the uses to which it is put. (See Table 5–3.) Only then can individual countries assess the

technical and economic feasibility of limiting emissions from specific markets.

Immediate reductions in CFC emissions can be achieved by banning CFC propellants in aerosols and by eliminating rapid evaporation of cleaning solvents. Intermediate savings are obtainable by capturing the blowing agents used to inflate flexible foams, by plugging the leaks in refrigeration and air-conditioning systems, and by recovering the refrigerants drained during system recharging. Long-term reductions involve alternative product disposal methods, use of substitute chemicals, and development of new process technologies.

When concern about the ozone layer first emerged in the seventies, some industrial-country governments responded. Since 455,000 tons (56 percent) of CFC-11 and CFC-12 produced

Table 5-3. Use and Emissions Profiles of Commonly Used Chemicals, 1985

Chemical	Emissions	Atmospheric Lifetime[1]	Applications	Annual Growth Rate	Share of Contribution to Depletion[2]
	(thousand tons)	(years)		(percent)	(percent)
CFC-11	238	76	Foams, Aerosols, Refrigeration	5	26
CFC-12	412	139	Air Conditioning, Refrigeration, Aerosols, Foams	5	45
HCFC-22	72	22	Refrigeration, Foams	11	0
CFC-113	138	92	Solvents	10	12
Halon 1211	3	12	Fire Extinguishers	23	1
Halon 1301	3	101	Fire Extinguishers	n.a.	4
Methyl Chloroform	474	8	Solvents	7	5
Carbon Tetrachloride	66	67	Solvents	1	8

[1]Time it takes for 63 percent of the chemical to be washed out of the atmosphere.   [2]Column does not total 100 due to rounding.
SOURCES: James K. Hammitt et al., "Future Emission Scenarios for Chemicals that May Deplete Stratospheric Ozone," *Nature*, December 24, 1987; U.S. Environmental Protection Agency, *Regulatory Impact Analysis: Protection of Stratospheric Ozone*, Volume II, Part I (Washington, D.C.: 1987); Douglas Cogan, *Stones in a Glass House: CFCs and Ozone Depletion* (Washington, D.C.: Investor Responsibility Research Center, 1988).

in 1974 were used in aerosols, spray cans were an obvious target. Under strong public pressure, Canada, Norway, Sweden, and the United States banned CFC propellants in at least 90 percent of their aerosol products. Because hydrocarbons, the replacement propellant, are less expensive than CFCs, the net savings to the U.S. economy was $165 million in 1983 alone. The European Community adopted a different approach. In 1980, the member countries agreed not to increase their already excessive capacity to produce these two CFCs and called for a 30-percent reduction in their use in aerosol propellants by 1982 (based on 1976 consumption figures).[53]

Cumulative reductions in CFC-11 and CFC-12 emissions due to lowered use in aerosols in the United States and the European Community amount to 2 million and 501,000 tons, respectively, the equivalent of six years of current CFC-11 production and one year of CFC-12 output. These figures are based on the assumption that CFC use in aerosols would have remained at the 1974 peak in the United States and the 1976 peak in the European Community.[54]

Worldwide, aerosol cans are still the largest source of CFC emissions, contributing 224,000 tons annually, some 33 percent of combined global emissions of CFC-11 and CFC-12. Rising concern about ozone depletion among consumers and governments should soon curtail this use. And because some nations took the lead, economical and often less expensive substitutes are already widely available.[55]

Denmark banned aerosol propellants in 1987, and voluntary industry cutbacks of 90 percent by the end of 1989 were announced recently in Belgium, the Netherlands, Switzerland, the United Kingdom, and West Germany. British and Swiss manufacturers will also label their products so consumers will know if they are ozone-friendly. The Soviet Union has declared its intention to switch to non-CFC aerosol propellants by 1993. France, Japan, and the nations of Eastern Europe and the Third World are the only major users that have not yet announced control measures.[56]

Worldwide, aerosol cans are still the largest source of CFC emissions.

Despite rapid growth, CFC-113 emissions may be some of the easiest and most economical to control. Since the chemical is only used to clean the final product and is not incorporated in it, emissions are virtually immediate; three quarters result from vapor losses, the remainder from waste disposal. A U.S. ban on land disposal of chlorinated solvents that took effect in November 1986, consideration of similar regulations elsewhere, the high cost of incinerating CFC-113 (because it contains toxic fluorine), and accelerating concern about ozone depletion have all created strong incentives for solvent recovery and recycling.[57]

Since CFC-113 costs about twice as much as other CFCs, investments in recovery and recyling pay off more quickly. Recycling of CFC-113 is now practiced on-site at many large computer companies. An IBM plant outside of Stuttgart, West Germany, has installed a recycling system that recovers 70–90 percent of the plant's solvents. Similar rates are being achieved by American Telephone and Telegraph (AT&T) in the United States. Smaller electronics firms, for whom in-house recycling is not economical, can sell their used solvents to commercial recyclers or the distributors of some chemical manufacturers.[58]

Rapid progress in emissions reductions over the past several years bodes well for more short-term savings. Hirotoshi Goto, director of the Stratospheric Protection Program in Japan, expects industries that use CFC solvents to achieve recycling rates of 95 percent. Such firms account for some 40 percent of total Japanese CFC consumption.[59]

Capturing CFC emissions from flexible foam manufacturing can also be accomplished fairly quickly, but requires investment in new ventilation systems. Current production processes result in the complete and immediate release of the blowing agent to the atmosphere. (When rigid foams are made, 90 percent of the CFC blowing agent remains in the closed cells of the product.) New suction systems coupled with carbon adsorption technologies are able to recover from 40 to 90 percent of the CFCs released.[60]

One technology operating in both Denmark and Norway traps CFCs at the blowing stage and recovers 40–45 percent of total emissions. A more comprehensive system designed by Hyman Development in the United Kingdom is able to recover almost twice as much. Traditionally, flexible foam is cured in an open room for several days, allowing CFCs to waft from the product. In the Hyman process, curing time is reduced to 40 minutes, occurs in an enclosed area, and the CFCs released are captured by the ventilating system. Unifoam, a Swiss company, is marketing a similar system able to recover 85 percent of the blowing agent for future use.[61]

Another area that offers significant savings, at a low cost, is improved design, operating, and maintenance standards for refrigeration and air conditioning equipment. These uses account for 30 percent of combined CFC-11 and CFC-12 consumption. Codes of practice to govern equipment handling are being drawn up by many major trade associations. Key among the recommendations are to require worker training, to limit maintenance and repair work to authorized personnel, to install leak detection systems, and to use smaller refrigerant charges. Another recommendation, to prohibit venting of the refrigerant directly to the atmosphere, requires the use of recovery and recycling technologies.

Careful study of the automobile air-conditioning market in the United States, the largest user of CFC-12 in the country, has found that 34 percent of emissions can be traced to leakage, 48 percent occur during recharge and repair servicing, and the remainder happen through accidents, disposal, and manufacturing, in that order. Equipment with better seals and hoses would curb emissions and result in less need for system maintenance.[62]

When car air conditioners are serviced, it is now standard practice to drain the coolant and let it evaporate. Several companies have seen the folly of this approach and designed recovery systems, known as "vampires." The refrigerant is pumped out of the compressor, purified, and reinjected into the automobile by equipment costing several thousand dollars. Because the coolant contains few contaminants, up to 95 percent of it can be reused. Refrigerant can also be stored and transported to a central recycler, though this option appears to offer less promise.[63]

Markets for the on-site equipment include mass transit companies, airplane manufacturers, government agencies, automobile dealerships, and high-volume service stations. The U.S. automobile industry is currently developing quality standards for recovery and recycling operations and should have the infrastructure and perhaps the equipment in place by the 1989 air-conditioning season. If the industry is not recycling at a satisfactory level by 1992, EPA will make the practice mandatory.[64]

To recover CFCs from junked automobiles and other appliances years after they are produced requires either a collection system or a bounty scheme to encourage reclamation by salvagers. Several towns in West Germany are starting to collect discarded household refrigerators in order to keep the CFCs in the refrigerant and the insulating foam from reaching the atmosphere. The refrigerants will be recycled and the foam will be incinerated in high-temperature furnaces. Although a few other countries are contemplating this approach, most view it as economical only for large commercial and industrial units, not for the small volumes that would be recovered from household appliances.[65]

Over the longer term, phasing out the use and emissions of CFCs will require the development of chemical substitutes that do not harm the ozone layer. The challenge is to find alternatives that perform the same function for a reasonable cost, that do not require major equipment modifications, that are nontoxic to workers and consumers, and that are environmentally benign.

Petroferm, a small company in Fernandina Beach, Florida, has developed a substitute solvent called BioAct EC-7. Made with terpenes found in citrus fruit rinds, the chemical is biodegradable, nontoxic, and noncorrosive. BioAct EC-7 has been tested by AT&T at three of its plants and was found to be effective and economically competitive, even counting the cost of replacing cleaning machinery. AT&T, which used some 1,400 tons of CFC-113 in 1986, expects to replace about one quarter of its CFC use with BioAct EC-7 over the next two years. An outside analysis estimates that the new compound could substitute for 30–55 percent of total projected CFC-113 use in the U.S. electronics industry.[66]

Du Pont and Imperial Chemical Industries (ICI), the world's two largest CFC producers, appear convinced that the replacement chemical for CFC-12 in air conditioners and refrigerators will be chlorine-free HFC-134a. Du Pont has already announced plans to build a commercial plant costing $25 million in Corpus Christi, Texas. The company says annual production will exceed 1,000 tons starting in 1990. The plant will be the fourth Du Pont facility for HFC-134a, and the seventh in the company's overall program to develop CFC alternatives. The substitute will likely sell for $2 a kilogram, some seven times the price of CFC-12.[67]

Several towns in West Germany are starting to collect discarded household refrigerators.

Work is also under way to develop new chemical blowing agents for both flexible and rigid foams. Union Carbide recently announced that it has found a substitute chemical for blowing the soft polyurethane foam used in furniture padding. According to the company, its new product, Ultracel, is already commercially available and could eliminate 70 percent of the CFCs employed in the flexible foam industry. Dow Chemical, a leading manufacturer of rigid foam insulation, has announced that it will stop using regulated CFCs by 1989.[68]

Many of the major chemical manufacturers are placing their bets on HCFC-22, -123, -141b, and -142b. The added hydrogen atom makes the ozone depletion potential of these compounds only 5 percent that of the chemicals they would replace. Their cost, on the other hand, would be three to five times greater.[69]

One major delay associated with the commercialization of new chemical compounds is the need for extensive toxicity testing; tests are run for five to seven years. To expedite this process, 14 CFC producers from Europe, Japan, South

Korea, and the United States have decided to pool their efforts in a multimillion-dollar joint testing program. HCFC-123 and HFC-134a are the first two chemicals chosen to undergo long-term testing. HCFC-22 has already passed. Results will be shared among members and, if promising, ought to be passed along to regulatory agencies to speed the approval process.[70]

Some alternative foam-blowing agents are already available and have been used for years. These include methylene chloride, pentane, and carbon dioxide. Although still viewed as possible substitutes, each has drawbacks. Methylene chloride is a carcinogen and difficult to dispose of, pentane is highly flammable and contributes to photochemical smog, and carbon dioxide results in denser flexible foams and has poorer insulating properties, meaning that rigid foams made with it alone must be 40–50 percent thicker to perform the same function.[71]

In some instances, new product designs can eliminate or reduce the need for CFCs and substitute chemicals while providing additional benefits. In automobiles, for instance, side vent windows, window glazings that slow solar absorption, and new solar ventilation systems can reduce interior heating and curb or eliminate the need for air-conditioning, thereby saving energy. Helium refrigerators, long used for space and military applications, have been adapted for civilian use in trucks and homes. Cryodynamics, a New Jersey company, will soon produce 9 million helium-cooled refrigerators in Shanghai. The units use less than half the energy of conventional systems. In Japan, ammonia refrigerants are used in energy-efficient commercial buildings.[72]

Rigid foam insulation in refrigerators and freezers may ultimately be replaced by vacuum insulation, the type used in thermos bottles. Work done at the U.S. Solar Energy Research Institute indicates that vacuum panels take up less space than foams and make appliances more energy-efficient.[73]

Halon emissions appear relatively easy to curtail, although there are no promising substitutes on the horizon. Most halons produced are never used, they just need to be available in case of emergency. At present, halon flooding systems are tested when first installed by releasing all the halon in the system. Discharge testing now contributes more emissions than fire fighting does. Using alternative chemicals or testing procedures that are acceptable to the insurance industry and eliminating accidental discharges would cut annual emissions by two thirds.[74]

Another large source of halon emissions is fire fighter training. The U.S. military, with one of the world's largest programs, has recently introduced the use of simulators that do not require actual chemical release. ICI is establishing a recycling service for halon 1211 so that contaminated supplies, and those that would otherwise be disposed of, can be recovered.[75]

The approach taken to reducing CFC and halon emissions varies greatly among nations and industries. Companies in Sweden, for example, view the development of alternative products and processes as an economic opportunity. They are poised to seize new international markets in a changing global economy. On the other hand, the major chemical producers in France, Japan, the United Kingdom, the United States, and West Germany have traditionally viewed emission controls as a threat to their international competitiveness. They have been loath to go along with unilateral control measures for fear of losing their market share.

The time has come to ask if the functions performed by CFCs are really necessary and, if they are, whether they can be performed in new ways. For example, must all computer chips be cleaned? For those that require cleaning, are water- or alcohol-based solvents sufficient? The U.S. Army and Navy will not allow the question to be asked. They require that electronic components be cleaned with CFCs, thereby discouraging manufacturers from exploring alternatives.[76]

If all known technical control measures were used, total CFC and halon emissions could be reduced by approximately 90 percent. Many of these control strategies are already cost-effective, and more will become so as regulations push up the price of ozone-depleting chemicals. The speed with which controls are introduced will determine the extent of ozone depletion in the years ahead and the date when stratospheric healing will begin.

Moving Beyond Montreal

On September 16, 1987, after years of arduous and heated negotiation, the Montreal Protocol on Substances that Deplete the Ozone Layer was signed by 24 countries. (As of mid-November 1988, that total had increased to 35 countries.) Provisions of the agreement include a freeze on CFC production (at 1986 levels) by 1989, a 20-percent decrease in production by 1993, and another 30-percent cut by 1998. Halon production is subject to a freeze based on 1986 levels starting in 1992.[77]

An international document calling for a 50-percent reduction in the production of a ubiquitous, invisible chemical feared responsible for destroying an invisible shield is unprecedented. The achievement is a tribute to the United Nations Environment Programme that spearheaded the effort; to government negotiators from all countries, especially those from the so-called Toronto group who kept pushing for tougher regulations; and to the many nongovernmental organizations and scientists who worked to build support among policymakers and the general public.

In order to take effect by the target date of January 1989, the protocol must have been ratified by 11 countries representing at least two thirds of international CFC consumption. By mid-November 1988, 14 countries had already approved the treaty—Canada, Egypt, Kenya, Japan, Luxembourg, Mexico, New Zealand, Nigeria, Norway, Portugal, the Soviet Union, Sweden, Uganda, and the United States. But the two-thirds consumption requirement will not be met until the treaty is ratified by the entire European Community—a step the group has pledged to take. Unfortunatley, even this level of support will not be enough to protect the fragile ozone layer.[78]

Ozone does not differentiate the source of chlorine and bromine emissions. All nations, including those in the Third World, must rapidly step up their reduction efforts. Developing countries are an important part of the control strategy because of their large and growing populations and their rapidly increasing CFC use. Some of the key developing countries are Brazil, China, India, Indonesia, and South Korea. In China, for example, only 1 household out of 10 now owns a refrigerator, but the government hopes that by 2000 every kitchen will have one. South Korea and Brazil are world-class automobile manufacturers.[79]

Some of the provisions that enhance the treaty's appeal to signatories include extended deadlines, allowances to accommodate industry restructuring, and loose definitions of the products that can legitimately be traded internationally. The Soviet Union and Eastern bloc countries, for example, are permitted to carry out the erection or expansion of any production facilities that are part of their current five-year plans before adopting restrictions, provided total consumption will not exceed 0.5 kilograms per capita. Developing countries have been given a 10-year grace period past the industrial-country deadline, during which CFC use can grow to meet "basic domestic needs," up to a limit of 0.3 kilograms per capita (one third the current per capita level in some industrial countries). After that, they too must freeze and then cut their use of controlled chemicals by 50 percent.[80]

The Montreal agreement will not arrest depletion, merely slow its acceleration.

The treaty also grants a country that enacts more than the prescribed measures the right to transfer production capacity to low-volume producers. And although imports of chemicals from nonsignatory countries are to cease within a year after the treaty takes effect, trade in products containing or manufactured with CFCs is permitted until at least the mid-nineties. The cumulative effect of these loopholes means that, even with widespread participation, the protocol's goal of halving worldwide CFC use by 1998 will not be met.[81]

Signatories of the Montreal Protocol were operating under the assumption that implementation of the treaty would result in a maximum ozone loss of 2 percent by the year 2075. Furthermore, because negotiations preceded results of the 1987 Antarctic expedition, delegates were effectively told not to consider the hole when adopting their positions. Yet less than one year later, there was widespread agreement that average global ozone concentrations had already fallen

by more than 2 percent, and by considerably more close to the poles. A recent EPA report concluded that by 2075, even with 100-percent global participation in the protocol, chlorine concentrations in the atmosphere would triple.[82] The agreement will not arrest depletion, merely slow its acceleration. In light of these findings, it is obvious that the treaty and other regulatory measures need to be strengthened.

Curtailing chlorine and bromine emissions enough to prevent widespread environmental damage requires a virtual phaseout of CFC and halon emissions by all countries as soon as possible. Releases of other compounds containing chlorine and bromine not currently covered under the treaty also need to be controlled and in some cases halted. According to EPA analyses, 45 percent of projected chlorine growth in the stratosphere by 2075 will stem from allowed use of controlled compounds, 40 percent will come from chlorine-containing chemicals that are not covered, and 15 percent will be from the emissions of nonparticipant nations.[83]

Methyl chloroform and carbon tetrachloride together contributed 13 percent of total ozone-depleting chemical emissions in 1985. As the use of controlled chemicals diminishes, the relative and absolute contribution of these two uncontrolled compounds will grow. Methyl chloroform is widely used as a solvent, especially for metal cleaning, and carbon tetrachloride (though used primarily to manufacture CFCs in western industrial countries) is still used as a solvent in Eastern bloc and developing nations. Although methyl chloroform emissions currently exceed those for any of the CFCs, its short atmospheric lifetime of eight years makes it one of the few chemicals whose control would provide short-term results.[84]

As noted, it is technically feasible to reduce CFC and halon emissions by 90 percent by 1995. The challenge is for governments to muster the political will to phase out CFC and halon emissions as soon as possible.

Timing is crucial. Analysts at EPA examined the effects of a 100-percent CFC phaseout by 1990 versus a 95-percent phaseout by 1998. Peak chlorine concentrations would differ by 0.8 parts per billion, some one third of current levels. Under the slower schedule, atmospheric cleansing would be considerably delayed: chlorine levels would remain higher than the peak associated with the accelerated schedule for at least 50 years.[85]

Sweden is the first country to move beyond endorsing a theoretical phaseout. In June 1988 the parliament, after extensive discussions with industry, passed legislation that includes specific deadlines for banning the use of CFCs in new products. Consumption is to be halved by 1991 and virtually eliminated by 1995. Sterilization uses and the small quantity remaining in aerosols were to be phased out by the end of 1988. Use in packaging materials is to cease a year later. CFCs used as an engineering solvent and for blowing flexible and extruded polystyrene foams are to be discontinued by the end of 1990. Blow-molding of rigid foams, dry-cleaning, and coolant uses are to cease by the end of 1994 at the latest. Under no circumstance may CFCs be replaced with chemicals that pose environmental or health hazards.[86]

If it becomes possible to phase any of these uses out earlier than planned, industry will be required to do so. In the interim, the Swedish government plans to offer incentives and provide financial support for the research and development of recovery and recycling technologies, of alternative products, and of means to keep discarded CFCs from reaching the atmosphere. The latter includes collection systems for coolants and incineration technologies for rigid foams. Sweden is currently responsible for less than 1 percent of global CFC use, however, so its approach will have to be adopted by many more countries before a significant dent is made in global emissions.[87]

Priming the research and development pump is a role for governments around the world. Although chemical manufacturers are spending some $100 million annually to develop safe chemical substitutes, they have no interest in alternative product designs that would cut into their markets.[88]

Research on new refrigeration, air-conditioning, and insulation processes is the most worthy of government support. Phasing out the use of CFCs in these applications would protect the ozone layer and delay the greenhouse effect—directly by reducing the emissions of CFCs that absorb infrared radiation, and indirectly by promoting more energy-efficient processes that would trim carbon dioxide emissions. Cooling cars, offices, and factories with equipment dependent on chemicals and powered by fuels that warm the earth is ludicrous. Unfortunately, international funding to develop new approaches is probably less than $5 million.[89]

As mentioned in the text of the Montreal Protocol, results of this research, as well as new technologies and processes, need to be shared with developing countries. Ozone depletion and climate warming are undeniably global in scope. Not sharing information on the most recent developments is like refusing to tell the driver of a car that is about to hit you where the brakes are. And it ensures that environmentally damaging and outdated equipment will continue to be used for years to come, further eroding the technology base in the Third World. Developing countries are also the most vulnerable to the effects of ozone depletion because they rely primarily on fish for their protein and have inadequate health care facilities.

Under the existing treaty, a scientific assessment of current ozone depletion is scheduled to occur from April to August of 1989. This is to be followed in April 1990 by a meeting of treaty negotiators to consider the evidence and decide what further actions are called for. Given recent developments, Mostafa Tolba, Executive Director of the United Nations Environment Programme, has been petitioned by many to expedite the process and is in favor of doing so. The United Kingdom, the United States, West Germany, and possibly Japan and the Soviet Union appear amenable to taking faster action. France is the only major producer country still dragging its feet.[90]

As with so many of the major environmental problems now facing policymakers, the timing and fortitude of their response is crucial. The ultimate goal of negotiators has always been the eventual phaseout of all ozone-depleting chemicals. The question is, How quickly are countries willing to act in order to protect human health, food supplies, and the global climate?

The scientific fundamentals of ozone depletion are known. Although current models of future change vary in their predictions, the evidence is clear enough to warrant an immediate response. Because valuable time was lost when governments and industries relaxed their regulatory and research efforts during the early eighties, a crash program is now essential. Given the relatively high degree of understanding and consensus surrounding ozone depletion, the support that can be garnered for putting an end to chlorine and bromine emissions may be indicative of the political will to protect the earth's habitability.

6

Rethinking Transportation

Michael Renner

The individual mobility, convenience, and status bestowed by the private passenger car hold a seemingly unbeatable allure. In 1987, a record 126,000 cars rolled off assembly lines each working day, and close to 400 million vehicles clog the world's streets today.[1]

But the car's utility to the individual stands in sharp contrast to the costs and burdens that society must shoulder to provide an automobile-centered transportation system. Since the days of Henry Ford, societies have enacted a steady stream of laws to protect drivers from each other and themselves, as well as to protect the general public from the unintended effects of massive automobile use. Legislators have struggled over the competing goals of unlimited mobility and the individual's right to be free of the noise, pollution, and physical dangers that the automobile often brings.

Prior to the seventies, the auto's utility

An expanded version of this chapter appeared as Worldwatch Paper 84, *Rethinking the Role of the Automobile.*

and assured role in society were hardly questioned. Even worries about escalating gas prices and future fuel availability subsided in the eighties almost as quickly as they had emerged. Car sales recovered, driving is up, and affluent customers are once more shopping for high-performance cars.

The motor vehicle industry's apparent success in dealing with the challenges of the seventies has obscured the adverse long-term trends of automobile-centered transportation. Rising gasoline consumption will before long put increased pressure on oil production capacities. In addition, as more and more people can afford their own cars and as mass motorization takes hold, congestion becomes an intractable problem. And motor vehicles are important contributors to urban air pollution, acid rain, and global warming.

Society's interest in fuel supply security, the integrity of its cities, and protection of the environment calls for a fundamental rethinking of the automobile's role. Stricter fuel economy and pollution standards are the most obvious and immediate measures that can be adopted. But they can only be part of the answer. In the years ahead, the challenge will be to develop innovative transportation policies.

WHITHER THE AUTOMOTIVE AGE?

During the postwar period, the automobile industry experienced its most dramatic and sustained expansion, buttressed by massive highway construction projects, fueled by cheap and abundant oil, and riding a wave of unprecedented affluence in industrial countries. Production grew a rapid 6 percent annually, from under 10 million vehicles a year in the fifties to almost 30 million in 1973.[2]

The first oil crisis, however, brought on an era of unprecedented volatility. (See Figure 6–1.) Global production did reach a new peak of 32.9 million vehicles in 1987. Yet had the pace recorded between 1950 and 1973 continued, annual output would now be twice as high.[3]

The world's car fleet has grown from about 50 million vehicles in the immediate postwar period to 386 million in 1986 (see Table 6–1), with still no sign of a real leveling-off. But if the pre-1973 pace of additions to the car fleet—not just replacements—had held, total passenger cars would now number close to 600 million.

The United States dominated the early stages of the automotive age. Only during the sixties and seventies did Western Europe and Japan, respectively, begin to catch up. The lure of owning a private passenger car has since proved irresistible everywhere.

Until the seventies, the Soviet Union and Eastern Europe gave production of

Table 6-1. Automobiles in Use, Worldwide and United States, 1950–87

Year	World	United States	U.S. Share
	(million passenger cars)		(percent)
1950	53	40	75
1955	73	52	71
1960	98	62	63
1965	140	75	54
1970	195	89	46
1975	260	107	41
1980	321	122	38
1981	331	123	37
1982	340	124	36
1983	352	127	36
1984	365	128	35
1985	375	132	35
1986	386	135	35
1987	. . .	139	. . .

SOURCE: Motor Vehicle Manufacturers Association, *World Motor Vehicle Data, 1988 Edition* and *Facts and Figures '88* (Detroit, Mich.: 1988).

Million Vehicles

Figure 6-1. World Passenger Car Production, 1950-87

Source: *MVMA*

trains, trucks, and buses priority over automobiles. But in response to growing consumer pressure, passenger car production more than tripled in the seventies. Between 1970 and 1985, the Soviet and East European car fleets grew fivefold—to 27 million vehicles. Long waiting lists indicate there is still enormous unmet demand. Access to car ownership remains regulated by bureaucratic allocation and heavy taxation.[4]

General Secretary Gorbachev's attempts at *perestroika,* the restructuring of the Soviet economy, may well lead to a stronger emphasis on consumer goods, with the automobile near the top of the list. The Soviet Union is currently studying plans to double its car production of 1.4 million vehicles per year. In Eastern Europe, on the other hand, an unresolved debt crisis may keep a lid on expansion of car ownership.[5]

The governments of many developing countries are also anxious to encourage the development of auto-centered transportation systems because they consider them an indispensable cornerstone of industrial development. Car ownership in the Third World has risen sharply, averaging an annual growth rate of 11 percent in the first half of the seventies and 8 percent in the second half, but only 5 percent in the eighties.[6]

With only a few exceptions, car ownership in the Third World is unlikely to reach the levels in industrial countries. Low per capita incomes mean buying and maintaining a car is simply beyond the reach of most people. The highly skewed wealth distribution patterns in most countries may foster a small, privileged class with ample purchasing power, but they effectively limit the number of potential car owners.

Third World car ownership is concentrated mainly in the newly industrializing countries of Latin America and Southeast Asia and in the major oil-exporting countries where appetites for cars were whetted by soaring oil revenues in the seventies and low gasoline retail prices. Argentina, Brazil, and Mexico together account for almost half the cars in the developing world.[7]

Yet the emergence of the debt crisis in 1982, coming on the heels of surging oil prices in the seventies, shattered the auto industry's expectations that the bulk of future growth would occur in Latin America. The debt crunch compelled these nations to marshall their financial resources for debt servicing, precipitating major recessions. Soaring interest rates and falling real wages eroded buying power. Car purchases in Argentina, Brazil, and Mexico fell by half in the eighties, and the once dynamic Brazilian auto industry stumbled from boom to bust and back. (See Figure 6-2.)[8]

Brazil and Mexico embraced automobile exports as an avenue to escape the debt morass. First encouraged in 1972 by generous government incentives to pay for ballooning oil imports, exports took a rising share of Brazil's car production and soared to 40 percent in 1987, when domestic demand collapsed. In Mexico, the share of production sold

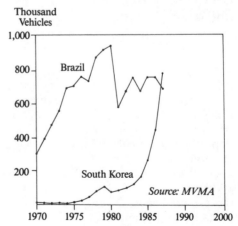

Figure 6-2. Car Production in South Korea and Brazil, 1970-87

abroad has grown from less than 5 percent in 1982 to 48 percent in 1987. These two countries are joined by India, Indonesia, Malaysia, Taiwan, and Thailand in growing competition in the world export market.[9]

South Korea, by contrast, has always depended on sales overseas, which currently claim two thirds of domestic production. With close to 800,000 units produced in 1987, South Korea is emerging as a serious challenger to Japan in the small-car market segment. But car ownership at home—currently one auto for every 65 people—has been hobbled through high taxes on purchases, registration, and gasoline and through low wages.[10]

China and India together account for 38 percent of the world's population, but they own scarcely half of 1 percent of its automobiles. Until the late seventies, these governments assigned cars one of the lowest development priorities. Both, however, have since embarked on policies that seek to emulate the motorized transport systems of the industrial West and to increase domestic car production dramatically.[11]

Cars now account for a larger portion of oil demand than they did at the time of the first oil crisis.

Production and ownership are thus still overwhelmingly concentrated in advanced industrial societies. They account for only 16 percent of the world's population but 88 percent of the car production and 81 percent of the global fleet. (See Table 6–2.) Put differently, by 1986 only a little more than 1 percent of the population in developing countries owned a car, compared with 40 percent in the western industrial countries, and with a world average of about 8 percent.

Between 1970 and 1986, the United States alone added as many cars to its roads as the entire Third World now possesses.[12]

SEARCHING FOR ALTERNATIVES TO OIL

Because cars run almost exclusively on petroleum-based fuels, the auto industry is understandably sensitive to changes in the price and availability of oil. As a means of transportation, the automobile is, after all, only as reliable as its fuel supplies. Since the first oil crisis, other sectors of the economy have reduced their reliance on petroleum. But no easy substitutes are available for automotive fuels. Thus, cars now account for a larger portion of oil demand than they did at the time of the first oil crisis. Since 1976, the United States has used more petroleum each year for transportation than it has produced. In 1985, the transport sector consumed 63 percent of the oil used in the United States (up from 50 percent in 1973), 44 percent of that used in Western Europe, 35 percent in Japan, and 49 percent in developing countries.[13]

The oil crises of the past 15 years reinforced the notion that a transport system centered on the private passenger car can impose tremendous costs on society, whether in the form of escalating fuel import bills or huge expenditures of capital and resources to tap domestic fuel sources. Higher prices made oil account for a rapidly growing share of total imports of most countries. The average fraction of Third World export earnings used to pay for oil imports tripled during the seventies. By 1981, Brazil spent over half such earnings to pay for imported

Table 6-2. Car Density, 1970–86, and Car Fleet in 1986, by Region

Region or Country	Density			1986 Fleet
	1970	1980	1986	
		(people per car)		(million vehicles)
United States	2.0	1.9	1.8	135
Western Europe	5.2	3.3	2.8	125
Oceania	4.0	3.3	2.8	8
Canada	3.0	2.6	2.2	11
Japan	12.0	4.9	4.2	29
South Africa	12	12	11	3
Eastern Europe	36	12	11	17
Latin America	38	18	15	26
Soviet Union	147	32	24	12
Asia[1]	196	95	62	12
Africa[2]	191	111	110	5
India	902	718	554	1.4
China	27,707	18,673	1,374	0.8
World	18	14	12	386[3]

[1]Excluding Japan, China, India. [2]Excluding South Africa. [3]Column does not add to total due to rounding.
SOURCE: Worldwatch Institute, based on Motor Vehicle Manufacturers Association, *Facts and Figures* (Detroit, Mich.: various editions).

oil. Kenya, South Korea, and Thailand spent close to one third and Bangladesh, two thirds.[14]

Brazil, by far the Third World's largest car market and oil importer, saw its oil bill skyrocket from $280 million in 1970 to $10.3 billion in 1980. Higher domestic oil production and a controversial program to generate ethanol fuel from sugar crops allowed the country to cut its reliance on imported oil by 60 percent between 1979 and 1986. Yet, providing the fuel from domestic sources carried a hefty price tag, requiring large-scale investment and government subsidies. The Brazilian government has spent an estimated $8 billion to prop up the country's ethanol industry alone. When international oil prices collapsed in 1986, annual subsidies grew to $2 billion from $650 million in the preceding year.[15]

The dark clouds cast over the auto's future by the two oil shocks in the seventies seemed to recede in the eighties. Car sales quickly resumed growth as concern over oil prices and supplies faded from memory. Cheaper gasoline served as a catalyst for increased and faster driving. Global gasoline consumption resumed its upward climb in 1983. (See Figure 6–3.) Unless car fuel efficiency is boosted further to offset these trends, gasoline consumption will continue to rise. Growing demand will eventually put increased pressure on production capacities.[16]

Warnings of a renewed oil crisis and concerns about the environmental effects of gasoline use have revived inter-

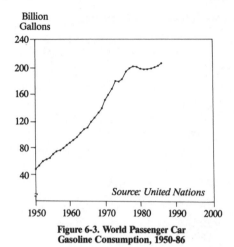

Billion Gallons

Source: United Nations

Figure 6-3. World Passenger Car Gasoline Consumption, 1950-86

est in alternative fuels. Attention currently centers on alcohol fuels (ethanol and methanol), natural gas, and, to a lesser degree, electricity. Alcohol fuels can be derived from agricultural waste and other biomass sources; methanol can also be produced from natural gas and coal.

Brazil's *Proalcool* program is widely regarded the "success story" of the ethanol industry, despite the hefty government support required. Sugarcane-derived ethanol provided roughly half the country's automotive fuel in 1986. The scope of Brazil's program, however, may not be readily replicable elsewhere, because of either insufficient crop surpluses, or a lack of government commitment, or an automotive fleet that is simply too large. If corn were used as a feedstock, for example, almost 40 percent of the entire U.S. annual harvest would have to be earmarked for ethanol production in order to meet 10 percent of the nation's automotive fuel demand. Sugar beets and, where it can be cultivated, sugarcane are more efficient in converting sunlight into stored energy, and therefore promise greater fuel yields than corn or other grains.[17]

But in most heavily auto-dependent countries, the production of alcohol fuels in large quantities would still require large inputs of agricultural land. Thus, transportation fuel needs could come in conflict with food requirements, particularly if both keep growing. The drought that befell different parts of the world during the summer of 1988 demonstrates how quickly surpluses can be transformed into shortages. (See Chapter 3.)

Coal and natural gas reserves are plentiful enough to produce methanol on a large scale in resource-rich countries. Abundant as these sources may be, however, ultimately they are as finite as petroleum. And their use on a large scale has serious implications for the trend toward global warming, as discussed later in this chapter.

A major drawback of all alcohol fuels is that some 30–40 percent of the original energy content of their potential feedstocks (biomass, coal, and natural gas) is lost in the conversion process. Numerous studies suggest that the total amount of energy inputs to obtain ethanol—including energy required to fuel farmers' vehicles, to produce fertilizer and pesticides, and to ferment and purify the alcohol—may be close to or even surpass the eventual energy output.[18]

Using natural gas directly as an automotive fuel, either in compressed (CNG) or in liquefied form (LPG), appears more practical than tapping it as a feedstock for alcohol fuels because less of the original energy is lost in the conversion process. Today, more than 680,000 CNG vehicles are on the road worldwide, with a similar number expected over the next 10–15 years.[19]

In the more distant future, hydrogen—the most common element in the universe—may become a widely used fuel in either liquid or compressed gaseous form. For environmental and supply reasons, hydrogen is best derived from water. Cost is still a major impediment to commercialization, and vehicle technology has not yet advanced beyond the prototype stage. Canada, Japan, and West Germany have made major commitments to promote hydrogen research and development. In the United States, however, hydrogen has yet to attract R&D funding commensurate with its enormous potential.[20]

Electric vehicles promise higher energy efficiency and quieter operation than conventional internal combustion engines. Barring major breakthroughs in battery technology and cost, however, electric vehicles will likely be confined to market niches where performance and range criteria are less important than in the overall passenger car market. Moreover, such vehicles can only be a viable alternative if the fuels used in electricity generation are renewable. Solar power, through the use of photovoltaic cells, is one main candidate. Fuel cells—which convert the chemical energy in hydrogen, methanol, and natural gas directly into electrical energy without mechanical losses—could some day hold the key to making electric vehicles more acceptable.[21]

Alternative fuels have to overcome considerable odds if they are to make more than just a dent in the motor fuel market. The most daunting obstacle is a "chicken and egg" dilemma: an infrastructure—fuels, vehicles, service stations—will not spring up unless there is adequate demand, while such demand is unlikely to materialize in the absence of an appropriate infrastructure.

ENHANCING FUEL EFFICIENCY

After the first oil crisis, car companies around the world took dramatic steps to boost fuel efficiency. New passenger cars in the United States today are almost twice as efficient as the gas-guzzling behemoths of the early seventies; as a result, the average fleet fuel usage rose from 13 miles per gallon (MPG) in 1973 to 18 MPG in 1986. (See Figure 6–4.)[22]

New U.S. cars travel an average of 26 miles per gallon, but continue to trail their European and Japanese competitors, whose models achieve 30 MPG or more. Due to lower efficiency and more driving, the average North American car still burns up more than twice as much gas each year as its counterpart in Japan or Western Europe. Annual gasoline consumption per car in countries belonging to the Organisation for Economic Co-operation and Develoment (OECD) fell by one quarter between 1973 and 1985. Thus, while the OECD fleet expanded by 45 percent, its total fuel consumption grew by only 4 percent.[23]

Fuel economy in the Soviet Union and East Germany is roughly on a par with that in Western Europe. Information on fuel efficiency in developing countries is spotty; most cars there are either imported or engineered and designed by western car manufacturers. However, because on average they rely on older designs and because maintenance is often poor, autos in the Third World are

Figure 6-4. Fuel Consumption of U.S. Automobiles, 1970-88

likely to be less efficient than those in industrial countries.[24]

Once the world passed the peak of the second oil crisis, fuel economy goals swiftly lost their urgency. Since 1983, gains in the United States and most other OECD member countries have fallen short of the impressive achievements between 1974 and 1982. Moreover, the growing popularity of light trucks in the United States—which are one-third less fuel-efficient than new U.S. passenger cars—limits the potential for future efficiency gains. Improvements in Europe and Japan have been partly offset by consumers' growing preference for larger and more powerful vehicles.[25]

But the world could make much greater strides toward fuel efficiency. Although technical solutions seem almost invariably to generate the greatest excitement and attention, simple human adjustments could double efficiency virtually overnight. For example, even a highly fuel-efficient car is inefficiently used when it carries only the driver, as is the case for over half the auto trips made in the United States; 87 percent of all trips have at most two passengers. In 1984, American cars used just as much energy for every passenger-mile of travel as in 1971.[26]

Still, technical opportunities to improve efficiency are far from exhausted. Weight reduction and improvements in engine and transmission efficiency hold the greatest promise. In addition, aerodynamics, tire rolling resistance, the energy dissipation of the brakes, and the energy consumption of accessories merit further improvement.[27]

On average, a 10-percent weight reduction will yield a 6-percent fuel economy gain. Past fuel-economy improvements in the United States have primarily been accomplished through lowered weights and shifts to front-wheel drive. Further gains will likely result from greater substitution of lighter-weight materials for steel and cast-iron components. These materials, in order of their potential contribution to lighter cars, include magnesium, plastics, aluminum, and high-strength low-alloy steel; they offer strength, heat and stress resistance, and design flexibility comparable to conventional materials.[28]

Even a highly fuel-efficient car is inefficiently used when it carries only the driver.

Due to low cost, plastics have exhibited the most dramatic growth of all new automotive materials. In 1985, some 8–11 percent of the vehicle weight of cars manufactured in Japan, the United States, and West Germany was accounted for by plastics; that share could grow to 18–20 percent by early next century.[29]

Reducing the weight of a car allows the use of smaller engines without having to sacrifice performance. Engine efficiency can also be improved by running the motor at more optimal loads, minimizing energy loss through exhaust gases, and improving fuel combustion. Reducing engine warm-up time is another important goal since fuel efficiency can drop by half when an engine is cold.[30]

Advanced engine designs such as the adiabatic diesel (which minimizes heat loss) and the stratified charge engine (which features a "rich" air-to-fuel mixture surrounding the spark plug while maintaining an efficient and cleaner-burning overall lean mixture) promise fuel economy improvements of 25–40 percent.[31]

Increases in the number of gears allow a motor to run at its most efficient speed.

Continuously variable transmissions (CVTs) essentially give a car an unlimited number of gears; they offer fuel savings of 20–24 percent, particularly in urban, stop-and-go, driving. Japan's Subaru, in its Justy subcompact model, was the first to introduce CVT technology commercially, to be followed by the Fiat Uno and Ford Fiesta.[32]

Energy losses due to braking and idling—which occur frequently during urban driving—can amount to as much as one third of a vehicle's original kinetic energy. Energy storage systems, such as a flywheel device, together with a CVT can alleviate this problem by capturing an engine's excess power whenever the driving requirements are less than its output. This power can then be tapped at some other time, thereby enabling smaller engines than in today's models. Researchers at the University of Wisconsin hope to double fuel economy with such a system.[33]

The most efficient cars currently available are about twice as efficient as the average new car on the road. At the top of the list is a Japanese model, the Suzuki Sprint, which gets 57 MPG. More advanced prototypes, such as the Peugeot ECO 2000, Toyota AXV, Volkswagen E80, and Volvo LCP 2000, achieve anywhere from 70 to over 100 MPG; Renault's VESTA scored a stunning 124 MPG in test runs.[34]

The prospects that innovations currently tested in prototypes will be commercialized in a timely fashion are not encouraging, however. Car companies around the world have responded to lower oil prices by slowing down their efforts to incorporate advanced fuel-economy technologies in mass-produced cars. Instead, consumers are offered styling changes and gadgetry. In fact, "muscle cars"—featuring eight cylinders and high horsepower—are back in style.

In the seventies, the United States held a research lead in advanced fuel efficiency projects such as energy storage systems and the lean-burn engine. But with the advent of the oil glut, the American car companies abandoned fuel economy as a strategic goal. At the same time, U.S. government support for various fuel economy R&D projects was terminated or reduced by the Reagan administration. This shortsighted attitude was compounded by the administration's rollback and proposed repeal of federally mandated standards for new cars—an idea bound to decrease national security, contrary to government predictions.[35]

Today, the Japanese and Europeans are the pacesetters in the quest for higher fuel efficiency. Japanese firms lead in developing lean-burn motors and ceramic engines, and European firms are strong contenders in energy storage systems. Even in aerodynamics, where American companies are still ahead, a research lead has not translated into practical advances.

In keeping with Henry Ford II's 1971 dictum that "mini-cars mean mini-profits," General Motors and Ford prefer to concentrate on big cars. In the small-car segment, all three U.S. companies increasingly rely on "sponsored" imports—marketing cars often designed, engineered, and manufactured abroad. As a result, they could find themselves without a sufficient manufacturing base to meet the demand for smaller cars when it develops again.[36]

One reason auto companies lag in commercializing highly fuel-efficient technologies is the current lack of consumer interest. In 1986, gasoline and motor oil accounted for only 15 percent of total car operating costs per mile in the United States, down from 26 percent in 1975. In addition, each fuel economy increment yields proportionally smaller savings. For someone driving 10,000 miles a year, an improvement from 10 to

20 MPG will save 500 gallons of fuel annually; but doubling that to 40 MPG promises "only" an additional savings of 250 gallons, and doubling again, a comparatively meager 125 gallons.[37]

Fuel taxes, collected per unit of consumption, have had some success in restraining gasoline consumption. But they have done so more by affecting driving patterns than by steering consumers toward the most efficient cars. A tax levied on the sale of a new vehicle could shape consumers' purchasing decisions if it were tailored to the car's fuel economy.[38]

Left to their own devices, both industry and consumers will enjoy the free ride currently afforded by low fuel prices and will neglect fuel economy. Governments need to adopt a strong framework—a set of new standards and taxes—to boost fuel efficiency. Given the range of advanced technologies now installed in prototypes, on the shelf, or on a drawing board, striving for 50 MPG in new cars by the end of the century is a reasonable goal.

IMPROVING AIR QUALITY

The most alarming effect of mass motorization may not be the depletion of fossil fuels but the large-scale damage to human health and the natural environment. Researchers at the University of California estimate that the use of gasoline and diesel fuel in the United States alone may cause up to 30,000 deaths every year. And the American Lung Association estimates that air pollution from motor vehicles, power plants, and industrial fuel combustion costs the United States $40 billion annually in health care and lost productivity.[39]

Cars, trucks, and buses play a prominent role in generating virtually all the major air pollutants, especially in cities. In OECD member countries, they contribute 75 percent of carbon monoxide emissions, 48 percent of nitrogen oxides, 40 percent of hydrocarbons, 13 percent of particulates, and 3 percent of sulfur oxides. Worldwide, the production and use of automotive fuels accounts for an estimated 17 percent of all carbon dioxide (CO_2) released from fossil fuels. Transportation is also the primary source of lead pollution. The adverse health effects of all these pollutants are fairly well established, though the threshold of effects remains uncertain.[40]

Perhaps more significant are the synergistic effects. The best known and most pervasive of these is photochemical smog—the brown haze that causes health disorders, restricts visibility, erodes buildings and monuments, reduces crop yields, and is at least partly responsible for the massive forest damage afflicting central Europe. Ozone, the most important component of smog, is the product of complex reactions between nitrogen oxides and hydrocarbons in the presence of sunlight.[41]

In 1986, between 40 million and 75 million Americans were living in areas that failed to attain National Ambient Air Quality Standards for ozone, carbon monoxide, and particulates. If these standards were in force elsewhere, they would routinely be exceeded in many cities: Athens, Budapest, Cairo, Mexico City, New Delhi, and São Paulo are among those with the world's most polluted air.[42]

Nitrogen and sulfur oxides, together with unburnt hydrocarbons, are the principal components of the phenomenon commonly known as acid rain. Acid precipitation is destroying freshwater aquatic life and forests throughout central Europe and North America and degrading marine life in Atlantic coastal waters.[43]

The most serious long-term consequence of automotive emissions, however, is the atmospheric buildup of CO_2 and other "greenhouse gases"—nitrous oxide, methane, and ozone. There is now virtual consensus among scientists that if the concentration of CO_2 in the atmosphere doubles from preindustrial levels, a substantial increase in average global temperature will occur. Indeed, such a rise is already under way. The impending climate change could shift global precipitation patterns, disrupt crop-growing regions, raise sea levels, and threaten coastal cities worldwide with inundation. (See Chapter 1.)[44]

Among all the auto-generated air pollutants, lead has been most successfully fought. Since it was purposely added to gasoline as an octane enhancer, it could just as well be eliminated from it. Reducing emissions of nitrogen and sulfur oxides, carbon monoxide, hydrocarbons, and particulates has proved more difficult because they are products of the combustion process. The most sophisticated exhaust control device at the moment is the three-way catalyst, which reduces emissions of hydrocarbons, carbon monoxide, and nitrogen oxides. Over the life of a vehicle, today's catalysts cut emissions of hydrocarbons by an average of 87 percent, of carbon monoxide by 85 percent, and of nitrogen oxides by 62 percent. But without proper maintenance, their effectiveness is likely to decrease rapidly. And catalysts are least effective when an engine is cold—a frequent situation given the prevalence of short trips in OECD member countries.[45]

Since the early sixties, the United States has set the pace in establishing and tightening emission limits and pioneering control devices. Japan's standards, implemented in 1975 and 1978, are roughly comparable. Australia, Canada, and South Korea recently established emission standards equivalent to those in force in the United States. Brazil initiated a 10-year phase-in of regulations that, by 1997, will allow it to match current U.S. standards. Emissions in Argentina, India, and Mexico, on the other hand, still go virtually uncontrolled. Controls in the Soviet Union and Eastern Europe are limited to engine modifications.[46]

The most serious long-term consequence of automotive emissions is the atmospheric buildup of "greenhouse gases."

Within Western Europe, there is a widening gulf between the so-called Stockholm group and the European Economic Community (EEC). Austria, Norway, Sweden, and Switzerland require installation of catalytic converters and compliance with emission levels comparable to those prevalent in the United States. EEC standards establish separate categories for large, medium, and small vehicles, and those for small cars in particular remain very lenient, due to the opposition of the French and Italian car industries. Because some 60 percent of all cars on the road in Europe are in that category, little reduction in emissions can be expected.[47]

Europe has also been slow to control diesel pollutants, which pose even greater health risks than gasoline emissions. Unlike in Japan and the United States, diesels are enjoying rising popularity among European motorists, capturing 18 percent of the new-car market in 1986. EEC diesel emissions standards are still considerably less stringent than those in the United States, which ironically many European-produced vehicles are already capable of meeting.[48]

Emission controls have been most

successful in reducing carbon monoxide and hydrocarbons. During the seventies, carbon monoxide emissions from mobile sources fell by more than 50 percent in Japan and by one third in the United States. But during the eighties progress has come to a virtual standstill, although emission levels remain unacceptably high; in most of Europe emissions are rising along with increasing traffic volume. A similar trend can be observed for hydrocarbons. Nitrogen oxides emissions stabilized or decreased modestly in the seventies and early eighties in the United States, Japan, and some European countries. But in many nations, these earlier gains are in danger of being wiped out by growing traffic and higher travel speeds.[49]

Athens, Budapest, and São Paulo have imposed restraints on motorized traffic in their inner cities.

The goal of clean air remains elusive. Even though U.S. emission standards are as strict as any in the world, the nation's enormous traffic volume simply overwhelms pollution control efforts. The average new gasoline-powered car could already meet considerably more stringent norms than those in force today. Yet there are no in-use standards for older cars, even though these often pollute far more than permitted by new-car standards. Some 62 American cities still fail to meet federal ozone and carbon monoxide standards, and one third of them have no prospect of ever meeting them.[50]

The U.S. Environmental Protection Agency (EPA) has been lax in enforcing Clean Air Act provisions that call for bans on federal funds for new highway and industrial construction in noncompliance areas. Since 1975, Congress has repeatedly rolled back the deadline for meeting ozone standards. An effort to reauthorize a stricter Clean Air Act became deadlocked in the fall of 1988 due to the opposition of the car, coal, and utilities industries.[51]

Tougher measures seem called for. EPA Administrator Lee Thomas has suggested that "the smog problem may well need to be dealt with by reducing the number of cars on the street, by telling people they can't drive nearly to the extent they have in the past." Indeed, in an effort to combat urban air pollution, Athens, Budapest, Florence, Milan, Rome, and São Paulo have recently imposed restraints of varying strictness on motorized traffic in their inner cities.[52]

Fuel efficiency has been largely neglected as a means of combating pollution. Doubling fuel economy will roughly halve CO_2 emissions. Efficiency could be of further help if legislated emission limits were expressed in units of fuel consumed rather than in units of distance traveled. One technology under development is a membrane that, by separating nitrogen from the air before it is drawn into the combustion chamber, would not only eliminate nitrogen oxides but also boost combustion efficiency.[53]

Pollution abatement efforts everywhere have focused almost entirely on tailpipe devices that seek to reduce exhaust emissions rather than on developing solutions that might prevent their formation in the first place. Some alternative engine designs described earlier as fuel savers—the stratified charge and adiabatic diesel engines—could fit that bill. Ceramic engines or engine components could also cut emissions. Unfortunately, government R&D support for these technologies in the United States was terminated or sharply curtailed under the Reagan administration.[54]

The use of nonpetroleum fuels to reduce emissions is garnering growing support among both public officials and auto industry managers. A bill passed by the U.S. Congress in the fall of 1988 strives to encourage automakers to mass-produce either "dedicated" alternative-fuel vehicles (designed to use a fuel mixture containing at least 85 percent ethanol or methanol) or fuel-flexible vehicles (capable of running on various blends of gasoline and alcohol fuels or of operating on natural gas and gasoline). But the legislation may end up eroding fuel economy standards while failing to induce the use of alcohol fuels.[55]

Colorado and several other states are or will be mandating alcohol blends (gasoline containing up to 10 percent ethanol or methanol) to meet Clean Air Act standards. California has taken the lead on pure methanol. The mecca of the automotive culture originally embraced methanol in 1979 in response to the oil crisis; the program has since gained fresh impetus as a way to meet air quality standards. In little more than a decade, California hopes to replace as much as 30 percent of gasoline consumption with methanol in areas violating federal air pollution standards.[56]

Tests for alcohol fuel vehicles show a wide range of air quality results, and there is considerable controversy, particularly over the merits of methanol use. Pure methanol yields only negligible amounts of highly reactive, ozone-producing hydrocarbons, but does not noticeably reduce carbon monoxide emissions; methanol blends decrease carbon monoxide emissions, but do not provide any tangible ozone benefit.[57]

A neglected aspect of turning to methanol is its impact on the greenhouse effect. Operating a vehicle on methanol emits less CO_2 than using gasoline would. But producing the fuel from coal would worsen the threat of climate change because converting coal into methanol could double CO_2-equivalent

emissions. Even ethanol combustion produces compounds—aldehydes and peroxyacetyl nitrate—that may contribute to global warming.[58]

The search for less polluting alternatives to petroleum extends beyond alcohol fuels. Outside the United States, natural gas vehicles are receiving growing attention, because they promise lower carbon monoxide and particulate emissions (but perhaps higher discharges of nitrogen oxides) than conventional vehicles. But emissions of greenhouse gases would hardly be lower.[59]

Electric vehicles essentially emit no pollutants. Their environmental acceptability, however, depends on how the electricity that powers them is generated. Unless nonfossil feedstocks are used, the CO_2 problem would remain untackled or could even be aggravated.[60]

Hydrogen may well be the most desirable fuel of the future. Unless it is based on fossil fuels, the production of hydrogen does not lead to CO_2 emissions. Its use does not generate carbon monoxide or unburnt hydrocarbons, and nitrogen oxides emissions are low.[61]

A NEW AGE OF TRANSPORT

The auto culture is so deeply ingrained in western society that alternatives to it seem virtually unthinkable. But excessive reliance on cars can actually stifle rather than advance societies. The very success of mass motorization has created conditions that cannot be ameliorated simply by making cars more efficient and less polluting.

The automobile exacts an enormous toll in human life. Despite safety improvements, an estimated quarter-million people die in traffic accidents around the world every year, with millions more suffering injuries of varying severity.[62]

Large stretches of land have been given over to the automobile and its infrastructure. Worldwide, at least a third of an average city's land is devoted to roads, parking lots, and other elements of a car infrastructure. In American cities, close to half the urban space goes to accommodate the automobile; in Los Angeles, the figure is two thirds.[63]

Cars confer on their owners virtually boundless freedom as long as their numbers remain limited. But instead of facilitating individual mobility, the proliferation of automobiles has bred a crisis of its own—congestion. The conventional approach to this problem has led to a vicious circle: building more roads simply attracts more cars, thus increasing the pressure for still more roads. In southern California, with probably more miles of freeways than anywhere in the world, the average travel speed is no higher than 33 miles per hour and is expected to drop to 15 miles per hour by 2000. The Commission on California State Government Organization and Economy, a panel of business and political leaders, recently warned that mounting congestion had placed California on the brink of "a transportation crisis which will affect the economic prosperity of the state."[64]

Those cities most reliant on automobiles face virtual paralysis, an "urban thrombosis," as Kirkpatrick Sale has put it, "that slowly deprives the city of its lifeblood." In U.S. cities like Denver, Houston, and Los Angeles, roughly 90 percent of people get to work by car; in the less auto-dependent cities like New York, cars still account for two thirds of all work-related trips. By comparison, in Europe, where communities are less extensively suburbanized and average commuting distances are half those in North America, only about 40 percent of urban residents use their cars. Some 37 percent use public transportation, and the remainder walk or bike. In Tokyo, just 15 percent of the population drives to work. The result is that residents of the highly car-oriented American cities use twice as much gasoline per capita as Australians, four times as much as Europeans, and 10 times as much as Asians.[65]

Congestion is no longer an exclusively urban phenomenon. In the United States, residential settlements and jobs are increasingly dispersed in sprawling suburbs. As a consequence, the number of commutes within central city areas has remained fairly stable since 1960, while the number of trips between central cities and suburbs and from suburb to suburb has doubled. When suburban communities are too scattered, public mass transit, biking, and walking are not feasible.[66]

The United States boasts of the highest degree of individual mobility in the world. But Americans' heavy reliance on the automobile is a peculiar blend of preference and necessity, a cross between an abiding love affair with the passenger car and a profound lack of alternatives to autos. Fewer than 20 percent of the miles traveled by car are for vacationing, "pleasure" driving, or visiting family or friends. The overwhelming majority of driving goes for such daily necessities as commuting to work and shopping.[67]

A full accounting of the manifold subsidies the automobile receives, plus the environmental and health costs it entails, might cool the passion felt for cars. In most if not all countries, car owners do not bear the full costs of road building and maintenance, municipal services (such as traffic regulation and costs borne by police and fire departments), accidents and related health care, and tax losses from land paved over for automotive purposes.

In the United States, total subsidies may surpass $300 billion each year—an amount equal to all personal auto-related expenditures. If these expenses were reflected in retail fuel prices, a gallon of gasoline might cost as much as $4.50. An environment tax, assessed either on automobiles or the fuels they burn, would help internalize the less quantifiable environmental costs. No doubt political opposition to such measures would be enormous. But societies cannot continue to ignore the true costs of cars.[68]

With a short reprieve from higher oil prices, it is time to build a bridge from an auto-centered society into an alternative transportation future characterized by greater diversity of transport modes, in which cars, buses, rail systems, bicycles, and walking all complement each other. Mass transit systems offer a host of advantages over automobiles. When fully used, they are considerably more energy-efficient and less polluting. In addition, they reduce congestion: a car requires roughly nine times more road space per passenger than a bus.[69]

If properly planned, public transit networks can approximate the flexibility provided by private passenger cars. By synchronizing schedules, multidestinational or grid systems allow convenient transfers between different transit lines. They enhance access throughout a metropolitan area and create a dense network of mass transit corridors that attracts more riders. Multidestinational systems are operating successfully in many European and some North American cities.[70]

The viability of public transit systems—particularly in suburban areas—can be enhanced by making them more accessible. Bike-and-ride stations and facilities to carry bicycles on buses and rail systems have proved enormously popular in Denmark, Japan, the Netherlands, and West Germany, but remain little used in the United States.[71]

Reorienting transport priorities can be successful only if the symbiotic relationship between land use patterns and transportation networks is recognized. Public transit systems can facilitate and reinforce more compact land use, while land use patterns frequently determine transportation needs. Zoning ordinances can encourage a higher density of urban activity while slowing development at the urban perimeter. The more concentrated both population and jobs are, the shorter are travel distances, the more mass transit becomes viable, and the more walking and biking occurs. In short, more compact cities foster less individual motorized transport.[72]

Societies cannot continue to ignore the true costs of cars.

Third World cities stand at a crossroads as they swell in size and as urban transportation needs rapidly multiply. In the view of Michael Replogle of the Institute for Transportation and Development Policy in Washington, D.C., "there is a growing transportation crisis in many lesser developed countries. This crisis is the product of . . . a mismatch between the supply of transportation infrastructure, services, and technologies and the mobility needs of the majority of Third World people."[73]

Governments frequently assign priority to motorized travel in traffic planning, budget decisions, and allocation of street space, marginalizing pedestrians and traditional modes of transportation. Similarly, the World Bank has helped to slant transportation projects toward motorized solutions. Between 1972 and 1985, rail and bus systems received less than one third of the funding for World Bank urban transportation projects. Nonmotorized modes have been virtually ignored.[74]

Alas, government policies favoring private car ownership by a tiny but affluent elite are squandering scarce resources and distorting development priorities. Bringing in fuel, car components, or already assembled autos stretches import budgets thin. Likewise, building and maintaining an elaborate system of roads, highways, bridges, and tunnels devours enormous resources.

The overwhelming majority of people in the Third World will never be able to own a car. The promotion of auto ownership thus entails sharp inequities: to make it happen, the resources of poor and wealthy alike need to be devoted, though only a small share of the population enjoys the benefits. Existing public transportation often is in poor repair and has failed to keep up with urban population growth. In India and Bangladesh, for example, the urban public transit sector may meet as little as 15 percent of transportation needs.[75]

To meet the mobility needs of the poor majority in the Third World, substantial improvements and expansion of public transport are required. But often the poor cannot even afford public transportation. They frequently spend a disproportionate share of their incomes on getting around the city. In New Delhi, the lowest income groups devote 20–25 percent of their household incomes to transport, while the wealthiest group spends only 8 percent. Walking accounts for two thirds of all trips in large African cities like Kinshasa, and for almost half the trips in Bangalore, India.[76]

Nonmotorized modes of transportation—rickshaws, bicycles, push-carts, and animal-drawn carts—that require little input of capital and energy can be an important complement to public transit. They are more affordable, mostly do not pollute, do not strain investment and import budgets, and also generate a significant amount of employment.[77]

Bicycles—considered mainly a recreational device in the industrial West—are the predominant means of short-distance urban vehicular transportation in Asia, although they are far less common in parts of the western hemisphere and Africa. There are 800 million bicycles in the world today, twice the number of cars. In China, there are 540 bikes for every car, with one bicycle for every four people.[78]

French philosopher André Gorz once remarked that "the automobile is the paradoxical example of a luxury object that has been devalued by its own spread. But this practical devaluation has not yet been followed by an ideological devaluation." The proliferation of automobiles has led to the multiple crises of oil depletion, air pollution, looming climate change, and congestion. The magnitude of these problems suggests the need for a fundamental rethinking of the automobile's role.[79]

The scope of the modern, auto-centered transportation system—from production and distribution to operation and repair—is so tremendous that fundamental change cannot occur quickly. A successful policy therefore needs to encompass various layers, ranging from those that can take effect more immediately, such as making cars more efficient and less polluting and discouraging auto use where possible, to others that will need more time to make their impact felt, such as identifying and developing renewable, environmentally acceptable fuels, and establishing efficient, flexible public mass transit systems.

A more comprehensive policy must recognize that transportation needs are not abstract. What people need is access to jobs, homes, and services. More compact and integrated communities can provide such access without long commutes. Making urban design an integral component of future transportation policies could reconcile the contrasting interests of individuals in mobility and of society in fuel supply security, urban integrity, and environmental protection.

7

Responding to AIDS

Lori Heise

Few tragedies in human history have captured the world's attention as has AIDS. No disease, past or present, has inspired an international response equal to the current AIDS mobilization of the World Health Organization (WHO). None in recent memory has provoked more anxiety, aroused such prejudice against the afflicted, or stimulated so many moral, ethical, and legal debates. And no disease has more pointedly forced societies to confront issues otherwise conveniently ignored: drug abuse, sexuality, and the plight of the poor.

This global response is all the more remarkable given the relatively small number of people affected by acquired immunodeficiency syndrome so far. WHO estimates that by the end of 1988, at least 350,000 cases of the disease had occurred worldwide. The U.N. agency expects 1 million more cases by 1992, but even then, other killers will dwarf AIDS' toll. Each year, 2.5 million people die of smoking-related illnesses and 5 million children succumb to chronic diarrhea. Tuberculosis alone claims 3 million lives annually, 10 times the number of AIDS cases to date.[1]

This incongruity of numbers more likely reflects gross underattention to diarrhea and tuberculosis than overreaction to AIDS. The world is rightly alarmed at AIDS' potential to surpass other killers if it continues to spread unchecked. Moreover, body counts alone do not reflect what sets AIDS apart. Unlike most diseases, AIDS is almost always fatal; there is no cure and no vaccine. Carriers may go for years without symptoms, evoking the paranoia and fear that accompany uncertainty. And AIDS deals with the most intimate of human activities, the most powerful of human emotions.

Together these factors give AIDS a psychological charge unmatched by any other illness. Significantly, though, AIDS is one of the few diseases that pose a substantial threat to both industrial and developing nations. This convergence of interests provides opportunities to forge new alliances and new models for international cooperation. As Jonathan Mann, Director of WHO's Global Programme on AIDS, observes: "AIDS has the potential to bring us together, if we can thwart those who would use it to drive us apart."[2]

THE PANDEMIC UNFOLDS

In 1981, astute physicians in California and New York began to recognize a strange clustering of symptoms among some of their male homosexual patients. Something was destroying the immune systems of these individuals, rendering them susceptible to an odd assortment of opportunistic infections and cancers. Almost simultaneously, doctors in Central Africa, Europe, and Haiti began to note patients with similar conditions. By 1982, the new disease had a name: AIDS. And one year later, it had a cause: the human immunodeficiency virus, or HIV.[3]

AIDS on average takes eight or nine years to develop.

HIV exhibits a unique combination of characteristics that makes it intrinsically hard to control. Like genital herpes, once caught, the virus stays with its carrier for life. Once disease develops, AIDS is almost always fatal—usually within two years. But instead of manifesting within a few days or weeks, like most viral diseases, AIDS on average takes eight or nine years to develop. During this interval, carriers look and feel healthy but can pass the virus to others. Researchers now believe that most if not all individuals infected with HIV will eventually develop AIDS.[4]

The good news, however, is that compared with other viruses—such as polio and the common cold—HIV is fragile and relatively difficult to transmit. AIDS is overwhelmingly a sexually transmitted disease, communicated through body fluids and blood during vaginal or anal intercourse. To a significant but lesser extent, the virus is also transmitted through blood transfusions, through the sharing or reusing of contaminated nee-

dles, and from mother to child during pregnancy or birth. Contrary to widespread fears, AIDS cannot be caught through casual contact, sneezes, kissing, toilet seats, or insects.

Although the virus is transmitted the same way everywhere—through blood, through sexual intercourse, or from mother to child—the pattern of transmission and infection varies among regions. Indeed, the international AIDS picture can best be understood in terms of three broadly defined subepidemics, each with its own dynamic.

In North America, Western Europe, and certain Latin American countries, AIDS is mainly transmitted through homosexual intercourse and the sharing of needles among drug addicts. As a result, those infected are overwhelmingly male, and transmission from mother to child is limited. Less than 1 percent of the population is thought to be infected, but the infection rate among intravenous (IV) drug users and homosexual men exceeds 50 percent in some cities. Heterosexual sex is responsible for a small but increasing proportion of cases. Interestingly, despite its potential, sex with prostitutes is not a major mode of transmission.[5]

By contrast, in sub-Saharan Africa and parts of the Caribbean, AIDS is primarily a heterosexually transmitted disease, with women infected as often as men. Because so many women are infected, transmission from mother to child is disturbingly common. Blood transfusions—a route largely eliminated in the industrial world—remain a source of infection in many countries where blood supplies still are not screened. Since intravenous drug use and homosexuality are rare, these modes of transmission are not significant, although reuse of contaminated needles by health workers remains a likely source of infection. In some countries, infection in the total population exceeds 1 percent, with 5–33 percent of sexually active adults in select urban areas infected. Male contact with prostitutes is thought to play a major role in the epidemic's spread.[6]

In the third set of countries, HIV has been introduced only recently. Infection rates remain extremely low even among people with multiple sex partners, such as prostitutes. Most cases have originated outside of the country either through sex with a foreigner or through imported blood products contaminated with HIV. Although there is increasing evidence of in-country spread, no strong pattern of heterosexual or homosexual transmission has emerged. Asia, Eastern Europe, northern Africa, the Middle East, and most of the Pacific all fall in this category.[7]

These variations evolve from a combination of factors, including when and where the virus first entered the population and the different social practices and behaviors that exist among cultures. In Africa, for example, the epidemic involved the heterosexually active population first, whereas in the United States the epidemic was initially introduced and amplified in predominately male populations: homosexuals, people with hemophilia, and IV drug users. Researchers also believe that the greater prevalence of untreated sexually transmitted diseases (STDs) in Africa has facilitated the spread of AIDS there and may largely explain the greater efficiency of heterosexual sex in transmitting the virus among Africans.[8]

It is becoming increasingly clear, for example, that chlamydia and STDs that cause genital sores (such as syphilis, herpes, and chancroid) make it easier for HIV to pass between sexual partners. Sadly, in developing countries where treatment is less accessible, STDs are far more endemic than in the industrial world. Laboratory evidence also suggests that an individual whose immune system has been activated by chronic infections might be more susceptible to HIV infection. This factor may operate to increase heterosexual transmission in the Third World, where viral and parasitic diseases are endemic. There is no convincing evidence that genetic differences or variations in viral strains account for the African pattern of transmission.[9]

Although scientists have mapped the virus's surface chemistry in minute detail, the world has only the vaguest notion of where HIV is and where it is going. As of December 1, 1988, 142 countries had reported a total of 129,385 AIDS cases to the World Health Organization. (See Table 7–1.) Due to gross underreporting and underrecognition, however, WHO suspects that the true global caseload is more than twice that figure. Moreover, AIDS cases represent only the tip of the iceberg: for every AIDS case, anywhere from 20 to 100 people may carry the virus but not yet show symptoms. All told, WHO estimates that 5 million to 10 million people worldwide may be infected with HIV.[10]

Lacking any better measure, many people have used WHO data on reported AIDS cases to compare the severity of the epidemic in different parts of the world. Such comparisons can be misleading, however, because countries vary greatly in the accuracy and completeness of their reporting. Also, because of the virus's long latency period, a country's current number of AIDS cases is actually a snapshot of the epidemic five to eight years ago, when those who now have AIDS first got infected. The severity of today's epidemic is best represented by studies that measure how many people are currently infected with HIV by testing individuals' blood for antibodies to the virus.

Because antibody testing is expensive and difficult to conduct on a large scale, only a handful of countries—including

Table 7-1. Officially Reported AIDS Cases, Selected Countries, December 1, 1988

Country	Prevalence	Rate
	(cases)	(cases per million population)
United States	78,985	321
Uganda	5,508	336
Brazil	4,436	31
France	4,211	75
Tanzania	3,055	126
Kenya	2,732	117
Malawi	2,586	336
West Germany	2,580	42
Italy	2,556	45
Canada	2,156	83
Mexico	1,502	18
Haiti	1,455	231
Burundi	1,408	271
Congo	1,250	568
Zambia	1,056	141
Rwanda	987	139
Switzerland	605	92
French Guiana	113	1,228
Japan	90	0.7
Bermuda	81	1,396
China	3	0.003

SOURCES: World Health Organization data base; Population Reference Bureau, *1988 World Population Data Sheet* (Washington, D.C.: 1988).

Uganda and Rwanda—have attempted to design and implement surveys that would yield national estimates of HIV prevalence. Even in these small countries, the logistical and design problems of testing "representative" cross sections of society have proved immense, making it unlikely that many countries will undertake similar ventures. Without systematic testing, epidemiologists will have to rely on small-scale blood surveys of select groups for estimating the scope of infection.[11]

By testing enough people with different backgrounds and risk factors—factory workers, prostitutes in cities, rural blood donors—epidemiologists can piece together a fairly accurate picture of the epidemic's extent. Researchers at WHO are now using such surveys to derive country-specific estimates of infection within different age-groups. Although estimates of infection by country are not yet available, the sum total of data lead WHO to believe that Africa is the most affected continent and Asia the least. (See Table 7–2.) Infection in Africa appears largely concentrated in the center, extending west from Tanzania to the Congo, and dipping south to include Zambia and Malawi. The United States is also severely affected, with an estimated 1–1.5 million infected individuals.[12]

Antibody surveys likewise reveal that throughout the world AIDS is primarily an urban disease, although it is gradually spreading from major urban centers to smaller cities and towns. In parts of Zambia, northwestern Tanzania, and southwestern Uganda, however, there are major rural outbreaks, emanating from the movement of people and disease along the Trans-African Highway and in areas of military conflict.[13]

Table 7-2. Estimated HIV Prevalence, Selected Regions, 1987/88

Region	Prevalence
	(number infected)
Africa	2–3 million
United States	1–1.5 million
Latin America	500,000–750,000
Europe	280,000–800,000
Asia	fewer than 100,000
World	5–10 million (probably closer to 5 million)

SOURCE: Worldwatch Institute, compiled from various World Health Organization sources.

Even more difficult than determining the world's current AIDS picture is predicting how the epidemic will evolve. Already there have been important shifts in the persons most at risk in various countries and in the relative significance of different transmission routes. Such shifts are meaningful because they indicate where new prevention activities should be focused and have important implications for the spread of infection beyond those presently affected.

The United States and Western Europe, for example, are now experiencing a second wave of epidemic among intravenous drug users. Whereas most AIDS cases used to involve homosexual men, evidence indicates that rates of new infection are declining among gay men but accelerating among drug addicts. In fact, in certain parts of Europe—including Italy, Spain, and Scotland—IV drug users now account for the majority of all cases. Overall, the proportion of total European AIDS cases involving drug injection rose from 2 percent in September 1984 to 24 percent in mid-1988.[14]

This new pattern is important because of both its impact on the drug-using community and its potential to facilitate the spread of AIDS into the general population. Although it is too early to predict whether AIDS will move into the heterosexual mainstream in these areas, addicts could facilitate this process by communicating the virus to their sexual partners who in turn could infect people outside the drug community. Seventy percent of heterosexually transmitted cases in native-born U.S. citizens currently occur in partners of IV drug users.[15]

Indeed, it is difficult to overemphasize the role that drug abuse could play in the future of the American and European AIDS epidemic. Already, more than 70 percent of cases in American children are due to IV drug use by their mother or her sexual partner. Half of all AIDS cases in American women are related to drug use, with even higher proportions among black and Hispanic women (70 and 83 percent, respectively). Even among female prostitutes, the likelihood of infection is more closely linked to IV drug use than to prostitution itself.[16]

Half of all AIDS cases in American women are related to drug use.

Certain Central American and Caribbean nations have also experienced shifts in AIDS epidemiology, with heterosexual sex gradually replacing homosexual activity as the dominant route of transmission. This change is best exemplified in Haiti, where the percentage of cases involving men who contracted AIDS through homosexual activity declined from 50 percent in 1983 to 1 percent in 1987, while the share transmitted heterosexually increased from 26 to over 80 percent. As a result, the proportion of cases among women has doubled since 1979, and the number of babies born with AIDS has increased greatly.[17]

Latin American health officials suspect that the high prevalence of bisexuality among some Latin men has contributed to this shifting epidemiology. Because homosexuality is less acceptable in Latin culture and the pressure to have children is acute, many men who engage in homosexual activity marry or have steady female lovers. This sets the stage for increasing AIDS incidence among women and children, a pattern already documented in Trinidad and Tobago, the Dominican Republic, and Honduras, among others. Health officials fear that other Latin American countries could follow Haiti's lead. In Brazil and Mexico, for example, bisexuals account for 23 percent of reported AIDS cases; in Ecuador, for 40 percent.[18]

THE IMPACT IN THE THIRD WORLD

Estimating the social and economic impact of AIDS in the Third World is an endeavor fraught with uncertainty. Scientists have too few data on the prevalence of HIV infection or on the conditions—both behavioral and social—that determine its spread to project with any confidence the future course of the epidemic. Even less information is available for translating rising death rates into potential impacts on overtaxed health care systems, economic output, or future population growth. Yet one thing is certain: AIDS will have a profound impact in the Third World, and one that exceeds the impact in the West, where resources are more plentiful and basic infrastructure better developed.

A look at existing health care systems in the Third World provides a glimpse of the disadvantage that developing countries face in responding to AIDS. In 1984, Haiti had $3.25 to spend on health care per citizen; Mexico had $11.50. Rwanda's pitiful annual budget of $1.60 per person would not even buy a bottle of aspirin in the industrial world. By contrast, Sweden annually spends over $1,100 on health care per person and the United States invests more than $760. Yet meager Third World health budgets must contend with existing epidemics of frightening proportion. Three million Third World children die each year from preventable diseases such as measles, tetanus, and whooping cough. In Africa alone, malaria annually claims 1 million lives.[19]

Data from countries already responding to AIDS confirm that the costs of prevention will be high. In 1988, for example, Brazil's prevention program was estimated to cost $28 million, $8 million of which went to screen blood at state-run blood banks. Health officials in Peru put the start-up costs of screening their national blood supply at $20 million in 1987, a sum that could otherwise cover the total annual health care bill for 1.5 million Peruvians. If borne alone by developing countries, these costs could derail already fragile and inadequate health care systems.[20]

Developing countries also have fewer options for treating AIDS patients than countries in the West do. Physicians in industrial countries largely respond by treating the secondary diseases, such as *Pneumocystis carinii* pneumonia, that accompany AIDS. It is an expensive ordeal that often involves frequent hospital stays. The only drug currently known to attack HIV directly—zidovudine, commonly known as AZT—costs roughly $8,000 per patient annually, and causes anemia so severe that over a quarter of recipients require blood transfusions. In the Third World, where per capita incomes are measured in hundreds of dollars and blood is in short supply, a life-prolonging drug like AZT might as well not exist.[21]

Indeed, preliminary cost data from around the world suggest that the amount spent per AIDS patient roughly correlates with a country's gross national product (GNP). As with health care in general, poor countries are forced to spend less on each patient. If Zaire spent at a level comparable to the United States, the cost of treating 10 AIDS patients would exceed the entire budget of Mama Yemo, the nation's largest public hospital. Although costs in industrial countries are inflated by higher salaries, more expensive equipment, and added malpractice insurance, AIDS treatment undoubtedly suffers in countries where even antibiotics and syringes are in short supply.[22]

Given such constraints, AIDS naturally raises the question of triage. Where hospital space and medical supplies are scarce and where people regularly die of treatable illnesses, diverting resources to AIDS treatment may actually cost lives by crowding out patients who can be cured. From a quarter to half of precious hospital beds in some central African hospitals are occupied by patients who are infected with HIV; Costa Rican officials predict a similar situation by the mid-1990s. Already, AIDS patients are being discharged from some health facilities in Africa, Haiti, and Brazil to give preference to patients with curable illnesses.[23]

In terms of overall health investment, however, AIDS prevention activities may actually deserve high priority, even in countries heavily burdened by other diseases. A World Bank/WHO research team of western and African researchers has estimated that preventing one case of HIV infection in Africa would save more years of life than would preventing a case of malaria, measles, tuberculosis (TB), or pneumonia. To determine the relative merits of investing in AIDS prevention versus other disease control programs, decision makers need to consider how many people are affected by each disease and the comparative costs of each prevention program. Significantly, preventing a case of AIDS stops secondary and tertiary transmission of the virus, whereas preventing a case of measles or malaria would affect transmission little if at all, because such diseases are already so pervasive in Africa.[24]

Not only does AIDS compete with other diseases for limited health budgets, HIV actually magnifies existing epidemics. By weakening the immune system of its host, the virus makes carriers more susceptible to renewed attack from other microbes lying dormant. For example, some 30–60 percent of adults in many developing countries are carriers of the tuberculosis bacteria, even though their bodies have conquered outward signs of the disease. By suppressing the immune system, HIV allows dormant TB bacteria to become active, leading to the contagious form of tuberculosis.[25]

Although it is too early to measure worldwide increases in TB prevalence, some evidence suggests that HIV may already be having a multiplier effect on this deadly disease. New York City—home to almost half of all U.S. AIDS patients—reported a 35-percent jump in TB cases between 1984 and 1986. Studies also document a close association between TB and HIV: in Kinshasa, Zaire, 38 percent of TB patients tested were HIV-positive, compared with only 2.5–8 percent of healthy adults. An HIV-TB link is especially worrisome in the Third World, where poverty, overcrowding, and lack of access to treatment make tuberculosis more lethal than in the West.[26]

From a quarter to half of precious hospital beds in some central African hospitals are occupied by patients infected with HIV.

It is in the area of child health, however, that AIDS has the greatest potential to erode hard-won health gains in the Third World. Over the last three decades, developing regions have inaugurated a "child survival revolution" through encouraging oral rehydration therapy for diarrhea, immunization, breast-feeding, and birth spacing. Together with economic growth and increased female literacy, these simple interventions have cut Third World child deaths by slightly more than half since 1955, with Southeast Asia making the greatest progress and Africa the least.[27]

Left unchecked, AIDS will undermine these gains as more and more pregnant women become infected and transmit the virus to their children *in utero*. Already 9–24 percent of pregnant women in some African cities—such as Kinshasa and Kampala—are infected. Up to half the children born to these women will contract the virus and die. Preliminary models of the most affected regions in Africa suggest that infant mortality could increase by more than 25 percent, eroding three decades of progress in infant and child health.[28]

These models also show that although adult death rates in Africa could rise dramatically, AIDS will likely have only modest impacts on population growth. The notion—advanced by some—that parts of Africa are already "lost" to AIDS or that the disease eliminates the need for family planning funds is not supported by the evidence. A model by John Bongaarts of the Population Council in New York, for example, predicts that a typical African growth rate of 3 percent could fall to 2 percent over 25 years if 20 percent of the total population became infected. Even if death rates were to double—with AIDS adding as many deaths as all other causes combined—population growth would not cease.[29]

AIDS eliminates the most productive segment of a population.

The demographic effects of AIDS may be small, but the economic impact of a fatal epidemic focused on sexually active adults could be immense. Unlike other diseases that cull the weakest members of society—the sick, the old, and the very young—AIDS eliminates the most productive segment of a population. In Africa, HIV infection in women peaks during their third decade—the prime childbearing years—and for males during their fourth decade, the most productive years at work and in the community. Where the ranks of people with

certain specialized skills and training may be small, the loss of even a handful of engineers, health planners, or agronomists can be debilitating.[30]

Although predicting AIDS' impact on specific economic sectors will require detailed country-by-country analysis, hints of what may be in store have started to emerge. Zambian researchers fear that labor losses due to AIDS could cripple their nation's copper mining industry, which accounts for one fifth of Zambia's GNP. One study in the nation's Copper Belt found that 68 percent of men testing positive were the skilled professionals upon whom the mining industry depends. Since the companies provide both retirement benefits and comprehensive medical and social services for miners and their families, Zambian researchers fear that the financial drain of AIDS could jeopardize the entire mining sector.[31]

These economic disruptions come at a time when developing nations—especially in Africa—are already laboring under severe economic hardship. Per capita income is declining and foreign debt is mounting. Against this backdrop, AIDS threatens to further complicate balance-of-payment problems. Foreign exchange will be lost as governments seek to import items necessary to combat the epidemic, tourist dollars may decline in response to travelers' fears, and economic growth will slow as people and governments divert savings from investment to treatment. Indeed, in industrial and developing countries alike, the indirect economic costs of AIDS will far exceed any direct costs related to prevention or treatment.[32]

Researchers at the Harvard Institute of International Development are attempting to quantify these indirect costs by modeling the impact of AIDS on certain central African economies. According to their projections, by 1995 the annual loss to Zaire's economy due to premature deaths and reduced savings will be between $350 million and $670 million—equal to 8 to 16 percent of the nation's GNP in 1984. Even without including direct treatment costs or losses due to illness, these figures exceed the $314 million that Zaire received from all sources of development assistance in 1984.[33]

In human terms, this economic slowing will mean that by 1995, the average Zairian will have roughly $18 less income per year than he or she would have had in an economy without AIDS (measured in constant 1984 dollars). A mere pittance in industrial societies, $18 represents a 10-percent loss in income for Zairians, who average only $170 per year. Tragically, this decline comes on top of an already seriously eroded income base: per capita income in Zaire declined roughly 42 percent between 1965 and 1985. AIDS is an added burden these people cannot afford.[34]

Even more devastating are the costs of caring for family members stricken with AIDS. Athough employers or the state pay health care costs in many developing countries, not all citizens have access to such assistance, either because they are unemployed or because they live in remote areas. In one study of children with AIDS in Kinshasa, over half the parents were either unemployed or dead, meaning that treatment costs fell to family and friends. Children's hospital expenses typically were three times their parents' average monthly wages, and funerals and burial cost almost a year's salary.[35]

Yet the true costs of AIDS are both economic and personal. Economists can count up the direct costs and calculate the indirect cost of lost wages from disability and death. But what of the psychological toll on those left behind? Economic tally sheets cannot capture the pain of a child left without parents or of a generation whose future is shortchanged by AIDS.

PROGRESS TOWARD PREVENTION IN INDUSTRIAL COUNTRIES

For a world used to solving problems with a technical fix, AIDS is frustrating. Today, prospects for a vaccine or cure seem even more distant than they did two years ago, when scientists were reeling from the thrill of rapid discovery. The AIDS virus has proved a wily opponent: It hides within the very immune cells that the body normally uses to ward off invaders, making vaccines and treatments exceedingly difficult to devise. And it mutates at a furious pace—perhaps even faster than the influenza virus that requires researchers to alter the flu vaccine every year. Prevention will likely remain the world's primary weapon against AIDS for at least the next decade.[36]

In the industrial world, where transmission through blood transfusions has essentially ceased, stopping AIDS means getting people to change high-risk behavior. Risky behavior includes unprotected sex, especially with multiple partners, and the sharing of contaminated needles among drug addicts. The best way to avoid AIDS is to have a mutually monogamous sexual relationship with a partner known to be uninfected. Short of that, condoms provide good, although not foolproof protection against HIV transmission. The spermicide nonoxyl-9 has also been shown to kill the virus in laboratory tests, but its ability to prevent HIV transmission between sexual partners has yet to be proved.[37]

It is important to recognize that it is

what people do, not who they are, that puts them at risk. As the Panos Institute has pointed out in its groundbreaking work *Blaming Others,* talk of "high-risk groups," such as Haitians, gay men, or prostitutes, tends to invite finger-pointing and erroneously suggests that anyone not in these groups is safe. Moreover, categorization fails to acknowledge that not all group members practice high-risk behavior. AIDS is not a "gay disease" or an "African disease" or a "disease of drug addicts." Anyone who engages in high-risk behavior can contract HIV.[38]

Given these risks, industrial countries have responded in a variety of ways, some constructive, others less so. In general, European governments were quicker than the United States to launch broad-based AIDS education programs, even though their epidemics were not yet as severe. Seven European countries sent information booklets to their citizens more than a year before the United States did so in June 1988. Across the board, these public information campaigns have achieved roughly the same result: people now know that sex, blood, and needles can transmit AIDS, but they still cling to many misperceptions. In 1987, 40 percent of Canadians polled, for instance, believed that AIDS could be transmitted through insects, as did 38 percent of Americans.[39]

Regrettably, some nations have also espoused superficially attractive but ineffective responses, such as screening and deportation of infected foreigners, premarital testing, and mandatory testing of those perceived to be at risk. For example, 29 countries—including various developing ones—now impose some form of travel restriction or mandatory screening of foreigners even though WHO has determined that such measures are costly, repressive, and will not stem the epidemic's tide. Entry restrictions are born of a desire to erect a bar-

rier between the virus and the uninfected, to label the afflicted as "foreign," "different," "not me." In reality, by providing a false sense of security, they allow the disease to spread unchecked.[40]

In the United States, bills for premarital screening for HIV have been introduced in 35 states and become law in Illinois, Louisiana, and Texas. (The law in Texas will not go into effect unless HIV prevalence exceeds a certain threshold.) Like travel restrictions, such bills are politically attractive because they are highly visible; yet they are dangerous because they deflect attention and resources from those truly at risk. Even premarital syphilis testing has never efficiently identified new syphilis cases: in 1978, premarital screening accounted for only 1.27 percent of all tests found positive, but the program cost $80 million annually. Not surprisingly, Louisiana has already repealed its AIDS law after realizing that it uncovered few cases and pushed couples to neighboring states to get married. Illinois likewise is having second thoughts.[41]

Other countries and constituencies have responded with calls for mandatory testing, compulsory reporting of HIV-positive individuals, or required partner tracing. The Soviet Union, Hungary, and Bavaria in West Germany, for example, all require testing of high-risk individuals, including prostitutes, drug addicts, and—with the exception of Bavaria—homosexuals. Yet health officials are unanimous in the view that mandatory measures merely drive underground those most in need of testing. In Charleston, South Carolina, the number of homosexual men seeking testing dropped by 51 percent after the state began requiring all those who tested positive to be reported to the public health department. When anonymous and voluntary, however, testing, counseling, and partner tracing have proved to be useful and effective tools for AIDS prevention.[42]

Despite these false starts, many countries now have innovative prevention programs in place, including school-based education, information campaigns aimed at the general public, condom promotion, and specialized outreach programs designed to reach those at highest risk. Many of the most impressive initiatives come from outside government and draw on the skills and energy of the homosexual community, which rallied early to protect its members. The Gay Men's Health Crisis in New York (founded in 1982) and the Terrence Higgins Trust in London (founded in 1983) probably still have more experience in AIDS education than any other groups in the world.[43]

So far it appears that among heterosexuals, prevention campaigns have increased knowledge but have changed sexual behavior only marginally. Change among gay men, however, has been dramatic and may well constitute the most rapid and profound behavioral response ever documented in public health. Studies throughout the United States and Western Europe have found that gay men have reduced their number of sexual partners, increased their use of condoms, and decreased their participation in unprotected anal intercourse. One review of 24 American and European studies concluded that, on average, gay men have 63 percent fewer sexual partners since AIDS. The incidence of receptive anal intercourse has similarly declined, by 59 percent.[44]

Because of HIV's long latency period, these behavior changes have not yet translated into fewer new AIDS cases, but in parts of the United States rates of new HIV infection among gay men have declined. Less than 1 percent of noninfected homosexual men in San Francisco, for example, were being infected annually by 1988, down from 18 percent

in 1983. AIDS-induced behavior change is also probably responsible for recent declines in the number of new gonorrhea and syphilis cases among gay men in Denmark, Finland, the Netherlands, Sweden, and the United Kingdom. Because these STDs have shorter incubation periods than HIV, reductions in high-risk behavior register more quickly with syphilis and gonorrhea than with AIDS.[45]

Mandatory measures merely drive underground those most in need of testing.

Unfortunately, studies on both continents confirm that a minority of gay men still engage in dangerous behavior despite understanding the risks involved. Risky behavior is most often associated with the use of uninhibiting drugs during sex, suggesting that programs aimed at alcohol and recreational drugs may be important for AIDS control. Moreover, gays living in lower risk areas do not seem to have modified their behavior as much, perhaps because they do not feel as personally at risk. It is unsafe to assume, therefore, that the entire gay male population in the United States and Europe has been educated and that attention is better placed elsewhere. Promising progress has been made, but much remains to be done.[46]

Intravenous drug users have also proved capable of change, although curbing HIV infection among drug addicts has received far too little attention, especially in the United States. Response has been hampered by debate over the moral and legal appropriateness of certain interventions, such as needle exchange programs, and the pervasive view that addicts somehow "deserve" AIDS. Inaction, however, is both inhumane to drug users and shortsighted, given that IV drug users are the most likely bridge between HIV and the general population.

Without a doubt, helping addicts kick their habit is the favored approach to stopping AIDS transmission among drug users, but in many countries treatment capacity is sorely lacking. The United States, for example, can treat only 15–20 percent of its more than 1.2 million needle addicts, and waiting lists of up to six months for treatment are not uncommon. During this time, addicts continue to shoot drugs, increasing their chances of contracting and spreading HIV and diminishing their resolve to fight their addiction. When treatment is affordable and accessible, IV drug users have shown that they will seek it out to reduce their risk of AIDS. In New Jersey, addicts redeemed 84 percent of 970 coupons for free treatment that AIDS outreach workers distributed. More than half said they were largely motivated by fear of AIDS.[47]

For those unable or unwilling to break their addiction, programs aimed at safer injection are important for AIDS control. Needle-sharing is deeply ingrained in the drug culture, both as a form of social bonding and because new syringes are expensive, hard to obtain, and illegal to possess in many areas. But studies confirm that addicts will reduce their use of contaminated needles, especially if given the means to do so, either through needle/syringe exchange programs or through the provision of bleach for cleaning syringes between uses. Indeed, several studies suggest that supplying the means to change behavior is critical; programs that provide information alone have tended to fail.[48]

Despite the importance of providing the hardware of behavior change, needle exchange programs have been extremely controversial, especially in the United States, where only two small pilot programs have been approved. On both sides of the Atlantic, people argue that to supply syringes is to condone drug use. To refuse addicts access to clean needles in the age of AIDS, however, is to deny them the opportunity to protect themselves—and eventually others—from a deadly infection.[49]

While still controversial, other countries have been more willing than the United States to experiment with needle exchange programs. So far, Switzerland, Denmark, the Netherlands, the United Kingdom, and Australia have initiated programs and all report significantly less needle-sharing among addicts. France has also liberalized its policy by making needles available for sale at pharmacies without prescription or identification. Despite widespread concern that increased availability of needles would encourage drug use, there is no evidence that this is occurring. Indeed, in the Netherlands the number of addicts actually decreased from roughly 8,500 in 1984 to 6,800 in 1988 after the government implemented a comprehensive AIDS prevention campaign aimed at addicts, including needle exchange, methadone treatment, and outreach.[50]

Prevention programs have been singularly ineffective at reaching U.S. minority communities.

Disturbing evidence indicates, however, that changes in sexual behavior among American and European drug addicts lag considerably behind changes in drug-use behavior. Even more distressing, the least amount of change has occurred within committed, heterosexual relationships, where HIV transmission is most likely to occur (because of frequency of intercourse) and where children are most likely to be conceived.

Given that three fourths of American IV drug users are male and have a primary partner who does not use drugs, there is clearly need for more education on safer sex among addicts as part of an effort to prevent the spread of HIV.[51]

AIDS prevention programs to date have also been singularly ineffective at reaching U.S. minority communities. Studies show that blacks and Hispanics are less well informed than whites about AIDS and that they have not modified their behavior as much. This is particularly worrisome because blacks and Hispanics are at extremely high risk. Already they account for 41 percent of AIDS cases, even though they constitute only 19 percent of the U.S. population. Eighty-five percent of children who acquired AIDS from their mother and 71 percent of all women with AIDS are black or Hispanic.[52]

This pattern of infection is partly due to the fact that a disproportionate number of IV drug users are black or Hispanic. But even among drug addicts, minorities are more likely to be infected than whites. The reasons for this are unclear, although for cultural and economic reasons, blacks and Hispanics may have less access to clean needles, drug treatment, and AIDS information. Particularly disturbing is evidence that blacks also account for a disproportionate share of new HIV infection occurring outside of big cities, where IV drug use would be less common.[53]

These trends emphasize the need for more culturally relevant AIDS information aimed at minorities. Recently, the Centers for Disease Control of the U.S. Public Health Service has attempted to fill this gap by earmarking almost $45 million for minority outreach projects in 1989, up from only $14 million in 1987. Experience suggests that initiatives arising from the minority communities themselves have the greatest chance of success.[54]

ALLIANCE FOR PREVENTION IN DEVELOPING COUNTRIES

Stopping AIDS in developing countries will take a worldwide alliance of professional skills, resources, and experience. Left unaided, the Third World would have to divert scarce resources from other essential development initiatives or be forced to accept ever-rising death tolls. Even industrial countries cannot fight this scourge alone. Barring a vaccine or a cure, no country can independently protect itself from HIV, for the disease respects no national boundaries. Like several of today's most pressing problems—global warming, ozone depletion, Third World debt—unless all nations work together against AIDS, there is little hope in acting separately.

Although nations have collaborated before on action aimed at disease control, there is no precedent for the level of cooperation that will be required to battle AIDS. Even WHO's successful effort to eradicate smallpox during the seventies is not fully analogous: Smallpox could be prevented with a single vaccine that was already available and relatively easy to deliver. Industrial nations had already conquered the disease, and carriers were easily identified by a characteristic rash. By contrast, HIV infection is invisible and insidious. And there is no vaccine. Stopping AIDS means getting people to change their behavior, a task that governments and international agencies are ill prepared to do.

With a threat this great and requiring so much coordination, central leadership is essential. WHO accepted this role in February 1987 when it formed the Special Programme on AIDS, later renamed the Global Programme on AIDS (GPA). Since then, the program has grown rapidly, largely due to the determined leadership of its director, Dr. Jonathan Mann. Starting with one secretary and a $580,000 budget, Mann has built the AIDS program into one of the agency's largest and most active, with a proposed budget of $95 million for 1989 and a year-end staffing target of 222 professionals.[55]

GPA acts primarily as a coordinating body for AIDS surveillance, prevention, and research and as a resource to governments trying to develop national AIDS control plans. With WHO's encouragement and assistance, more than 150 nations now have national AIDS committees, and 119 have developed short-term plans for combatting the disease (including every country in sub-Saharan Africa). Forty-eight countries, mostly in the Third World, have gone on to develop three- to five-year plans. WHO also serves as an intermediary between donors and developing countries hoping to arrange funding for their national AIDS programs. As of December 1988, $99 million had been raised to support 30 medium-term plans, mostly in Africa and the Caribbean.[56]

That so many nations have mobilized is a testament to WHO's effectiveness, given that two years ago most governments still denied the presence or extent of AIDS. The challenge now is to translate these paper plans into functioning programs, a task that will be particularly hard in developing countries. Most experts agree that it is preferable to integrate AIDS prevention activities into existing health and educational systems rather than develop "vertical" AIDS programs that would compete for resources and attention. But it is impossible to graft AIDS control programs onto nonexistent or rudimentary rural health care systems or to introduce blood screening in countries without adequate labs, trained technicians, or functioning blood banks. Indeed, to be successful in some poorer countries, the whole health infrastructure will have to be expanded and fortified.

WHO's leadership has clearly inspired some countries to act, but many nations had nascent education campaigns even before WHO entered the scene. As in industrial countries, many of the earliest efforts were implemented by nongovernmental groups, the vanguard of AIDS education. In Kenya, for example, the Red Cross distributed over a million leaflets counseling "Help Crush AIDS" and "Spread facts . . . not fear." The Rwandan Red Cross launched an impressive campaign using radio announcements, posters, and leaflets. And in the Dominican Republic, the government distributed free condoms, printed hundreds of thousands of brochures, posters, and bumper stickers, and passed legislation requiring all motels to provide complimentary condoms.[57]

Indeed, the picture that emerges from the Third World is one of many small acts that combine to form a growing tide of prevention activities. In Guatemala, the Association for Sexual Education has produced two pamphlets and a series of wallet-sized cards that describe how to protect oneself from AIDS. In Mexico, a dynamic woman named Gloria Ornelas Hall runs an AIDS hotline that handles over 70 calls a day. And in Uganda, a physiotherapist and a doctor whose lives were personally touched by AIDS have formed a counseling service for sufferers and their families. With few resources but much foresight, these individuals are reaching out into their communities to educate others about AIDS.[58]

As WHO has helped mobilize outside funds, Third World governments have become more involved in prevention. Often one of their first priorities has been to secure the nation's blood supply, primarily because it is one route that can be eliminated with a technical fix. In 1985, when a blood test for HIV first became available, from 8 to 18 percent of blood donors in the capitals of Uganda, Rwanda, and Zaire were infected. With screening units costing up to $10,000 apiece and each test costing on average $1–4, developing countries could not afford screening and hospitals became part of the chain of infection. In Central Africa, transfusions probably account for 5–10 percent of HIV transmission among adults and up to a quarter of all AIDS cases in children.[59]

The majority of developing countries now have at least some screening capacity, mostly in major urban areas. By the end of 1988, limited testing equipment was available in most capital cities in Africa and Latin America and some countries—such as Zimbabwe, Zambia, and Mexico—had nearly universal screening. Blood screening should become considerably more common in the near future as a new generation of simple, rapid blood tests for HIV become available. Field tests are nearing completion on several that yield results in 2–4 minutes, and that use only a slide and medicine dropper instead of expensive equipment and reagents. The ability to screen quickly is especially important in developing countries where blood is often not banked but donated as needed when an emergency arises.[60]

Although worth doing, screening blood will have a relatively small impact on the spread of AIDS because at least 80 percent of transmission in the Third World is through heterosexual sex. Thus the bulk of prevention must come from encouraging fidelity and greater use of condoms. Also important is expanding access to treatment for other sexually transmitted diseases that may be facilitating the spread of HIV.

The best strategy for curtailing sexual transmission depends in part on whether HIV has infiltrated the general population or not. In countries where the virus is already widely dispersed, prevention activities must be broad in scope. But where HIV prevalence is still low, as in West Africa and Asia, countries have an opportunity to target interventions and thereby save vital resources. Experience has shown that HIV generally spreads outward from pockets of infection among individuals whose behavior increases their risk of contracting and transmitting the virus, such as prostitutes, men in the military, and IV drug users. By helping such groups to protect themselves, governments can prevent HIV from gaining a foothold in their country.[61]

Programs that use peers as AIDS educators seem the most promising.

The speed at which the virus can infiltrate unsuspecting populations argues persuasively for acting before HIV is an obvious problem. Studies in Bangkok, Thailand, for example, show that among the city's estimated 60,000 IV drug users, HIV prevalence rose from 1 percent in 1987 to over 30 percent by mid-1988. Had prevention programs been in place, this precipitous rise might have been avoided. These individuals now represent a large pool for spread of HIV both within the drug community and, through sexual contact, outside of it.[62]

Even where HIV is already widespread, there is urgent need for more community-based programs designed to reach populations at highest risk: clients of STD clinics, long-distance truck drivers, and bisexual men in Latin America, among others. The message must be delivered in their own language and by a source they can trust. So far, programs that use peers as AIDS educators seem the most promising. In Accra, Ghana, for example, prostitutes trained as AIDS educators increased condom use significantly within their community: 67 percent of prostitutes now use condoms all the time and another 24 percent report frequent or occasional use. (Only 13 percent used condoms before the program.) Similar gains have been achieved by peer educators working with prostitutes in Nairobi, Kenya, and in Santo Domingo, Dominican Republic.[63]

Encouraging though this may be, these results are but small victories in what is destined to be a protracted and expensive war. Consider the challenge of expanding condom use alone. Programs to supply condoms vary greatly in cost depending on how the condoms will be distributed and how actively they will be promoted. Even the least expensive option—subsidizing their sale through existing commercial outlets—costs roughly $12 per couple annually, half of which is the cost of the condoms themselves. Just to ensure that commercial channels supply enough condoms for one third of all couples in the nine hardest-hit countries of Africa would cost $110 million annually, more than WHO's total AIDS budget for 1989.[64]

Yet the bigger challenge—both in terms of difficulty and expense—is getting couples to use condoms in cultures where birth control itself is not readily accepted and where condoms are especially disdained. In most African countries, less than 5 percent of married women practice any form of modern contraception and only 0.3 percent use condoms. Efforts to promote condoms throughout the Third World will have to overcome strong cultural and religious prohibitions as well as daunting logistical problems.[65]

Such observations capture the magnitude of the prevention task at hand and raise the question, Are we doing enough? The answer is most certainly no if the number of lives at risk is considered. Yet world priorities have seldom bowed to the exigencies of body counts. In 1988, industrial countries probably spent in the neighborhood of $100–150 million on AIDS control in the Third World, a reasonable amount when compared with other health, nutrition, and population assistance. But the world spent more than $100 million *each hour* on the global military apparatus. It is not that AIDS deserves a bigger share of the health and development pie, but that health and development themselves have been vastly underattended.[66]

Admittedly, money alone will not solve the AIDS dilemma. But money is an important catalyst for action. The challenge ahead is to find new international funds for AIDS control with an eye toward helping the Third World develop the infrastructure and indigenous human talent necessary to sustain the effort over the long haul. So far donors have been forthcoming with development assistance to fight AIDS, but this money appears largely to have been subtracted from other development accounts. If AIDS control comes at the expense of other life-promoting initiatives, we will have won the battle, but lost the war.

AIDS AS SOCIAL CRUCIBLE

AIDS is both a product of social change and its instrument. Rapid urbanization in Africa, the rise of gay liberation in the West, and the advent of modern air travel have all fueled this pandemic. In turn, AIDS has already triggered profound changes in every aspect of human endeavor, from how we care for the dying to how we relate to the living. Perhaps most significant, AIDS compels societies to confront issues and aspects of the human condition that are otherwise easily ignored. While heightening awareness, the disease does not dictate our response. How societies choose to act on the issues raised by AIDS may stand as a key measure of our time.[67]

Like all crises, AIDS has brought out the best and the worst of human nature. The pulling together of the American gay community to respond to a crisis within its ranks, the generous and often courageous actions of thousands of professional and voluntary caregivers, and the outpouring of global resources and talent to fight the disease are all expressions of human compassion at its best. But if compassion has been at work, so too have fear and denial.[68]

AIDS has aroused mean-spirited and irrational responses, often provoked by gross misperceptions about how the disease can be transmitted. American children with AIDS have been barred from school, despite repeated assurances by health professionals that they pose no risk to other students. In Colombia, one man with AIDS was forced to guard his house with a shotgun to keep villagers from burning it down to avoid "contamination." And in the United States, gay rights groups note that physical attacks against homosexuals have risen sharply since the epidemic began.[69]

AIDS has thrown into sharp relief inadequacies and inequities in the existing social order.

These panic responses have been made worse by the fact that AIDS first struck already stigmatized populations—gay men, IV drug users, and foreigners in the West; prostitutes and those with multiple sex partners in developing countries. This has reinforced thinly veiled prejudices and encouraged scapegoating. Regrettably, the global mobilization against AIDS has been hampered by the human tendency to blame others for a problem rather than

tackle the problem itself. AIDS has been blamed on everything from Western decadence to sexual promiscuity among Africans. Such accusations have merely bred resentment, encouraged denial, and thwarted the global cooperation so desperately needed to fight this disease.[70]

The potential for discrimination and persecution is so great, in fact, that Jonathan Mann recently made an unprecedented call for an international human rights network to monitor discrimination and abuse against HIV-infected individuals. Without a supportive and tolerant social environment, fear and retribution will undermine communication, reinforce prejudice, and make infected people unwilling to come forward. Indeed, health officials consider tolerance so important to AIDS control that the London World Summit of Health Ministers and the U.S. Presidential Commission on the Human Immunodeficiency Virus Epidemic both endorsed antidiscrimination policies as a top AIDS priority.[71]

In addition to exposing human vulnerabilities, AIDS has thrown into sharp relief certain inadequacies and inequities in the existing social order. The crisis has underscored the dismal state of health infrastructure in the developing world, where even syringes are in short supply. It has highlighted the structural flaws in economic systems that fail to provide gainful alternatives to prostitution and drug dealing. And in the United States, it has made painfully obvious shortcomings in the nation's health care system: the underfunding of preventive health measures, the lack of care options for the chronically ill, and the plight of the poor and uninsured.

By highlighting these flaws and adding a sense of urgency, AIDS may galvanize societies to tackle the underlying problems that allow HIV to flourish. Stopping AIDS among drug users, for example, may have more to do in the long term with fighting unemployment, poverty, and welfare dependence than with needle exchange or more treatment. As Harvey Fineberg, Dean of Harvard's School of Public Health, observes: "Jobs, schools and housing . . . would go a long way toward creating the individual self-respect, dignity and hope for the future that can forestall the turning to drugs in the first place." Similarly, societies may come to realize that prostitution is seldom a profession of choice, but one of economic necessity. Already, a family planning association in Ghana is fighting AIDS by retraining prostitutes in other types of work.[72]

AIDS has also forced societies to look again and with new eyes at issues such as sex education in schools, drug addiction, and the standards of public discourse. The urgency of AIDS has encouraged reappraisal of the appropriateness of certain interventions and has tabled debates over offending "public sensibilities." Formerly taboo subjects such as condoms are now topics of conversation in settings as diverse as western dinner parties and village tea stalls. In the Soviet Union, Vadim Pokrovskiy, director of the Moscow AIDS Clinic, appeared on television in August 1987, strongly urging the use of condoms. Such frankness in Soviet broadcasting would have been unthinkable in a world without AIDS.[73]

Indeed, AIDS has forged is own special form of *glasnost* in the Eastern bloc. For the first time, governments are responding with candor about the existence of drug abuse, prostitution, and homosexuality within their societies. Bulgaria, for example, now acknowledges some 600 addicts in a population of 9 million. The Soviet Union has gone from denying that drug addiction exists to implementing a program to register addicts. And the Polish weekly *Polityka* now reports that Poland has approximately 270,000 homosexual men—

about 1.5 percent of the male population—and twice as many bisexuals.[74]

It is in the area of health care, however, that AIDS will likely catalyze the greatest changes. In both industrial and developing countries, for example, AIDS is already encouraging a shift from hospital to community- or home-based care to limit cost and preserve vital hospital beds. Interestingly, AIDS' influence to date appears to be operating through its ability to overwhelm local health care services rather than through its impact on national health care expenditures. In the United States, the cost of AIDS treatment and prevention accounted for only 0.4 percent of total medical spending in 1986. Even by 1991, AIDS will likely account for only 1.5 percent of U.S. health expenditures, largely because deaths from other diseases will still overwhelm those from AIDS.[75]

In the world's hardest-hit cities, however, the financial and health impacts of AIDS are already substantial. By 1991, AIDS patients will occupy one out of every four hospital beds in New York City, a proportion already exceeded in some central African cities. In fiscal year 1988, San Francisco spent $17 million of city funds on AIDS; New York plans to spend $170 million in 1989. Medical care alone for San Francisco's AIDS patients in 1991 is expected to cost some $350 per city resident. Of course, city taxpayers will share these costs with private insurers, the federal government, and the patients themselves, but the local burden will still be great.[76]

Faced with such burdens, cities around the world are experimenting with new models of community-based care that may forever change how societies cope with chronic illness. San Francisco, which pioneered this approach, now has expanded hospice care, improved home nursing, residential facilities for patients who are homeless, and outpatient clinics for AIDS treatment. Cost per patient has declined, as has the percentage of patients requiring hospitalization and the average hospital stay. Likewise, in southern Zambia, Chikankata Hospital has cooperated with the Salvation Army to establish roving health teams that care for and counsel AIDS patients in their homes. In 1987, the program avoided an estimated 35 hospital admissions, more than paying for itself.[77]

Ultimately, the power of AIDS lies in its ability to reveal ourselves to ourselves. AIDS raises the questions, and the quality of our response may define our humanity. What if scientists develop a solution to AIDS that works in industrial nations but is either impractical or too costly for the developing world? Will western nations consider further AIDS research a priority? Or will AIDS become like schistosomiasis and other Third World diseases that can be ignored because Americans and Europeans are not dying? What if AIDS becomes largely a disease of minorities and drug users? Will money for treatment and prevention still be forthcoming? As Jonathan Mann observes, "AIDS will . . . put our global conscience to the test." Let us hope that compassion and tolerance prevail.

8

Enhancing Global Security

Michael Renner

National security has traditionally been defined almost exclusively in military terms. As a concept, it is invoked to justify the expenditure of enormous sums of money, the maintenance of large armed forces, the deployment of ever-newer weapons systems, the intervention by stronger powers in the affairs of weaker nations, or even the violation of human rights at home. After 1945, the cold war elevated such considerations to new heights.

But perceived in these terms, national security is an outmoded concept. Indeed, we are now witnessing an era in which the old bipolar, superpower-dominated system seems to be evolving into a multipolar and more interdependent world, undermining the foundations of the cold war; in which there are more stirrings than cohesion within the military blocs; in which "geo-economics" seems to rival geopolitics as a focus of concern; and in which ecological threats are ascending to the top of the international agenda. There are still no widely accepted ways to measure what consti-

tutes security. But the debate is in flux: the essence of security, the threats to it, and the means to achieve and preserve it need to be reappraised.

Military means are no longer adequate to provide tangible security benefits. Although they may at times in the past have been too weak to repel an attacker, ironically now they are often too strong. In the age of weapons of mass destruction, the world faces a fundamental security dilemma. The accumulation of weapons and the growth of military power tends to diminish the security of an opponent more than it adds to a nation's own security. National security policies have yielded international insecurity.[1]

No doubt nuclear weapons are the most extreme example. Gene Sharp, director of the Program on Nonviolent Sanctions in Conflict and Defense at Harvard University, has perceptively said that "the capacity to defend in order to deter [an attacker] has been replaced by the capability to destroy massively without the ability to defend." Warfare is no longer limited to a delineated battle-field, and the distinction between combatants and civilians has become blurred. Modern technology has given even so-called conventional weapons a degree of range, accuracy, and destructive power that renders a viable defense difficult if not impossible. In the Iran-Iraq war, for example, both belligerents' cities were vulnerable to escalating missile attacks.[2]

But military prowess has not lost its usefulness in the eyes of those who wield it. By using it, or threatening to, governments still hope to coerce other nations, to influence their economic policies and political systems, or to secure desired resources on their own terms. The world community has accepted a definition of security that focuses almost exclusively on this attitude.

Yet the security of nations depends at least as much on economic well-being, social justice, and ecological stability. Environmental problems—climate change, ozone depletion, transboundary air pollution, land degradation, deforestation, and soil erosion—threaten to destroy the human habitat and undermine economies everywhere. Pursuing military security at the cost of social, economic, and environmental well-being is akin to dismantling a house to salvage materials to erect a fence around it.

In an age in which civilian and military technology has given governments and corporations a global reach, purely national means are fast becoming obsolete, while real security is increasingly to be found in global cooperation. If the world's nations want true security, they need to devote greater energies to developing reliable mechanisms for nonviolent dispute settlement. If security policies are to be relevant to society's future security needs, they need to be reoriented to meet looming environmental dangers.

A World at War

Through the course of human history, the ability to wage war, in either defensive or offensive fashion, has become more organized and institutionalized. "Progressing" from standing armies to launch-on-warning, war preparation has become a permanent endeavor, often no longer related to any particular, identifiable threat. The notion that countries should be able to defend themselves from any conceivable threat at all times has found near-universal acceptance. As a result, the war-making institutions—the armed forces, the national security bureaucracy, the military intelligence agencies—have become fixtures of national life, supported by a permanent war economy.

The world has spent an estimated $16 trillion for military purposes since World War II; annual expenditures reached $825 billion in 1986 (both in 1984 dollars). (See Figure 8-1.) Adjusted for inflation, industrial countries have doubled their outlays since 1960, while the Third World has increased its expenditures more than sixfold. Developing countries' share of world military spend-

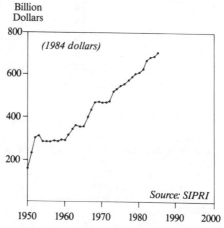

Figure 8-1. World Military Expenditures, 1950-85

ing rose from 6 percent of the world total in 1965 to 18 percent by the mideighties.[3]

The world's armed forces are some 29 million strong, equivalent to the population of Argentina; a further 11 million people at least are employed in the world's arms industries. (See Table 8-1.) These numbers understate the real extent of militarization because they do not include militias and other paramilitary forces and because there are no estimates for employment in arms indus-

tries of such important producers as China.

Although the superpowers and their European allies are responsible for three quarters of global military spending, militarization is spreading worldwide along numerous avenues: military alliances, bases on foreign territories (with at least 1.8 million military personnel stationed in some 68 countries), and military training programs and joint maneuvers. Perhaps most important, though, is the burgeoning arms trade.

Table 8-1. Armed Forces and Employment in Military Industry, Selected Countries, Early to Mid-Eighties

Country	Workers[1]	Soldiers[2]	Country	Workers[1]	Soldiers[2]
	(thousands)			(thousands)	
Soviet Union	4,800	4,500	Israel	90	195
United States	3,350	2,289	Thailand	5	270
India	280	1,515	South Africa	100	95
United Kingdom	700	335	Argentina	60	129
France	435	563	Philippines	5	157
North Korea	55	784	Peru	5	128
West Germany	290	495	Chile	3	124
Italy	160	531	Malaysia	3	124
Pakistan	40	644	Netherlands	18	103
South Korea	30	600	Sweden	28	69
Brazil	75	496	Singapore	11	59
Egypt	75	466	Austria	16	40
Taiwan	50	440	Norway	15	41
Spain	66	411			
Indonesia	26	281			
			Total	10,791	15,884
			World	n.a.	29,260

[1]Employed in arms-producing industries.   [2]Military and civil service personnel employed by national defense ministries.

SOURCES: P. Wilke and H. Wulf, "Manpower Conversion in Defence-Related Industry," Disarmament and Employment Programme, Working Paper No. 4 (Geneva: International Labour Organisation, June 1986); Peter Southwood, "The UK Defence Industry," Peace Research Reports No. 8, University of Bradford, September 1985; U.S. Department of Defense, *National Defense Budget Estimates for FY 1988/1989* (Washington, D.C.: Office of the Assistant Secretary of Defense (Comptroller), 1987); Michael Brzoska and Thomas Ohlson, "Trade in Major Conventional Weapons: The Changing Pattern," *Bulletin of Peace Proposals*, Vol. 17, No. 3–4, 1986; U.S. Arms Control and Disarmament Agency, *World Military Expenditures and Arms Transfers 1987* (Washington, D.C.: U.S. Government Printing Office, March 1988); Vicenç Fisas Armengol, *Les Armes de la Democràcia* (Barcelona, Spain: Fundación Jaume Bofill, 1988).

Deals worth an estimated $635 billion, (in 1984 dollars) were concluded between 1967 and 1986. Since 1984 the monetary value of weapons transfers has declined somewhat, no doubt as a result of worsening economic conditions in many Third World countries. A growing number of countries, however, are acquiring the capacity to produce sophisticated weaponry domestically.[4]

Throughout history, governments have sought to develop and acquire more numerous and more effective arms. Every major scientific discovery has been checked for possible military application. Possession of the "perfect" weapon, it was (and still is) believed, would mean absolute security, unquestioned superiority, and thus leverage over other nations. But ultimately, unilateral advantages prove short-lived, fueling destabilizing arms races and degenerating into warfare.

Ironically, the nation that pioneered nuclear weapons development is now more vulnerable than ever. A country separated from most of the world's other nations by oceans, for more than 165 years the United States has had no reason to fear an invasion of its territory. But its possession of the atomic bomb spurred the Soviets and other powers to acquire such weapons as well. Later innovations like the intercontinental bomber, the ballistic missile, the multiple warhead delivery vehicle, and the cruise missile resulted in only transitory advantages.

Particularly since 1945, modern military technology has dramatically increased the destructive power of weapons, the range and speed of delivery vehicles, and the sophistication of targeting technologies. In less than 30 minutes, a single MX missile or its Soviet counterpart can deliver a destructive force equivalent to more than 200 Hiroshima bombs to within 90 meters of a target 11,000 kilometers away.[5]

The quest for the ultimate weapon has delivered the global community to an all-encompassing state of insecurity. An arsenal of 55,000 nuclear warheads worldwide possesses the explosive power of 160 million Chernobyls. As Ruth Sivard writes in *World Military and Social Expenditures 1987–88:* "Every hamlet has been brought within the orbit of conflict, every inhabitant made a potential victim of random annihilation. Militarization presumably designed to insulate and protect the nation state has in fact united the world's population in a precarious mutual vulnerability."[6]

National military power is at unprecedented levels, yet—or perhaps as a result—the number of wars and war deaths has steadily increased over the centuries. Some 22 wars have been raging in the eighties, more than in any previous decade in recorded military history. Some 120 armed conflicts in the Third World since 1945—in terms of death, collectively the equivalent of World War II—have killed at least 20 million people. Many of these conflicts are far removed from the minds of westerners, but some may be the tinderboxes from which a future conflict might rapidly spread to global conflagration.[7]

Civilians constitute a rapidly growing share of war victims.

Interestingly, military aggression has become less successful. In the twentieth century, aggressors have won only 4 out of 10 wars; in the eighties, that ratio is down to 1 out of 10. Irrespective of the outcome of wars, the prime losers have been the civilians whom the military supposedly is protecting. Whether through direct war actions or war-induced starvation, civilians constitute a rapidly growing share of war victims: they accounted for 52 percent of all deaths in the fifties, but for 85 percent in the eighties. It is without exaggeration that economist Kenneth Boulding says: "National defense is now the greatest enemy of national security."[8]

The conventional view of armed forces guarding against external enemies is becoming increasingly irrelevant. By far the most conflicts (and approximately half of all war deaths) since World War II have been in the form of "civil wars," pitching armies controlled by unrepresentative elites against their domestic opponents. These conflicts arise from a host of social (ethnic, class, religious), political, economic, and ecological disputes and are fueled by sharp inequalities. But while resort to military means may succeed in suppressing those expressing grievances, it is unlikely to eliminate the causes of conflict.[9]

When Third World governments actually do engage in warfare against another state, the combat is usually of short duration because their staying power is severely circumscribed by limited financial resources, weak civic institutions, and a lack of regime legitimacy. Wars of attrition risk major political and economic breakdown. As Mohammed Ayoob of the National University of Singapore explains: "These constraints soon outweigh the perceived political or military benefits for which the wars were launched." The exceptions are found where outside powers stoke the fires or, as in the Iran-Iraq war, where large oil revenues foot the bill.[10]

Countries lack a reliable international framework and mechanism on which to depend for security. Robert Johansen, former president of the World Policy Institute, points out that "the very nature of the system of sovereign states encourages armed rivalry between governments. Because the system provides no impartial, dependable way to prevent one government from violently coercing another, governments seek arms as a means of self-help."[11]

Governments frequently comprehend military prowess as the ultimate expression of national sovereignty. But reasons for the continuing arms race can also be found at home. Keeping a nation in a state of constant war preparation gives politicians, bureaucrats, and generals command over an enormous share of a society's resources and lets arms merchants derive a steady stream of profits.

THE DRAIN OF A PERMANENT WAR ECONOMY

Even in the absence of armed conflict, preoccupation with building military power can drain the vitality of nations and lead to social neglect. On average, the world's nations spend some 6 percent of their gross national product (GNP) on defense, although countries at war allocate a considerably higher portion. (See Table 8–2.) Such a share is routinely considered too small by many economists to elicit concern. In fact, some observers even argue that "military Keynesianism"—a steady stream of large government contracts for weapons—is a perfect tool for stimulating the economy.

But GNP is a poor yardstick against which to measure the impact of military spending on the civilian economy. A statistical aggregate of monetary values, GNP tells little about the productive capacities of an economy and nothing about how they are being used. The military sector saps productive capacities far beyond the effect suggested by a simple comparison with GNP.[12]

In fact, as a new cold war chilled relations between the world's nations during the eighties, global military expenditures rose rapidly, while GNP growth

Table 8-2. Military Share of Gross National Product, Selected Countries, 1984

Country	Share
	(percent)
Iraq	50.0
Israel	27.1
Saudi Arabia	21.7
Syria	16.6
Angola	14.2
Iran	13.3
Libya	12.9
Nicaragua	12.4
Soviet Union	11.5
Chad	10.4
North Korea	10.2
Ethiopia	9.3
Egypt	8.5
China	7.0
Afghanistan	7.0
United States	6.4
South Korea	5.4
United Kingdom	5.4
East Germany	4.9
France	4.1
South Africa	4.0
West Germany	3.3
India	3.2
Japan	1.0
Brazil	0.8
World Average	5.6

SOURCE: Ruth Leger Sivard, *World Military and Social Expenditures 1987–88* (Washington, D.C.: World Priorities, 1988).

continued its downward trend. For the first time since 1960, the growth in global military outlays exceeded that of world economic output. (See Table 8–3.)

Although the military expenditures of most Third World countries are minute compared with those of the superpowers—either one of which spends more than developing countries combined—they nonetheless entail a heavy burden for their economies and populations.

When improving people's living standards requires all available resources for productive investment, every dollar, rupee, peso, or naira spent for the military is money forgone for human development.

When arms take precedence over needs basic to human development, people are not secure. The present priorities of the international system deplete scarce resources required for meeting basic human needs: they leave some 770 million persons malnourished, 14 million children dying of hunger-related causes each year, some 1.3 billion people without access to safe drinking water, 100 million individuals without adequate shelter, and 880 million adults unable to read and write. President Dwight D. Eisenhower put it eloquently 36 years ago: "Every gun that is made, every warship launched, every rocket fired represents, in the final analysis, a theft from those who hunger and are not fed, who are cold and are not clothed."[13]

Soaring arms imports have contributed to bloated foreign debt: had non-oil-exporting developing countries made no foreign arms purchases during 1972–82, their accumulated debts by the end of that period would have been at least 15 percent smaller, and perhaps as much as 25 percent. Cumulative Third World military expenditures between 1977 and 1982 alone were greater than their total debt outstanding in 1982—the year the debt crisis first erupted. Lloyd Dumas, Professor of Political Economy at the University of Texas, has pointed out that "if the Third World's *share* of world military spending had been the same in those years as it was in the early sixties, the less developed nations as a group would have saved enough money from this one source to finance repayment of nearly two-thirds of their outstanding debt."[14]

Huge foreign debts, no matter what their origin, are serious threats to the

Table 8-3. Annual Growth of World Economic Output and Military Expenditures, 1960–85[1]

Region	1960–70	1970–80	1980–85	1960–85
	(percent)			
Western Industrial Countries				
Gross National Product	4.9	3.1	2.2	3.6
Military Spending	2.9	−0.8	5.7	2.0
Third World[2]				
Gross National Product	7.6	6.2	3.1	6.1
Military Spending	11.7	2.7	2.1	6.1
Centrally Planned Economies[3]				
Gross National Product	4.4	3.3	1.7	3.4
Military Spending	3.2	3.9	1.3	3.1
World Average				
Gross National Product	5.0	3.5	2.2	3.9
Military Spending	4.1	1.6	3.2	2.9

[1]Military spending figures are for 1961; annual growth rates calculated from data expressed in constant 1986 dollars. [2]Includes China. [3]Estimates for centrally planned economies are likely to have a wide margin of error.
SOURCES: Worldwatch Institute, based on U.S. Central Intelligence Agency, *Handbook of Economic Statistics 1987*, (Springfield, Va: National Technical Information Service, 1987), and U.S. Arms Control and Disarmament Agency, *World Military Expenditures and Arms Transfers* (Washington, D.C.: U.S. Government Printing Office, various editions).

economic security of many Third World countries. By siphoning off financial resources needed for investment and social spending, debt servicing impairs economic development and sacrifices economic well-being.

For wealthy, industrialized countries, the negative consequences of maintaining a permanent war economy are less dramatic, but no less pervasive. Both the United States and the Soviet Union, for example, have spent enough on the military to cause a deterioration of vital infrastructure, a retardation of civilian research and development, and a loss of competitiveness. Soviet leader Mikhail Gorbachev is well aware that the arms race with the United States needs to be brought under control if the ailing Soviet economy is to be invigorated. The nation's chronic shortages of consumer goods and their low quality are widely

recognized. Civilian R&D and capital and consumer goods production have suffered enormously as the prerogatives of the arms race assigned top priority in resource allocation and high-quality inputs to military projects.

The tremendous demands of military spending share a good deal of the blame for transforming the Soviet and East European economies into economic backwaters. In the late fifties, according to Seymour Melman, Professor Emeritus of Industrial Engineering at Columbia University, the Soviet Union was on the verge of becoming an efficient mass producer of machine tools, with the prospect of assuming a world leadership role in the field. That promise never materialized, however, because the money and talent to develop a competitive industry were redirected to a massive military space program. Today, the Soviets find they are unable to compete in world industrial markets, having been bypassed in high-tech development by newly industrialized countries such as Brazil and South Korea.[15]

The United States, too, faces trouble across its economic landscape. While the military has enjoyed a cornucopia, civilian infrastructure has been starved of funds. The amount of capital devoted by the United States to building military power of colossal proportions ($8.4 trillion between 1948 and 1988, in 1984 prices) exceeds the cumulative money value of all human-made wealth in the United States. An estimated two thirds of the products of this civilian "fixed reproducible tangible wealth"—industrial plants and machinery, communications and transport systems, buildings, bridges, water and sewage systems, and so on—are now in dire need of reconstruction.[16]

The most critical impact of military spending is perhaps in the area of research and development. The research intensity of military products has been estimated to be about 20 times that of civilian products. A heavy emphasis on defense-related R&D impairs a country's innovative capacity by pointing scientific talent toward the military. A large pool of a nation's talents are then unavailable to keep industry at the competitive edge, or to develop less polluting production technologies, improve energy efficiency, and advance renewable sources of energy.[17]

World military R&D—estimated to total at least $80 billion in 1985—accounts for roughly a quarter of all R&D funds and for a comparable portion of all the scientists and engineers engaged in research. The share of public R&D outlays that goes to the military is as high as 70 percent in the United States, 60 percent in the Soviet Union, and 50 percent in the United Kingdom. It demands much lower shares, however, in most other countries, such as 19 percent in

India, 13 percent in West Germany and Australia, and below 5 percent in Switzerland, Norway, and Japan.[18]

The military share is lower when private R&D funds are taken into consideration, but the discrepancy in priorities between different countries remains. (See Table 8–4.) Overall, some 25–30 percent of U.S scientists and engineers are engaged in military-related work. This is a much higher proportion than, for example, in either West Germany or Japan.[19]

Heavy emphasis on defense-related R&D impairs a country's innovative capacity.

Proponents of large-scale military spending contend that while resources are diverted from the civilian economy, scientific breakthroughs from defense-related research more than offset that disadvantage. But relative to the lavish resources devoted to military R&D, the "spinoffs" have been minimal. Generally, the results of applied research, which constitutes the bulk of military research, are less transferable than those of basic R&D. In the military realm, product specifications are geared to maximum performance, with little attention devoted to cost. These criteria are increasingly divergent from those of civilian products, for which durability and low cost, not the extreme demands of combat conditions, are key.[20]

Simon Ramo, a cofounder of TRW Inc., one of the leading U.S. military contractors, admitted in 1980 that "in the past thirty years, had the total dollars we spent on military R&D been expended instead in those areas of science and technology promising the most economic progress, we probably would be today where we are going to find ourselves arriving in the year 2000."[21]

Table 8-4. Military and Civilian R&D[1] in Selected Countries, 1971 and 1986

Country	1971 Expenditures			1986 Expenditures		
	Military	Civilian	Military Share	Military	Civilian	Military Share
	(billion dollars)		(percent)	(billion dollars)		(percent)
United States	8.50	18.2	31.8[2]	37.3	79.4	32.0[2]
United Kingdom[3]	0.80	2.3	26.1	3.5	8.5	29.3
France	0.60[4]	3.0[4]	16.8	3.5	14.6	19.5
West Germany	0.40	4.7	7.3	1.4	26.1	5.1
Japan	0.03	4.8	0.5	0.3[5]	44.0[5]	0.7

[1]Includes government and privately funded R&D. [2]Understates the total military share because military-related R&D of the federal space program is not included; including space, the military share may be as high as 40 percent in 1986. [3]British data are for 1972 and 1985. [4]1972. [5]1985.
SOURCE: Worldwatch Institute, calculated from International Monetary Fund, *International Financial Statistics Yearbook 1987* (Washington, D.C.: 1987), and from National Science Board, *Science and Engineering Indicators 1987* (Washington, D.C.: U.S. Government Printing Office, 1987).

To the extent that spinoffs are achieved, they could be accomplished more directly and at considerably lower cost through civilian scientific studies. Research by Professor David Noble of Drexel University in Philadelphia, for example, demonstrates that the U.S. Air Force's sponsorship of computer-controlled machine tools resulted in an overly complex and expensive technology that failed to keep American industry competitive with Japan.[22]

Large-scale military spending preempts capital from civilian investments. In the United States, according to Professor Dumas of the University of Texas, the physical capital controlled by the Pentagon in 1983—valued conservatively at $475 billion—was equivalent to almost half that owned by all U.S. manufacturers, *including* the 20,000 prime military contractors and over 100,000 subcontractors. The military's net investment in plant and equipment in 1982 equaled nearly 38 percent of the investments in plant equipment undertaken by all U.S. manufacturers.[23]

The effects of long years of military priorities are also apparent in the areas of unemployment and inflation. A 1988 study by Michael Dee Oden of Employ-ment Research Associates in Michigan found that military outlays generate less employment per dollar spent than civilian expenditures do. There is also strong evidence that large-scale military spending "accelerates inflation in periods of full employment and limits the fall in the inflation rate in deflationary periods."[24]

Military largesse cannot alone be blamed for all the troubles of the U.S. economy. But it has strongly contributed. A combination of record peacetime military spending and tax policies that reduced federal revenues triggered a dramatic rise in federal budget deficits in the eighties. These deficits have primarily been financed by an enormous inflow of foreign capital. If this capital inflow were to stop, the Federal Reserve would be confronted with a dilemma, Dumas points out: either "to finance the huge deficits and risk inflation, or refuse to finance them and risk depression."[25]

Decades of heavy military spending have strongly contributed to a deterioration in civilian productivity growth, which in turn has undermined the ability of U.S. industry to remain cost-competitive. Compounded by a strong dollar in the early eighties, this led to a loss of domestic and overseas markets and hence to a growing trade gap. (See Figure 8–2.) Between 1981 and 1984, 42 percent of the growth of U.S. domestic consumer spending went to imports. But the bloated dollar masked the erosion of the country's fundamental competitiveness. Its value against other western currencies fell by 30 percent between 1985 and 1987, but did virtually nothing to shrink the trade deficit.[26]

Until 1980, the United States never registered a trade deficit in manufactured goods. Today, imports are no longer restricted to low-tech, labor-intensive industries, but are booming in areas of traditional U.S. strength—such as automobiles, consumer electronics, metal-cutting machine tools, steel, and semiconductors. In 1984, the United States experienced its first-ever trade deficit in electronics.[27]

It is no surprise that the disproportionate amount of resources and talent devoted to military purposes in the United States has adversely affected its competitiveness in the world market. Countries such as Japan, which has kept its military spending within tight

Figure 8-2. U.S. Military Expenditures and Budget Deficits, 1950-88

bounds, are the only winners of the superpower arms race.

ENVIRONMENT AND SECURITY

Countries are prepared to make considerable sacrifices in order to defend their national sovereignty and territory. Environmental degradation is a more fundamental, if sometimes subtler, threat to the security of virtually all nations. It undermines the very support systems on which human activity depends and eventually manifests itself as a threat to economic well-being. But most countries are doing precious little to preserve their environmental security. The United States, for example, spent some $273 billion in 1986 to defend against poorly defined foreign military threats, but only $78 billion (of which $60 billion were private funds) to deal with very concrete environmental pollution threats.[28]

It may be that ecological threats generate less attention because often they are homespun. As Wendell Berry, noted American writer and farmer, has asked: "To what point . . . do we defend from foreign enemies a country that we are destroying ourselves? In spite of all our propagandists can do, the foreign threat inevitably seems diminished when our air is unsafe to breathe, when our drinking water is unsafe to drink, when our rivers carry tonnages of topsoil that make light of the freight they carry in boats, when our forests are dying from air pollution and acid rain, and when we ourselves are sick from poisons in the air. Who *are* the enemies of this country?"[29]

But pollution respects no human-drawn borders; it jeopardizes not only the security of the country from which it emanates, but also that of its neighbors. There is thus a fundamental contradiction between the illusion of national sovereignty and the reality of transboundary environmental degradation. *Our Common Future,* the report of the World Commission on Environment and Development (the Brundtland Commission), put the dilemma succinctly: "The Earth is one but the world is not. We all depend on one biosphere for sustaining our lives. Yet each community, each country, strives for survival and prosperity with little regard for its impact on others."[30]

Throughout human history, struggles over access to and control over natural resources—land, water, energy, and minerals—have been a root cause of tension and armed conflict. But disputes over the allocation of resources are increasingly aggravated by the rapid deterioration of resource quality. In some cases, environmental degradation is rapidly becoming a prominent source of international tension.

Border-transcending environmental degradation most immediately affects neighboring countries, as illustrated by disputes over water resources. An estimated 40 percent of the world's population depends on the 214 major river systems shared by two or more countries for drinking water, irrigation, or hydropower; 12 of these basins are shared by five or more countries. Disputes revolve around water diversion or reduced water flow, industrial pollution, the salination or siltation of streams, and floods aggravated by soil erosion.[31]

For example, control over the Nile waters is a matter that casts a long shadow over relations between Egypt, the Sudan, and Ethiopia. Butros Ghali, Egypt's Foreign Minister, warned in early 1985: "The next war in our region will be over the waters of the Nile, not politics." Similar disputes simmer in virtually all parts of the world. (See Table 8–5.)[32]

Soil erosion might seem less directly implicated as a source of tension between nations, yet silt accumulation can lead to more frequent and devastating floods. This has happened in Bangladesh, for instance, where years of deforestation in the Himalayas have led to increased soil erosion and, as a consequence, to siltation of the rivers entering that country. The latest flood, in September 1988, is now considered to be the worst ever. Such catastrophes can only be effectively counteracted if Bangladesh, India, Nepal, and China all agree to cooperate in reforestation and reduction of soil erosion—a task that seems daunting indeed.[33]

Environmental degradation is rapidly becoming a source of international tension.

The rapid evaporation of the Aral Sea in the central Asian region of the Soviet Union (due to excessive draining for irrigation purposes of rivers feeding the sea) is having detrimental effects on regional agriculture, fisheries, vegetation, and climate patterns. The climatic impact might well be felt as far away as Afghanistan and Iran, for the Aral Sea absorbs solar energy, thus moderating winters and making possible a longer growing season.[34]

Transboundary air pollution provides another example, with perhaps even more worrisome consequences. Acid rain is destroying aquatic life and forests throughout central Europe and North America. Massive damage from acid deposition in Canada (more than 50 percent of which comes from U.S. sources) has caused considerable diplomatic frictions between Canada and the United States, because the latter has doggedly refused to consider additional measures to reduce emissions of sulfur and nitrogen oxides.[35]

Table 8-5. International Water Disputes, Mid-Eighties

Body of Water	Countries Involved in Dispute	Subject of Dispute
Nile	Egypt, Ethiopia, Sudan	Level of water flow
Euphrates, Tigris	Iraq, Syria, Turkey	Dams, water flow
Jordan, Litani, Yarmuk	Israel, Lebanon, Jordan, Syria	Water flow
Indus, Sutlei	India, Pakistan	Irrigation
Ganges	Bangladesh, India	Siltation, flooding
Mekong	Kampuchea, Laos, Thailand, Vietnam	Water flow
Paraná	Argentina, Brazil	Dam, land inundation
Lauca	Bolivia, Chile	Dam, salinization
Rio Grande, Colorado	Mexico, United States	Salinization, water flow, agrochemical pollution
Great Lakes	Canada, United States	Water diversion
Rhine	France, Netherlands, Switzerland, West Germany	Industrial pollution
Elbe	Czechoslovakia, East Germany, West Germany	Industrial pollution
Szamos	Hungary, Romania	Industrial pollution

SOURCE: Worldwatch Institute, based on various sources.

"Toxic clouds" carrying hazardous substances can traverse the entire globe before dispersing or falling down to earth. A case in point is the pesticide DDT. Though its use has been prohibited in the United States since 1972, it is nevertheless still produced and exported to many developing countries, where no laws govern its use. DDT sprayed in Central America is known to have contaminated the upper Great Lakes, and the pesticide even returns in imported agricultural produce. Simi-larly, insecticides from Asia and southern Europe are found in Arctic and Antarctic waters.[36]

Increasingly, environmental degradation is having a truly all-encompassing, global effect, in the sense that no single nation can hope to escape the danger. The growing hole in the ozone layer poses grave threats to human health, agricultural productivity, and marine fisheries. (See Chapter 5.) Similarly, the buildup of carbon dioxide and other trace gases is leading to rising global temperatures and potentially catastrophic climate shifts. (See Chapters 1 and 10.) The security of entire nations is compromised by the impending dangers of shifting precipitation patterns, rising sea levels, and disrupted crop-growing regions. While all of humanity will suffer from the repercussions, ozone depletion and global warming are caused primarily by industrial countries, which account for 84 percent of chlorofluorocarbon (CFC) production and 69 percent of carbon dioxide emissions.[37]

Nuclear power provides an important example of both the global effects of environmental destruction and the transboundary political problems it can cause. The powerful explosion at Chernobyl on April 26, 1986, hurled radioactive debris far into the atmosphere and across large areas of the planet's northern hemisphere. The recriminations against the Soviet Union for failing to provide an adequate and timely warning of the accident have demonstrated the potential of such incidents for raising international tensions.

Military means cannot reverse resource depletion or restore lost ecological balance.

As popular awareness of the dangers of nuclear power has grown, so have strains between nations over the construction and siting of reactors, enrichment and reprocessing facilities, and radioactive waste dumps. In Europe, 119 nuclear power plants are located within 100 kilometers of a national border. The Danish parliament decided to ask Sweden to close a plant 30 kilometers from Copenhagen. The French government rejected a similar plea by local West German authorities to cancel construction of four reactors at Cattenom. Tensions

on similar issues run high between Ireland and the United Kingdom, between Austria (whose nuclear program was abandoned in 1978) and both West Germany and Czechoslovakia, between Hong Kong and China, and between Argentina and Chile.[38]

The contradiction between national sovereignty and the international impact of environmental degradation is exacerbated by the wide discrepancies in the stage of industrial development and the capacity for effective action that different countries find themselves in. For example, strict regulations, increased public opposition to landfills and incinerators, and consequently rising costs for hazardous waste disposal in industrial countries have led to a proliferation of legal and illegal shipments to developing nations—particularly those on the African continent—with little or no environmental legislation. The dumping of Italian toxic wastes in Nigeria in 1988 cast a spotlight on such shadowy deals.[39]

Conflicts over the allocation of natural resources have lent themselves, at least in the view of competing governments, to military solutions. But in the face of transnational pollution, a zero-sum game is transformed into a no-win situation. National defense establishments are powerless against environmental threats. As technologically sophisticated as they may be, military means cannot reverse resource depletion or restore lost ecological balance. In fact, an emphasis on military strength compounds the problem. As described in the previous section, the ability to deal effectively with the challenges arising from environmental degradation is compromised by the continued global arms race.

Predictably, national governments are reluctant to relinquish any of their hard-won sovereign rights. At a conference of European environmental ministers convened to work out a cleanup program for the Rhine, for example, France, Switzerland, and West Germany objected to a Dutch recommendation for international inspection of suspected pollution sites, arguing that such action would violate national sovereignty.[40]

But absolute sovereignty is no longer a workable concept. Exclusively national policies are ill suited for a world that faces border-transcending environmental destruction of an unprecedented scope. Without effective "environmental diplomacy" that yields multinational agreements to limit or ban the production of substances inimical to the environment, each country is left at the mercy of others' actions. Environmental security depends critically on international coordination and cooperation.

FROM OFFENSE TO DEFENSE AND PEACEKEEPING

After a decade of runaway military spending, the nineties may provide an opportunity for redirecting security policies. More-stringent U.S. federal spending limits, Gorbachev's disarmament overtures, the onerous debt burden in the Third World, and, perhaps most important, the popular yearning for a less heavily armed world could set the stage for far-reaching arms reductions. Reversing the global arms race not only promises greater security, but also allows governments to free the resources needed to address pressing social, economic, and environmental problems across the globe.

The record of traditional arms control is not reassuring. Instead of putting a brake on military competition, superpower agreements have served as a smokescreen for relentless war preparation: tailored to establish weak limits for aging weapons systems, they stimulated

the development and deployment of more-sophisticated technology. Since 1972, the Strategic Arms Limitation Talks treaties allowed the superpowers to add almost 13,000 warheads to their strategic nuclear stockpiles.[41]

A Strategic Arms Reductions Talks (START) accord, if it becomes reality, would cut strategic nuclear weapons by 30–35 percent, returning warhead numbers to the level prevalent in the late seventies. But fixation on numerical limits alone—however "deep" a cut may be envisioned—will fail to arrest the most dynamic aspects of the arms race. Scientists never stop conceiving of new technologies, and military strategists always seem to discover new security threats and new weapons "gaps" to justify their deployment. As currently envisioned, a START accord would in no way slow the tide of new weapons planned or on the drawing board. Terminating the arms race and releasing substantial resources for productive use requires a curb on further development, production, and deployment of new warheads and delivery systems.[42]

Cloaked in secrecy, arms negotiations tend to get bogged down because there is little pressure to compromise. "Independent initiatives" may prove more fruitful. Taken outside the realm of formal bargaining sessions, they seek to bring the weight of world public opinion to bear on the process. Either the U.S. or the Soviet government, for example, might publicly announce it will refrain from testing and deploying any new nuclear weapons for a specified period. If reciprocated by the other government, that constraint could be extended for an indefinite period, and at a later point be codified in a formal accord.[43]

General Secretary Gorbachev has in fact taken this approach in an effort to break the arms control stalemate. Unfortunately, his initiatives have been brushed aside by western leaders as mere propaganda ploys. A constructive American response—testing the sincerity of these proposals—might create a positive dynamic in the superpower relationship. If such initial steps proved successful, they could build the trust necessary to move toward disarmament.[44]

As frightening as a world wired with explosives is, many people find it hard to conceive of a practical alternative to it. This is a profound obstacle to disarmament. Governments and ordinary citizens alike need a roadmap that gives them a measure of confidence that they can navigate this largely uncharted territory. Although most governments employ not a single person for such purposes, nongovernmental groups have put their imaginations to work.

The debate over alternative defense has simmered for many years within academic and peace movement circles. But it has gathered momentum in Europe, as denuclearization and a reduction of conventional forces have suddenly become serious options in the wake of the Intermediate-Range Nuclear Forces treaty. A "nonprovocative defense" would involve a fundamental restructuring of the armed forces—weapons, personnel, and strategies—so that they can defend but lack the ability to attack. It may be difficult to determine whether a particular weapon has defensive or offensive properties, but the litmus test is whether a defensive system increases a nation's security *without* threatening the security of others.[45]

In the eighties, alternative defense has, in the words of Hal Harvey, director of the security program at the Rocky Mountain Institute, "graduated from theory to politics." The Danish parliament has established a research center to study nonoffensive defense, and the Social Democratic Party in West Germany and the Labour Party in the United Kingdom are advocating such policies. Similar concepts have entered the vocabulary of Soviet generals and party leaders. Gorbachev has coined the term "reasonable sufficiency" to guide the transition of Soviet military doctrine from offense to defense. In July 1988 the Warsaw Pact nations formally proposed a three-step conventional arms reductions process in Europe.[46]

A defensive footing not only promises greater military stability, it also is an important way station on the path toward disarmament. A sober reassessment of mutual intentions, interests, and security needs would likely show that the assumptions that have guided security policies in the post–World War II era are seriously outdated. If so, reduced reliance on weapons may become more palatable.

It may seem unrealistic to envision a world without war. But it is perhaps less reasonable to expect humanity to survive with a nuclear sword of Damocles hanging over it indefinitely. A world in which the use of force becomes increasingly delegitimized does not abolish nation-states; rather, it would enable states to resolve internal and external disputes more safely, without resort to armed conflict and the prospect of mutual annihilation.

It has been a quarter-century since the superpowers seriously contemplated general and complete disarmament. In 1961, they agreed on the McCloy-Zorin Joint Statement of Agreed Principles for Disarmament Negotiations, the terms of which were unanimously adopted by the U.N. General Assembly that September. The statement contained guidelines for multilateral negotiations to design and implement an internationally acceptable disarmament program. In 1962, the Kennedy administration presented a treaty outline to an international conference and distributed its provisions in a document entitled *Blueprint for the Peace Race.* By late 1963, however, that approach had been shunted aside in favor of arms control.[47]

Almost three decades and an inconclusive arms race later, the merits of disarmament are worth reconsidering. Recognizing the dire military and economic implications of the arms race, in January 1986 Mikhail Gorbachev presented a plan to rid the world of all nuclear weapons by the end of the century. It remains to be seen whether the new administration under George Bush is prepared to take up the Gorbachev challenge and bring the cold war to an end.

Meanwhile, Marcus Raskin, a senior fellow at the Institute for Policy Studies in Washington, D.C., and former member of President Kennedy's National Security Council, has launched an effort to revive the McCloy-Zorin Principles. He has formulated, and submitted to American and Soviet analysts for comment, a detailed and careful draft treaty that spells out a 15-year process for disbanding the world's armed forces, eliminating all stockpiles of weapons and their delivery vehicles, and converting arms industries to civilian use.[48]

One reason governments resist disarmament is that they distrust each other's intentions. An international satellite monitoring agency—proposed in 1962 and 1978, and currently revived as an idea—could help build greater trust. Undertaking modest tasks at first, it might eventually provide impartial information to verify arms treaties, confirm or deny alleged border violations, deter surprise attacks, monitor cease-fires, discourage clandestine missile tests, and assist U.N. peacekeeping missions. According to a U.N. General Assembly study, start-up and operating costs would be well under 1 percent of world military expenditures annually.[49]

The General Assembly is currently considering the establishment of a monitoring center of limited scope that, for the time being, would not involve satellite monitoring. In the United States, Representative Robert Mrazek has introduced a bill to investigate how satellite monitoring can increase international security and stability.[50]

The greatest hope for reining in the arms race lies with the vocal and insistent pressure that has emerged from the grassroots, paralleling the movement in the environment and development field. (See Chapter 9.) People everywhere are less and less inclined to leave the responsibility for defining security to governments. Their agenda ranges from traditional peace movement actions to innovative acts of citizen diplomacy. The Natural Resources Defense Council, by persuading Soviet authorities to let it establish seismic monitoring stations near the nuclear testing grounds at Semipalatinsk, helped compel the Reagan administration to reopen talks with Moscow about nuclear test ban verification. The Campaign for Peace and Democracy/East and West and the European Nuclear Disarmament Campaign seek to counter the arms race by building a grassroots alliance of peace and human rights groups straddling the military blocs in Europe.

An international satellite monitoring agency could help build greater trust.

While Third World conflicts arise from a multitude of causes, they often are exacerbated by the involvement of outside powers. In the absence of foreign intervention, such disputes may be easier to resolve. For the superpowers, the lessons of Vietnam and Afghanistan suggest that military intervention has reached a point of diminishing returns. Either the United States or the Soviet Union could offer to refrain from sending armed forces or weapons into any nonaligned country, in return for similar self-restraint from the other superpower. Such a nonintervention policy was in effect endorsed by a panel of former and current American and Soviet officials in a report on "The Requirements for Stable Coexistence in United States-Soviet Relations." In a similar vein, Gorbachev proposed removing Soviet naval forces from Cam Ranh Bay in Vietnam, if the United States in return agreed to close down its military bases in the Philippines.[51]

The best hope for impartially resolving Third World conflicts rests with the United Nations. The history of U.N. peacekeeping efforts shows that the organization has been an effective conciliator of conflicts that did not directly involve any of the major powers. Even though those who had high hopes invested in the United Nations have largely been disappointed during the first four decades of its existence, the organization's reputation has lately improved.[52]

The changing Soviet attitude toward the United Nations is a particularly encouraging development, as reflected in Soviet payment of past membership dues, Moscow's proposals for a U.N. flotilla in the Persian Gulf, and its acceptance of U.N.-mediated talks that initiated the withdrawal of Soviet troops from Afghanistan. If the incoming administration in Washington can reverse the hostile U.S. stance toward this world body, both superpowers could jointly make the United Nations what its founders envisioned: an organization at the center of a collective security system.

Meanwhile, the United Nations is receiving a boost from an unexpected corner. This decade has seen numerous conflicts around the globe that seem to have no victors but only vanquished—the Iran-Iraq war, Soviet forces pitched against the Afghan *mujahedeen*, the Viet-

namese occupation of Kampuchea, and the struggle between the Sahrawi people and Morocco over control of the Western Sahara. Sheer exhaustion and war weariness have driven these combatants to see the United Nations as a peacemaker of last resort. Cease-fire negotiations sponsored by the United Nations offer a face-saving way out of a stalemated conflict. And in southern Africa, the world body may soon play a crucial role in overseeing Namibia's transition to independence.

If the world body's current peacekeeping efforts continue to be successful, it can capitalize on its new prestige, reputation, and trust to cope with an even more daunting challenge: to move from organizing cease-fires and creating buffer zones to preventing the outbreak of hostilities in the first place. The announcement that U.N. Peacekeeping Forces received the 1988 Nobel Peace Prize may be just the boost the organization needed to take on this new role.

In the future, armed conflict may well be prevented by having either unarmed observers or peacekeeping forces already in place. Indeed, as part of a proposal for a comprehensive security system, the Soviet Union recently urged the United Nations to set up "observation posts in explosive areas of the world." Deputy Foreign Minister Vladimir F. Petrovsky suggested that any country seeking to protect itself from outside interference should be able to call on the United Nations to send observer teams to patrol borders.[53]

In 1983, Nicaragua proposed that an eight-nation Latin American contingent patrol its border with Honduras to deter Contra mercenary incursions. In 1988, Honduran Foreign Minister Lopez Contreras called for a similar force. If a U.N. team or another international force had been available, it might have prevented much of the bloodshed in the region. It would also have been much cheaper. A Pentagon estimate concluded that a force of 1,300 observers could monitor the borders separating Nicaragua from Honduras, El Salvador, and Costa Rica for less than $40 million a year. By contrast, the United States spends some $3 billion to project military force into the region, and the Central American countries together spend another $1 billion on their armies.[54]

The world may therefore want to consider creating a more permanent peacekeeping force. To solidify the impartiality of such a force—and therefore its acceptability—it should ideally consist of individually recruited persons, trained in the unique skills of peacekeeping, whose loyalty to the United Nations is beyond question.[55]

Annual outlays for seven U.N. peacekeeping operations come to about $380 million currently. A stepped-up role for the United Nations would require greater expenditures. The organization may soon be spending $2 billion a year if it assumes an active role in Kampuchea, the Western Sahara, and southern Africa. That would still be less than what the world spends on the arms race on a single day.[56]

BEATING SWORDS INTO PLOWSHARES

As far back as in the Bible, people have been urged to cast down their arms, to be done with war and to labor instead with plows and pruning hooks. The advice is even more appropriate today, when threats to natural life-support systems are the whole world's enemy.

To rechannel resources from the military to the civilian economy and to provide sufficient resources for reversing environmental degradation, a planned conversion process must be set in motion in parallel to a disarmament process. Conversion seeks to protect defense-dependent workers and communities from the social and economic dislocation that otherwise would arise during disarmament. Worldwide, perhaps as many as 50 million people—either as soldiers or as workers in military industry—are on the military payroll.[57]

A planned conversion process must be set in motion in parallel to a disarmament process.

Conversion is a critical component in reordering the priorities of a nation's security policy. First of all, it helps identify existing innovative and productive capabilities—the capital, raw materials, machinery, and human skills and expertise—now tied up in military-related production. Second, it provides the framework and mechanism for rechanneling these capabilities into civilian use. Legislation proposed by Representative Ted Weiss, for example, would mandate the formation of local alternative-use committees in every military plant, base, or laboratory, and entrust them with the responsibility for developing a blueprint for civilian product development and marketing; the bill further provides for occupational retraining of managers, engineers, and workers to help them adapt to the requirements of the civilian market.[58]

Third, as a deliberate planning process, conversion enables societies to anticipate the availability of capital and other resources for alternative civilian uses. Their reclamation from the military sector is badly needed to assist in repairing deteriorating public infrastructure, revitalizing the economy, and improving living standards. But conver-

Table 8-6. Trade-Offs Between Military and Social or Environmental Priorities

Military Priority	Cost	Social/Environmental Priority
Trident II submarine and F-18 jet fighter programs	$100,000,000,000	Estimated cost of cleaning up the 10,000 worst hazardous waste dumps in the United States
Stealth bomber program	$68,000,000,000	Two thirds of estimated costs to meet U.S. clean water goals by the year 2000
Requested SDI funding fiscal years 1988–92	$38,000,000,000	Disposal of highly radioactive waste in the United States
2 weeks of world military expenditure	$30,000,000,000	Annual cost of the proposed U.N. Water and Sanitation Decade
German outlays for military procurement and R&D, fiscal year 1985	$10,750,000,000	Estimated costs to clean up West German sector of the North Sea
3 days of global military spending	$6,500,000,000	To fund Tropical Forest Action Plan over 5 years
Development cost for Midgetman ICBM	$6,000,000,000	Annual cost to cut sulfur dioxide emissions by 8–12 million tons/year in the United States to combat acid rain
2 days of global military spending	$4,800,000,000	Annual cost of proposed U.N. Action Plan to halt Third World desertification, over 20 years

sion also frees up the money and brains required for reversing environmental degradation. Table 8–6 provides a sample of the trade-offs between military and social and environmental priorities.

In 1978, for example, the University of California Nuclear Weapons Labs Conversion Project studied the possibilities of switching the Lawrence Livermore Laboratory to work on alternative production in the energy field. Another such proposal envisioned transforming the Fort Detrick biological warfare facility into a center for cancer and related biomedical research. Or a chemical weapons factory could become a laboratory working on toxic waste treatment.[59]

Conversion is more than just a theory. At the close of World War II, 30 percent of U.S. GNP was transferred from the war industry into civilian uses. Today, China stands as an example. The post-Mao leadership assigned the military sector the lowest priority of the "four modernizations" (the others being agriculture, industry, and science and tech-

Military Priority	Cost	Social/Environmental Priority
6 months of U.S. outlays for nuclear warheads, fiscal year 1986	$4,000,000,000	U.S. government spending on energy efficiency, fiscal years 1980–87
SDI research, fiscal year 1987	$3,700,000,000	Enough funds to build a solar power system serving a city of 200,000
10 days of European Economic Community military spending	$2,000,000,000	Annual cost to clean up hazardous waste sites in 10 European Economic Community countries by the year 2000
1 Trident submarine	$1,400,000,000	Global 5-year child immunization program against 6 deadly diseases, preventing 1 million deaths a year
3 B-1B bombers	$680,000,000	U.S. government spending on renewable energy, fiscal years 1983–85
2 months of Ethiopian military spending	$50,000,000	Annual cost of proposed U.N. Anti-Desertification Plan for Ethiopia
1 nuclear weapon test	$12,000,000	Installation of 80,000 hand pumps to give Third World villages access to safe water
1-hour operating cost, B-1B bomber	$21,000	Community-based maternal health care in 10 African villages to reduce maternal deaths by half in one decade

SOURCE: Worldwatch Institute, based on various sources.

nology). In 1985, the country decided to slice its 4-million-strong armed forces by one quarter and to utilize part of the military-industrial capacity to manufacture civilian goods. Civilian production now accounts for 20 percent of the output of China's 30,000 military factories; that share is projected to reach 50 percent by the year 2000.[60]

It is important for nations to devote greater resources to environmental protection. But in the face of transnational environmental problems, national efforts are likely to prove fruitless without the cooperation of neighbors. Indeed, as awareness of the transnational character of environmental degradation has grown and as remedies became more urgent, an increasing number of international conventions have been concluded, with varying degrees of national commitment and success. (See Chapter 1.)

The United Nations Environment Programme (UNEP) has served a useful function in laying the groundwork for additional treaties. Its most celebrated achievement to date is the Montreal Protocol that calls for a 50-percent cut in CFC production by 1999. But UNEP's mandate remains limited, and there are no firmly established international mechanisms to address ecological problems. For example, several of UNEP's attempts to draft rules on international responsibility for transboundary environmental damage have failed.[61]

Ironically, transnational coordination of environmental policies can occasionally even be a two-edged sword. The consensus-building process within the European Economic Community, for example, has at times inhibited individual member countries from taking stricter national action. This was the case with automotive emissions. (See Chapter 6.)

As in the field of disarmament, the inertia of formal international conferences may be overcome by the independent actions of one or more like-minded countries. They could commit themselves to reduce their fossil fuel consumption, cut their CFC production, or stop ocean dumping, and then invite other nations to adopt similar policies. Such environmental alliances—formed to act against a common threat—could tie together nations that share ecosystems, countries that are geographically distant but bear primary responsibility for global environmental threats, or political, ideological, or military rivals that may have little else in common than an interest in avoiding environmental catastrophes.

These alliances are already becoming a reality. In 1984, nine European countries and Canada formed a "30 percent club." Aware that vast amounts of airborne pollutants drift across national borders, these nations committed themselves to reduce their 1980 levels of sulfur dioxide emissions, a chief culprit in the formation of acid rain, by at least 30 percent by 1993. A total of 19 countries (including the Soviet Union but not the United States) have joined the club so far. A similar pledge to cut nitrogen oxides by 30 percent by 1998 was made by 12 European nations in 1988.[62]

Environmental alliances that run across adversarial military alliances can fulfill a valuable role by strengthening the common interests of opposing camps. Europe has been divided into East and West for four decades now, but joint policies to cope with environmental threats may help in breaking down ideological barriers. Tanks and planes *might* fend off a military attack, but no technology exists to repel the air- and waterborne pollutants that cross borders with impunity. East-West environmental cooperation first became manifest in the 1979 Convention on Long-Range Transboundary Air Pollution, which gave rise to the "30 percent club." Both sides are now showing considerably greater interest in enhanced cooperation.[63]

One specific alliance might evolve among the countries that share the Elbe. This river—severely polluted with cadmium, mercury, lead, phosphates, and nitrates—flows through heavily industrialized parts of Czechoslovakia and East Germany before streaming through Hamburg, West Germany, and emptying into the North Sea. Because West Germany has an obvious interest in seeing the river cleaned up, it is considering funding a water treatment plant in East Germany. By similar logic, the country earlier agreed to pay for some sulfur dioxide scrubbers on Czechoslovakian power plants in an effort to reduce the air pollution wafting across the border.[64]

The newfound urgency to counteract global problems like the greenhouse effect and ozone depletion may also bring change in U.S.-Soviet relations. As early as 1972, the superpowers signed an Agreement on Cooperation in the Field of Environmental Protection. But activities carried out under the accord have been starved for funds. Now, without governmental sponsorship, scientists from the Soviet Union and the United States are beginning to collaborate more closely on measures to cope with the greenhouse effect, in an effort dubbed greenhouse *glasnost*.[65]

A unique environmental alliance is shaping up in war-torn Central America. Governments agreed in 1988 to establish a series of "peace parks"—designed to preserve the region's fast-disappearing rain forests and to help promote sustainable development—straddling the borders of Costa Rica, El Salvador, Honduras, Guatemala, Nicaragua, and Panama. Nicaraguan official Lorenzo Cardenal hopes these biosphere reserves will become "a worldwide model of sustainable tropical forest development."[66]

In the final analysis, *all* countries must become part of an earth-spanning environmental coalition. In June 1988, the prime ministers of Norway and Canada called for a global "law of the air" analogous to the Law of the Sea—a treaty to protect the earth's atmosphere from ozone depletion and the buildup of greenhouse gases. A world atmosphere fund, financed by a tax on fossil fuel consumption in the industrial countries, could provide the financial support for improving energy efficiency, switching to more benign fuels, and taking other remedial actions. (See Chapter 10.)[67]

As with war and peace issues, citizen diplomacy is playing an increasingly important role in pushing governments to stem environmental degradation. In widely divergent ways, environmental groups have sought to link up with overseas counterparts or influence national policies affecting the global environment. The Rainforest Action Network, for instance, is pressuring development banks not to fund projects that destroy the remaining rain forests. The Environmental Project on Central America is organizing American support for the Central American "peace parks."

Conservation International and the World Wildlife Fund have pioneered innovative financial arrangements known as debt-for-nature swaps (though their impact is too minuscule to solve the debt crisis). Survival International is concerned with preserving the habitat on which endangered peoples depend. Greenpeace has developed a truly globe-spanning network of activists mobilized on a wide range of issues. Environmental links across the East-West divide on the grassroots level are still in their infancy. But Friends of the Earth, among others, is busy building contacts with a budding East European environmental movement.

Today's threats to environmental security may supplant concerns about intractable issues of military security, even as the world takes halting steps toward disarmament and economic conversion. Growing environmental awareness is spawning a new willingness to collaborate on a global basis. If nations can work together to solve common ecological problems, if multilateralism works, then we stand a chance of overcoming the many other issues that divide us.

9

Mobilizing at the Grassroots

Alan B. Durning

Villagers in the parched hinterlands of Senegal may never have heard the word desertification, yet they know better than any agronomist that their soil is exhausted and that hunger is on their heels. Women on the banks of the Ganges may not know what an infant mortality rate is, but they know all too well the helpless agony of holding a child as it dies of diarrhea. Forest dwellers in the heart of the Amazon may never have been told about the mass extinction of species now occurring around them, but they know far better than any research biologist what it is to watch their primeval homeland go up in smoke before advancing waves of migrants and developers.

The men and women of Senegal, Bangladesh, and Brazil understand global deterioration in its rawest forms. To them, creeping degradation of ecosystems has meant declining health, failing

An expanded version of this chapter appeared as Worldwatch Paper 88, *Mobilizing at the Grassroots: Local Action on Poverty and the Environment.*

livelihoods, and lengthening workdays. But they are not standing idle. In villages, neighborhoods, and shantytowns around the world, people are coming together to discuss and respond to the tightening ecological and economic conditions that confront them. Viewed in isolation, these initiatives are modest—10 women plant trees on a roadside, a dozen youths dig a well, an old man teaches neighborhood children to read—but from a global perspective their scale and impact are monumental. Indeed, local organizations form a sort of ragtag front line in the worldwide struggle to end poverty and environmental destruction.

Although most individual groups are little known outside their own locality, the overall movements they form can be studied by piecing together insights from scores of interviews, field visits, grassroots newsletters, official documents, press reports, and academic papers. The resulting picture reveals an expanding latticework of human organizations that, while varying from place to place in many of the particulars, share basic characteristics.[1]

The particulars include cooperatives, mothers' clubs, peasant unions, religious groups, savings and credit associations, neighborhood federations, collective work arrangements, tribal networks, and innumerable others. The universals include the capacities to tap local knowledge and resources, to respond to problems rapidly and creatively, and to maintain the institutional flexibility necessary in changing circumstances. In addition, although few groups use the words sustainable development, their agendas in many cases embody its ideal. They want economic prosperity without sacrificing their health or the prospects for their children.

At the grassroots, and particularly among the close to 4 billion humans in developing lands, it appears that the world's people are better organized in 1989 than they have been since European colonialism disrupted traditional societies centuries ago. Alone, however, this new class of organizations is far from powerful enough to single-handedly set the world on a sustainable course. The tasks required—from putting the brakes on population growth to reforesting the planet's denuded watersheds—will necessitate an unprecedented outpouring of human energy. (See Chapter 10.) Community groups, whose membership now numbers perhaps into the hundreds of millions, can show the world how to tap that energy. But national governments and international agencies, which have all too often excluded or sought to control popular organizations, must learn to work with them. Development institutions in particular will need fundamental reorientation if they are to fulfill their potential as supporters of and complements to local efforts.[2]

The difficulty of forging an alliance between powerful, often rigid institutions and the world's millions of fledgling community groups can scarcely be underestimated, yet neither can its importance. To succeed, sustainable development will have to come from both the bottom and the top.

AN UNNOTICED TIDE

In an anthropological sense, social organization is always present. Kinship, peer relations, division of labor, social hierarchies, and religious structures form the scaffolding of human community in traditional societies. Yet traditional organizations, first disturbed by European colonialism, have been stretched and often dismantled by the great cultural upheavals of the twentieth century: population growth, urbanization, the advent of modern technology, and the spread of western commercialism.[3]

In the resulting organizational vacuum, a new generation of community and grassroots groups has been steadily, albeit unevenly, developing, particularly over the past two decades. This emergence is driven by a shifting constellation of forces, including stagnant or deteriorating economic and ecological conditions for the poor, the failure of many governments to respond adequately, and the spread in some regions of new social ideologies and new interpretations of religious doctrines. In contrast to traditional organizations and mass political movements, this rising tide of community groups is generally pragmatic, self-consciously focused on development, nonaligned in party politics, and concerned primarily with self-help.

At the same time, in much of the world a second layer of institutions has jelled atop the first. This diverse class of intermediary organizations serves the groups at the base by facilitating the flow of information, materials, and funds between the grassroots and broader institutions such as church, state, and development donors. The groups go by many names: in Europe they are called nongovernmental organizations (NGOs), in the United States private voluntary organizations (PVOs), and in Asia voluntary agencies or "Volags." Here they will be called "independent development organizations" or simply "independent groups."[4]

Numbers only crudely capture the vitality of the world's grassroots movements since data are sketchy and groups fluid, yet the explosive growth is unmistakable. Although at mid-century community development projects existed mainly where traditional self-help customs remained intact, today dynamic local organizations are found throughout the world. (See Table 9–1.)[5]

Asia has by many accounts the most active community movement. India's self-help movement has a prized place in society, tracing its roots to Mahatma Gandhi's pioneering village development work 60 years ago. Gandhi aimed to build a just and humane society from the bottom up, starting with self-reliant villages based on renewable resources. After independence in 1948, Gandhi's disciple Vinoba Bhave sparked the influential Village Awakening movement and, when that peaked in 1964, a new wave of community organizing commenced, spurred by a generation of committed middle-class youths. Tens if not hundreds of thousands of local groups in India now wage the day-by-day struggle for development.[6]

Across the subcontinent, community activism runs high. Self-help in Bangladesh has risen sharply since independence in 1971, and 3 million Sri Lankans participate in Sarvodaya Shramadana, a community development movement that combines Gandhian teachings with social action tenets of Theravada Bud-

dhism. Sarvodaya mobilizes massive work teams to do everything from building road networks to draining malarial ponds, and their achievements have garnered international praise.[7]

After Asia, Latin American communities are perhaps the most active. There, the bulk of the continent's experience dates to the 1968 conference of Catholic Bishops in Medellín, Colombia, where the church fundamentally reoriented its social mission toward improving the lot of the poor. Since that time, millions of priests, nuns, and laypeople have fanned out into the back streets and hinterlands from Tierra del Fuego to the Rio Grande, dedicating themselves to creating a people's church embodied in neighborhood worship and action groups called Christian Base Communities. Brazil alone has 100,000 base communities, with at least 3 million members, and an equal number are spread across the rest of the continent. In Central America, they play an important role in movements for peace and human rights.[8]

In Latin America, past political movements also lay the groundwork for current community self-help efforts. In Colombia, the rise and subsequent violent repression of the National Association of Small Farmers in the seventies gave peasants experiences with organizing that led to the abundance of community efforts today, including everything from cooperative stores to environmental "green councils." In Nicaragua, the national uprising that overthrew the Somoza dictatorship in 1979 created a fount of grassroots energy that flowed into thousands of local groups.[9]

Community self-help organizations are relative newcomers to Africa, though traditional village institutions are stronger than in other regions. Nevertheless, in parts of Africa where political struggles have led to dramatic changes in political structures, local initiatives

Table 9-1. Grassroots Organizations in Selected Developing Countries, Late Eighties

Country	Description
India	Strong Gandhian self-help tradition promotes social welfare, appropriate technology, and tree planting; local groups number in at least the tens of thousands; independent development organizations estimated at 12,000.
Indonesia	600 independent development groups work in environmental protection alone.
Bangladesh	1,200 independent development organizations formed since 1971, particularly active with large landless population.
Philippines	3,000–5,000 Christian Base Communities form focal points for local action.
Sri Lanka	Rapidly growing Sarvodaya Shramadana village awakening movement includes over 8,000 villages, one third of total in country; 3 million people involved in range of efforts, particularly work parties, education, preventive health care, and cooperative crafts projects.
Kenya	16,232 women's groups with 637,000 members registered in 1984, quadruple the 1980 number; 1988 estimates range up to 25,000; many start as savings clubs.
Zimbabwe	Informal small-farmer groups throughout country have estimated membership of 276,500 families (2.3 million people); active women's community gardens multiplying.
Burkina Faso	Naam grassroots peasant movement has 2,500 groups participating in dry-season self-help; similar movements forming in Senegal, Mauritania, Mali, Niger, and Togo.
Brazil	Enormous growth in community action since democratization in early eighties: 100,000 Christian Base Communities with 3 million members; 1,300 neighborhood associations in São Paulo; landless peasant groups proliferating; 1,041 independent development organizations.
Mexico	Massive urban grassroots movement active in squatter settlements of major cities; at least 250 independent development organizations.
Peru	Vital women's self-help movement in Lima's impoverished shantytowns with 1,500 community kitchens; 300 independent development organizations.

SOURCE: Worldwatch Institute, based on various sources.

have sprung up in abundance. In Kenya, the harambee ("let's pull together") movement began with independence in 1963 and, with encouragement from the national government, by the early eighties was contributing nearly one third of all labor, materials, and finances invested in rural development. With Zimbabwe's transfer to black rule in 1980, a similar explosion in community organizing began, as thousands of women's community gardens and informal small farmer associations formed. Senegal and Burkina Faso are well organized at the grassroots level as a result of traditions of joint action.[10]

With Zimbabwe's transfer to black rule in 1980, thousands of women's community gardens and small farmer associations formed.

For lack of space, this chapter concentrates on Third World self-help movements, yet local action seems to be on the rise everywhere. In the Soviet Union, Eastern Europe, and China, officially sanctioned local organizations are numerous but largely controlled by state and party hierarchies, and as such cannot be equated with the nonaligned self-help movements of other countries. Nevertheless, the Soviet Union and Eastern Europe have witnessed over this decade the emergence, often at considerable risk to the founders, of independent community groups battling nuclear power reactors and industrial pollution.[11]

In western industrial nations, grassroots action for sustainability is a formidable force, setting its sights on everything from local waste recycling to international trade and debt issues. The U.S. environmental movement took a decidedly grassroots turn in the early

eighties, as momentum switched from national to local campaigns on toxic waste and groundwater protection. Estimates of nationwide participation range up to 25 million. In West Germany, meanwhile, the ascent of the Green Party, whose roots go back to the "citizen initiative" movement of the sixties and seventies, fostered broad public environmental awareness and pushed national leaders toward institutionalizing concern for the environment.[12]

A final noteworthy characteristic of community movements is the central role that women play. As the majority of participants in many regions, they form the backbones of the movements. In Africa the sheer enormity of women's burden unites them: women bear exclusive responsibility for child care, cooking, cleaning, processing food, carrying water, and gathering fuel; they grow 80 percent of the food, raise half the livestock, and have 27 million babies a year. Worldwide, women's traditional nurturing role may give them increased concern for the generations of their children and grandchildren, while their subordinate social status gives them more to gain from organizing.[13]

THE GENESIS OF LOCAL ACTION

Poverty is an economic condition, but its effects ripple deep into the human psyche, devastating self-confidence and self-respect. One consequence, according to sociologists, is that organizing comes more naturally to the fortunate than to the dispossessed. Despite activist priests and Gandhian workers, the poor remain the least organized of the world's people. The multiple causes of this inertia are critical obstacles to progress against hunger, poverty, and environmental decline.

For those who live on the brink of starvation, generations of misfortune and injustice have bred an often overwhelming fatalism. As Zimbabwean organizer Sithembiso Nyoni has pointed out, Third World people are not at the dawn of their history. Life experience counsels them that change is impossible and that those who offer to help have ulterior motives—proselytization, political patronage, or simple greed. Further, living hand-to-mouth, the poor have little margin for risky experiments and new undertakings. Change must go inch by inch.[14]

If fatalism and risk-aversion account for some of the world's grassroots inertia, social structures account for the rest. The poor of the world are not, as First World myth has it, an undifferentiated "peasant mass" or a "sea of need." Social and economic roles are as intricately stratified in Bombay slums as they are in New York or Berlin. Research on a Bangladeshi village of 150 households, for example, revealed 10 distinct social classes. Many communities are further torn apart by personality conflicts, factional frictions, and turbulent squabbles.[15]

Springing the trap of fatalism and division usually requires a catalyzing influence from outside the community— "some experience," in the words of development theorist Albert Hirschman, "dispelling isolation and mutual distrust."[16] Sometimes broad-based political upheaval has this effect, as in Zimbabwe or Nicaragua, but more frequently an organizer is involved.

Experience from India suggests that with training and support from independent groups, the most effective organizers are natural leaders from the area itself. These individuals, who often hold no official position, know community members and their strengths, quirks,

and failings well. Indian independent organizations find that the most reliable organizers are middle-aged mothers: they have good rapport with villagers, especially other women, but are likely to stay put while younger people often migrate to cities after completing organizer training.[17]

Another lesson from India is that social stratification often makes all-inclusive community organizations counterproductive. Lumping male farmers with landless women almost guarantees that the men will reap the bulk of rewards. Many government community development programs have treated all villagers as essentially equal in interests and status, allowing the more powerful to co-opt projects for their own benefit.[18]

The two basic paths out of fatalism and divisiveness are, in essence, forms of education, but education need not mean schooling. The first path is typified by Brazilian educator Paulo Freire's learning process, now practiced by independent groups worldwide. It uses informal teachers who guide illiterate adults through discussions of basic concepts from everyday life—such as food, school, and landlord—to foster a critical awareness of the predicament of poverty. Similar techniques include street theater, revitalization of traditional dance and music, and oral history. By promoting a sense of identity and self-worth, these methods of "popular education" all aim to break what Freire termed the "culture of silence" that traps large classes in powerlessness and vulnerability.[19]

In 1975, the Catholic diocese of Machakos, Kenya, initiated a Freirian literacy program that, by 1984, involved some 60,000 participants. Program coordinator Francis Mulwa reports, "Literacy-class discussions became the springboard to other development," generating ventures in handicrafts, tree planting, primary health care, cooperative farming, soil conservation, savings and credit, and water supply. Albert Hirschman calls this pervasive springboard effect "social energy": once a group gets started, projects proliferate and momentum builds.[20]

Because actions speak louder than words, many organizers prefer the second path out of fatalism: they organize to produce something tangible early on, be it a school building, a well, or a paint job for the church. Again, momentum builds once people see what joint action can achieve. A variation is the method of such appropriate technology groups as India's Centre of Science for Villages and the Philippine Palawan Center for Appropriate Rural Technology. Devendra Kumar of Science for Villages describes the philosophy well: "Technology can be a tool of rural change, because by introducing one simple device, such as a pulley with ball bearings for hauling water out of a well, rural people begin to see possibilities that they did not see before." People rarely seek relief from hardships they consider inevitable.[21]

Many organize to produce something tangible early on, be it a school building or a paint job for the church.

In Sri Lanka, Sarvodaya Shramadana combines the two paths in massive work parties and communal feasts, where villages come together to speak, listen, and learn. The philosophy is all in the name. Shramadana means "gift of labor," and Sarvodaya means "village awakening." By giving their labor, people awaken the talents within their village and set it on a course of self-development.[22]

Even in the best of circumstances, popular action is difficult; the odds weigh heavily against the poor. In average conditions, failure to achieve goals is a normal part of the process. Working together, however, has its own rewards. Indeed, the intangible benefits of grassroots action are as important as the latrines dug and trees planted, for as Chilean dissident Ariel Dorfman so eloquently put it, "How do you measure the amount of dignity that people accumulate? How do you quantify the disappearance of apathy?"[23]

MEETING HUMAN NEEDS

In September 1988, World Bank president Barber Conable flew to Berlin to report to the governors of the Bank and the International Monetary Fund. Poverty, he announced, "prevents a billion people from having even minimally acceptable standards of living." The ranks of the dispossessed, moreover, appear to be growing.[24]

Thus, the world's self-help movements are arising amidst increasing desperation; the poor take action as best they can on many fronts and all too often they lose. Although the cultural, economic, and political factors that determine the effectiveness of community action are too complex to be condensed into a universal "recipe for success," experiences from around the world reveal the strengths and weaknesses of grassroots groups.

The most essential lesson is that community groups organize to respond, on the one hand, to a felt need or threat and, on the other hand, to *perceived* opportunities. There is, in other words, both a "push" and a "pull" to community action, and neither is sufficient in itself. Depending on local needs and the awareness of opportunities to meet those needs, communities focus on a variety of areas, most commonly securing rights to their land, providing education, improving health, generating income, and protecting their resource base.[25]

In the mushrooming shantytowns of the southern hemisphere, neighborhood movements have grown dramatically; São Paulo alone has 1,300 organizations. A typical sequence of development for such a squatter community begins when individuals or an organized group invades a vacant area—the push is the obvious need for shelter and the pull is seeing empty land. Once settled, the community's top priority is to protect itself from expulsion, a difficult and dangerous job. In Manila's Tondo slum, one of Asia's largest, residents formed massive "human barricades" in the late sixties to halt government bulldozers bent on demolishing homes. The land tenure struggle can also be protracted: the 40,000 inhabitants of Klong Toey in Bangkok, for example, prevailed only after a three-decade campaign.[26]

Natural disasters and similar crises can throw open the floodgates to old grievances between popular groups and powerful institutions. The Mexican government seized on the opportunity of the 1985 Mexico City earthquake to relocate thousands of squatters from the prime real estate they occupied, but the city's neighborhood organizations unleashed what writer Octavio Paz called "a social tide" to halt the relocations and demand reconstruction assistance. Later, with the symbolic leadership of wrestling star Superbarrio, hero of society's underdogs, the unprecedented movement pressured government to extend housing programs.[27]

As often as not the poor are evicted, but where they are able to establish land tenure, they generally move on to other priorities. They pressure authorities to supply services including water, waste disposal, and schools, or they provide

them for themselves. In Rio de Janeiro, tenure is largely secure and half of Rio's *favelas,* where at least 2 million live, are at some stage of organization, according to lawyer-organizer Eliana Athayde. One of the most successful is Santa Marta, where 11,500 live in precarious structures clinging to a steep slope above Rio's city council offices. The local organization, which started with an informal day care program, evolved into a vocal and effective neighborhood association. As of June 1988, the accumulated social energy had brought water, paved stairways (in lieu of roads), and health clinics into the *favela,* along with drainage systems against mud slides, which had wiped out two dozen homes in February 1988. The people of Santa Marta built some of it themselves; the rest they pressed the city to construct.[28]

Perhaps the world's greatest success story in self-help community building is Lima's Villa El Salvador, where citizens have planted a half-million trees; built 26 schools, 150 day care centers, and 300 community kitchens; and trained hundreds of door-to-door health workers. Despite the extreme poverty of the town's inhabitants and a population that has shot up to 300,000, illiteracy has fallen to 3 percent—one of the lowest rates in Latin America—and infant mortality is 40 percent below the national average. The major contributors to success have been a vast network of women's groups and the neighborhood association's democratic administrative structure, which extends down to representatives on each block. Together, they match a high degree of base-level organization with a responsive system of governance to yield maximum participation in designing and implementing community efforts.[29]

In Recife, the metropolis of Brazil's poor northeast region, 2.5 million people live in shantytowns where barely half the population can read. The state government, under leadership first from the right and then from the left, has been unwilling or unable to respond to the crisis in education, leaving the public school system with a 70-percent dropout rate in the elementary grades alone. Sixty of Recife's *favelas* have completed the mammoth organizational task of opening their own elementary schools, with teachers and lesson plans drawn from local life. By 1988, the popular education movement was spreading like wildfire across Brazil. Rio de Janeiro, Belém, and Salvador each had over a dozen community schools, and the *favelas* of São Luis had already opened 40.[30]

In Peru, international debt and the economic crisis it drives can be measured in the height of the children.

At least 1.5 billion people worldwide still lack clean water, although hundreds of communities are bucking the odds of government complacence and international neglect to confront this need. In Dhandhuka, on the barren coastal plane of India's Gujarat state, a generation of excessive fuelwood gathering and overgrazing led to desertification, which in turn triggered social and economic disintegration. Conflicts erupted over water that seeped into brackish wells, and in the worst years, four fifths of the population had to migrate to survive.[31]

As in much of the world, fetching water in Dhandhuka is women's work, and it was the women who decided, upon talking with community organizers in 1981, to construct a permanent reservoir to trap the seasonal rains. In this case, an idea from migrant laborers provided the pull that complemented the push of water scarcity. They had seen

irrigation channels lined with plastic sheets and reasoned that a reservoir could be similarly sealed. After lengthy discussion and debate, the community agreed to the plan, and in 1986, all but a few stayed home during the dry season to get the job done. Moving thousands of tons of earth by hand, they finished the pool before the rains and were soon the envy of their neighbors, who promptly made plans to build their own.[32]

Food scarcity may be similarly tackled by community groups. In Peru, international debt and the economic crisis it drives can be measured in the height of the children: malnutrition now stunts the growth of one in four. The mothers of the shantytowns that encircle Lima have found an innovative way to combat hunger. In more than 1,500 community kitchens, they buy in bulk to cut costs and rotate cooking duties to save time. The kitchens improve nutrition for all while building solidarity among women, long subdued in the *machismo* of Latin culture.[33]

As these examples show, community groups are good at attacking sources of disease with an identifiable cause, such as contaminated water or malnutrition. On their own, however, they are unaware of, and therefore cannot promote, other low-cost preventive techniques that public health experts believe could save millions of lives in the Third World each year, such as oral rehydration for diarrhea, extended breast-feeding, and mother and child immunization. The push of illness is there, but there is no pull of perceived opportunities. Most campaigns that promote these measures, therefore, are initiated by independent health groups or governments.[34]

Nevertheless, such large-scale programs usually make use of community health workers, who need the support of local groups to be effective. Millions of community health workers have been trained since 1980; China alone had 1 million "barefoot doctors" and 4 million health aides in 1981. In Bangladesh, where 250,000 children die each year from diarrhea, the nongovernmental Bangladesh Rural Advancement Committee has gone door-to-door to teach 9 million mothers the use of diarrhea rehydration fluids made from sugar, water, and salt.[35]

Most grassroots groups around the world also neglect family planning, again because they lack knowledge of the opportunities. Spreading the word about the benefits of contraception, therefore, generally falls to a class of specialized government bodies and independent family planning agencies. Where family planning has effectively turned the tide on excessive population growth, however, it has done so through collaboration between local and central institutions. Thousands of mothers' clubs in Indonesia and South Korea are the foot soldiers of those countries' highly effective family planning campaigns. In Thailand, the Population and Community Development Association has trained representatives in 16,000 of the country's estimated 48,000 villages.[36]

Community groups' indirect contribution to family planning, moreover, is substantial. Data from around the world show that as female education, health, employment, and legal rights improve, birth rates decline. Large families are frequently a sign of the subordination of women. Thus, although community groups have had a small role in distributing contraceptives and family planning information, they play what is in many ways a more fundamental role: liberating women.[37]

Through the weekly meetings of mothers' clubs, church groups, health committees, and cooperatives, women emerge from the isolation of home and field to try their voices. Gradually demystifying age-old taboos against discussing sexuality and mistreatment at the hands of men, women gain perspective on the hardships of their lives. The growing women's movements of Kenya and Nigeria—where birth rates have remained high since the sixties—may presage falling fertility in the nineties. Since the eighties began, rural Brazil has also seen explosive growth in women's groups, many of them anxious to better inform themselves of their legal, economic, and reproductive rights.[38]

In the area of economic development, grassroots efforts fail perhaps more commonly than those in the social development areas of health and education. The basic unit of community economic development is often the cooperative, an association of worker-owners who form a business together and manage it jointly. Unfortunately, the majority of worker cooperatives survive only a few years; their members are generally inexperienced in managing capital and equipment, and they often face volatile markets, skyrocketing inflation, and policies unsupportive of small producers.[39]

Success is more common in groups that join forces to accomplish well-defined, mutually beneficial tasks, without collectivizing production. A striking example of this comes from the extreme north of Pakistan, where 800,000 peasants live in one of the earth's most rugged terrains. In 1982, the nongovernmental Aga Khan Rural Support Program began resuscitating the tradition of local self-help through a partnership arrangement.[40]

At thousands of mass meetings, Aga Khan organizers offered support and assistance if the village would form an organization, begin a saving scheme, and select priority projects. By the end of 1987, 764 of the 1,280 villages had battled their way through day-long meetings to qualify. Villagers have cleared new farmland, bored irrigation lines through mountains, and suspended pipes across gaping chasms. They have saved 34 million Rupees ($1.9 million), enough to start a regional village bank, and have sharpened their skills in everything from poultry production to accounting. Meanwhile, dozens of women's groups have sprung up parallel to the male-dominated village organizations. Community organizing for economic progress works in Pakistan, so long as no attempt is made to collectivize production.[41]

Similar wisdom has arisen around the world. In Taiwan and South Korea, small farmers' associations that facilitate the flow of information and improved seed have been the foundation of agricultural productivity for over a generation. In Zimbabwe, corn production on black farmers' land increased from 5 percent of the national harvest in 1980 to 45 percent in 1985, thanks in part to the services provided by small farmers' groups, which grew dramatically during that period. Case studies from Sri Lanka, India, and the Philippines demonstrate the critical role of peasant associations in managing irrigation systems.[42]

Since most of the Third World's urban poor are involved in what development specialists call the "informal sector"— buying, trading, and selling the litter of goods that flow through the world's cities—that is where most urban grassroots economic development efforts are concentrated. Judith Tendler performed an in-depth review of independent organizations' economic development initiatives, and found that those groups best able to provide large numbers of people with substantial economic gains were not the common "integrated" small projects that include credit, management training, equipment, and advice. Rather, the successful groups tended to be highly specialized ones that began by de-

veloping a profound understanding of existing conditions in a particular sector of the economy. Although grassroots-oriented, they were centralized enough to bring their force to bear on specific legal and institutional obstacles that hinder progress for the poor.[43]

Many of them work primarily with women. The 22,000-strong Self-Employed Women's Association (SEWA) based in Ahmadabad, India, was formed in 1971 as a trade union to battle for continued access to sidewalk space for street vendors and to stop police harassment. After each success, they have consciously worked to widen their impact, now extending to trash collectors, cigarette rollers, and farm laborers. SEWA provides a heartening contrast to most grassroots economic projects for women, which establish crafts, sewing, and weaving cooperatives, activities where markets are usually flooded and profit margins slim.[44]

Community organizing for economic progress works, so long as no attempt is made to collectivize production.

Many of the most effective grassroots economic programs revolve around credit. The Grameen Bank of Bangladesh, for example, has attracted worldwide attention for its distribution of over 400,000 tiny loans, averaging $60 apiece. The funds go largely to women for investment in micro-enterprises that involve the purchase of a goat, for example, or a rice-huller, or tools for wood cutting. On first entering a village, Grameen's "bicycle bankers" simply tell landless peasants about the bank's credit offer. Those interested must find four others and form a "solidarity group" to apply. The neediest two are given loans first, and if they make their weekly payments on time, the others get theirs; peer pressure takes the place of loan collateral.[45]

Grameen is not in the business of community organizing, but it has had that effect nonetheless: dozens of loan groups have begun community schools, gardens, and sanitary latrines. With over 100 new branches added each year, Grameen's track record is truly extraordinary and has inspired a bevy of imitators on other continents. As Grameen president Muhammad Yunus points out, however, short-term credit is no substitute for necessary reforms in national tax, investment, and tenure policies. It would be unfortunate if effective credit programs such as Grameen's became viewed as a panacea—the latest fad to sweep development institutions.[46]

In particular, for those who are excluded from access to productive resources, self-help of necessity takes on a more confrontational style. The Bhoomi Sena land movement of *adivasis* (tribal people) in Maharashtra, India, for instance, has struggled for 15 years to regain the tribal land base that was appropriated by moneylenders and timber barons early this century. In the Philippines and El Salvador, maldistribution of farmland fuels grassroots action in its most violent form—civil war. And in Brazil, gross inequality in tenure hamstrings agricultural production. Brazil's 10 million landless and marginal peasants began mass occupations of unused private estates in the early eighties and have, in turn, suffered fierce reprisals from landowners. Amnesty International reports that 1,000 Brazilian peasants have been killed since 1980, mostly by hired guns.[47] All too often, grassroots initiatives run into the brick wall of oppressive political and economic power.

PROTECTING THE EARTH

In November 1987, 2,000 low-caste laborers and farmers from Karnataka, India, performed one of the most peculiar acts of civil disobedience in that nation's long Gandhian history: they uprooted 100 trees planted as part of a massive government reforestation campaign. That villagers should destroy trees in such a fuelwood-starved land appears little less than self-destructive; in fact, it was perfectly reasonable. The trees, eucalyptus to be used in production of rayon, were planted by a private company on what had been common land where the poor gathered wood. The poor were defending what was theirs.[48]

As officials in northern and southern capitals alike grow increasingly aware that a sound resource base is crucial for real social and economic progress, a stream of self-described "sustainable development" projects has begun to flow from the pens of development planners. Notwithstanding their good intentions, this round of ventures could fail as badly as earlier ones if they disregard the lesson of Karnataka. The fundamental questions of sustainable development are, *by whom* and *for whom?* Sustainable development imposed from on high is rarely sustainable; it may not even be development.

Environmental quality is not a luxury. Those who live beyond the borders of the world's industrial economy subsist on nature's surplus—on organic soil fertility for food, on stable hydrological cycles for water, and on forests for fuel. Environmental degradation, consequently, has a direct, tangible meaning: hunger, thirst, and fuel scarcity. No line can be drawn between economic development and environmental protection.

Many communities have traditional resource management systems that effectively husband natural systems, but when authority over ranges, forests, or fisheries is vested in distant institutions, the tragedy of the commons all too often sets in. Nepal nationalized its forests in 1957, ostensibly "to protect, manage, and improve" them. The result, however, was disastrous, as villagers' time-honored management systems broke down and the welter of unchecked individual interests overwhelmed government forest institutions. Twenty years later, the Nepalese government reversed itself, slowly handing over woodlands to intervillage councils. The reform has not decentralized control far enough, yet local mechanisms of restraint seem to be recuperating, with dramatic forest restoration in several cases.[49]

Traditional resource management mechanisms can also be overrun by forces internal to the community, such as population growth, or external to it, such as commercial interests. Communities are most apt to protect their environment against the latter, which provide a visible adversary against which to mobilize. For example, traditional fishers of northeastern Brazil, the Philippines, and the Indian states of Goa and Kerala have built vocal movements for safeguarding ocean fisheries against commercial trollers and industrial polluters.[50]

In the world's disappearing tropical forests, community action is also accelerating. Every tropical forest, from the Congo to Kalimantan, has human residents who live from its natural surplus. The traditional inhabitants of the world's largest rain forest, in the Amazon Basin, include dozens of tribes of Indians and perhaps a half-million rubber tappers, a guild of workers who trace their roots and their residence in the forests to the cyclical rubber booms of the late nineteenth and early twentieth centuries. They earn their keep by tapping the rubber trees spread liberally through the forests. Since the sixties, a series of powerful economic and political forces have thrown waves of landless peasants and wealthy land speculators into the jungles, where they have driven the rubber tappers out—sometimes at gun point.[51]

In the remote Brazilian state of Acre on the Bolivian border, by contrast, 30,-000 rubber tappers took a stand in the late seventies, using improvised nonviolent methods. Where clear-cutting had begun, men, women, and children peacefully occupied the forest, putting their bodies in the path of destruction. More recently they have taken their protests into the courthouse, the legislative chamber, and the governor's mansion. They have helped reshape World Bank and Inter-American Development Bank lending policy by showing that, over the long run, natural rubber production is more profitable per hectare than cattle ranching or farming.[52]

Bolstered by an unprecedented alliance with indigenous tribes and the scattered beginnings of a nationwide rubber tappers movement, Acre's union has pushed hard for an end to the destruction of their land base—and to violence against their members. (In June 1988, a landlord's hired assassins killed Ivair Higino de Almeida, a local peasant running for county council with rubber tapper support.) With help from international environmental groups, the union has called on the Brazilian government to set off large "extractive reserves" where rubber tappers can carry on their way of life in perpetuity. It has also given the tappers the strength to open a dozen community schools, a health program, and a marketing cooperative.[53]

Across the Pacific, Borneo's dense woodlands have become a foundation of Malaysia's foreign-exchange strategy, providing the country with most of the $1.6 billion worth of tropical hardwoods it exported in 1986. The forest is home to the Dayak tribes, however, who want it cut only on a sustainable basis and have battled state-supported timber companies by constructing roadblocks and appealing to European consumers to boycott Malaysian hardwoods. To date, unfortunately, they have had less success than the rubber tappers, due to greater government intransigence. The official attitude is summed up by state minister of the environment Datuk James Wong, himself a timber tycoon: "There is too much sympathy for the Dayaks. Their swidden lifestyle must be stamped out."[54]

The world's most famous community movement for forest protection, Chipko, was born in the Garhwal hills of Uttar Pradesh, India. One movement story has now virtually ascended into mythology. In March 1973, as a timber company prepared to fell trees above impoverished Gopeshwar village, local men, women, and children rushed to the woods and hugged the trees, daring the loggers to let the axes fall on their backs.[55]

Less well known is that Chipko is now far more than a rearguard action. The movement has deepened its ecological understanding and, in the words of movement-follower Vandana Shiva, "widened from embracing trees to embracing mountains and waters." In 1987, for example, activists erected a seven-month blockade at a limestone quarry that was destroying the Doon Valley ecosystem. Expanding geographically to all points of the compass, Chipko has gone beyond resource protection to ecological management, restoration, and what members call "eco-development." The women who first guarded trees from loggers now plant trees, build soil retainer walls, and prepare village forest plans.[56]

Groups organize most readily to de-

fend their resource base against the incursion of others, but they may also organize to reverse deterioration driven by forces internal to the community. As Kenya's forests shrink, for instance, thousands of women's groups, youth clubs, and harambee societies have mounted local tree planting drives. The National Council of Women of Kenya inaugurated its Greenbelt Movement in 1977, calling on women's groups across the country to turn open spaces, school grounds, and road sides into forests. Over a million trees in 1,000 greenbelts are now straining skyward, 20,000 mini-greenbelts have taken root, and upwards of 670 community tree nurseries are in place. Meanwhile, Kenya's largest women's development network, Maendeleo Ya Wanawake, with its 10,000 member groups, initiated a campaign in 1985 to construct wood-saving improved cookstoves.[57]

Chipko has gone beyond resource protection to restoration and "eco-development."

Kenya takes soil conservation as seriously as tree planting, and again women are the mainstay of the crusade. Writer Paul Harrison relates a tale representative of the achievements of Kenyan women's groups. Kimakimu hill, which towers over the town of Machakos, was so badly eroded from forest clearing and plowing that gaping chasms had opened on its face. "In 1981, the Kaluodi women's group began an ambitious series of conservation works on the hillside. By 1985 all but a handful of farms were terraced, and the whole hillside was notched with zigzagging cut-off drains to channel rainwater away from the fields."[58]

The Naam movement of Burkina Faso, which now spills over under different names into Mauritania, Senegal, Mali, Niger, and Togo, is remarkable in a number of ways. Reviving pre-colonial self-help traditions, the movement unleashes vast stores of peasant knowledge, creativity, and energy to loosen the grip of poverty and ecological deterioration in the drought-prone Sahel. (See Chapter 2.) Each year during the dry season, thousands of villages undertake projects that they choose and design with minimal assistance from outsiders. Along with five neighboring communities, for example, Somiaga built a large dam and a series of check dams to trap drinking and irrigation water and to slow soil erosion. Villagers piled caged rocks by hand to form a dam 180 meters long and 4 meters high. Meanwhile, hundreds of Naam farmers have adopted a simple technique of soil and water conservation developed by Oxfam-UK, in which stones are piled in low rows along the contour to hold back the runoff from torrential rains. While halting soil loss, these *diguetes* increase crop yields dramatically.[59]

As deterioration of the resource base pushes environmental issues to the fore of many communities' concerns, the foundations of a new international environmental movement are in place. Local and national groups are extending tentative feelers out around the world, forming effective communication channels around issues of common interest. Just in the last year, international environmental networks have been formed in Africa and Latin America, adding to that already existing in Asia. Environmentalism in Brazil has taken off in the eighties, and Sri Lanka has an environmental congress with 100 member groups. New regional, continental, and global alliances form each year, adding strands to the thickening web.[60]

REFORMING DEVELOPMENT

Despite the heartening rise of grassroots action, humanity is losing the struggle to halt ecological decline. For every peasant league that staunches the hemorrhage of topsoil from a watershed, dozens more fail. Hundreds of communities remain mired in fatalism for each one that rallies to the common cause.

Deep reforms in broader institutions are the key to unleashing a wider grassroots mobilization, because no popular effort exists in an institutional vacuum. An intricate matrix of human structures shapes the local space where grassroots groups work, a matrix that includes churches, political parties, and social clubs, as well as international development agencies and governments. Whether intentionally or not, these institutions create many of the opportunities and incentives for organized action; they also create many of the obstacles. In almost every case cited in the chapter thus far, larger institutions played an important role at different points in the process.[61]

Local groups eventually collide with forces they cannot control. Peasant associations cannot enact supportive agricultural policies or build roads to distant markets. Women's groups cannot develop and test modern contraceptive technologies or rewrite bank lending rules. Forest people cannot give themselves a seat at the table in national forest planning. Thus, perhaps the greatest irony of community action for sustainability is that communities cannot do it alone. Small may be beautiful, but it can also be insignificant.[62]

The prospects for grassroots self-help are further limited in a world economy in which vested interests are deeply entrenched and power is concentrated in a few nations. Federal budget deficits in Washington drive up interest rates worldwide, and protectionism in Europe and Japan reduces markets for many Third World exports. The combination of international debt payments and industrial-country trade barriers costs developing nations about three times what they receive in development assistance each year. Thus reforms at the international level are as important as those at the village level.[63]

The paradox of the relationship between community movements and international development institutions is that both subscribe to the same goals and both need what the other has, yet only rarely have they worked effectively together. Many community organizations have deep misgivings about what they perceive as heavy-handed interventionism on the part of multilateral and bilateral bodies such as the World Bank and U.S. Agency for International Development (AID). Development agencies, for their part, generally view community organizations as unstable amateurs, junior partners in the serious business of development.

A simple distinction untangles the issues that hog-tie foreign assistance—the distinction between aid and development. Much that passes as aid does not foster development, while much development has nothing to do with aid. Real development is the process whereby individuals and societies build the capacity to meet their own needs and improve the quality of their own lives. Physically, it means finding solutions to the basic necessities of nutritious food, clean water, adequate clothing and shelter, and access to basic health care. Socially, it means developing the institutions that can promote the public good and restrain individual excess. Individually, it means self-respect, for without personal dignity economic progress is a charade.

On a rhetorical level, international development institutions began singing the praises of community development and popular participation in the fifties, but practice has been another matter. For most governments and development agencies, "grassroots participation" means getting peasants and slum dwellers to build their own roads and schools—things they would never dream of demanding of the rich. The critical element, control over the goals and process of development, has never gone to the communities themselves. Some European agencies and many charitable donors go further toward putting participation into practice, but still, development assistance that is truly responsive to the initiatives of the poor is rare.[64]

Small may be beautiful, but it can also be insignificant.

This cautionary note notwithstanding, many development assistance institutions do seem to be in the midst of a period of re-evaluation. A track record over decades that can at best be termed disappointing has prompted them to look for more people-centered approaches. A growing fraction of bilateral assistance is already channeled through northern charities such as CARE, seen by development agencies as a cost-effective alternative to weak or corrupt government ministries.[65]

Indeed, grassroots development seems to have proved its effectiveness to such an extent that large aid donors want to jump on the bandwagon. The problem is, they want to jump on with all their weight—without first undergoing the necessary restructuring and reorientation. Within assistance agencies, administrators are rewarded for the number of dollars they move across their desks rather than their sensitive support of the local process of change. It is no surprise that they choose large, capital-intensive endeavors. Most development projects are, in this sense, "funding-led"; *development,* by contrast, is people-led.[66]

Those closest to the process of grassroots development rightfully warn that indiscriminately pumping money into community organizations and independent groups would be as bad as not supporting them at all. Overfunding can subvert local control, distort community priorities, promote capital-intensive technologies over effective local ones, and fuel jealousy between organizations that should be allies.[67]

Most development projects are "funding-led"; development, by contrast, is people-led.

The central lesson of Naam, Sarvodaya, harambee, and Chipko is that while money is necessary, it is far from the most important ingredient. What counts is organization, and the local momentum, initiative, and control it generates; although the organizing process cannot be forced from the outside, it can be nurtured and catalyzed. Funding should match and grow with a group's capacity to employ those funds effectively.

Another problem created by money-centered development programs is a paralyzing burden of paperwork. An institutionalized fear of misappropriation and graft creates what one AID employee terms an "ambience of pre-emptive cowardice." Required to account for every cent distributed and tabulate every benefit delivered, aid agencies demand reams of accounts and reports, prior approval for all decisions, and elaborate planning that extends to minutiae. A British researcher reports that the quarterly accounts a German agency required of a tiny Bengali independent group "weighed over two kilograms and

included . . . a line item and supporting vouchers for the food supplied to the dog that guards the stores."[68]

If bureaucracy is the organizational culture of aid agencies, the culture of community groups and the independent groups that support them could be called "visionary ad hoc-racy." Operating in the context of marginalized villages and slums, they confront constant change, unstable priorities, and short-lived opportunities. Working relations are founded not on contractual obligations but on mutual trust. The logical but unfortunate result of combining bureaucracy with community groups is a clash of organizational cultures that leaves both sides resentful and discontent. The creative energy and commitment of community workers is wasted filing reports and stifled by arbitrary planning periods. Aid administrators' technical training, meanwhile, is frustrated by attempting to manage such an unpredictable process.

The "project"—nearly universal in the field of aid—is another source of problems. For development agencies, a project is a discrete, defined entity: an elaborately planned and budgeted undertaking in a limited time frame with a long list of prescribed procedural steps and stages. For community groups, by contrast, development is a process that at various points may involve particular efforts such as digging wells or planting trees, but that has neither a beginning nor an end, nor a final evaluation or project document.[69]

With leadership from the independent sector, the outlines of a new assistance compact between grassroots groups and northern donors are beginning to take shape. Third World independent and grassroots groups will shoulder more and more of the responsibility for direct work, as their northern partners gradually retreat to a funding and support role. Simultaneously, northern groups will work harder to educate the public of industrial nations about the reality of life in the Third World and to pressure industrial-country governments to pursue policies that further the prospects of the poor majority, not only in assistance but more significantly in international debt, finance, trade, and military policy. Their most important role will be as a voice for the world's poor in the nations of the world's wealthy.[70]

As this transition evolves, action is also called for to overcome "project-itis." Specifically, funding should be process-oriented, given to an organization on the basis of its past record and an agreement on goals and principles of operation. Initial funding would be small—sometimes less than $10,000—and would increase steadily as the local group developed a capacity to use larger sums. The relationship would involve more than funding, however, moving toward a long-term goal of equal partnership through information sharing, training, and building of an international network.[71]

The U.S.-funded Inter-American Foundation, which grants sums generally under $100,000 to grassroots groups and independent development organizations through a highly qualified field staff, is protected by institutional autonomy from foreign policy priorities. In 1980, Congress created a parallel body called the African Development Foundation, which is now getting off the ground after surviving several attempts at political sabotage from the Reagan administration. Oxfam-UK and its namesakes in Belgium, Canada, and the United States have been committed to promoting local initiatives for perhaps longer than any other major charitable donor. Ashoka, an American foundation, has seen the importance of process funding. It provides no-strings-attached grants to rising community organizers

and creative advocates in the world's most populous developing nations.[72]

If aid is to support development, institutions need nothing less than to be turned on their heads; they must learn to take their lead from the village water committees, health workers, and tree planting brigades. For particular institutions this will mean different things. Bilateral agencies should be isolated from the yearly shifts of foreign policy, as are the Inter-American Foundation and the Swedish International Development Authority. In addition to drastically cutting paperwork, they can progressively decentralize operations so that their staff is on the ground with the development process itself.[73]

Multilateral development banks, which increasingly lend to governments not for projects but to implement certain policies, such as "structural adjustment" austerity measures, could use that same leverage on governments to create an institutional environment supportive of grassroots action—a critical condition for local success. They can also open their planning process and policy dialogue to grassroots participation. Designing major development programs and policies without consulting local people is like prescribing medicine without asking what hurts.[74]

Northern charities can accelerate their progress along the spectrum from giving out groceries to supporting the efforts of the poor to help themselves. Equally important, they can educate policymakers and the public in industrial nations about the true conditions and priorities of the poor. Charities can also pioneer international forms of participation in development assistance policy, by putting grassroots representatives on their boards of directors, and by refining flexible funding relations.

Deep down, working with the grassroots is a philosophical attitude, an allegiance. "Grassroots development is a way of traveling, more than a goal," writes Pierre Pradervand, a French collaborator with Naam. "It means being ready to travel in a mammie wagon *with* people—with all the delays, punctures, breakdowns, and sweat that implies—rather than driving along in one's air-conditioned Range Rover with two spare wheels, cool Coke in the icebox, and a fixed timetable."[75]

FROM THE BOTTOM AND THE TOP

Reforming the world's development assistance agencies, official and unofficial, will be a monumental task. But the larger challenge in reversing global deterioration will be to forge an alliance between local groups and national governments. Only governments have the resources and authority to create the conditions for full-scale grassroots mobilization—and nothing less will now suffice if sustainability is to be achieved. As grassroots development theorist Sheldon Annis writes: "It may well be that wildflowers grow by themselves. But grassroots organizations do not. They are cultivated, in large measure, by just policies and competent government agencies that do their job."[76]

In the rare cases where a national-local alliance has been forged, extraordinary gains have followed. South Korea and China have used village-level organizations to plant enormous expanses of trees, implement national population policies, and boost agricultural production. Zimbabwe has trained over 500 community-selected family planners to improve maternal and child health and control population growth. In the year after the 1979 Nicaraguan revolution, a massive literacy campaign sent 90,000

volunteers into the countryside; in one year, they raised literacy from 50 to 87 percent. In 1984, Burkina Faso immunized three quarters of its children against measles, meningitis, and yellow fever in the space of three months. Kenya is waging war on soil erosion, as thousands of women's groups terrace mountainsides with crude shovels and hoes.[77]

During World War II, millions of Soviet, American, Asian, and European civilians recycled materials, conserved energy, and planted victory gardens to boost food production. Today, the threat to global security from ecological degradation merits a similar mobilization. (See Chapter 8.) Although unprecedented in scope, the actions necessary are far from mysterious; in fact, millions have been engaged in them for years. What is required is an enormous number of simple acts: organizing local groups, teaching literacy and preventive health care, spreading family planning, and planting trees.

Many things can be accomplished, of course, short of a wholesale government-grassroots mobilization. No state is monolithic: even in Marcos's Philippines, the National Irrigation Administration transformed itself into a people-centered institution, cooperating with peasant associations. Such changes are already promoted by grassroots groups and could be supported by multilateral institutions like the International Monetary Fund, which currently uses its leverage to impose austerity plans on Third World governments.[78]

In many cases, the mobilization required is not one of performing a certain task but of enacting a policy. Grassroots energy spent collecting bottles for recycling, for example, might be better spent campaigning for citywide recycling collection. Because western industrial countries have such disproportionate power in the international economic system, their citizens have a special responsibility in applying pressure on lawmakers to establish farsighted policies on international debt and trade. They can also use the power of their pocketbooks to support socially conscious and environmentally sustainable enterprises.

Full-scale grassroots-government partnership can only come about when a motivated and organized populace joins forces with high-caliber leadership, a prospect that is unlikely in many countries without political change. Unrepresentative elites rule many nations and all too often they crush popular movements rather than yield their prerogatives; elsewhere, powerful interests vehemently defend the status quo. In the end, self-help will clash with these forces. Like all development, self-help merges into politics: it is the struggle to control the future. Particularly where governments are nondemocratic, that struggle holds the potential to erupt in conflict, confrontation, and violence.

In the final analysis, the most lasting contribution of community groups may not be the direct benefits they provide their members but the fundamental changes they bring to the world's political landscape. Self-help organizations formed in Philippine slums in the seventies, for example, played an important role in the "people's power" revolution that toppled the Marcos dictatorship in 1986.[79]

The time has come—indeed it may be slipping away—for grassroots mobilization worldwide to put our civilization on a sustainable base. Until governments and international institutions join the struggle, it cannot succeed, but in the meantime hope lies with individual citizens. Our most gifted, young and old, have a critical role to play in the communities where they live. To be seeds of change, these men and women will need a clear personal vision and deep determination mixed with patience, humility, pragmatism, and insight.

They will join a grassroots campaign already being waged in the villages and shantytowns of the Third World: In the war-ravaged south of Zimbabwe, villagers gather at dusk to plan the wells and ditches they will dig to combat drought. In a Brazilian *favela* called People of God, two young doctors work with a team of neighborhood women to teach preventive health care. In a remote Bolivian jungle, a band of Indians demands an end to clear-cutting by timber exporters in favor of sustainable forestry by local people.[80]

Whether these heartening beginnings become a global ground swell depends only on how many more individuals commit their creativity and energy to the challenge. One truth becomes clearer with each passing year: we humans are the only force in the world powerful enough to end global poverty and environmental degradation. The inescapable lesson for each of us is best distilled in the words of Angeles Serrano, a grandmother and community activist in Manila's Leveriza slum—"Act, act, act. You can't just watch."[81]

10

Outlining a Global Action Plan

Lester R. Brown, Christopher Flavin,
and Sandra Postel

Many societies have been severely tested over the several thousand years since civilization began. Some successfully met the challenges confronting them and thrived; others did not. But the world as a whole has never been so challenged as it is today. The questions humanity now faces are profound ones: Can we protect this and future generations from harmful doses of ultraviolet radiation? Can we avoid the biological impoverishment of the earth projected for the next two decades? Can we head off runaway climate change? Can we bring population and food supplies into balance so that famine does not persistently stalk the land?

An affirmative answer to these questions depends on restoring and preserving the conditions that make the earth habitable, a place capable of supporting a diversity of life and modern civiliza-

tion. Human activities have pushed the planet's natural support systems dangerously out of kilter. Continuing on a business-as-usual path thus virtually assures severe economic disruption, social instability, and human suffering.

In these last few years of the twentieth century, difficult questions are emerging of social equity, national sovereignty, and individual rights and responsibilities. A person may be able to afford a large, energy-consumptive automobile, but can the planet afford it? Indeed, how many carbon-emitting automobiles can the atmosphere tolerate without the planet's habitability being threatened? Similarly, a couple may desire and be able to support several children, but can the planet afford several children per family?

Issues of equity also span the generations. Does our generation have the right to extinguish plant and animal species that have evolved over millions of years? Do we not have an obligation to preserve our biological heritage for future generations?

Like it or not, we find ourselves in a world where we are responsible for each other's well-being. Inefficient use of fossil fuels in the Soviet Union and the United States contributes to global warming and thus to the eventual inundation of rich cropland in the Nile River delta of Egypt. Uncontrolled air pollution by any country in central Europe threatens forests throughout the region. The use of chlorofluorocarbons anywhere puts the ozone layer at risk everywhere.

In the end, it is we as individuals who are being tested.

Never have national governments and international institutions faced problems more difficult than those now before them. Our agenda for action focuses on four areas: developing energy strategies that have climate protection as their cornerstone; expanding the earth's forest cover so as to meet basic economic and environmental needs in the Third World and to slow global warming; redoubling efforts to meet food needs in light of an ominous trend of declining per capita grain production; and braking the tremendous momentum of population growth that already is undermining living standards in large parts of the world.

Obviously, a comprehensive global action plan would include many other issues—infant mortality, inequitable wealth distribution, and industrial pollution, to name a few. But failure to meet the challenges outlined in this chapter will make dealing with other pressing problems virtually impossible. While reducing Third World debt and demilitarizing the global economy are not addressed in this agenda, they are prerequisites for successful implementation of the specific measures we are suggesting.

The capacity of national leaders and of international institutions will be severely tested in the effort to put the world on a firm ecological and economic footing. Yet in the end, it is we as individuals who are being tested. Our values collectively shape social priorities—what policies are formulated, how resources are used, and when change begins to occur.

A CLIMATE-SENSITIVE ENERGY STRATEGY

There can be little doubt that energy production is now changing the earth's climate—and with it many of the natural systems on which humanity depends. (See Chapter 1.) Food production, water supplies, forest products industries, and fisheries will all be at risk if global warming continues to accelerate during the next several decades. The huge quantities of oil, coal, and natural gas that fueled the modern age may well lead to its decline.

There are no quick fixes to this problem. Avoiding destructive climate change will require a fundamental reordering of national energy priorities within the next decade. Carbon dioxide (CO_2) accounts for about half of the global warming now occurring. Producing less CO_2 requires using less fossil fuels, which means that other energy sources must be found to run the global economy.

What would a serious effort at slowing climate change look like? There are essentially three ways to displace fossil fuels: improving energy efficiency, thereby accomplishing the same tasks using less oil and coal; developing renewable sources of energy; and expanding the use of nuclear power. Our conclusion is that the simultaneous pursuit of renewables and efficiency—and the abandonment of the nuclear power "option"—is the only safe and cost-effective way to slow global warming. Meanwhile, natural gas has an important role to play as a transition fuel since it produces less carbon per unit of energy than do the other fossil fuels.

The problem with nuclear power is that over the past 40 years it has absorbed the preponderance of government energy investments and diverted attention from other attractive options. Nuclear power does provide about 15 percent of the world's electricity, and could in theory be used to replace coal-fired power plants and reduce carbon emissions. But this is not a practical response. Since its troubled start, nuclear power has been a problem-ridden technology; unlike renewable energy, its problems are growing. It has become increasingly expensive and accident-prone in the past decade. And the critical problem of disposing of radioactive wastes has yet to be solved.[1]

To replace *all* coal-fired power plants with nuclear ones by 2025 would require building a minimum of one plant every two and a half days for 38 years. The world would have 18 times as many nuclear plants as it does today at a minimum cost of $144 billion annually, and carbon emissions would still be higher than they are now. Nuclear power could of course be pursued as one of a long list of options, but for this it is poorly suited. Even on a limited scale, this energy source requires vast financial resources and technical skills, curtailing the development of other options. As construction, operating, and decommissioning costs have grown, nuclear power has

become a prohibitively expensive way of providing electricity or displacing carbon emissions. Throughout most of North America, Western Europe, and even the Soviet Union, people are rejecting the expansion of nuclear power. Unless the technology is completely revamped and there is a sea change in public attitudes, both of which are still remote, that scale of expansion is impossible.[2]

Improved energy efficiency can have a much larger and more immediate impact on carbon emissions and global warming. For example, the efficiency of U.S. buildings, industry, and transportation improved 26 percent between 1973 and 1987; this kept carbon emissions at 1.2 billion tons per year instead of reaching 1.6 billion tons annually. An additional output of 300 million tons of carbon emissions was avoided by efficiency improvements in other countries. Similar gains in efficiency are possible in the future using already available technologies.[3]

No other approach offers as cost-effective an opportunity for limiting carbon emissions as energy efficiency does.

Shifting to more fuel-efficient transportation can sharply reduce carbon emissions. The world's nearly 400 million cars currently spew 547 million tons of carbon into the atmosphere each year, 10 percent of the total from fossil fuels. Projections based on recent trends would have these emissions nearly doubling by 2010. However, if a combination of improved mass transit, greater use of bicycles for short trips, and a carbon tax kept the world fleet to 500 million cars by the year 2010, and if these vehicles averaged 50 miles to the gallon rather than the current 20, automobile carbon emissions would fall to 274 million tons, half of what they are today. (Prototype cars have already been developed that get over 70 miles per gallon.)[4]

Carbon emissions can also be lowered by improving the efficiency of electricity-using devices. Currently, 64 percent of the world's electricity is produced using fossil fuels (chiefly coal), accounting for 27 percent of global carbon emissions from fossil fuels (1.5 billion tons annually). Electricity is used in many different ways, all of which can become far more efficient. Based on current technologies, for example, electric motors can be made at least 40 percent more efficient than they are today, and refrigerators 75 percent.[5]

More-efficient lighting systems have a particularly large potential. Worldwide, lighting accounts for about 17 percent of electricity use or 250 million tons of annual carbon emissions. These emissions continue to grow rapidly as electric lighting is used more widely in developing countries. If the world were to double the efficiency of these systems by the year 2010, it could cut a projected 450 million tons of carbon emissions from lighting in half, to 225 million tons. For common household use, compact fluorescent bulbs using 18 watts of electricity can already provide the same illumination as incandescent bulbs that use 75 watts. Improved bulbs and ballasts can cut the electricity use of commercial buildings' lighting by 75 percent using existing technology.[6]

Cogeneration (the combined production of heat and power) also has enormous potential to improve the efficiency with which electricity is generated. This technology, already extensively used in some countries, allows the inevitable waste heat from electricity generation to be used directly by buildings or industry or for further electricity generation in a combined cycle system.[7]

Switching from a conventional 1,000-megawatt coal-fired power station to a combined cycle system allows a 30-percent improvement in efficiency and a commensurate cut in carbon emissions of 568,000 tons per year. However, switching to a natural-gas-fired, steam-injected turbine permits a 70-percent cut in carbon emissions. For the world as a whole, improving the average efficiency of today's 1 million megawatts of coal-fired capacity by 30 percent could cut carbon emissions by 312 million tons.[8]

About 5.5 billion tons of carbon were emitted through fossil fuel use in 1988; this will go as high as 10 billion tons in 2010 if it grows at just 3 percent annually. Overall, energy efficiency improvements worldwide between 1990 and 2010 could make a 3-billion-ton difference in the annual amount being released to the atmosphere. A study by Irving Mintzer of the World Resources Institute suggests that a continuing reduction in emissions of this magnitude could make a difference of 0.5–1.5 degrees Celsius in the global average temperature by 2075. There is simply no other approach that offers as cost-effective an opportunity for limiting carbon emissions as energy efficiency does.[9]

Renewable sources of energy do not have nearly as large a potential to displace fossil fuels in the years immediately ahead as energy efficiency improvements do. However, that potential will grow as the technologies are improved. The outlines of a successful strategy already exist. Solar, hydro, wind, and geothermal power have been pursued with notable successes by governments and private companies since the mid-seventies. Across a broad spectrum of technologies, costs have fallen steadily and performance has improved. If renewable sources are to supply a large share of the world's energy by mid-century, then they must be vigorously developed today.[10]

Hydropower supplies about 21 percent of the electricity produced worldwide, displacing 539 million tons of carbon that would otherwise be emitted each year. Solar collectors are a major source of hot water in Israel, wind power has taken hold in California, and geothermal energy is a major electricity source in the Philippines.[11]

Solar photovoltaic cells, the cost of which has fallen 90 percent in the past decade, are already being widely used on remote communications systems and portable electronic devices. Photovoltaics are already an economical electricity source for Third World villages, and as costs fall further in the next decade they will become economical for large power grids everywhere. The world now has approximately 2,000 megawatts of wind power in place, which produces about 2 billion kilowatt-hours of electricity, displacing 540,000 tons of carbon annually. If wind power and photovoltaic electricity development were accelerated, reaching 150,000 megawatts in the year 2010, they could displace 71 million tons of carbon emissions a year.[12]

If policymakers do not grasp the link between energy efficiency, renewable energy, and global warming, climate stabilization will not be possible. Although governments have supported these technologies for over a decade, their commitment has been inconstant. This is particularly true in the United States, where research and development budgets for renewables and efficiency soared in the late seventies and then were each cut by four fifths between 1981 and 1988. The U.S. Department of Transportation's recent decision to lower fuel economy standards for automobiles and light trucks will exacerbate global warming, as will the choice of Chinese officials to emphasize extensive coal mining rather than efficiency.[13]

A serious and lasting government commitment to the development and use of energy-efficient and renewable technologies is a prerequisite to stabilizing world climate. So too are individual decisions about the kind of refrigerator to buy, the amount of home insulation to install, and how much to drive a car.

For policymakers, the essential challenge today is to improve energy efficiency in a period of low energy prices. The costs of climate change and other environmental effects of fossil fuels can be reflected in prices that consumers pay by raising taxes on gasoline and other carbon-based fuels. The United States, for example, could raise $100 billion annually by hiking its gasoline taxes by $1 per gallon to the European average tax of about $1.50 per gallon. In addition, governments could levy a "carbon tax" on fossil fuels, with the tax corresponding to the amount of carbon in each fuel. This would hit coal appropriately hard, since it produces more carbon per unit of energy used than do either oil or natural gas. Energy prices would rise and efficiency would improve. Renewable energy sources would become more competitive.[14]

Ideally, such taxes should be agreed on globally so that the additional costs would not affect the international competitiveness of national economies. The revenues could be used in part to offset other taxes and in part to develop permanent and stable funding for energy efficiency and renewable energy programs. If industrial-country governments devoted 10 percent of the revenues of such a tax to energy efficiency, renewable energy development, and reforestation in the Third World, it would encourage a broad-based assault on the problem of climate change.

Large-scale investments in energy-efficient buildings can also help stabilize climate. Governments can provide building owners with technical assistance and utility companies can invest in improved building efficiency rather than new plants. These investments can be essentially self-financing via a revolving fund since they pay for themselves in lowered fuel bills.[15]

Efficiency standards for automobiles, appliances, and other energy-using devices are another proven way to reduce fossil fuel use. U.S. appliance efficiency standards already enacted will cumulatively displace over 300 million tons of carbon emissions by the year 2000. The broad international market for technologies and the common interest in climate stabilization argue for international efficiency standards for automobiles, trucks, lighting systems, appliances, and electric motors. For example, reaching a minimum new-car fuel efficiency of 50 miles per gallon by the year 2000 and 60 miles per gallon by 2010 would be an important step toward restoring climate stability.[16]

To slow global warming significantly, hundreds of billions of dollars of investments in improved energy efficiency will ultimately be required. Although it might seem that in a debt-swamped world such levels are impossible, many energy efficiency options are inherently cost-effective. Companies and individuals save money via reduced fuel bills. Ultimately, the more energy-efficient economies tend to be more competitive in world markets. Government's role is to set the framework that allows these kinds of cost-effective investments to proliferate.

In other areas, government has a more direct role to play. It would, for example, make sense for the international community to devise a program to use photovoltaics rather than coal to electrify all Third World villages by 2010. The United Nations and the World Bank could thereby spur sustainable development and help slow global warming.

The challenge of raising sufficient funds to invest in efficiency in the Third

World is particularly severe. Carbon emissions there are growing at annual rates as high as 5 percent, driven by rapid population growth and expanding economies. China, for example, has plans to more than double its use of coal by sometime after the turn of the century, an "achievement" that could well push it past the United States and the Soviet Union as the world's number one carbon emitter. Already deeply in debt, most developing countries are chronically short of capital. One answer is to redirect a portion of the enormous flow of international lending currently devoted to building power plants and electric lines. The World Bank has just begun to consider major loans for improved efficiency.[17]

Global warming has already opened a new chapter in the debates over energy policy in many national capitals. Old battle lines, first established when high oil prices commanded attention, have in many cases been redrawn. Many politicians still seem to be hoping for technical fixes that will allow them to avoid making hard choices. This resistance will have to be overcome if effective energy policy is to be forged out of the global warming threat.

Global warming has opened a new chapter in the debates over energy policy in many national capitals.

Unfortunately, the challenge of making global warming a central concern of national energy planners is far from being realized. Energy policymaking is often driven by self-interested industries and unions, and some, such as the oil and coal lobbies, push for policies that accelerate global warming. Key legislative committees are dominated by provinces or states that produce fossil fuels;

many of the laws and tax breaks that emerge are intended to propel their growth. In Eastern Europe, ossified energy ministries continue to emphasize meeting their five-year plans, regardless of the ecological costs.

The tendency is simply to add global warming to a long list of considerations that go into making energy policy. This is not enough. If energy policymaking continues to be the domain of short-term thinking and narrow political considerations, there can be little hope. If the climate is to be stabilized, it must become the cornerstone of national energy policies.

Encouragingly, three global warming bills were introduced in the U.S. Congress in 1988, and two included "least-cost" energy plans designed to ensure that the most cost-effective means to displace carbon emissions (chiefly energy efficiency) are pursued first. Government programs to improve the efficiency of automobiles, to step up research on efficient technologies, and to accelerate the development of renewable energy technologies are good first steps.[18]

To redirect world energy trends in the absence of direct market pressures is an unprecedented challenge. Politicians will have to rise above the parochial interests that often motivate them, and companies and individuals will have to focus on the real bottom line, which shows that improved efficiency is both cost-effective and can slow global warming. Action will be facilitated if governments adopt short- and long-term carbon reduction goals along the lines of the 20-percent reduction by 2005 suggested at the 1988 Toronto climate conference. Perhaps more productive would be energy efficiency targets either by sector or for the economy as a whole. In any case, there is a clear need both for early national initiatives and eventual international agreements to reduce carbon emissions from fossil fuels.[19]

A New Future for Forests

The grim state of much of the world's forests and the consequences of their destruction came to light in numerous, unsettling ways in 1988. Hills stripped of trees in the Himalayan watershed contributed to the worst flooding on record in Bangladesh. New satellite data showed that 8 million hectares of Brazilian rain forest were burned in 1987 alone, which means that the widely cited figure of 11.3 million hectares for annual forest clearing in all of the tropics is probably at least 50 percent too low. In industrial countries, forests continued to deteriorate under the stresses of air pollution and acid rain.[20]

Evidence that global warming has begun underscores the importance of forests worldwide. The earth's vegetation and soils store roughly triple the amount of carbon held in the atmosphere. When cleared or burned, forests release much of their carbon, adding to carbon dioxide buildup and hastening global warming. Though estimates are uncertain, deforestation probably released a fifth to half as much carbon in 1988 as the burning of fossil fuels did.[21]

Only vigorous efforts to protect the remaining forests and to plant billions more trees each year can reverse these worrisome trends. Yet many tropical countries—plagued by debt, weak economies, and burgeoning populations—see few alternatives to clearing forests as ways to earn quick foreign exchange, to spur regional development, or to open up new areas for settlement. They continue to promote wasteful and destructive logging and the clearing of primary forest for cropping and grazing, even though such activities are not economically or ecologically sustainable. Much forest has been cleared in Brazil, for example, because of government subsidies that encourage cattle ranching, even though depletion of the pasture-land's fertility causes the ventures to be abandoned in a matter of years.[22]

Developing alternatives is thus crucial to a broad-based strategy of expanding global forest cover. One approach is the exchange of some debt relief for more conservation-oriented resource policies. Tropical countries would benefit economically from the easing of their debt burdens as well as from the more sustainable use of their resources. Commercial banks and industrial-country governments, which are beginning to realize that some debt will never be repaid, have little to lose from the cancellation of "bad debt" from their books. Thus, the time could be ripe for such a linkage. Among the terms of these debt-relief packages would be the elimination of policies that promote destructive logging and the clearing of forests for unsustainable uses.[23]

Another important step is for development institutions, especially the World Bank, to exercise their leverage in promoting sounder strategies. The Bank needs not only to stop funding projects that promote senseless forest destruction, but to more actively support sustainable agriculture and forestry efforts that can relieve pressures on primary forests. The current pace of deforestation warrants more drastic action than has yet been considered—including, perhaps, making certain development aid contingent on the elimination of policies and programs leading to forest destruction. Pressure from aid institutions seems to have played a role, for example, in Brazilian President José Sarney's October 1988 decision to temporarily suspend government incentives that have promoted forest clearing.[24]

Stepped-up support for the International Tropical Timber Organization (ITTO) could also help slow deforestation. The agreement setting up the ITTO, ratified in 1985, calls for national policies that "encourage sustainable utilization and conservation of tropical forests and their genetic resources." At the group's meeting in Rio de Janeiro in June 1988, funding was approved for a major project to study the feasibility of sustainable forest management in the Brazilian state of Acre. By demonstrating economic alternatives to wasteful logging and forest conversion practices, such projects can help pave the way for forest protection.[25]

Reforesting 130 million hectares would cut the release of carbon from all human activities by 8 to 11 percent.

A major global reforestation effort is the other key component of a strategy to preserve and expand the world's forest cover. In 1988 we estimated that trees need to be planted on the equivalent of 130 million hectares—an area slightly larger than Ethiopia—in order to meet growing demands for fuelwood and industrial wood products and to stabilize soil and water resources in the Third World. Accomplishing this goal over the next 15 years would require planting some 15 billion trees annually.[26]

Besides helping meet basic economic and environmental needs, such an unprecedented reforestation effort is critical to a global strategy of slowing the pace of climate change. As trees grow, they remove carbon dioxide from the atmosphere through photosynthesis, thereby slowing the CO_2 buildup. Successfully reforesting 130 million hectares would reduce net carbon emissions from tropical forests by some 660 million tons annually until the trees reach maturity (after subtracting 10 million hectares of trees that would be burned quickly for fuel), cutting the current release of carbon from all human activities by 8 to 11 percent.[27]

Although forest cover in much of the industrial world is fairly stable, the urgency of climate change warrants greater efforts to capture more carbon by increasing forest productivity and planting more trees there as well. Curbing acid rain and air pollutants is crucial to safeguarding forest health and assuring that trees can obtain their maximum carbon-fixing potential. Beyond that, governments can design tree-planting initiatives to turn their national landscapes—urban and rural—into greater sinks for atmospheric carbon.

If industrial countries collectively planted trees on an additional 40 million hectares—an area roughly the size of Japan, or two-and-a-half times the area slated to be planted in grass or trees between 1986 and 1990 under the U.S. Conservation Reserve Program—they would remove some 200 million tons of carbon from the atmosphere annually while the trees were growing. That would offset the carbon released annually by 211 average-sized coal-burning power plants.[28]

Once the newly planted stands matured, carbon released by the decomposition of dead trees over time would balance carbon fixed by replacement growth. At this point, mature trees could be harvested on a sustainable yield basis to replace coal in electrical generation. Using half that harvest to generate electricity, for example, could reduce coal-burning by some 100 million tons annually. In contrast to energy produced from fossil fuels, a wood-energy system managed in this way helps fix carbon in the short term and makes a continuous contribution to stabilizing the earth's climate.

Collectively, a global strategy of halving tropical deforestation and of planting the equivalent of 130 million hec-

tares of trees in developing countries and 40 million hectares in industrial ones could reduce worldwide carbon emissions from all human activities by about a fourth of current levels. (See Table 10–1.) This would slow the pace of warming for several decades, buying precious time to adapt and respond to climate change in other ways. And this expansion of forest cover is vital for other reasons in any case—including preserving biological diversity, meeting fuelwood needs, and rehabilitating degraded environments. (See Chapter 2.)[29]

In Kenya, the Greenbelt Movement has mobilized farmers and school-children in planting more than 2 million trees.

Successfully reforesting such large areas will require sustained and secure sources of funding. One possibility is for governments to levy a reforestation tax on some forest- or energy-related activity they desire to discourage. Some tropical countries, for example, might tax timber harvested for export by private contractors, generating funds for reforestation while simultaneously discouraging damaging "timber booms" of the sort that have ravaged forests in Côte d'Ivoire, Ghana, the Philippines, and elsewhere.

Industrial-country governments might levy the tax on gasoline consumption, fossil-fuel generated electricity, or some other carbon-emitting activity and, as suggested earlier in this chapter, use part of the revenues to support reforestation either domestically or abroad. In the United States, such an initiative could be linked with the Conservation Reserve Program, under which highly erodible land is being removed from

Table 10-1. Projected Net Reductions in Carbon Emissions from Expanded Forest Protection and Reforestation Efforts

Target	Net Carbon Emission Reductions	Share of Total Carbon Emissions from Fossil Fuels and Deforestation[1]
	(million tons)	(percent)
Halving tropical deforestation rates	830[2]	12
Planting equivalent of 130 million hectares of trees in Third World	660[3]	9
Planting equivalent of 40 million hectares of trees in industrial countries	200[4]	3
Total	1,690	24

[1]Total estimated at 7.1 billion tons per year, 5.5 billion from fossil fuels and 1.6 billion from deforestation. [2]Midpoint of estimated range. [3]Assumes average annual carbon-fixing rate of 5.5 tons per hectare, and that 10 million hectares would yield no carbon-fixing benefits because trees would be burned quickly for fuel. [4]Assumes average annual carbon-fixing rate of 5 tons per hectare.
SOURCES: Worldwatch Institute, based on R.A. Houghton et al., "The Flux of Carbon from Terrestrial Ecosystems to the Atmosphere in 1980 Due to Changes in Land Use: Geographic Distribution of the Global Flux," *Tellus,* February/April 1987; Sandra Postel and Lori Heise, *Reforesting the Earth,* Worldwatch Paper 83 (Washington, D.C.: Worldwatch Institute, April 1988); Sandra Brown et al., "Biomass of Tropical Tree Plantations and its Implications for the Global Carbon Budget," *Canadian Journal of Forest Research,* Vol. 16, No. 2, 1986.

crop production under 10-year contracts and planted in trees or grass. Daniel Dudek of the Environmental Defense Fund has suggested such a linkage for offsetting future carbon emissions from planned fossil fuel power plants. He estimates that a decade's worth of new emissions could be balanced by planting one quarter of the Conservation Reserve in trees. The utilities building the power plants would foot the bill, possibly with some assistance from the government through the reserve program.[30]

Orchestrating large-scale reforestation worldwide presents major challenges. It will require the support and energy of national leaders, development agencies, corporations, nongovernmental organizations, community groups, and—most importantly—individual citizens.

Examples of the diverse kinds of actions needed already exist. In Kenya, the Greenbelt Movement, sponsored by the National Council of Women, has mobilized more than 15,000 farmers and a half-million schoolchildren in planting more than 2 million trees. Virginia-based Applied Energy Services, an independent U.S. power company, is voluntarily helping fund a reforestation project in Guatemala with the explicit intent of offsetting the carbon emissions resulting from a new cogeneration power plant to be built in Connecticut. And the American Forestry Association has proposed an urban reforestation program with a target of planting some 100 million trees in cities and suburbs around the country by 1992.[31]

Finally, a strategy aimed at expanding the earth's forest cover and stabilizing climate needs as a foundation much better data on the status of forests than now exist. While worldwide carbon emissions from fossil fuels can be plotted with a good degree of confidence each year, those from deforestation cannot. Huge uncertainties remain about how fast tropical forests are being cleared, how much regrowth is taking place on lands formerly cleared, and how much biomass (and therefore carbon) is contained in forested areas. Increased and sustained funding to resolve these issues is crucial. A promising step forward is the undertaking of a new forest assessment using remote sensing technologies by scientists from the National Aeronautics and Space Adminstration's Goddard Institute for Space Studies, the Woods Hole Research Center in Massachusetts, the U.N. Environment Programme's Global Environmental Monitoring System, and the U.N. Food and Agriculture Organization (FAO). The first stage, expected to have begun in late 1988, will pinpoint deforestation "hot spots"—areas of rapid forest clearing, such as those documented in parts of the Brazilian Amazon—which will help focus forest protection efforts.[32]

National governments, with the help of international development organizations, also need to engage in more long-term forest planning. Tropical forests rarely are managed as the multipurpose, renewable resources they are, even though such management is the key to maximizing their benefits to society over the long term. With the late 1985 launch of the Tropical Forestry Action Plan, jointly sponsored by FAO, the U.N. Development Programme, the World Resources Institute, and the World Bank, a framework was established for improved planning and management, and for stepped-up forest protection and tree planting efforts. The action plan's ultimate impact, however, will depend on individual governments making the hard choices to restructure forest policies and invest in reforestation.

MEETING FUTURE FOOD NEEDS

In many ways, the nineties will be unlike any decade that the world's farmers have ever faced. There will be little opportunity for expanding cultivated area; irrigated area, while growing slowly worldwide, is declining in some key countries. For the world's more advanced farmers, there are few new technologies to draw upon. In many countries, returns on the use of additional fertilizer—which has been the driving force behind the worldwide expansion of food output over the past four decades—are diminishing. And, finally, the prospect of global warming now hangs over the future of agriculture.[33]

On the demand side, the annual increment in world population is projected to climb to record highs in the years immediately ahead. The 86 million added in 1988 are expected to joined by at least 90 million annually during the early nineties. And most of the added millions will live in countries where nutrition is already inadequate and, in many cases, deteriorating.[34]

Meeting future food needs is a far more complex undertaking today than it was 20 years ago. During the sixties, outlining a strategy for expanding food output was relatively simple in most countries. The key was assuring farmers a price for their harvest that would make investments in fertilizer, irrigation, and improved varieties profitable. In many developing countries this required reversing food price policies that had traditionally catered to urban interests, substituting food price supports for food price ceilings. When governments adopted these price support policies and ensured that yield-raising inputs were available, farmers could often double or triple the productivity of their land.

Restoring the rapid growth in world

food output that existed from 1950 to 1984 will not be easy. In some countries and regions, massive gains in output are still possible. In others, the potential for large jumps in the near future is limited. Achieving a satisfactory balance between food and people is becoming more difficult and may not be possible without raising the efficiency of feedgrain use and dramatically lowering birth rates in countries where population is still growing rapidly.

Among the areas where massive increases in output are unlikely, because yields are already high and response to the use of additional fertilizer is low, are Japan, China, Western Europe, and North America. Some regions, such as the semiarid West African Sahel, have no technologies available that will sharply boost output.[35]

India, Argentina, Brazil, and the Soviet Union, on the other hand, all have a large potential to raise yields. In India, where grain yield per hectare is less than half that in China, a combination of incentive prices, investment in irrigation, and the use of more fertilizer should greatly boost output in the years ahead. At present, India's farmers use less than half as much fertilizer per hectare as do their Chinese and U.S. counterparts.[36]

Policy adjustments could also spur output in Argentina, which still taxes food exports, thus discouraging farmers by reducing the prices they receive to levels well below those of the world market.[37]

Brazil, too, has a large unrealized potential, one that may reside as much in land reform as in expanding the cultivated area. In few countries is landownership as concentrated as in Brazil, where 70 percent of rural households are essentially landless. World Bank studies in several countries demonstrate that farmers with small holdings produce more per hectare than those with large holdings. In part this is because

small farmers, using family labor, can boost output by continuing to use more labor per hectare even though the value of the resultant additional output is less than the prevailing wage. Large landowners who rely on hired labor cannot afford to do this.[38]

In the Soviet Union, reforms that strengthen the link between effort and reward for those working the land could substantially increase the productivity of agriculture. A plan to lease land to individual farmers for up to 50 years, announced in Moscow in August 1988, could measurably lift farm output, perhaps reducing the need to import grain.[39]

For some countries, many of which are in Africa, local rainfall is too low and irrigation water too scarce to permit the extensive use of fertilizer. Fortunately, alternatives exist for many of these countries, which may never develop a fossil-fuel-based agriculture. While these will not lead to the dramatic gains in yield of the Green Revolution technologies, they can boost production markedly among subsistence farmers, where the need is greatest. In many tropical and subtropical regions, agroforestry (the incorporation of trees and field crops into a single farming system) is proving to be highly productive. (See Chapter 2.) The trees can provide food, forage, fuel, organic matter in the form of leaf drop, and, if they are nitrogen-fixing, nitrogen for the crops grown in the immediate vicinity.[40]

One type of agroforestry involves a technique known as alley cropping, in which strips of fast-growing leguminous trees are alternated with rows of food crops, making it possible to sustainably cultivate some soils that otherwise would quickly deteriorate once plowed. The leguminous trees provide nitrogen and, through their leaf drop, organic material to nourish the soil; the alternate strips also control soil erosion.[41]

Where labor is abundant relative to

land, labor-intensive agricultural techniques such as multiple cropping (growing more than one crop per year) and intercropping (simultaneously planting more than one crop on a piece of land) can make a big difference. So can the composting of organic wastes, including straw, livestock manure, and leaves. In densely populated parts of Africa and Asia, the stall feeding of livestock, also labor-intensive, both helps control land degradation from random grazing and concentrates livestock manure, making composting easier.[42]

As population pressures build, land can be farmed more intensively using such techniques as biointensive gardening. This has figured prominently in efforts to expand production of vegetables to supplement cereals and tubers on the Philippine island of Negros. The technique, involving hand-tillage of the seedbed to one foot or more in depth, relies on local materials to improve and maintain soil fertility. Among the local inputs used in these highly productive plots are compost manure, wood ash, bonemeal, leucaena leaves (from a fast-growing nitrogen-fixing tree), and crushed eggshells. Like the high-yielding rices that originated in the Philippines, this technology has a potentially broad application in other countries.[43]

With cropland becoming scarce, future food security depends on safeguarding it from conversion to nonfarm uses and from erosion.

One of the keys to raising output on a sustainable basis is protecting the resource base. With cropland becoming scarce, future food security depends on safeguarding it both from conversion to nonfarm uses and from the erosion that reduces its inherent productivity. Nearly

a decade ago, U.S. Assistant Secretary of Agriculture Rupert Cutler observed that "asphalt is the land's last crop." Once productive cropland is lost to suburban development, shopping malls, or roads, it is difficult to restore it to food production.[44]

A few countries, such as Japan, have carefully crafted programs designed to protect cropland. In 1968, Japan adopted a comprehensive zoning plan that put all land in one of three categories—industrial, agricultural, or other—and made it illegal to build on cropland. Faced with acute land pressures, Japan confronted the issue early and in doing so established an approach to cropland preservation that is simple, effective, and easily adapted to conditions in other countries.[45]

National success stories in the effort to conserve topsoil are few. Among the major food-producing countries, the United States is the only one systematically reducing excessive soil erosion. Its Conservation Reserve Program both encourages conversion of highly erodible cropland to grassland or woodland and penalizes farmers who do not manage their soil responsibly by denying them the benefits from farm programs. In 1987, the program's second year, U.S. soil losses were reduced by 460 million tons, the greatest year-to-year reduction on record for any country.[46]

In a world where fresh water is becoming more scarce, future growth in irrigation may depend on greater investments in the efficiency of water use. Stopping leakage from irrigation canals and ditches and abandoning the use of wasteful irrigation technologies present obvious opportunities. Israel, with its underground drip system and other advanced irrigation technologies, has expanded its irrigated area by using available water supplies more carefully. In many countries, the key to such gains is the elimination of water subsidies, which actually encourage the inefficient use of irrigation water.[47]

Early international agricultural research efforts concentrated heavily on raising yields of wheat and rice, the world's principal staple foods. In recent years, the Consultative Group on International Agricultural Research—a network of 13 ably staffed agricultural research centers, all but one in the Third World—has shifted its attention to raising output of such minor staples as millet, chickpeas, and cassava, crops produced by low-income, subsistence farmers. Although a far more demanding undertaking, this research effort is responsive to the needs of a large group of farmers, many of whom do not have access to fertilizer.[48]

In a warmer world, where fresh water is becoming scarce, scientists can help push back the physical frontiers of cropping by developing varieties that are more drought-resistant, salt-tolerant, and early-maturing. The payoff on the first two could be particularly high. It is in this area that biotechnology may be helpful in speeding up the plant breeding process.

Events of the last two years suggest that the time also has come to rethink international grain reserve policies. Two or more consecutive drought-reduced harvests could easily wipe out a normal level of reserves. Had there not been a record amount of grain in storage at the beginning of the 1987 crop year, back-to-back declines in the world grain harvests since then would by now have created a world food emergency. As it is, world grain prices in late 1988 had risen by half since late 1987.[49]

Ensuring an adequate level of grain stocks requires taking into account not only year-to-year variations in the weather but the uncertain effects of rising temperatures as well. Global warming will deepen the uncertainty surrounding each year's crop and probably increase the frequency of reduced harvests. (See Chapter 1.) For example, the three drought-reduced U.S. harvests in the eighties could increase to four or five in the nineties and even more thereafter. With much of the 20 million hectares of cropland idled under U.S. supply management programs scheduled to return to production in 1989, the need to establish a more formal set of guidelines for managing world grain reserves will become increasingly urgent.

If world food supplies tighten in the years ahead, the distribution of available supplies will become even more important than when the world was plagued with surpluses. High on the list of questions will be how much of the world's grain supply can be fed to livestock. At present, roughly 500 million tons of an annual harvest of usually 1.6 billion tons is consumed this way.[50]

If the U.S. cropland now set aside under the supply management programs were returned to production, the only remaining major food reserve to fall back on if carryover stocks of grain are depleted would be the grain consumed by livestock. When grain prices rise sharply, as they did in 1973, higher meat prices and the resulting drop in consumer demand force a reduction in the amount of grain fed to livestock. Tragically, by the time grain prices actually affect affluent consumers' consumption of meat, milk, and eggs, the world's poorest may not be getting enough grain to survive.[51]

The relative efficiency of converting grain to various types of animal protein also affects the world grain supply-and-demand balance. The least efficient livestock product is beef produced in feedlots, where it takes roughly seven pounds of grain to produce a pound of meat. The grain used in producing a quarter-pound hamburger could feed a person in a low-income country for two days. The production of broilers, much more efficient than beef, requires roughly two pounds of grain per pound of meat. Thus, shifts from beef to poultry, already under way in some societies for health reasons, help stretch the world supply of grain.[52]

Shifts from beef to poultry, under way in some societies for health reasons, help stretch the world supply of grain.

Perhaps the principal conclusion in this year's analysis of the world food prospect is that future food security may lie more in the hands of family planners than farmers. Agricultural policymakers and farmers acting alone may not be able to ensure adequate food supplies in the years ahead. What is needed is a major assist of the sort that China's family planning ministry has provided that country's farmers over the last two decades, a lift that, when combined with economic reforms in agriculture, helped raise food output per person by nearly half between 1976 and 1984.[53]

STABILIZING POPULATION

At the annual meeting in Berlin in September 1988, World Bank President Barber Conable urged developing countries to "renew and expand efforts to limit population growth," saying that rapid population increase was contributing to persistent and widespread poverty, which he described as a "moral outrage." Conable's comments reflected growing frustration within the Bank over the inability of many of its member countries to raise living standards. In most countries in Africa, and several in Latin America, average food consumption is falling and living conditions are deteriorating. In many of these countries, the restoration of economic and social progress now depends on quickly reducing population growth.[54]

Population stabilization is the only acceptable goal in a world where growth in human numbers is leading to a life-threatening deterioration of environmental systems. In 13 countries, home to some 266 million people, birth rates have already fallen to the point where births and deaths are in balance. Except for Czechoslovakia, East Germany, and Hungary, all are in Western Europe. They range from tiny Luxembourg to three of the four largest countries in Western Europe—Italy, the United Kingdom, and West Germany.[55]

Balancing birth and death rates was not an explicit goal in any of these countries. Fertility declined as economic and social conditions improved. As incomes rose and employment opportunities for women expanded, couples chose to have fewer children. The wide availability of family planning services and liberal abortion laws provided the means for them to do so.

The contrasting prospects of these countries and those where populations are projected to double, triple, or quadruple (see Table 10–2) is alarming. The experience of recent years indicates that rapid population growth and social progress are not compatible over the long term. Countries either make the shift to smaller families, as China has done, or their life-support systems begin to break down, as is occurring in many African countries. Given the conditions of these systems and the trends in per capita food production and income, many countries may have delayed too long in implementing effective family planning policies. They may now face a choice: adopt a one-child family goal or accept a decline in living standards. It is

Table 10-2. Projected Population Size at Stabilization and Increase Over Current Level, Selected Countries

Country	1988 Population	Projected Population When Stationary State is Reached	Ratio
	(million)	(million)	
Kenya	23	121	5.3
Uganda	16	82	5.1
Tanzania	24	123	5.1
Nigeria	112	529	4.7
Ethiopia	48	205	4.3
Zaire	33	142	4.3
Sudan	24	101	4.2
Ghana	14	58	4.1
Pakistan	107	423	4.0
Syria	11	42	3.8
Algeria	24	81	3.4
Bolivia	7	24	3.4
Iran	52	169	3.2
Bangladesh	109	342	3.1
South Africa	35	90	2.6
Egypt	53	132	2.5
Peru	21	48	2.3
Philippines	63	137	2.2
Mexico	83	187	2.2
India	817	1,698	2.1

SOURCE: World Bank, *World Development Report 1988* (New York: Oxford University Press, 1988).

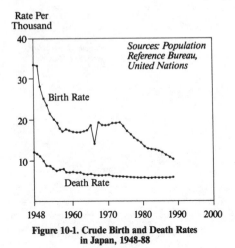

Figure 10-1. Crude Birth and Death Rates in Japan, 1948-88

hard to imagine anything more difficult for a society than striving for acceptance of a one-child family goal except suffering the consequences of failing to do so.

At this point, the only socially responsible step for the United Nations, the World Bank, and the international development community is to call for a sharp reduction in the world growth rate, one patterned after the rapid declines in fertility that occurred in both Japan and China. (See Figures 10–1 and 10–2.) In effect, each of these countries halved its rate of population growth within a matter of years.[56]

Following the loss of its wartime empire, Japan was faced with the reality of living largely on the resources within its own national borders. Living conditions deteriorated, leading many Japanese couples to want smaller families. This in turn prompted public discussion about population control. The Japanese government responded by legalizing abortion in 1948 and creating a national family planning program to provide contraceptive information and counseling. The result was a drop in fertility "unprecedented in the annals of world demography." Between 1949 and 1956, Japan cut its population growth rate from just under 2.2 percent to scarcely 1 percent. Remarkably, Japan made this demographic advance before the advent of modern contraceptives, such as the pill and the intrauterine device.[57]

Two decades later, the Chinese government also concluded that its fast-falling population/land ratio was threatening its future economic progress. This led to a decision to lower its birth rate. Between 1970 and 1976, China's popu-

Figure 10-2. Crude Birth and Death Rates
in China, 1949-87

lation growth rate dropped from 2.6 percent per year to 1.3 percent. Although
starting from a slightly higher point than
Japan, it nonetheless cut its growth rate
in half.[58]

These family planning breakthroughs
in Japan and China are indicative of what
nations can do if they are serious about
slowing population growth. Countries
that now want to reduce their birth rate
can draw upon the experience of these
two pioneers. And they have the advantage of a wider range of modern contraceptive technologies.

Given the experience of Japan and
China, a global effort to cut world population growth in half by the year 2000
does not seem out of the question. The
birth rate for the world of 28 per thousand population in 1988 is lower than
the 33 per thousand that prevailed in
Japan and China when they launched
their fertility reduction campaigns. The
1988 world death rate is 10, midway between the 12 in Japan and the 8 in China
when their efforts began. If national governments become serious, it is possible
to lower the global birth rate of 28 to 19
by the end of the century, a decline of
one third. Assuming that the death rate
for the world remains at roughly 10 per

thousand, this would cut the rate of
world population growth in half, dropping it below 1 percent per year. (See
Figure 10-3.)[59]

Much of this decline would have to
occur, of course, where population
growth is most rapid—Africa, Latin
America, and the Indian subcontinent.
Industrial countries, such as the United
States, the Soviet Union, and Japan,
where population growth is now well
below 1 percent per year, can easily follow the industrial societies of Western
Europe to zero population growth.[60]

Countries that have made the shift to
small families typically have four things
in common: an active national population education program, widely available
family planning services, incentives for
small families (and in some cases, disincentives for large ones), and widespread
improvements in economic and social
conditions.[61]

The starting point for an effective national population education program is a
careful look into the future, a set of alternative projections that relate population
growth to environmental support systems and economic trends. The model
for this continues to be the projections
undertaken in China in the mid-seven-

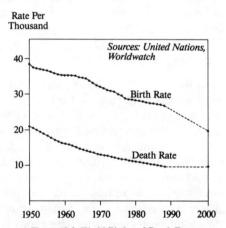

Figure 10-3. World Birth and Death Rates,
1950-88, With Projected Goal for 2000

ties as part of the post-Mao reassessment. One of the questions asked was, What will the future be like if each couple has two children? Under this assumption, the country would have added some 700 million people, roughly another India, to its population. When related to the future availability of soil, water, forest, energy resources, and jobs, it became clear that a two-child family would lead to a decline in living standards. China's leaders realized that only a one-child family was compatible with the goals and aspirations of the Chinese people.[62]

This information was then used in public discussions and debates, all the way down to the village level. People were involved in considering whether to accept two or more children per family and a decline in living conditions or to move quickly to a one-child family program and a more promising future. However difficult the choice, China opted for the latter, enabling it to achieve levels of infant mortality and life expectancy that approach those of affluent industrial societies.[63]

Undertaking these studies is an area in which international development agencies can be of major assistance. The key to meaningful projections is the integration of national demographic, economic, and ecological trends. Only when the three are combined can a useful view of the future be achieved. Only then do the choices become clear.

Another step with a potentially high payoff is the provision of family planning services to those not yet reached by existing service networks. Recent surveys in developing countries indicate that many women who wish to limit family size do not have access to family planning services. Few efforts to improve the human condition will pay a higher return on investment than filling this family planning gap.[64]

Societies that have quickly reduced family size have often relied heavily on a combination of incentives for small families or disincentives for large ones. Countries such as China, Singapore, and South Korea have typically offered free health care and in some cases free education through secondary school if couples agree to have only the one child or two children that circumstances call for. This approach is appealing because the free health care helps assure children's survival and the free education helps enhance their earning power, thus increasing the long-term financial security of parents in societies where people depend on their children in old age.[65]

In developing countries, many women who wish to limit family size do not have access to family planning services.

Any meaningful effort to slow population growth quickly will thus depend on heavy additional investments in the provision of family planning services, improvements in education and health, and financial incentives that encourage couples to have smaller families. Although such a broad-based effort could easily involve additional expenditures of $30 billion per year, it can be viewed by industrial societies, who would help provide financing, as a down payment on a sustainable future, an effort to protect the habitability of the planet.[66]

The formulation of population policies and the design of family planning programs are both handicapped by a lack of information. Although changes in birth rates may have a far greater effect on future economic and social trends in developing countries than any other economic trends will, few such countries regularly collect and publish these data. The U.N. *Monthly Bulletin of Statistics* normally includes data on birth and death rates for only 34 countries, nearly all industrial ones.

If the United Nations could launch a monthly report on population and population-related issues and indicators, it would help fill an information gap that handicaps many family planners. Such a report could include information on national goals to reduce family size and progress in extending family planning services. A monthly population report could also provide national analyses of the characteristics of successful family planning efforts, material on the kinds of contraceptives that work best under various conditions, and country-by-country progress in restoring a balance between births and deaths.

At the national level, it now seems reasonable to expect governments to set family planning goals that will lead to improved living conditions. Some countries may find it necessary to press for one child per couple until the momentum of their population growth is checked. But for the world as a whole, two children may now be a more realistic goal. Accumulating evidence suggests that this is the only population policy that is consistent with restoring a worldwide improvement in living conditions. It is time for international leaders, such as the Secretary General of the United Nations and the President of the World Bank, to urge adoption of such a goal by all governments.

A TURNAROUND DECADE

In an address before the American Institute of Biological Sciences in August 1988, biologist Thomas Lovejoy, Assistant Secretary for External Affairs of the Smithsonian Institution, stated: "I am utterly convinced that most of the great environmental struggles will be either won or lost in the 1990s. And that by the next century it will be too late." Lovejoy is not alone. Thousands of other scientists around the world who are tracking changes in the planet's health share his sense of urgency.[67]

Viewing the world from a very different vantage point, but reaching a similar conclusion, was Eduard Shevardnadze, foreign minister of the Soviet Union. He observed in an address to the U.N. General Assembly in September, that "all the environmental disasters of the current year have placed in the forefront the task of pooling and coordinating efforts in developing a global strategy for the rational management of the environment." He then went on to emphasize the lack of time, saying that "we have too little of it, and problems are piling up faster than they are solved."[68]

The 1989 annual report of the United Nations Children's Fund gets to the heart of what is at stake: "For almost nine hundred million people, approximately one sixth of mankind, the march of human progress has now become a retreat."[69]

By many measures, time is running out. Circumstances call for major shifts on several fronts simultaneously to restore the equilibria that make the planet habitable: a global balance between births and deaths, carbon emissions and carbon fixation, soil erosion and soil formation, tree cutting and tree planting.

It is now clear that we are moving into a new age, for the current situation simply will not prevail for much longer. The outlines of this new age will be defined by choices made in the years immediately ahead. We will either mobilize to reestablish a stable relationship with the earth's natural support systems or continue down the path of environmental deterioration.

If societies successfully mobilize for change, the new age will be one in which forest cover is expanding, hunger is diminishing, and life expectancy is everywhere increasing. This age will see the evolution of transportation systems that rely heavily on bicycles and mass transit, as well as on more fuel-efficient automobiles. It will be an age in which most residential hot water comes from rooftop solar collectors, more windmills and fewer polluting power plants dot the landscape, and Third World villages are electrified by photovoltaic solar cells. It will be an age in which population growth slows because birth rates fall, not because death rates rise. It will, by necessity, be a more equitable world, and, by consequence, a more peaceful world.

If instead societies persist with business as usual, letting current trends continue, the new age will look very different. Climate change will accelerate, causing untold economic disruption. Summertime heat waves will bring more water shortages, power blackouts, and crop failures. The hunger and malnutrition that has engulfed much of Africa and parts of Latin America during the eighties will spread. In more countries, infant mortality will rise and life expectancy will fall, as is already happening in Ghana, Madagascar, and Peru. As food riots and famine become more commonplace, and as the chasm between the haves and have-nots widens, social and political institutions will begin to unravel. At some point, a mounting preoccupation with the unstable present will begin to obliterate hopes for reclaiming the future.[70]

There is little precedent for the scale of action needed over the next decade. In recent history, the only time when change even remotely approached that needed now was in the early forties, when countries mobilized for war. There are, however, important differences. Despite its name, World War II scarcely touched parts of the world. The dangers were clear and immediate for those involved, and they knew the military effort was temporary. This made the sacrifices and adjustments easier to bear.

We are moving into a new age, for the current situation simply will not prevail for much longer.

By contrast, the battle to protect the earth's life-support systems lacks definition in the minds of many. The danger is not so clear and present. Climate change, ozone depletion, population growth, and soil erosion are gradual processes, and therefore difficult to mobilize against. And the adjustments needed are permanent, for they are the prerequisites for long-term progress. Given these characteristics, a timely response to environmental threats depends less on emotion and more on reason—which may explain the growing gap between what needs to be done to secure the future and what is being done.

Social change on the scale needed will take society into uncharted territory. It will require converting a global economy now using 6 percent of its resources for means of destruction into one devoted to the reconstruction of the planet. In essence, the task is to organize and sustain a survival economy much the way countries today maintain permanent standing armies and strategic weapons in the hope of deterring war. Rather than sitting idle, however, the investments in our planet's future will be used productively—for planting trees, developing renewable energy sources, and expanding food production, among other vital tasks.[71]

Launching and carrying through on the initiatives needed to safeguard the planet will place extraordinary demands on political leaders and a high premium on imaginative leadership. As shown by the progress of air pollution control in Europe or protection of the ozone layer globally, action by just a few countries can inspire many others to join in. When the prime ministers of Canada and Norway publicly embraced the goal of reducing carbon dioxide emissions by 20 percent by 2005, they helped move concerns about climate change from research institutes into legislatures, where they now need to be.[72]

Whether the nineties becomes a turnaround decade will also depend heavily on the response of scientists and the communications media, for both play key roles in broad-based public education. As important as scientists' findings in their laboratories will be their ability and willingness to translate these findings into terms understandable by nonscientists. Similarly, the media will better serve the public's need for information when it begins reporting, for example, that deforestation rates are as important an indicator of societal health as inflation rates are.

Up until now, environmental organizations, both national and local, have provided the impetus for efforts to restore and protect the planet. Numerous citizens' groups have organized to remedy problems directly touching their lives, whether it be planting trees in a Third World village or opposing the siting of a toxic waste dump in a U.S. community. The challenge now is for other groups to get involved. Collectively, churches, civic groups, and professional societies represent an enormous potential for planetary reclamation. Rotary International, Girl Scouts, the International Association of Agricultural Economists, the Lutheran Church, the International Society of Tropical Foresters, the American Medical Association, and the International Jaycees are but a few of the thousands of groups that could play a part.

Ultimately, responsibility for the future rests with individuals. Our values, choices, and behaviors shape social and political change. Unless more of us join the effort, there is little hope of halting the planet's deterioration.

By the end of the next decade, the die will pretty well be cast. As the world enters the twenty-first century, the community of nations either will have rallied and turned back the threatening trends, or environmental deterioration and social disintegration will be feeding on each other.

The ultimate rationale for a massive social mobilization to safeguard the earth is summed up in a bit of graffiti painted on a bridge in Rock Creek Park in Washington, D.C. It says, "Good planets are hard to find."

Notes

Chapter 1. A World at Risk

1. James E. Hansen, Director, NASA Goddard Institute for Space Studies, "The Greenhouse Effect: Impacts on Current Global Temperature and Regional Heat Waves," Testimony before the Committee on Energy and Natural Resources, U.S. Senate, June 23, 1988.

2. Edward A. Gargan, "Flash Floods and Drought Ravage China," *New York Times*, August 3, 1988; Noel Fletcher, "China's Drought Boosting Food-Import Needs," *Journal of Commerce*, July 25, 1988; "Killing Heat Wave Hits South China," *Beijing Review*, July 25-31, 1988; numerous articles on the drought in *China Daily*, Summer 1988.

3. National Aeronautics and Space Administration, "Executive Summary of the Ozone Trends Panel," Washington, D.C., March 15, 1988.

4. Richard M. Weintraub, "Flooding Worsens in Bangladesh," *Washington Post*, September 5, 1988.

5. Alberto W. Setzer et al., "Relatório de Atividades do Projeto IBDF-INPE 'SEQE'—Ano 1987," Instituto de Pesquisas Espaciais, São Jose dos Campos, Brazil, May 1988; Robert J. McNeal, Testimony before the Committee on Energy and Natural Resources, U.S. Senate, September 20, 1988.

6. David C. Anderson, "The Medical Trash That's on the Beach Is Only the Start," *Washington Post*, August 7, 1988; Keith Schneider, "Rain Revives Crops but Experts say Drought Persists," *New York Times*, July

26, 1988; David S. Wilson, "U.S. Forest Fires Worst Since 1919," *New York Times*, September 1, 1988; Sam Howe Verhovek, "The Long Heat Also Polluted the Air," *New York Times*, August 26, 1988.

7. Karen DeYoung, "European Seal Herd Perishing," *Washington Post*, August 7, 1988; "Italy Promises Remedial Steps Against Eutrophication in Adriatic," *International Environment Reporter*, September 14, 1988; David Remnick, "Foul Air, Water Problems Wake Soviets to Ecology," *Washington Post*, July 31, 1988; James Brooke, "African Nations Barring Toxic Waste," *New York Times*, September 25, 1988; Arshad Mahmud, "In Bangladesh, Too Much Water and Not Enough," *New York Times*, September 18, 1988.

8. Christopher Flavin, *Reassessing Nuclear Power: The Fallout From Chernobyl*, Worldwatch Paper 75 (Washington, D.C.: Worldwatch Institute, March 1987).

9. Christopher Flavin, "The Case Against Reviving Nuclear Power," *World Watch* (Washington, D.C.), July/August 1988; Bill Keller, "Public Mistrust Curbs Soviet Nuclear Power Efforts," *New York Times*, October 13, 1988.

10. Sandra Postel, *Air Pollution, Acid Rain, and the Future of Forests*, Worldwatch Paper 58 (Washington, D.C.: Worldwatch Institute, March 1984).

11. Sandra Postel, "Protecting Forests from Air Pollution and Acid Rain," in Lester R. Brown et al., *State of the World 1985* (New York: W.W. Norton & Co., 1985); Peter H.

Sand, "Air Pollution in Europe: International Policy Responses," *Environment*, December 1987.

12. Sand, "Air Pollution in Europe."

13. Catherine Fitzpatrick and Janet Fleischman, *From Below: Independent Peace and Environmental Movements in Eastern Europe and the USSR* (New York: Helsinki Watch Committee, 1987).

14. Remnick, "Foul Air, Water Problems Wake Soviets to Ecology"; Barbara Jancar, "The Politics of Pollution in the Soviet Union and Eastern Europe: Two Years after Chernobyl," Testimony before Commission on Security and Cooperation in Europe, U.S. Congress, April 26, 1988; Fitzpatrick and Fleischman, *From Below.*

15. Green Party, "The Green Party of Sweden," Stockholm, 1988.

16. Lynn White, Jr., "The Historical Roots of Our Ecologic Crisis," *Science*, March 10, 1967.

17. Jeremy Brecher, "The Opening Shot of the Second Ecological Revolution," *Chicago Tribune*, August 16, 1988.

18. Elizabeth Kemf, "The Re-greening of Vietnam," *New Scientist*, June 23, 1988.

19. "Conference Statement," The Changing Atmosphere: Implications for Global Security, Toronto, June 27–30, 1988; "Global Environmental Protection Act of 1988," S. 2666, U.S. Senate, introduced by Senator Robert Stafford, July 28, 1988; "National Energy Policy Act of 1988," S. 2667, U.S. Senate, introduced by Senator Timothy Wirth, July 28, 1988; "Global Warming Prevention Act of 1988," H.R. 5460, U.S. House of Representatives, introduced by Representative Claudine Schneider, October 5, 1988.

20. Hansen, "The Greenhouse Effect."

21. World Resources Institute/International Institute for Environment and Development, *World Resources Report 1988/1989* (New York: Basic Books, 1988); Pieter Tans, Group Chief, Carbon Cycle Group, National Oceanic and Atmospheric Administration, Boulder, Colo., private communication, October 28, 1988; Eric T. Sundquist, "Ice Core Links CO_2 to Climate," *Nature*, October 1, 1987.

22. V. Ramanathan et al., "Trace Gas Trends and Their Potential Role in Climate Change," *Journal of Geophysical Research*, June 20, 1985; F. Sherwood Rowland, "Chlorofluorocarbons, Stratospheric Ozone, and the Antarctic 'Ozone Hole'," *Environmental Conservation*, Summer 1988; Irving R. Mintzer, Senior Associate, World Resources Institute, Testimony before Subcommittee on Energy and Power, Committee on Energy and Commerce, U.S. House of Representatives, September 22, 1988.

23. Worldwatch estimate from Gregg Marland, Environmental Science Division, Oak Ridge National Laboratory, Oak Ridge, Tenn., unpublished printout and private communication, September 9, 1988; the lower estimated range for carbon addition from deforestation is from R.P. Detwiler and Charles A.S. Hall, "Tropical Forests and the Global Carbon Cycle," *Science*, January 1, 1988; the higher one is from R.A. Houghton et al., "The Flux of Carbon from Terrestrial Ecosystems to the Atmosphere in 1980 Due to Changes in Land Use: Geographic Distribution of the Global Flux," *Tellus*, February/April 1987; George M. Woodwell, "How Does the World Work?" presented to World Wildlife Fund (WWF) Conference on Consequences of the Greenhouse Effect for Biological Diversity, Washington, D.C., October 4–6, 1988 (hereinafter cited as WWF Conference); fossil fuel projections are Worldwatch Institute estimates.

24. Philip D. Jones et al., "Evidence for Global Warming in the Past Decade," *Nature*, April 28, 1988; James E. Hansen et al., "Global Climate Changes as Forecast by the GISS 3-D Model," *Journal of Geophysical Research*, August 20, 1988; data for 1988 are preliminary, based on recordings for the first nine

months of the year, according to James E. Hansen, private communication, October 26, 1988.

25. Hansen, "The Greenhouse Effect."

26. U.S. National Academy of Sciences, *Changing Climate,* Report of the Carbon Dioxide Assessment Committee (Washington, D.C.: National Academy Press, 1983); James E. Hansen, "Prediction of Near-Term Climate Evolution: What Can We Tell Decision-Makers Now?" Testimony before Committee on Energy and Natural Resources, U.S. Senate, November 9, 1987; John W. Firor, Director, Advanced Study Program, National Center for Atmospheric Research, Boulder, Colo., Testimony before Subcommittee on Energy and Power, Committee on Energy and Commerce, U.S. House of Representatives, July 7, 1988.

27. Hansen, "The Greenhouse Effect"; Syukuro Manabe, Geophysical Fluid Dynamics Laboratory, National Oceanic and Atmospheric Administration, Princeton, N.J., Testimony before Committee on Energy and Natural Resources, U.S. Senate, November 9, 1987.

28. World Climate Programme, *Developing Policies for Responding to Climate Change* (Geneva: World Meteorological Organization, 1988); Firor, Testimony.

29. Woodwell, "How Does the World Work?"; Margaret B. Davis and Catherine Zabinski, University of Minnesota, "Rates of Dispersal of North American Trees: Implications for Response to Climatic Warming," presented to WWF Conference.

30. W.D. Billings, Duke University, "Effects of Predicted Climatic Warming on Arctic Tundra Ecosystems on the Alaskan North Slope," and Daniel B. Botkin and Robert A. Nisbet, University of California, Santa Barbara, "Projecting the Effects of Climate Change on Biological Diversity in Forests," both presented to WWF Conference.

31. James G. Titus, U.S. Environmental Protection Agency, "Causes and Effects of Sea Level Rise," presented to the First North American Conference on Preparing for Climate Change: A Cooperative Approach, Washington, D.C., October 27–29, 1987.

32. Tom Goemans and Pier Vellinga, "Low Countries and High Seas," presented to the First North American Conference on Preparing for Climate Change: A Cooperative Approach, Washington, D.C., October 27–29, 1987.

33. John D. Milliman et al., "Environmental and Economic Impact of Rising Sea Level and Subsiding Deltas: The Nile and Bengal Examples," Woods Hole Oceanographic Institution, Woods Hole, Mass., unpublished, 1988.

34. J. Christopher Walker et al., "Impact of Global Climate Change on Urban Infrastructure" (draft), The Urban Institute, Washington, D.C., July 1988.

35. Ibid.

36. Debora MacKenzie, "Winds of Change May Be Harbingers of Drought," *New Scientist,* August 27, 1987; Dennis Wamsted, "Hyper-Hurricanes—A New Threat from the Greenhouse Effect?" *Energy Daily,* September 15, 1988.

37. U.N. World Food Council (WFC), "The Global State of Hunger and Malnutrition: 1988 Report," 14th Ministerial Session, Nicosia, Cyprus, March 24, 1988.

38. U.S. Department of Agriculture (USDA), Economic Research Service (ERS), *World Grain Harvested Area, Production, and Yield 1950–87* (unpublished printout) (Washington, D.C.: 1988); USDA, Foreign Agricultural Service (FAS), *World Grain Situation and Outlook,* Washington, D.C., October 1988.

39. USDA, ERS, *World Grain 1950–87;* 1988 per capita grain production estimate derived from production estimates in USDA, FAS, *World Grain Situation,* and from population projections in Francis Urban and Philip Rose, *World Population by Country and Region,*

1950–86, and Projections to 2050 (Washington, D.C.: USDA, ERS, 1988).

40. USDA, ERS, *World Grain 1950–87;* "Farmers Turn Down the Irrigation Tap," *Farmline,* August 1988; Frederick W. Crook, *Agricultural Statistics of the People's Republic of China, 1949–86* (Washington, D.C.: USDA, ERS, 1988).

41. USDA, ERS, *World Grain 1950–87.*

42. World Bank, *Report of the Task Force on Food Security in Africa* (Washington, D.C.: 1988).

43. Ibid.

44. Population Reference Bureau, *1988 World Population Data Sheet* (Washington, D.C.: 1988); USDA, ERS, *World Grain;* Michael Griffin, "Harsh Times for Madagascar's Growing Numbers," *People* (London), Vol. 15, No. 2, 1988.

45. U.N. Food and Agriculture Organization, *FAO Production Yearbook* (Rome: various years); USDA, ERS, *World Grain 1950–87;* WFC, "Global State of Hunger and Malnutrition."

46. International Monetary Fund, *International Financial Statistics,* Washington, D.C., various issues; World Bank, *Task Force on Food Security in Africa.*

47. Cost of the wheat in a loaf of bread calculated using a wheat price of U.S.$3 per bushel.

48. USDA, FAS, *World Rice Reference Tables* (unpublished printout)(Washington, D.C.: July 1988).

49. USDA, FAS, *World Grain Situation.*

50. Hansen, "The Greenhouse Effect"; Syukuro Manabe, "Climate Warming Due to Greenhouse Gases," Testimony before the Subcommittee on Toxic Substances and Environmental Oversight, Committee on Environment and Public Works, U.S. Senate, December 10, 1985; Hansen et al., "Global Climate Changes."

51. S. Manabe and R.T. Wetherald, "Reduction in Summer Soil Wetness Induced by an Increase in Atmospheric Carbon Dioxide," *Science,* May 2, 1986; Hansen et al., "Global Climate Changes."

52. USDA, FAS, *World Grain Situation;* R.H. Shaw, "Estimates of Yield Reductions in Corn Caused by Water and Temperature Stress," in C. D. Raper and P. J. Kramer, eds., *Crop Reactions to Water and Temperature Stresses in Humid, Temperate Climates* (Boulder, Colo.: Westview Press, 1983); R. F. Dale, "Temperature Perturbations in the Midwestern and Southeastern United States Important for Corn Production," in ibid.

53. Linda O. Mearns et al., "Extreme High-Temperature Events: Changes in Their Probabilities with Changes in Mean Temperature," *Journal of Climate and Applied Meteorology,* December 1984.

54. USDA, ERS, *World Grain 1950–87;* USDA, FAS, *World Grain Situation.*

55. USDA, ERS, *World Grain 1950–87;* USDA, FAS, *World Grain Situation.*

56. Hansen, "The Greenhouse Effect."

57. USDA, FAS, *World Wheat and Coarse Grains Reference Tables* (unpublished printout) (Washington, D.C.: August 1988); USDA, FAS, *World Rice;* USDA, FAS, *World Grain Situation.*

58. Eduard A. Shevardnadze, Minister for Foreign Affairs of the USSR, Statement before the Forty-third Session of the U.N. General Assembly, New York, September 27, 1988.

59. William Hively, "Global Change," *American Scientist,* March/April 1988; June S. Ewing, Staff Officer, National Research Council, Washington, D.C., private communication, June 22, 1988; "The International Geosphere—Biosphere Programme (IGBP): Towards a Plan for Action," *EarthQuest,* University Corporation for Atmospheric Research, Boulder, Colo., Summer 1988.

60. Denise Claveloux, "Tighter Control of Waste Management, Disposal of Toxic Waste

Envisioned in Proposals Made by European Community Commission," *International Environment Reporter,* August 10, 1988; "Tougher Small-Car Emissions Limits Being Sought By European Parliament," *International Environment Reporter,* October 12, 1988; "European Commission Considers Directive on Freedom of Information on Environment," *International Environment Reporter,* October 12, 1988; Steven Greenhouse, "Making Europe a Mighty Market," *New York Times,* May 22, 1988.

61. U.N. Economic Commission for Europe, *ECE 1947–1987* (New York: United Nations, 1987); Sand, "Air Pollution in Europe"; "12 Nations Agree to Cut Pollution," *Washington Post,* November 1, 1988.

62. Richard Mott, "An Acid Rain Summons from Europe," *The Environmental Forum,* March/April 1988.

63. Information on signatories from U.N. Office for Ocean Affairs and the Law of the Sea, New York, private communication, October 11, 1988; Elisabeth Mann Borgese, "The Law of the Sea," *Scientific American,* March 1983; Department of Public Information, *A Quiet Revolution: The United Nations Convention on the Law of the Sea* (New York: United Nations, 1984).

64. Clyde Sanger, *Ordering the Oceans: The Making of the Law of the Sea* (London: Zed Books Ltd., 1986); Ann L. Hollick, "Managing the Oceans," *The Wilson Quarterly,* Summer 1984; Karl Sullivan, "Overfishing and the New Law of the Sea," *OECD Observer,* July 1984; "United States Acceptance of MARPOL Annex Will Lead to Ban on Dumping Plastics at Sea," *International Environment Reporter,* February 10, 1988; "Global Stop to At-Sea Incineration Approved," *Multilateral Environmental Outlook,* October 13, 1988.

65. Douglas G. Cogan, *Stones in a Glass House: CFCs and Ozone Depletion* (Washington, D.C.: Investor Responsibility Research Center, 1988); Mostafa K. Tolba, "The Ozone

Agreement—and Beyond," *Environmental Conservation,* Winter 1987.

66. Cogan, *Stones in a Glass House;* Mark Crawford, "Landmark Ozone Treaty Negotiated," *Science,* September 25, 1987; U.N. Treaty Office, New York, various private communications; Philip Shabecoff, "E.P.A. Chief Asks Total Ban on Ozone-Harming Chemicals," *New York Times,* September 27, 1988.

67. World Climate Programme, *Developing Policies;* "Conference Statement," The Changing Atmosphere.

68. Toufiq A. Siddiqi, East-West Center, Honolulu, Hawaii, "A Comprehensive Law of the Atmosphere as a Framework for Addressing Carbon Dioxide and Climate Change Issues," presented to the Workshop on Global Climate Change, Woods Hole, Mass., September 23, 1988; Brian Mulroney, Prime Minister of Canada, Speech at The Changing Atmosphere: Implications for Global Security, Toronto, Canada, June 27–30, 1988; Kilaparti Ramakrishna, "Steps Toward an International Convention for Stabilizing the Greenhouse Gas Composition of the Atmosphere" (draft), Woods Hole Research Center, Woods Hole, Mass., September 2, 1988.

69. Jane Rosen, "Suddenly, Everyone's Talking About the Weather," *The Interdependent,* Fall 1988; Shevardnadze, Statement at U.N. General Assembly.

70. Mulroney, Speech at The Changing Atmosphere; Ed H.T.M. Nijpels, Minister of Housing, Physical Planning and Environment, the Netherlands, Speech at The Changing Atmosphere: Implications for Global Security, Toronto, Canada, June 27–30, 1988; Gro Harlem Brundtland, Prime Minister of Norway, "Our Common Future—A Climate for Change," Speech at The Changing Atmosphere: Implications for Global Security, Toronto, Canada, June 27–30, 1988; Shevardnadze, Statement at U.N. General Assembly; Draft Summary of Workshop

(200) *Notes (Chapters 1 and 2)*

on Global Climatic Change, Woods Hole Research Center, Woods Hole, Mass., September 23, 1988.

71. Richard N. Gardner, "The Case for Practical Internationalism," *Foreign Affairs,* Spring 1988; John M. Goshko, "United Nations Finds Itself 'Back in Fashion'," *Washington Post,* September 25, 1988; George D. Moffett III, "Peacekeepers Win Peace Prize," *Christian Science Monitor,* September 30, 1988.

72. Paul Lewis, "Soviet Announces Shift on U.N. Staff Demand by U.S.," *New York Times,* June 4, 1988; Elaine Sciolino, "Reagan, in Switch, Says U.S. Will Pay Some Old U.N. Dues," *New York Times,* September 14, 1988; Steven Greenhouse, "Japan Is Seeking Larger Role in World's Financial System and Debt Crisis," *New York Times,* September 27, 1988; Hilary F. French, "Restoring the U.N.," *World Watch* (Washington, D.C.), July/August 1988.

73. Maurice F. Strong, "Beyond Foreign Aid—Towards a New World System," presented to the International Development Conference, Washington, D.C., March 19, 1987.

74. Brundtland, "Our Common Future—A Climate for Change."

Chapter 2. Halting Land Degradation

1. Michel M. Verstraete, "Defining Desertification: A Review," *Climatic Change*, No. 9, 1986; H.E. Dregne, *Desertification of Arid Lands* (New York: Harwood Academic Publishers, 1983).

2. U.N. Environment Programme (UNEP), *General Assessment of Progress in the Implementation of the Plan of Action to Combat Desertification 1978-1984* (Nairobi: 1984).

3. F. Kenneth Hare, "Recent Climatic Experience in the Arid and Semi-arid Lands," *Desertification Control Bulletin,* No. 10, 1984.

4. Edward C. Wolf, "Managing Rangelands," in Lester R. Brown et al., *State of the*

World 1986 (New York: W.W. Norton & Co., 1986).

5. Dregne, *Desertification of Arid Lands.*

6. Peter H. Freeman and J.K. Rennie, *Desertification in the Sahel: Diagnosis and Proposals for IUCN's Response* (Gland, Switzerland: International Union for Conservation of Nature and Natural Resources, 1985).

7. Dregne, *Desertification of Arid Lands;* Wolf, "Managing Rangelands"; Jack A. Mabbutt, "A New Global Assessment of the Status and Trends of Desertification," *Environmental Conservation,* Summer 1984.

8. Thomas M. Painter, "Bringing Land Back In: Changing Strategies to Improve Agricultural Production in West African Sahel," in Peter D. Little et al., eds., *Lands at Risk in the Third World: Local Level Perspectives* (Boulder, Colo.: Westview Press, 1987); UNEP, *General Assessment of Progress.*

9. D. Pimentel et al., "World Agriculture and Soil Erosion," *BioScience,* April 1987.

10. The total is a modification of the estimate made by D.E. Walling, "Rainfall, Runoff and Erosion of the Land: A Global View," in K.J. Gregory, ed., *Energetics of Physical Environment* (New York: John Wiley & Sons, 1987), using a new figure for the Ganges-Brahmaputra system (as referenced in the next note), which increased the total from 19 billion tons to 20.3 billion.

11. Sediment load and area of sediment fan from Ocean Drilling Program, news release, Texas A&M University, College Station, September 4, 1987.

12. Degraded area of Loess Plateau from Men Qinmei, Vice Chief of Bureau of Middle Reach of Huang He, Xian, Shaanxi Province, private communication, June 9, 1988; average erosion rate from U.N. Food and Agriculture Organization (FAO)/World Food Programme (WFP) project report, "Improved Land Use of the Loess Plateau, Mizhi County, Shaanxi Province," Rome, July 11, 1984.

13. Sandra Postel, *Conserving Water: The Untapped Alternative*, Worldwatch Paper 67 (Washington, D.C.: Worldwatch Institute, September 1985).

14. Anupam Mishra, "An Irrigation Project That Has Reduced Farm Production," Centre for Science and Environment, New Delhi, 1981.

15. UNEP, *General Assessment of Progress*.

16. Ibid.; areas affected from Sandra Postel, *Water: Rethinking Management in an Age of Scarcity*, Worldwatch Paper 62 (Washington, D.C.: Worldwatch Institute, December 1984); Celestine Bohlen, "Cotton Measures Fortunes in Soviet Turkmenistan," *Washington Post*, May 13, 1986; Philip P. Micklin, "Desiccation of the Aral Sea: A Water Management Disaster in the Soviet Union," *Science*, September 2, 1988.

17. For an overview of deforestation trends and consequences, see Sandra Postel and Lori Heise, *Reforesting the Earth*, Worldwatch Paper 83 (Washington, D.C.: Worldwatch Institute, April 1988); Brazil figure from Alberto W. Setzer et al., "Relatório de Atividades do Projeto, IBDF-INPE 'SEQE'— Ano 1987," Instituto de Pesquisas Espaciais, São José dos Campos, Brazil, May 1988.

18. Jean Eugene Gorse and David R. Steeds, *Desertification in the Sahelian and Sudanian Zones of West Africa* (Washington, D.C.: World Bank, 1987).

19. Ibid.

20. Population projections from Population Reference Bureau (PRB), *1988 World Population Data Sheet* (Washington, D.C.: 1988).

21. Area of potentially productive land from B.B. Vohra, "Neglect of Natural Resource Management," *Mainstream*, January 16, 1988; National Land Use and Wastelands Development Council, "Strategies, Structures, Policies: National Wastelands Development Board," New Delhi, February 6, 1986; D.R. Bhumbla and Arvind Khare, "Es-timate of Wastelands in India," Society for Promotion of Wastelands Development, New Delhi, India, undated.

22. Maria Elena Lopez, "The Politics of Lands at Risk in a Philippine Frontier," in Little et al., *Lands at Risk in the Third World*.

23. Ibid.

24. John Hanks, "Southern Africa's Abused Environment," *Earthwatch*, No. 31, in *People* (London), Vol. 15, No. 2, 1988.

25. Dhira Phantumvanit and Khunying Suthawan Sathirathai, "Thailand: Degradation and Development in a Resource-Rich Land," *Environment*, January/February 1988.

26. Annar Cassam, "Prospects for African Development," *Journal für Entwicklungspolitik*, Special Issue 1, 1987; Leopold P. Mureithi, "Crisis and Recovery in African Agriculture: Priorities for Dialogue and Action," *Development: Seeds of Change*, No. 2/3, 1987; see also Jodi L. Jacobson, "The Forgotten Resource," *World Watch* (Washington, D.C.), May/June 1988.

27. World Commission on Environment and Development, *Our Common Future* (New York: Oxford University Press, 1987); see also Piers Blaikie and Harold Brookfield, "Retrospect and Prospect," in Piers Blaikie and Harold Brookfield, eds., *Land Degradation and Society* (New York: Methuen & Co., 1987).

28. Postel and Heise, *Reforesting the Earth*; Lester R. Brown, "Sustaining World Agriculture," in Lester R. Brown et al., *State of the World 1987* (New York: W.W. Norton & Co., 1987).

29. S. Manabe and R.T. Wetherald, "Reduction in Summer Soil Wetness Induced by an Increase in Atmospheric Carbon Dioxide," *Science*, May 2, 1986; for a general discussion of the impacts of climate change on agriculture, see Sandra Postel, *Altering the Earth's Chemistry: Assessing the Risks*, Worldwatch Paper 71 (Washington, D.C.: Worldwatch Institute, July 1986).

30. Piers J. Sellers, "Modeling Effects of Vegetation on Climate," in Robert E. Dickenson, ed., *The Geophysiology of Amazonia* (New York: John Wiley & Sons, 1987); Hare, "Recent Climatic Experience in the Arid and Semi-arid Lands."

31. J. Shukla and Y. Mintz, "Influence of Land-Surface Evapotranspiration on the Earth's Climate," *Science,* March 19, 1982.

32. Sharon Nicholson, Florida State University, Tallahassee, private communication, June 13, 1985, as cited in Lester R. Brown and Edward C. Wolf, *Reversing Africa's Decline,* Worldwatch Paper 65 (Washington, D.C.: Worldwatch Institute, June 1985); Sharon E. Nicholson, "Sub-Saharan Rainfall in the Years 1976–80: Evidence of Continued Drought," *Monthly Weather Review,* August 1983.

33. Ann Henderson-Sellers, "Effects of Change in Land Use on Climate in the Humid Tropics," in Dickenson, *Geophysiology of Amazonia;* Hare, "Recent Climatic Experience in the Arid and Semi-arid Lands."

34. Eneas Salati, "The Forest and the Hydrologic Cycle," in Dickenson, *Geophysiology of Amazonia;* see also Eneas Salati and Peter B. Vose, "Amazon Basin: A System in Equilibrium," *Science,* July 13, 1984.

35. Salati, "The Forest and the Hydrologic Cycle"; Salati and Vose, "Amazon Basin."

36. Eneas Salati, Inter-American Development Bank, Washington, D.C., private communications, August 4 and 11, 1988; 12 percent figure from Dennis Mahar, *Government Policies and Deforestation in Brazil's Amazon Region* (Washington, D.C.: World Bank, 1988); for a discussion of modeling studies on tropical deforestation's links to rainfall, see Henderson-Sellers, "Effects of Change in Land Use on Climate."

37. Jean-Paul Malingreau and Compton J. Tucker, "Large-Scale Deforestation in the Southeastern Amazon Basin of Brazil," *Ambio,* Vol. 17, No. 1, 1988.

38. Setzer et al., "Relatório de Atividades do Projeto, IBDF-INPE 'SEQE'."

39. G.P. Shrivastava, APS. University, REWA, Madya Pradesh, India, private communication, July 1, 1988; Jayanta Bandyopadhyay, "Political Ecology of Drought and Water Scarcity: Need for an Ecological Water Resources Policy," *Economic and Political Weekly,* December 12, 1987; see also J. Bandyopadhyay and Vandana Shiva, "Drought, Development and Desertification," *Economic and Political Weekly,* August 16, 1986.

40. Bandyopadhyay, "Political Ecology of Drought and Water Scarcity."

41. Michael Mortimore, "Shifting Sands and Human Sorrow: Social Response to Drought and Desertification," *Desertification Control Bulletin,* No. 14, 1987.

42. Ibid.

43. U.S. Department of Agriculture, Economic Research Service, *Cropland, Water, and Conservation Situation and Outlook Report,* Washington, D.C., September 1988; "Sixth CRP Signup Adds 3.4 Million Acres," *Agricultural Outlook,* August 1988; for historical background to the program, see also Lester R. Brown, "Breakthrough on Soil Erosion," *World Watch* (Washington, D.C.), May/June 1988.

44. Author's visit to China's Loess Plateau, June 1988; Men, private communication; FAO/WFP, "Improved Land Use of the Loess Plateau"; Qi Ying, "Erosion Controls are a Success," *China Daily,* March 10, 1987.

45. FAO/WFP, "Improved Land Use of the Loess Plateau"; author's visit to Mizhi County Experiment Station, Shaanxi Province, June 14, 1988.

46. FAO/WFP, "Improved Land Use of the Loess Plateau"; author's visit to Mizhi County Experiment Station.

47. Author's visit to two experimental villages and discussions with the Governor of Mizhi County and scientists at the Mizhi Experiment Station, Shaanxi Province, China, June 14 and 15, 1988.

48. Cost cited is upper end of range for projects of this type in Loess Plateau, according to Men, private communication; also, similar efforts in a nearby village cost $60 per hectare, according to Governor of Mizhi County, private communication, June 15, 1988.

49. Lengths of bunds and terraces from Hans Hurni, "Degradation and Conservation of the Resources in the Ethiopian Highlands," *Mountain Research and Development,* Vol. 8, Nos. 2/3, 1988; number of food-for-work projects from Paul Harrison, *The Greening of Africa* (New York: Viking/Penguin, 1987); Debora MacKenzie, "Can Ethiopia be Saved?" *New Scientist,* September 24, 1987; share of land protected from Debora MacKenzie, "Ethiopia's Hand to the Plough," *New Scientist,* October 1, 1987.

50. Rattan Lal, "Managing the Soils of Sub-Saharan Africa," *Science,* May 29, 1987.

51. Ibid.

52. Ibid.; for more information on agroforestry, see Postel and Heise, *Reforesting the Earth.*

53. Michael J. Dover and Lee M. Talbot, "Feeding the Earth: An Agroecological Solution," *Technology Review,* February/March 1988.

54. World Bank, *Vetiver Grass (Vetiveria zizanioides): A Method of Vegetative Soil and Moisture Conservation* (New Delhi: 1987); John C. Greenfield, seminar on the vetiver system presented at the World Bank, Washington, D.C., August 4, 1988.

55. World Bank, *Vetiver Grass.*

56. Author's discussion with officials at the State Land Administration, Beijing, China, June 7, 1988; Mizhi County figures from FAO/WFP, "Review of Project 2744," unpublished paper, Rome, August 1987.

57. Harrison, *Greening of Africa;* Lindsey Hilsum, "Aggravating Ethiopia's Environmental Disaster," *Panoscope* (London), August 1987; Robert M. Press, "Dash of Capitalism Brightens Ethiopia Food Picture," *Christian Science Monitor,* June 24, 1988.

58. Harrison, *Greening of Africa;* see also Wolf, "Managing Rangelands."

59. Secretariat of the Independent Commission on International Humanitarian Issues, *The Encroaching Desert: The Consequences of Human Failure* (London: Zed Books Ltd., 1986); Wolf, "Managing Rangelands."

60. Sam H. Johnson III, "Large Scale Irrigation and Drainage Schemes in Pakistan," in Gerald T. O'Mara, ed., *Efficiency in Irrigation: The Conjunctive Use of Surface and Groundwater Resources* (Washington, D.C.: World Bank, 1988).

61. Asit K. Biswas, "Environmental Concerns in Pakistan, with Special Reference to Water and Forests," *Environmental Conservation,* Winter 1987; Egypt figure from Janet Raloff, "Salt of the Earth," *Science News,* November 10, 1984.

62. Mostafa K. Tolba, "A Harvest of Dust?" *Environmental Conservation,* Spring 1984; Mostafa K. Tolba, "The Tenth Anniversary of UNCOD," *Desertification Control Bulletin,* No. 15, 1987; Harold E. Dregne, "Combating Desertification: Evaluation of Progress," *Environmental Conservation,* Summer 1984; Daniel Stiles, U.N. Sudano-Sahelian Office, private communication, New York, October 6, 1988.

63. Judith Gradwohl and Russell Greenberg, *Saving the Tropical Forests* (London: Earthscan Publications Ltd., 1988).

64. Tim Magee, "Trees for Farmers," *VITA News,* October 1987.

65. "India's 'People's Forestry Programme'—A Decentralized Approach to Reafforestation," in "News from UNEP," *Desertification Control Bulletin,* No. 14, 1987;

"Project Evaluation Mission in Southern India," in "News from UNEP," *Desertification Control Bulletin,* No. 16, 1988.

66. UNEP/African Ministerial Conference on the Environment (AMCEN), "Compendium of Project Fact Sheets Prepared in Connection with the AMCEN Donors Meeting," Nairobi, Kenya, January 1988; Tolba, "Tenth Anniversary of UNCOD."

67. Tolba, "Tenth Anniversary of UNCOD."

68. Ibid.; William Mansfield, UNEP's Deputy Executive Director, private communication, Washington, D.C., August 17, 1988; UNEP/AMCEN, "Compendium of Project Fact Sheets"; number of projects funded from Stiles, private communication.

69. Richard R. Pelleck, Senior Agroforestry Advisor, U.S. Agency for International Development (AID)/Haiti, private communication, March 1988; AID, *The Environment: Managing Natural Resources for Sustainable Development* (Washington, D.C.: 1987).

70. Pelleck, private communication; AID, *The Environment.*

71. Laura Tangley, "Fighting Central America's Other War," *BioScience,* December 1987.

72. Ibid.

73. Idriss Jazairy, "How to Make Africa Self-Sufficient in Food," *Development: Seeds of Change,* No. 2/3, 1987; number of projects from "Most Efficient and Successful," *World Development Forum,* December 15, 1987.

74. Jazairy, "How to Make Africa Self-Sufficient in Food."

75. Cowpea and sorghum figures from N.C. Brady, "Science and Technology for Development," *Global Development Report,* Fall 1987.

76. Population projections from PRB, *1988 World Population Data Sheet.*

Chapter 3. Reexamining the World Food Prospect

1. World grain stocks from U.S. Department of Agriculture (USDA), Foreign Agricultural Service (FAS), *World Grain Situation and Outlook,* Washington, D.C., July 1988.

2. Grain output in 1987 from USDA, Economic Research Service (ERS), *World Grain Harvested Area, Production, and Yield 1950-87* (unpublished printout) (Washington, D.C.: 1988); output in 1988 is a Worldwatch estimate.

3. U.S. grain production from USDA, FAS, *World Grain Situation and Outlook,* Washington, D.C., November 1988.

4. USDA, National Agricultural Statistics Service (NASS), *Crop Production,* Washington, D.C., August 1988; James E. Hansen, Director, NASA Goddard Institute for Space Studies, "The Greenhouse Effect: Impacts on Current Global Temperature and Regional Heat Waves," Testimony before the Committee on Energy and Natural Resources, U.S. Senate, June 23, 1988; Syukuro Manabe, "Climate Warming Due to Greenhouse Gases," Testimony before the Subcommittee on Toxic Substances and Environmental Oversight, Committee on Environment and Public Works, U.S. Senate, December 10, 1985.

5. USDA, ERS, *World Grain 1950-87.*

6. Gary A. Margheim, *Implementing Conservation Compliance* (Washington, D.C.: USDA, Soil Conservation Service (SCS), 1986); "Farmers Turn Down the Irrigation Tap," *Farmline,* August 1988; Gordon Sloggett and Clifford Dickason, *Ground-Water Mining in the United States* (Washington, D.C.: USDA, ERS, 1986).

7. Worldwatch Institute estimate based on irrigation data from Sloggett and Dickason, *Ground-Water Mining,* on soil erosion data from USDA, ERS, *An Economic Analysis of USDA Erosion Control Programs* (Washington, D.C.: 1986), and on grain production data from USDA, ERS, *World Grain 1950-87.*

8. Francis Urban and Philip Rose, *World Population by Country and Region, 1950–86, and Projections to 2050* (Washington, D.C.: USDA, ERS, 1988); USDA, ERS, *World Grain 1950–87.*

9. Per capita data through 1987 from USDA, ERS, *World Grain 1950–87;* per capita figure for 1988 derived from USDA, FAS, *World Grain Situation*, August 1988, and from Urban and Rose, *World Population.*

10. USDA, ERS, *World Grain 1950–87.*

11. Ibid.; Bruce E. Goldstein, "Indonesia Reconsiders Resettlement," *World Watch* (Washington, D.C.), March/April 1988.

12. USDA, ERS, *World Grain 1950–87.*

13. Ibid.; USDA, ERS, *China: Agriculture and Trade Report*, Washington, D.C., June 1988; "China Grain Yield Likely to Drop Below Target," *Journal of Commerce*, June 15, 1988.

14. Projected output from USDA, ERS, *China: Situation and Outlook Report*, Washington, D.C., July 1986.

15. USDA, ERS, *World Grain 1950–87.*

16. USDA, FAS, *World Rice Reference Tables* (unpublished printout) (Washington, D.C.: July 1988); USDA, FAS, *World Wheat and Coarse Grains Reference Tables* (unpublished printout) (Washington, D.C.: August 1988).

17. USDA, ERS, *World Grain 1950–87;* World Bank, *World Development Report 1988* (New York: Oxford University Press, 1988); USDA, ERS, *China: Situation and Outlook Report;* USDA, ERS, *China: Agriculture and Trade;* "Midsummer Heat Brings Problems," *China Daily,* August 4, 1988.

18. USDA, ERS, *China: Situation and Outlook;* USDA, ERS, *World Grain 1950–87.*

19. USDA, FAS, *World Rice;* USDA, FAS, *World Wheat and Coarse Grains.*

20. USDA, FAS, *World Rice;* USDA, FAS, *World Wheat and Coarse Grains.*

21. USDA, FAS, *World Rice;* USDA, FAS, *World Wheat and Coarse Grains;* United Nations World Food Council (WFC), "The Global State of Hunger and Malnutrition: 1988 Report," 14th Ministerial Session, Nicosia, Cyprus, March 24, 1988.

22. Calculations based on data in USDA, ERS, *World Grain 1950–87.*

23. Ibid.

24. Ibid.

25. Ibid.; USDA, ERS, *An Economic Analysis.*

26. USDA, ERS, *World Grain 1950-87;* Ye. F. Zorina et al., "The Role of the Human Factor in the Development of the Gullying in the Steppe and Wooded Steppe of the European USSR," *Soviet Geography,* January 1977.

27. Gorbachev quoted in Vera Rich, "Soil First," *Nature,* February 12, 1982.

28. Jiang Deqi et al., *Soil Erosion and Conservation in the Wuding River Valley* (Beijing: Yellow River Conservancy Commission, 1980), cited in S.A. El-Swaify and E.W. Dangler, "Rainfall Erosion in the Tropics: A State-of-the Art," in American Society of Agronomy, *Soil Erosion and Conservation in the Tropics,* Special Publication No. 43 (Madison, Wis.: 1982); Josef R. Parrington et al., "Asian Dust: Seasonal Transport to the Hawaiian Islands," *Science,* April 8, 1983.

29. U.S. Agency for International Development, "Fiscal Year 1980 Budget Proposal for Ethiopia," Washington, D.C., 1978.

30. USDA, ERS, *China: Agriculture and Trade;* USDA, ERS, *China: Situation and Outlook;* World Bank, *World Development Report 1988;* USDA, ERS, *World Grain 1950–87.*

31. Kenneth Newcombe, *An Economic Justification for Rural Afforestation: The Case of Ethiopia,* Energy Department Paper No. 16 (Washington, D.C.: World Bank, 1984); Kenneth Newcombe, "Household Energy Supply: The Energy Crisis That Is Here To Stay!" presented to the World Bank Senior Policy

Seminar—Energy, Gabarone, Botswana, March 18–22, 1985.

32. K. G. Tejwani, Land Use Consultants International, private communication, July 3, 1983; USDA, ERS, *An Economic Analysis;* Centre for Science and Environment, *The State of India's Environment 1982* (New Delhi: 1982).

33. Margheim, *Implementing Conservation Compliance.*

34. USDA, ERS, *World Grain 1950–87;* U.N. Food and Agriculture Organization (FAO), *Current World Fertilizer Situation and Outlook 1985/86–1991/92* (Rome: 1987).

35. Sidy Gaye, "Glaciers of the Desert," *Ambio,* Vol. 16, No. 6, 1987; Asim I. El Moghraby et al., "Desertification in Western Sudan and Strategies for Rehabilitation," *Environmental Conservation,* Autumn 1987; Djibril Diallo, "Saving Timbuktu," *Africa Recovery,* December 1987.

36. Lester R. Brown and Christopher Flavin, "The Earth's Vital Signs," in Lester R. Brown et al., *State of the World 1988* (New York: W.W. Norton & Co., 1988); USDA, ERS, *Cropland, Water, and Conservation: Situation and Outlook Report,* September 1988.

37. W.R. Rangeley, "Irrigation and Drainage in the World," paper presented at International Conference on Food and Water, Texas A&M University, College Station, May 26–30, 1986; irrigated area 1980 to present is Worldwatch Institute estimate based on ibid.

38. Frederick W. Crook, *Agricultural Statistics of the People's Republic of China, 1949–86* (Washington, D.C.: USDA, ERS, 1988).

39. Centre for Monitoring the Indian Economy, Economic Intelligence Service, *Basic Statistics Relating to the Indian Economy, Vol. 1: All India* (Bombay: 1984).

40. FAO, *Production Yearbooks* (Rome: various years); Sloggett and Dickason, *Ground-Water Mining;* USDA, ERS, *USSR: Agriculture and Trade Report,* Washington, D.C., May 1988.

41. David Fraser, "Water Crisis Threatens to Dry Up China's Future," *New Straits Times,* May 8, 1986; Sandra Postel, *Water: Rethinking Management in an Age of Scarcity,* Worldwatch Paper 62 (Washington, D.C.: Worldwatch Institute, December 1984); Sloggett and Dickason, *Ground-Water Mining.*

42. USDA, ERS, *Cropland, Water, and Conservation.*

43. Sloggett and Dickason, *Ground-Water Mining.*

44. Chinese irrigated area fell from nearly 45 million hectares in 1978 to an estimated 44 million hectares in 1987, according to data in USDA, ERS, *China Situation and Outlook Report,* Washington, D.C., July 1987; Fraser, "Water Crisis Threatens to Dry Up China's Future"; Postel, *Water: Rethinking Management;* Li Rongxia, "Irrigation System in Central Shaanxi," *Beijing Review,* December 14–20, 1987; Nie Lisheng, "State Organizes Farmers to Work on Irrigation," *China Daily,* January 16, 1988.

45. Salamat Ali, "Adrift in Flood and Drought," *Far Eastern Economic Review,* August 27, 1987; Navin C. Joshi, "Ground Water Crisis Swells Up," *Business Standard,* April 26, 1988; B. B. Vohra, *When Minor Becomes Major: Some Problems of Ground Water Management* (New Delhi: Advisory Board on Energy, 1986).

46. Martin Walker, "Sea Turning Into Desert," *Manchester Guardian Weekly,* April 24, 1988.

47. Philip P. Micklin, "Desiccation of the Aral Sea: A Water Management Disaster in the Soviet Union," *Science,* September 2, 1988; Walker, "Sea Turning Into Desert."

48. Walker, "Sea Turning Into Desert."

49. U.S. trend from "Farmers Turn Down the Irrigation Tap"; Chinese trend from Crook, *Agricultural Statistics.*

50. Rangeley, "Irrigation and Drainage."

51. USDA, ERS, *World Grain 1950–87.*

52. Yields 1984–88 from USDA, FAS, *World Grain Situation,* August 1988.

53. FAO, *Fertilizer Yearbooks* (Rome: various years); Elliot Berg, "Fertilizer Subsidies" (draft), World Bank, Washington, D.C., December 1985.

54. World fertilizer use from FAO, *Fertilizer Yearbooks;* world grain area per person from USDA, ERS, *World Grain 1950–87.*

55. FAO, *Fertilizer Yearbooks;* Anthony M. Tang and Bruce Stone, *Food Production in the People's Republic of China* (Washington, D.C.: International Food Policy Research Institute, 1980).

56. USDA, ERS, *World Grain 1950–87.*

57. Ibid.; Duane Chapman and Randy Barker, *Resource Depletion, Agricultural Research, and Development* (Ithaca, N.Y.: Cornell University, 1987).

58. USDA, ERS, *World Grain 1950–87.*

59. Robert W. Herdt, "Technological Potential for Increasing Crop Productivity in Developing Countries," paper presented to the meeting of the International Trade Research Consortium, December 14–18, 1986.

60. Fertilizer returns 20 years ago and projections from Lester R. Brown with Erik P. Eckholm, *By Bread Alone* (New York: Praeger Publishers, 1974); Chapman and Barker, *Resource Depletion;* FAO, *Current World Fertilizer Situation and Outlook.*

61. USDA, ERS, *World Grain 1950–87.*

62. Ibid.; 1988 per capita production is a Worldwatch estimate.

63. USDA, ERS, *World Grain 1950–87;* 1988 Worldwatch estimate; human caloric intake derived from data in FAO, *Production Yearbook, 1986* (Rome: 1986), from USDA, ERS, *World Grain 1950–87,* and from USDA, FAS, *World Grain Situation,* August 1988.

64. USDA, ERS, *World Grain 1950–87.*

65. Ibid.

66. Data on the carryover stocks of grain in Table 3–3 differ from those in earlier *States of the World* because USDA recently recalculated the historical data on this item using better information on China.

67. World cropland area figure from USDA, ERS, *World Grain 1950–87.*

68. USDA, FAS, *World Grain Situation,* November 1988; data on oil exports from British Petroleum Company, *BP Statistical Review of World Energy* (London: 1987).

Chapter 4. Abandoning Homelands

1. "Plan to Raze Chernobyl Reported," *New York Times,* October 9, 1988.

2. U.S. Committee For Refugees, *World Refugee Survey, 1987 in Review* (Washington, D.C.: American Council for Nationalities Service, 1988).

3. Worldwatch Institute estimate of the current number of environmental refugees worldwide assumes at least 8 million refugees from land degradation throughout Africa, Asia, and Latin America, including conservative estimates of migrants to cities due to declining land productivity; about 2 million displaced over the long term by natural disasters whose effects are exacerbated by human activity; and several thousand displaced by toxic poisoning of land, including the aftereffects of Chernobyl. Based on information obtained from the U.S. State Department, the United Nations High Commissioner for Refugees, and various other sources listed elsewhere in notes.

4. John Steinbeck, *The Grapes of Wrath* (New York: Viking Press, 1939).

5. Standing Committee on Agriculture, Fisheries and Forestry, *Soil At Risk: Canada's Eroding Future,* A Report on Soil Conservation to the Senate of Canada (Ottawa: 1984).

6. Paul Harrison, *The Greening of Africa* (New York: Viking/Penguin, 1987); Robert M. Press, "Ethiopia Appears to Stay One

Small Step Ahead of Famine," *Christian Science Monitor,* June 15, 1988.

7. Essam El-Hinnawi, *Environmental Refugees* (Nairobi: United Nations Environment Programme (UNEP), 1985).

8. UNEP, *General Assessment of Progress in the Implementation of the Plan of Action to Combat Desertification 1978–1984* (Nairobi: 1984); figure on earth's total land surface from James H. Brown, *Biogeography* (St. Louis: C.V. Mosby Company, 1983); UNEP, "Sands of Change: Why Land Becomes Desert and What Can be Done About It," *UNEP Environment Brief No. 2,* Nairobi, 1988; H.E. Dregne and C.J. Tucker, "Desert Encroachment," *Desertification Control Bulletin,* No. 16, 1988.

9. UNEP, "Sands of Change"; H.E. Dregne, *Desertification of Arid Lands* (New York: Harwood Academic Publishers, 1983).

10. UNEP, "Sands of Change"; for information on the ecology of the Sahelian region, see Harrison, *Greening of Africa;* James Brooke, "Some Gains in West Africa's War on the Desert," *New York Times,* September 13, 1987.

11. UNEP, "Sands of Change"; Brooke, "Some Gains in West Africa's War"; Carolyn M. Somerville, *Drought and Aid in the Sahel* (Boulder, Colo.: Westview Press, 1986); Anders Wijkman and Lloyd Timberlake, *Natural Disasters: Acts of God or Acts of Man* (London: International Institute for Environment and Development, 1984).

12. El-Hinnawi, *Environmental Refugees;* Wijkman and Timberlake, *Natural Disasters.*

13. El-Hinnawi, *Environmental Refugees;* Harrison, *Greening of Africa.*

14. Harrison, *Greening of Africa;* Wijkman and Timberlake, *Natural Disasters;* UNEP, "Sands of Change"; William S. Ellis, "Africa's Sahel: The Stricken Land," *National Geographic,* August 1987; Sidy Gaye, "Glaciers of the Desert," *Ambio,* Vol. 16, No. 6, 1987.

15. Oakland Ross, "Where the Water Was," *Globe and Mail,* April 23, 1988.

16. UNEP, *Desertification Control in Africa: Actions and Directory of Institutions* (Nairobi: 1985).

17. Harrison, *Greening of Africa;* Anne Charnock, "An African Survivor," *New Scientist,* July 3, 1986; Susan Ringrose and Wilma Matheson, "Desertification in Botswana: Progress Toward a Viable Monitoring System," *Desertification Control Bulletin,* No. 13, 1986.

18. Mary Anne Weaver, "India: The 'Greening' of a Bad Drought," *Christian Science Monitor,* May 25, 1983; UNEP, "Sands of Change"; J. Bandyopadhyay and Vandana Shiva, "Drought, Development, and Desertification," *Economic and Political Weekly,* August 16, 1986; Jayanta Bandyopadhyay, "Political Ecology of Drought and Water Scarcity: Need for an Ecological Water Resources Policy," *Economic and Political Weekly,* December 12, 1987; Steven R. Weisman, "India's Drought Is Worst in Decades," *New York Times,* August 16, 1987; Anthony Spaeth, "Harshest Drought in Decades Devastates India's Crops, Slows Economic Growth," *Wall Street Journal,* August 19, 1987.

19. Lester R. Brown and Jodi L. Jacobson, *The Future of Urbanization: Facing the Ecological and Economic Constraints,* Worldwatch Paper 77 (Washington, D.C.: Worldwatch Institute, May 1987).

20. Mark Kurlansky, "Haiti's Environment Teeters On the Edge," *International Wildlife,* March/April 1988; refugee figure from U.S. Committee For Refugees, *World Refugee Survey.*

21. Richard M. Weintraub, "Flooding Worsens in Bangladesh," *Washington Post,* September 5, 1988; "Bangladesh Intensifies Appeal for Flood Aid," *New York Times,* September 4, 1988.

22. Per capita income figure from World Bank, *World Development Report 1988* (New York: Oxford University Press, 1988); Popu-

lation Reference Bureau (PRB), *1988 World Population Data Sheet* (Washington, D.C.: 1988); "Life in Bangladesh Delta: A Race Bred By Disaster," *New York Times,* June 21, 1987.

23. Narul Huda, "Bangladesh Blames Neighbors for its Floods," *Panoscope* (London), December 1987.

24. International Task Force, *Tropical Forests: A Call to Action, Part 2: Case Studies* (Washington, D.C.: World Resources Institute, 1985).

25. Huda, "Bangladesh Blames Neighbors"; "Misery Rising in the Floods in Bangladesh," *New York Times,* September 5, 1987; S. Kamaluddin, "Flood of Woes," *Far Eastern Economic Review,* November 8, 1984.

26. Hans Hurni, "Degradation and Conservation of the Resources in the Ethiopian Highlands," *Mountain Research and Development,* Vol. 8, Nos. 2–3, 1988.

27. Blaine Harden, "Nile Floods in Sudan Termed Record, Could Deepen," *Washington Post,* August 10, 1988.

28. Debora MacKenzie, "Man-made Disaster in the Philippines," *New Scientist,* September 13, 1983.

29. "120 Die in Avalanche of Mud in Colombian Slum," *New York Times,* September 29, 1987.

30. Mac Margolis, "Rio's Mudslides Partly Self-inflicted," *Washington Post,* February 28, 1988.

31. Sally Johnson, "Toxic Waste Uprooting Elderly From Trailer Park," *New York Times,* July 17, 1988; for information on hazardous waste problems in the developing world, see H. Jeffrey Leonard, "Hazardous Wastes: The Crisis Spreads," *National Development,* April 1986.

32. Love Canal Homeowners Association, *Love Canal: A Chronology of Events That Shaped a Movement* (Arlington, Va.: Citizen's Clearinghouse for Hazardous Wastes, Inc., 1984).

33. Ibid.; Michael Weisskopf, "EPA to Complete Love Canal Cleanup but Habitability Remains Uncertain," *Washington Post,* October 27, 1987.

34. Federal Emergency Management Agency (FEMA), "Superfund Relocation Assistance," Washington, D.C., 1985; Charles Robinson, FEMA, Washington, D.C., private communication, February 22, 1988.

35. "Summary of Superfund Activity," unpublished memorandum, FEMA, Washington, D.C., 1988; "8 From Contaminated Town Lose Illness Suit," *New York Times,* June 9, 1988; Michael Weisskopf, "Buyouts Replacing Cleanups as Remedy for Polluted Communities," *Washington Post,* September 3, 1987.

36. Weisskopf, "Buyouts Replacing Cleanups."

37. David Maraniss and Michael Weisskopf, "Jobs and Illness in Petrochemical Corridor," *Washington Post,* December 22, 1987.

38. Ibid.

39. Mike Leary, "Poisoned Environment Worries Eastern Europe," *Philadelphia Inquirer,* October 4, 1987; Hilary F. French, "Industrial Wasteland," *World Watch* (Washington, D.C.), November/December 1988.

40. "Soviet Environmental Official Urges Punishment for Polluters," *Journal of Commerce,* July 6, 1988.

41. UNEP, "Hazardous Chemicals," *UNEP Environment Brief No. 4,* Nairobi, 1988.

42. Jon Nordheimer, "Dioxin's Effects in Italy Less Severe Than Had Been Feared," *New York Times,* January 31, 1983; Michael H. Brown, *The Toxic Cloud* (New York: Harper & Row, 1987); Thomas W. Netter, "Dioxin of '76 Italian Accident Reported Destroyed," *New York Times,* July 14, 1986.

43. Jane H. Ives, ed., *The Export of Hazard* (Boston: Routledge & Kegan Paul, 1985); Sandra Postel, *Defusing the Toxics Threat: Controlling Pesticides and Industrial Waste,* World-

watch Paper 79 (Washington, D.C.: World-watch Institute, September 1987).

44. UNEP, "Hazardous Chemicals"; Michael Isikoff, "Twice Poisoned," *The Washington Monthly,* December 1987.

45. Christopher Flavin, *Reassessing Nuclear Power: The Fallout From Chernobyl,* Worldwatch Paper 75 (Washington, D.C.: Worldwatch Institute, March 1987); George M. Woodwell, "Chernobyl: A Technology That Failed," *Issues in Science and Technology,* Fall 1986.

46. Flavin, *Reassessing Nuclear Power.*

47. Wendy Grieder, U.S. Environmental Protection Agency (EPA), quoted in Nathaniel Sheppard Jr., "U.S. Companies Looking Abroad for Waste Disposal," *Journal of Commerce,* July 20, 1988.

48. Blaine Harden, "Outcry Grows in Africa Over West's Waste-dumping," *Washington Post,* June 22, 1988; Steven Greenhouse, "Toxic Waste Boomerang: Ciao Italy!" *New York Times,* September 1, 1988.

49. "Waste Imports Alarm Lebanese," *Journal of Commerce,* June 27, 1988; Harden, "Outcry Grows."

50. Hilary F. French, "Combating Toxic Terrorism," *World Watch* (Washington, D.C.), September/October 1988.

51. Tom Goemans and Pier Vellinga, "Low Countries and High Seas," presented to the First North American Conference on Preparing for Climate Change: A Cooperative Approach, Washington, D.C., October 27–29, 1987; J.E. Prins, *Impact of Sea Level Rise on Society* (Delft, Netherlands: Delft Hydraulics Laboratory, 1986).

52. Robert C. Cowen, "Man-made Gases Increase the Chance of Major Weather Change," *Christian Science Monitor,* June 30, 1988; warming projections from U.S. National Academy of Sciences, *Changing Climate,* Report of the Carbon Dioxide Assessment Committee (Washington, D.C.: National Academy Press, 1983).

53. James G. Titus, EPA, "Causes and Effects of Sea Level Rise," presented to the First North American Conference on Preparing for Climate Change: A Cooperative Approach, Washington, D.C., October 27–29, 1987.

54. Maumoon Abdul Gayoom, speech before the Forty-second Session of the U.N. General Assembly, New York, October 19, 1987.

55. John D. Milliman et al., "Environmental and Economic Impact of Rising Sea Level and Subsiding Deltas: The Nile and Bengal Examples," Woods Hole Oceanographic Institution, Woods Hole, Mass., unpublished, 1988.

56. Ibid.; Daniel Jean Stanley, "Subsidence in the Northeastern Nile Delta: Rapid Rates, Possible Causes, and Consequences," *Science,* April 22, 1988.

57. Milliman et al., "Environmental and Economic Impact"; for further information, see Clyde Haberman, "A Steamy, Crowded Bangkok is Sinking Slowly Into the Sea," *New York Times,* May 1, 1983.

58. Information on Bangladesh and Egypt in this section from Milliman et al., "Environmental and Economic Impact," unless indicated otherwise.

59. Year 2100 population from PRB, *1988 World Population Data Sheet.*

60. Number of people affected in 2050 from PRB, *1988 World Population Data Sheet.*

61. Prins, *Impact of Sea Level Rise;* Gayoom, speech before U.N. General Assembly.

62. Goemans and Vellinga, "Low Countries and High Seas"; U.S. coastline figure from *The 1988 Information Please Almanac* (New York: Houghton Mifflin Co., 1987).

Chapter 5. Protecting the Ozone Layer

1. Joseph C. Farman et al., "Large Losses of Total Ozone in Antarctica Reveal Seasonal

ClO$_x$/NO$_x$ Interaction," *Nature,* May 16, 1985; Paul Brodeur, "Annals of Chemistry: In the Face of Doubt," *New Yorker,* June 9, 1986.

2. Subcommittees on Environmental Protection and on Hazardous Wastes and Toxic Substances, *Implications of the Findings of the Expedition to Investigate the Ozone Hole Over the Antarctic,* Committee on Environment and Public Works, U.S. Senate, October 27, 1987.

3. National Aeronautics and Space Administration (NASA), "Executive Summary of the Ozone Trends Panel," Washington, D.C., March 15, 1988.

4. United Nations Environment Programme (UNEP), "Montreal Protocol on Substances that Deplete the Ozone Layer," 1987; country updates from U.N. Treaty Office, New York, various private communications; Office of Technology Assessment (OTA), U.S. Congress, "An Analysis of the Montreal Protocol on Substances that Deplete the Ozone Layer," Washington, D.C., December 10, 1987 (rev. February 1, 1988); James E. Hansen, Director, NASA Goddard Institute for Space Studies, "The Greenhouse Effect: Impacts on Current Global Temperature and Regional Heat Waves," Testimony before the Committee on Energy and Natural Resources, U.S. Senate, June 23, 1988; Linda J. Fisher, U.S. Environmental Protection Agency (EPA), Testimony before the Subcommittee on Energy and Power, Committee on Energy and Commerce, U.S. House of Representatives, September 22, 1988; T.M.L. Wigley, "Future CFC Concentrations Under the Montreal Protocol and Their Greenhouse-Effect Implications," *Nature,* September, 22, 1988.

5. Farman et al., "Large Losses"; Mario Molina and F. Sherwood Rowland, "Stratospheric Sink for Chlorofluoromethanes: Chlorine Atom Catalysed Destruction of Ozone," *Nature,* June 28, 1974.

6. Douglas G. Cogan, *Stones in a Glass House: CFCs and Ozone Depletion* (Washington,

D.C.: Investor Responsibility Research Center, 1988); Richard S. Stolarski, "The Antarctic Ozone Hole," *Scientific American,* January 1988.

7. Susan Solomon, National Oceanic and Atmospheric Administration (NOAA), interview on "The Hole in the Sky," *NOVA,* WGBH-Boston, February 24, 1987.

8. Stolarski, "The Antarctic Ozone Hole"; "Airborne Antarctic Ozone Experiment," NASA, Washington, D.C., July 1987; Shirley Christian, "Pilots Fly Over the Pole into the Heart of Ozone Mystery," *New York Times,* September 22, 1987.

9. Mario J. Molina et al., "Antarctic Stratospheric Chemistry of Chlorine Nitrate, Hydrogen Chloride, and Ice: Release of Active Chlorine," *Science,* November 27, 1987; Mario Molina, "The Antarctic Ozone Hole," *Oceanus,* Summer 1988; F. Sherwood Rowland, University of California at Irvine, Testimony before the Committee on Environment and Public Works, U.S. Senate, September 14, 1988.

10. James G. Anderson, Harvard University, Testimony before the Environmental Protection and the Hazardous Wastes and Toxic Substances Subcommittees, Committee on Environment and Public Works, U.S. Senate, October 27, 1987.

11. Molina, "The Antarctic Ozone Hole"; NASA, "Ozone Trends."

12. Fisher, Testimony; Wigley, "Future CFC Concentrations"; Michael McElroy, "The Challenge of Global Change," *New Scientist,* July 28, 1988; Donald R. Blake and F. Sherwood Rowland, "Continuing Worldwide Increase in Tropospheric Methane, 1978 to 1987," *Nature,* March 4, 1988.

13. Pamela S. Zurer, "Studies on Ozone Destruction Expand Beyond Antarctic," *Chemical and Engineering News,* May 30, 1988.

14. Ibid.; Malcolm W. Browne, "New Ozone Threat: Scientists Fear Layer is Erod-

ing at North Pole," *New York Times,* October 11, 1988.

15. Zurer, "Studies on Ozone Destruction Expand Beyond Antarctic"; Molina, "The Antarctic Ozone Hole"; John Gribben, "Satellite Failure Threatens Ozone Probe," *New Scientist,* July 14, 1988.

16. Rowland, Testimony; R. Monastersky, "Arctic Ozone: Signs of Chemical Destruction," *Science News,* June 11, 1988; Robert T. Watson, NASA, Testimony before the Environmental Protection and the Hazardous Wastes and Toxic Substances Subcommittees, Committee on Environment and Public Works, U.S. Senate, October 27, 1987.

17. NASA, "Ozone Trends."

18. Ibid.

19. Ibid.; McElroy, "Challenge of Global Change."

20. Robert T. Watson, "Present State of Knowledge of the Ozone Layer," presented to The Changing Atmosphere: Implications for Global Security, Toronto, June 27–30, 1988; Rowland, Testimony.

21. James Gleik, "Even With Action Today, Ozone Loss Will Increase," *New York Times,* March 20, 1988.

22. NASA, "Ozone Trends"; EPA, *Regulatory Impact Analysis: Protection of Stratospheric Ozone,* Volume I (Washington, D.C.: 1987).

23. J.C. van der Leun, "Health Effects of Ultraviolet Radiation," draft report to the UNEP Coordinating Committee on the Ozone Layer, Effects of Stratospheric Modification and Climate Change, Bilthoven, Netherlands, November 19–21, 1986 (hereinafter cited as UNEP Coordinating Committee).

24. Ibid.; Paul Strickland et al., "Sunlight, Ozone, and Skin Cancer," *Health & Environment Digest,* May 1988; "Effects of Ozone Layer Modification," UNEP Coordinating Committee; EPA, *Regulatory Impact Analysis;* Polly Penhale, National Science Foundation, Washington, D.C., private communication,

September 28, 1988; Peter Wilkness, National Science Foundation, Testimony before the Environmental Protection and the Hazardous Wastes and Toxic Substances Subcommittees, Committee on Environment and Public Works, U.S. Senate, October 27, 1987.

25. National Cancer Institute, *1987 Annual Cancer Statistics Review: Including Cancer Trends: 1950–1985* (Bethesda, Md: National Institutes of Health, 1987); Arjun Makhijani et al., *Saving Our Skins: Technical Potential and Policies for the Elimination of Ozone-Depleting Chlorine Compounds* (Washington, D.C.: Environmental Policy Institute/Institute for Energy and Environmental Research, 1988); EPA, *Regulatory Impact Analysis.*

26. Robin Russell Jones, "Ozone Depletion and Cancer Risk," *Lancet,* August 22, 1987; Janice Longstreth, "Health Effects Associated with Stratospheric Ozone Depletion," in Dr. Karola Taschner, ed., *The Sky is the Limit* (Brussels: European Environmental Bureau, 1987); Darrel Rigel, New York University Medical Center, Testimony before the Subcommittee on Health and the Environment, Committee on Energy and Commerce, U.S. House of Representatives, March 9, 1987.

27. EPA, *Regulatory Impact Analysis.*

28. Margaret Kripke, M.D., Anderson Hospital and Tumor Institute, Testimony before the Environmental Protection and the Hazardous Wastes and Toxic Substances Subcommittees, Committee on Environment and Public Works, U.S. Senate, May 12, 1987; EPA, *Regulatory Impact Analysis;* Janice Longstreth, ICF Inc., Fairfax, Va., private communication, September 28, 1988.

29. EPA, *Regulatory Impact Analysis;* Longstreth, private communication; "Chlorofluorocarbons: A Valuable Chemical Threatens the Atmosphere," *Health & Environment Digest,* May 1988.

30. "Risks to Crops and Terrestrial Ecosystems From Enhanced UV-B Radiation,"

draft report to the UNEP Coordinating Committee; Alan Teramura, "The Potential Consequences of Ozone Depletion Upon Global Agriculture," in J. Titus, ed., *Effects of Changes in Stratospheric Ozone and Global Climate* (Washington, D.C.: EPA, 1986); Alan H. Teramura and N.S. Murali, "Intraspecific Differences in Growth and Yield of Soybean Exposed to Ultraviolet-B Radiation Under Greenhouse and Field Conditions," *Environmental and Experimental Botany,* Vol. 26, No. 1, 1986.

31. James Falco, Director, Office of Environmental Processes and Effects Research, EPA, Testimony before the Subcommittee on Natural Resources, Agriculture Research and Environment, Committee on Science, Space and Technology, U.S. House of Representatives, March 10, 1987.

32. Robert C. Worrest, "What Are the Effects of UV-B Radiation on Marine Organisms?" Testimony before the West German Bundestag Commission on Preventive Measures to Protect the Earth's Atmosphere, April 27, 1988.

33. Robert C. Worrest, "Solar Ultraviolet-B Radiation Effects on Aquatic Organisms," draft report to the UNEP Coordinating Committee; "Dinosaurs Doomed by a Dearth of Plankton," *New Scientist,* March 17, 1988.

34. Worrest, "Solar Ultraviolet-B Radiation Effects on Aquatic Organisms."

35. Office of Air and Radiation, *Assessing the Risks of Trace Gases that Can Modify the Stratosphere* (Washington, D.C.: EPA, 1987).

36. Raymond J. Kopp and Alan J. Krupnick, "Agricultural Policy and the Benefits of Ozone Control," *American Journal of Agricultural Economics,* December 1987.

37. Philip Shabecoff, "Ozone Pollution is Found at Peak in Summer Heat," *New York Times,* July 31, 1988; Marjorie Sun, "Tighter Ozone Standard Urged by Scientists," *Science,* June 24, 1988.

38. Shabecoff, "Ozone Pollution"; Harold Dovland, "Monitoring European Transboundary Air Pollution," *Environment,* December 1987.

39. Private communications with officials at EPA, National Science Foundation, U.S. Department of Agriculture, and National Institutes of Health; Hartmut Keune, Ecological Research Division, West German Ministry for Research and Technology, Bonn, private communication, June 28, 1988.

40. EPA, *Regulatory Impact Analysis.*

41. Cogan, *Stones in a Glass House.*

42. Chemical Manufacturers Association (CMA), "Production, Sales, and Calculated Release of CFC-11 and CFC-12 Through 1986," Washington, D.C., November 18, 1987.

43. Michael Weisskopf, "CFCs: Rise and Fall of Chemical 'Miracle'," *Washington Post,* April 10, 1988; EPA, Addenda to *Regulatory Impact Analysis*; Alliance for Responsible CFC Policy, *The Montreal Protocol: A Briefing Book* (Rosslyn, Va.: 1987).

44. Steve Risotto, Halogenated Solvents Industry Alliance, Washington, D.C., private communication, August 31, 1988.

45. Cogan, *Stones in a Glass House.*

46. Ron Wolf, "Ozone Layer Negotiations Target Chlorofluorocarbons," *Journal of Commerce,* August 13, 1987; Alliance for Responsible CFC Policy, *Briefing Book*.

47. Cogan, *Stones in a Glass House;* P.H. Gamlen et al., "The Production and Release to the Atmosphere of CCl_3F and CCl_2F_2 (Chlorofluorocarbons CFC 11 and CFC 12)," *Atmospheric Environment,* Vol. 20, No. 6, 1986; Elizabeth Festa Gormley, CMA, Washington, D.C., private communication, August 31, 1988; Christopher F.P. Bevington, Metro Consulting Group Limited, London, private communication, May 23, 1988; Risotto, private communication.

48. EPA, *Regulatory Impact Analysis;* Richard Monastersky, "Decline of the CFC Em-

pire," *Science News,* April 9, 1988; House of Commons Environment Committee, *Air Pollution* (London: Her Majesty's Stationery Office, 1988); Cogan, *Stones in a Glass House;* "White Paper on the Environment in Japan 1988," Japanese Environment Agency, Tokyo, May 1988.

49. CMA, "Production, Sales, and Calculated Release."

50. Cogan, *Stones in a Glass House.*

51. CMA, "Production, Sales, and Calculated Release"; Risotto, private communication.

52. Michael Weisskopf, "EPA Urges Halt in Use of CFCs," *Washington Post,* September 27, 1988; John S. Hoffman and Michael J. Gibbs, *Future Concentrations of Stratospheric Chlorine and Bromine* (Washington, D.C.: EPA, 1988).

53. Cogan, *Stones in a Glass House;* CMA, "Production, Sales, and Calculated Release"; Michael Kavanaugh et al., "An Analysis of the Economic Effects of Regulatory and Non-Regulatory Events Related to the Abandonment of Chlorofluorocarbons as Aerosol Propellants in the United States From 1970 to 1980, with a Discussion of Applicability of the Analysis to Other Nations," ICF Inc., Washington, D.C., February 1986 (rev.); Nigel Haigh, *EEC Environmental Policy & Britain* (Harlow, Essex: Longman Group UK Ltd, 1987).

54. Cumulative emissions reductions from EPA, *Regulatory Impact Analysis;* CMA, "Production, Sales, and Calculated Release."

55. CMA, "Production, Sales, and Calculated Release."

56. "The Aerosol Industry and CFCs: A Parting of the Ways," *ENDS Report,* January 1988; Mark Vandenreeck, Belgian embassy, Washington, D.C., private communication, April 14, 1988; Wolf Dieter Garber, Umweltbundesamt, Berlin, West Germany, private communication, June 24, 1988; "Aerosol Makers to Offer Voluntary Labeling for Prod-

ucts Without CFCs, Association Says," *International Environment Reporter,* June 8, 1988; Vera Rich, "Growing Reaction to Ozone Hole in Soviet Union," *Nature,* August 25, 1988.

57. F. Camm et al., "The Social Cost of Technical Control Options to Reduce Emissions of Potential Ozone Depleters in the United States: An Update," The Rand Corporation, Santa Monica, Calif., May 1986; Alan S. Miller and Irving M. Mintzer, "The Sky *Is* the Limit: Strategies for Protecting the Ozone Layer," World Resources Institute, Washington, D.C., November 1986.

58. M. Drechsler, Umweltbundesamt, Berlin, West Germany, private communication, June 24, 1988; L.R. Wallace, AT&T, Princeton, N.J., private communication, March 9, 1988; Maurice Verhille, Atochem, Paris, private communication, June 17, 1988; Kevin Fay, Alliance for Responsible CFC Policy, Rosslyn, Va., private communication, October 14, 1988; J. Rodgers, Allied-Signal, "Recycling and Recovery of Solvents in the Electronics Industry," in "Proceedings of Conference and Trade Fair: Substitutes and Alternatives to CFCs and Halons," EPA, Washington, D.C., January 13–15, 1988 (hereinafter cited as Substitutes and Alternatives Conference).

59. "Takeshita Cabinet Approves Ozone Bill Including Tax Incentives for CFC Recycling," *International Environment Reporter,* April 13, 1988.

60. C.H. Mueller, "Report on Realisation and Results with a Full Scale CFC 11 Recovery Unit in the Flexible Foam Slabstock Production at Recticel in Kesteren Holland," Escher Hoogezand, Netherlands, March 11, 1987; Dr. H. Creyf, Recticel, Testimony before the West German Bundestag Commission on Preventive Measures to Protect the Earth's Atmosphere, April 13, 1988; National Swedish Environmental Protection Board, *CFCs/Freons: Proposals to Protect the Ozone Layer* (Solna, Sweden: 1987); "Foam Plastics: Next in Line for the CFCs Cam-

paign," *ENDS Report,* March 1988; N.C. Vreenegoor, "Environmental Considerations in the Production of Flexible Slabstock," Substitutes and Alternatives Conference.

61. Mueller, "Report on Realisation and Results with a Full Scale CFC 11 Recovery Unit"; Creyf, Testimony; National Swedish Environmental Protection Board, *CFCs/Freons;* "Foam Plastics: Next in Line," *ENDS Report;* Vreenegoor, "Environmental Considerations in the Production of Flexible Slabstock."

62. EPA, Addenda to *Regulatory Impact Analysis.*

63. Sarah L. Clark, "Protecting the Ozone Layer: What You Can Do," Environmental Defense Fund, New York, 1988; Jean Lupinacci, EPA, Washington, D.C., private communication, October 14, 1988; Kenneth Manz, Robinair, Montpelier, Ohio, private communication, August 11, 1988.

64. Clark, "Protecting the Ozone Layer"; Lupinacci, private communication.

65. Mr. Pautz, Umweltbundesamt, Berlin, West Germany, private communication, June 24, 1988.

66. John R. Fisher, "A New Rosin Defluxing Alternative," AT&T, Princeton, N.J., 1988; Philip Shabecoff, "New Compound Is Hailed as Boon to Ozone Shield," *New York Times,* January 14, 1988; Pamela S. Zurer, "Search Intensifies for Alternatives to Ozone-Depleting Halocarbons," *Chemical and Engineering News,* February 8, 1988; Sudhakar Kesavan, "Overview of CFC-113 Use in the Electronics Industry and Control Options Available," Substitutes and Alternatives Conference.

67. Laurie Hays, "Du Pont Plans Plant to Produce Refrigerant Harmless to Ozone," *Wall Street Journal,* September 30, 1988; "Du Pont Plans Commercial-Scale Plant for Production of CFC-12 Substitute," *Journal of Commerce,* September 30, 1988; Malcolm

Gladwell, "Du Pont Plans to Make CFC Alternative," *Washington Post,* September 30, 1988.

68. "Carbide Easing an Ozone Peril," *Washington Post,* August 6, 1988; "Dow to Curtail CFCs," *Washington Post,* May 14, 1988.

69. Thomas P. Nelson, "Findings of the Chlorofluorocarbon Chemical Substitutes International Committee," EPA, Washington, D.C., 1988; Meirion Jones, "In Search of Safe CFCs," *New Scientist,* May 26, 1988; U. Bohr, Du Pont, Testimony before the West German Bundestag Commission on Preventive Measures to Protect the Earth's Atmosphere, April 25, 1988; Imperial Chemical Industries (ICI), Testimony before the West German Bundestag Commission on Preventive Measures to Protect the Earth's Atmosphere, April 29, 1988.

70. "Du Pont Sees Progress in Replacing Fluorocarbons," *Chemical Marketing Reporter,* January 11, 1988; "Korean Firm Joins in International Effort to Pool Knowledge on CFC Toxicity Testing Studies," *International Environment Reporter,* April 13, 1988; Greg Freiherr, "Can Chemists Save the World from Chemists?" *The Scientist,* May 16, 1988.

71. Camm et al., "Social Cost of Technical Control Options"; National Swedish Environmental Protection Board, *CFCs/Freons.*

72. Makhijani et al., *Saving Our Skins;* Nick Sundt, OTA, Washington, D.C., private communication, July 28, 1988.

73. Tom Potter, "Potential for Offsetting CFCs with Advanced Insulation," Substitutes and Alternatives Conference.

74. John W. Mossel, "Uses of Halons and Opportunities for Emission Reductions: Size and Structure of the Market," Substitutes and Alternatives Conference.

75. Ibid.; Tom Moorehouse, "The Air Force Halon/Ozone Research Program," Substitutes and Alternatives Conference.

76. Gregory C. Munie, AT&T Bell Laboratories, "Experience with the Use of Aqueous Cleaning in the Electronics Industry," Substitutes and Alternatives Conference; Leo Lambert, "Digital Equipment Corporation Experience with Aqueous Cleaning," Substitutes and Alternatives Conference; Eileen B. Claussen, "Moving Forward Together," *The Environmental Forum*, July/August 1988; Kathi Johnson, U.S. Navy, "Alternative Cleaning Materials: Research Topics for the Military," Substitutes and Alternatives Conference.

77. UNEP, "Montreal Protocol"; U.N. Treaty Office, private communication.

78. U.N. Treaty Office, private communication.

79. Refrigerator use in China from National Swedish Environmental Protection Board, *CFCs/Freons.*

80. UNEP, "Montreal Protocol."

81. Ibid.; OTA, "An Analysis of the Montreal Protocol."

82. Hoffman and Gibbs, *Future Concentrations.*

83. Ibid.

84. James K. Hammitt et al., "Future Emission Scenarios for Chemicals that May Deplete Stratospheric Ozone," *Nature*, December 24, 1987; Arjun Makhijani, Institute for Energy and Environmental Research, Takoma Park, Md., private communication, October 26, 1988.

85. Hoffman and Gibbs, *Future Concentrations.*

86. Government of Sweden, "Environmental Policy for the 1990s," Environmental Bill, March 4, 1988; Makhijani et al., *Saving Our Skins.*

87. National Swedish Environmental Protection Board, *CFCs/Freons;* Government of Sweden, "Environmental Policy for the 1990s."

88. $100-million figure from Fay, private communication.

89. Mark Ledbetter, American Council for an Energy Efficient Economy, Washington, D.C., private communication, October 12, 1988; Terry Statt, U.S. Department of Energy, Washington, D.C., private communication, October 12, 1988.

90. Suzanne Butcher, U.S. Department of State, Washington, D.C., private communication, September 1988; Joan Martin-Brown, UNEP, Washington, D.C., private communication, November 1, 1988.

Chapter 6. Rethinking Transportation

1. Motor Vehicle Manufacturers Association (MVMA), *Facts and Figures '88* (Detroit, Mich.: 1988).

2. Production and ownership data from MVMA, *World Motor Vehicle Data, 1987 Edition* (Detroit, Mich.: 1987) and MVMA, *Facts and Figures '87* (Detroit, Mich.: 1987).

3. MVMA, *World Motor Vehicle Data, 1987.*

4. Toli Welihozkiy, "Automobiles and the Soviet Consumer," in *Soviet Economy in a Time of Change*, Vol. 1, Compendium of Papers Submitted to the U.S. Congress, Joint Economic Committee, October 10, 1979; "Russian Cars: French Accent," *The Economist*, December 3, 1983; MVMA, *World Motor Vehicle Data* (Detroit, Mich.: various editions).

5. Clyde H. Farnsworth, "Rise in Allies' Lending to Soviets Divides U.S.," *New York Times*, October 21, 1988.

6. Worldwatch Institute, based on MVMA, *Facts and Figures* (Detroit, Mich.: various editions).

7. MVMA, *Facts and Figures '87.*

8. Pedro-Pablo Kuczynski, "The Outlook for Latin American Debt," *Foreign Affairs*, Fall 1987; William A. Orme, "End of Mexico's Oil Boom Era Has Meant Hardships for Citizens," *Washington Post*, August 16, 1987;

James Bruce, "Autolatina Braces For Further Clash," *Journal of Commerce,* October 15, 1987; MVMA, *World Motor Vehicle Data, 1987.*

9. "The Giants Ship Out to Shape Up," *Gazeta Mercantil,* July 13, 1987; James V. Higgins, "Mexico Pins Economic Recovery on Auto Exports," *Detroit News,* June 10, 1988.

10. Alan Altshuler et al., *The Future of the Automobile: The Report of MIT's International Auto Program* (Cambridge, Mass.: MIT Press, 1984); export and car density data based on MVMA, *World Motor Vehicle Data, 1987* and *Facts and Figures '87.*

11. Population data from United Nations, *World Population Prospects: Estimates and Projections as Assessed in 1984* (New York: 1986); MVMA, *Facts and Figures '87;* "A Great Drive Forward," *Asiaweek,* December 11, 1987; "How China Boosts Her Car Industry," *China Daily,* July 3, 1987; "China Plans to Build More Cars," *China Daily,* June 25, 1987; John Elliott, "A 1950s Comeback," *Financial Times Motor Industry Survey,* October 14, 1986.

12. United Nations, *World Population Prospects;* additions to U.S. car fleet calculated from MVMA, *World Motor Vehicle Data, 1987.*

13. U.S. Department of Energy (DOE), *Assessment of Costs and Benefits of Flexible and Alternative Fuel Use in the U.S. Transportation Sector—Progress Report One: Context and Analytical Framework* (Washington, D.C.: 1988); transport sector consumption based on Philip Patterson, "Periodic Energy Report, No. 2/1987," DOE, Washington, D.C., December 1987, and on Mary C. Holcomb et al., *Transportation Energy Data Book: Edition 9* (Oak Ridge, Tenn.: Oak Ridge National Laboratory, 1987). Comparative international data for passenger cars only are not available.

14. International Monetary Fund (IMF), *International Financial Statistics Yearbook 1987* (Washington, D.C.: 1987); José Goldemberg et al., *Energy for Development* (Washington, D.C.: World Resources Institute, 1987).

15. On Brazilian oil import bills, see "Brazil Survey," *The Economist,* April 25, 1987; IMF, *International Financial Statistics, 1987.* A barrel of alcohol fuel costs about $45 to provide (compared with oil prices currently barely above $10), but its retail price is kept to no more than 65 percent of gasoline prices. Moreover, a reduced fuel import bill is at least partially offset by the need to import some $3 billion worth of foodstuffs that farmers stopped planting in order to grow sugarcane as an ethanol feedstock; Mark Kosmo, *Money to Burn? The High Costs of Energy Subsidies* (Washington, D.C.: World Resources Institute, 1987).

16. United Nations, *1985 Energy Statistics Yearbook* (New York: 1987).

17. Cynthia Pollock Shea, *Renewable Energy: Today's Contribution, Tomorrow's Promise,* Worldwatch Paper 81 (Washington, D.C.: Worldwatch Institute, January 1988). Even in Brazil, demand is growing for gasoline-powered cars, particularly since the government decided to reduce the subsidy for ethanol; "Gasoline-Powered Cars: Output on the Upswing," *Gazeta Mercantil,* July 25, 1988. Corn as feedstock discussed in "PMAA Makes a Case for Methanol," *Energy Daily,* July 30, 1987; Barry Commoner, "Economic Growth and Environmental Quality: How to Have Both," *Social Policy,* Summer 1985.

18. J.R. Kenworthy and P.W.G. Newman, "The Potential of Ethanol as a Transportation Fuel: A Review Based on Technological, Economic, and Environmental Criteria," Discussion Paper No. 6/86, Murdoch University, Australia, August 1986; "Energy: Another Deficit," *The Economist,* November 14, 1987.

19. DOE, *Costs and Benefits of Flexible and Alternative Fuel Use.*

20. Peter Hoffmann, "Hydrogen: Power to Burn?" *Not Man Apart,* November/December 1987; "Hydrogen Drives Prototype Van," *New Scientist,* February 27, 1986.

21. Mark A. DeLuchi et al., "A Comparative Analysis of Future Transportation

Fuels," Institute of Transportation Studies, University of California, Berkeley, October 1987; Paul J. Werbos, *Oil Dependency and the Potential for Fuel Cell Vehicles,* Technical Paper Series (Warrendale, Pa.: Society of Automotive Engineers (SAE), 1987).

22. Average fleet fuel economy from DOE, Energy Information Administration, *Monthly Energy Review,* October 1987; new-car fuel economy from MVMA, *Facts and Figures '87.*

23. Fuel efficiency has been responsible for an estimated two thirds of the reduced gasoline consumption per car in countries that are members of the Organisation for Economic Co-operation and Development (OECD), with the remainder due to reduced driving; International Energy Agency (IEA), *Energy Conservation in IEA Countries* and *Energy Policies and Programmes of IEA Countries, 1986 Review* (Paris: OECD, 1987).

24. Soviet and East German fuel economy from William U. Chandler, *Energy Productivity: Key to Environmental Protection and Economic Progress,* Worldwatch Paper 63 (Washington, D.C.: Worldwatch Institute, January 1985).

25. MVMA, *Facts and Figures '87;* IEA, *Energy Conservation in IEA Countries;* R.M. Heavenrich et al., *Light Duty Automotive Trends Through 1986,* Technical Paper Series (Warrendale, Pa.: SAE, 1986). On light trucks, see Philip Patterson, "Analysis of Future Transportation Petroleum Demand and Efficiency Improvements," presented at IEA Energy Demand Analysis Symposium, Paris, October 12–14, 1987; Patterson, "Periodic Energy Report." The trend toward larger cars in Europe is particularly strong in West Germany; Bundesministerium für Verkehr, *Verkehr in Zahlen 1987* (Bonn: 1987).

26. Holcomb et al., *Transportation Energy Data Book.*

27. Deborah Lynn Bleviss, *The New Oil Crisis and Fuel Economy Technologies: Preparing the Light Transportation Industry for the 1990's* (New York: Quorum Press, 1988).

28. Ibid.

29. Klaus Müller, "The Increasing Use of Plastics and its Impacts on the Recyclability of Automobiles and on Waste Disposal in West Germany, the United States and Japan," presented at the Second Recycling Conference, Washington, D.C., June 18–19, 1987; Bleviss, *The New Oil Crisis.*

30. Bleviss, *The New Oil Crisis.*

31. OECD, *Environmental Effects of Automotive Transport* (The Compass Project) (Paris: 1986).

32. Bleviss, *The New Oil Crisis.*

33. Ibid.

34. Ibid.; Dan McCosh, "Automotive Newsfront," *Popular Science,* December 1987.

35. "Burnley Pushes Repeal of Fuel Economy Rules," *Journal of Commerce,* October 24, 1988.

36. Ford quote is from Robert J. Golten et al., eds., *The End of the Road: A Citizen's Guide to Transportation Problemsolving* (Washington, D.C.: National Wildlife Federation/Environmental Action Foundation, Inc., 1977).

37. Worldwatch estimates, based on MVMA, *Facts and Figures '87.*

38. The U.S. "gas guzzler" tax is assessed on the basis of a particular vehicle's fuel economy. However, it fails to encourage car buyers to purchase the most fuel-efficient models available: A 1986 car achieving a rating of more than 22.5 miles per gallon (MPG) was not subject to any levy, even while the government's own standards dictated a minimum corporate average fuel efficiency standard of 26 MPG. See Holcomb et al., *Transportation Energy Data Book;* Gary Klott, "Rise in 'Gas Guzzler' Tax Approved by Senate Panel," *New York Times,* March 22, 1988.

39. DeLuchi et al., "Comparative Analysis of Future Transportation Fuels"; "Auto Overuse — Dirty Air," *National Association of Railroad Passengers News,* February 1988.

40. Ariel Alexandre and Christian Avér-
ous, "Transport's Toll on the Environment,"
OECD Observer, February/March 1988; carbon dioxide (CO_2) estimate from DeLuchi et
al., "Comparative Analysis of Future Transportation Fuels." In the United States, highway transportation accounts for about 27
percent of all fossil-fuel-released CO_2.

41. Rose Marie Audette, "It Only Hurts
When You Breathe," *Environmental Action,*
March/April 1988; U.S. Environmental Pro-
tection Agency (EPA), *The Economic Effects of
Ozone on Agriculture* (Corvallis, Ore.: 1984).
Recent studies indicate that several hours of
exposure at lower levels may be dangerous to
human health; see Michael Weisskopf,
"Ozone Dangers Upgraded," *Washington
Post,* July 8, 1988.

42. EPA, *National Air Quality and Emissions
Trends Report, 1986* (Research Triangle Park,
N.C.: 1988); "Central Budapest Car Ban
Seeks to Curb Air Pollution," Reuters, March
30, 1988; Alan Cowell, "War on Smog is
Rude Awakening for Athens," *New York
Times,* February 14, 1988.

43. Sandra Postel, *Air Pollution, Acid Rain,
and the Future of Forests,* Worldwatch Paper 58
(Washington, D.C.: Worldwatch Institute,
March 1984); Diane Fisher et al., "Polluted
Coastal Waters: The Role of Acid Rain," Environmental Defense Fund, New York, April
1988.

44. Laura Tangley, "Preparing for Cli-
mate Change," *BioScience,* January 1988;
Philip Shabecoff, "Temperature for World
Rises Sharply in the 1980's," *New York Times,*
March 29, 1988.

45. OECD, *Energy and Cleaner Air* (Paris:
1987); EPA, *Compilation of Air Pollutant Emis-
sion Factors—Volume II: Mobile Sources,* 4th ed.
(Ann Arbor, Mich.: 1985); Jeff Alson, EPA,
Emission Control Technology Division, Ann
Arbor, Mich., private communications, Feb-
ruary 24 and April 14, 1988; Michael P.
Walsh, technical consultant on automotive

emissions, private communications, March
15 and April 7, 1988.

46. On U.S. standards, see Holcomb et al.,
Transportation Energy Data Book; OECD, *Energy
and Cleaner Air;* Japanese standards from T.
Karasudani, Japan External Trade Organization, New York, N.Y., private communication, February 24, 1988; Michael P. Walsh,
"Worldwide Developments in Motor Vehicle
Pollution Control—A 1987 Overview," and
Alfred Szwarc and Gabriel Murgel Branco,
"Automotive Emissions—The Brazilian Control Program," in SAE, *Motor Vehicle Pollution
Control—A Global Perspective* (Warrendale, Pa.:
1987). Different driving cycles and types of
instrumentation used make precise comparisons of national standards difficult.

47. Merrill Korth, EPA, Ann Arbor, Mich.,
private communication, February 24, 1988;
H. Henssler and S. Gospage, "The Exhaust
Emission Standards of the European Community," in SAE, *Motor Vehicle Pollution Control.*

48. Walsh, "Worldwide Developments";
Alson, private communication.

49. OECD, *OECD Environmental Data—
Compendium 1987* (Paris: 1987); World Re-
sources Institute/International Institute for
Environment and Development, *World Re-
sources 1987* (New York: Basic Books, 1987);
Commission of the European Communities,
*The State of the Environment in the European Com-
munity 1986* (Brussels: 1987); EPA, *National
Air Pollutant Estimates, 1940–1986* (Research
Triangle Park, N.C.: 1987).

50. EPA, *Air Pollutant Estimates, 1940–
1986;* Alson, private communication.

51. Audette, "It Only Hurts When You
Breathe"; "EPA Punts on Construction Sanc-
tions for City Ozone Violators," *Not Man
Apart,* November/December 1987; Michael
Weisskopf, "Hill Group Seeks to Clear the
Air With Compromise on Smog Control,"
Washington Post, March 18, 1988; Dennis
Wamsted, "Au Revoir to an Acid Rain Bill,"
Energy Daily, October 5, 1988.

52. Thomas quoted in "EPA Chief Sees Auto Use Curbs," *Journal of Commerce,* March 9, 1988; Cowell, "War on Smog"; "Central Budapest Car Ban," Reuters; "Air Pollution in Brazil," *Multinational Environmental Outlook,* July 21, 1988; Clyde Haberman, "Is It Over Then? The City Closes Its Heart to the Car," *New York Times,* October 10, 1988.

53. DeLuchi et al., "Comparative Analysis of Future Transportation Fuels"; Bleviss, *The New Oil Crisis.*

54. Barry Commoner, "A Reporter at Large: The Environment," *The New Yorker,* June 15, 1987; OECD, *Environmental Effects of Automotive Transport.* On ceramics, see Robert P. Larsen and Anant D. Vyas, "The Outlook for Ceramics in Heat Engines, 1990–2000: Results of a Worldwide Delphi Survey," Center for Transportation Research, Energy and Environmental Systems Division, Argonne National Laboratory, Argonne, Ill., March 1988.

55. U.S. Senate, Committee on Commerce, Science and Transportation, *Report on Methanol and Alternative Fuels Promotion Act of 1987* (Washington, D.C.: U.S. Government Printing Office, 1987); John Young, "Methanol Moonshine," *World Watch* (Washington, D.C.), July/August 1988.

56. "Colorado Alternative Fuels Program to be Watched Carefully by Other States: Herman," *International Solar Energy Intelligence Report,* July 28, 1987; "Air Quality Concerns Buoy Hopes for U.S. Makers of Alcohol Fuels," *Oil & Gas Journal,* February 9, 1987; Philip Shabecoff, "California Acts to Promote Switch From Gasoline to Methanol Fuel," *New York Times,* May 23, 1987; California Energy Commission, Air Resource Board, South Coast Air Quality Management District, "Report of the Three-Agency Methanol Task Force," Sacramento, Calif., May 15, 1986.

57. De Luchi et al., "Comparative Analysis of Future Transportation Fuels"; California Council for Environmental and Economic Balance, *Alternative Fuels as an Air Quality Improvement Strategy—Prospects, Options, and Implications for California* (Sacramento, Calif.: November 1987); California Energy Commission, "Report of the Methanol Task Force." EPA and California state officials disagree about whether pure methanol helps reduce nitrogen oxide; Alson, private communication.

58. Coal contains 1.4 times as much carbon per unit of stored energy as oil; Jim MacKenzie, "Relative Releases of Carbon Dioxide from Several Fuels," World Resources Institute, Washington, D.C., mimeographed, June 10, 1987. For detailed calculations of CO_2 emissions from methanol production, transmission, and use, see Mark DeLuchi et al., "Transportation Fuels and the Greenhouse Effect," University of California, Davis, December 1987. On ethanol, see "US–Brazilian Study Says Gasohol Creates 'Greenhouse Gases'," *Christian Science Monitor*, November 21, 1988.

59. OECD, *Environmental Effects of Automotive Transport;* DeLuchi et al., "Comparative Analysis of Future Transportation Fuels." On greenhouse gases, see DeLuchi et al., "Transportation Fuels and the Greenhouse Effect"; MacKenzie, "Relative Releases of Carbon Dioxide."

60. DeLuchi et al., "Comparative Analysis of Future Transportation Fuels"; DeLuchi et al., "Transportation Fuels and the Greenhouse Effect."

61. Peter Hoffmann, "Fueling the Future With Hydrogen," *Washington Post,* September 6, 1987; Hoffmann, "Hydrogen: Power to Burn?" Producing hydrogen from coal, however, would produce significant nitrogen and sulfur oxide emissions, and more than double the CO_2 emissions, compared with gasoline vehicles; DeLuchi et al., "Transportation Fuels and the Greenhouse Effect."

62. Worldwide fatality figure based on International Road Federation, *World Road Sta-*

tistics 1981–1985 (Washington, D.C.: 1986), and on MVMA, *Facts and Figures '87.*

63. Global average of land devoted to cars from Lester R. Brown and Jodi L. Jacobson, *The Future of Urbanization: Facing the Ecological and Economic Constraints,* Worldwatch Paper 77 (Washington, D.C.: Worldwatch Institute, May 1987); U.S. urban figure from Kirkpatrick Sale, *Human Scale* (New York: Coward, McCann, & Geoghegan, 1980), and from Richard Register, "What is an Ecocity?" *Earth Island Journal,* Fall 1987.

64. Peter W.G. Newman and Jeffrey R. Kenworthy, "The Use and Abuse of Driving Cycle Research: Clarifying the Relationship Between Traffic Congestion, Energy and Emissions," *Transportation Quarterly,* October 1984; Charles Lockwood and Christopher B. Leinberger, "Los Angeles Comes of Age," *Atlantic Monthly,* January 1988; California Commission quoted in Robert Lindsay, "California Now Sees Cars as a Threat," *New York Times,* April 5, 1988.

65. Sale, *Human Scale;* Peter Newman and Jeffrey Kenworthy, "Gasoline Consumption and Cities—A Comparison of U.S. Cities With a Global Survey and Some Implications," Transport Research Paper 8/87, School of Environmental and Life Sciences, Murdoch University, Australia; Peter Newman and Jeffrey Kenworthy, "Transport and Urban Form in Thirty-Two of the World's Principal Cities," Paper for International Symposium on Transport, Communication and Urban Form, Monash University, Australia, August 24–26, 1987.

66. "Jam Sessions," *U.S. News and World Report,* September 7, 1987; Christopher B. Leinberger and Charles Lockwood, "How Business is Reshaping America," *Atlantic Monthly,* October 1986.

67. Worldwatch Institute, based on MVMA, *Facts and Figures '87.*

68. In the United States, some $17 billion in contributions to 1986 highway construction and maintenance funds, or almost one third, was subsidized; subsidies in the form of municipal services could be as high as $60 billion annually. Furthermore, auto commuters are frequently reimbursed by employers for travel expenses and enjoy free parking at their workplace. "Huge Highway Subsidies . . . ," *National Association of Railroad Passengers News,* June 1985; Federal Highway Administration, *Highway Statistics 1986* (Washington, D.C.: U.S. Department of Transportation, 1987); Stanley Hart, "Huge City Subsidies for Autos, Trucks," *California Transit,* July/September 1986. Per-car and per-gallon subsidy estimates are from Stanley Hart, Sierra Club, San Francisco, Calif., private communication, April 12, 1988.

69. In the United States in 1984, urban rail and bus transit systems used 20 percent less energy per passenger mile than the average car on the road, Amtrak used 40 percent less energy, and intercity buses used less than one third as much energy. If public transit systems were used to fuller capacity, the advantages would increase further. Holcomb et al., *Transportation Energy Data Book.* On road space requirements, see Frederick C. Dunbar and Richard T. Rapp, "Urban Transport Economics: Analysis for Development Banks," presented at First Annual Meeting, International Mass Transit Association, Washington, D.C., February 16–17, 1986.

70. Citizens for Better Transit, "Multi-Destinational Transit," Portland, Ore., mimeographed, 1977.

71. Michael A. Replogle, *Bicycles and Public Transportation: New Links to Suburban Transit Markets,* 2nd ed. (Washington, D.C.: The Bicycle Federation, 1988).

72. Juri Pill, "Land Development: The Latest Panacea for Transit?" *Mass Transit,* January/February 1988.

73. Michael Replogle, "Sustainable Transportation Strategies for Third World Development," prepared for session on Human-Powered Transportation and Transportation Planning for Developing Countries, Transport Research Board 1988 An-

nual Meeting, National Research Council, Washington, D.C.

74. The World Bank accounts for by far the largest share of international development banks' spending on transportation projects; Dunbar and Rapp, "Urban Transport Economics: Analysis for Development Banks." Replogle, "Sustainable Transportation Strategies."

75. Brown and Jacobson, *The Future of Urbanization.*

76. V. Setty Pendakur, "Formal and Informal Urban Transport in Asia," *CUSO Journal,* December 1987; Replogle, "Sustainable Transportation Strategies."

77. Replogle, "Sustainable Transportation Strategies"; Pendakur, "Urban Transport in Asia."

78. Replogle, "Sustainable Transportation Strategies"; Neal R. Peirce, "China's Bike Boom Backward?" *China Daily,* March 9, 1988; Marcia D. Lowe, "Pedaling Into the Future," *World Watch* (Washington, D.C.), July/August 1988.

79. André Gorz, *Ecology as Politics* (Boston: South End Press, 1980).

Chapter 7. Responding to AIDS

1. Smoking-related deaths from William U. Chandler, *Banishing Tobacco*, Worldwatch Paper 68 (Washington, D.C.: Worldwatch Institute, January 1986); diarrhea figure from Katrina Galway et al., *Child Survival: Risks and The Road to Health* (Columbia, Md.: Institute for Resource Development/Westinghouse, 1987); tuberculosis figure from G. Slutkin et al., "Effect of AIDS on the Tuberculosis Problem and Programmes and Priorities for Control and Research," abstract of paper presented at the IV International Conference on AIDS, Stockholm, Sweden, June 12-16, 1988 (hereinafter cited as Stockholm Conference).

2. Quote from "Interview: Jonathan Mann," *AIDS Patient Care* (New York), June 1988.

3. Renée Sabatier, *Blaming Others: Prejudice, Race and Worldwide AIDS* (Philadelphia: New Society Publishers, for Panos Institute in association with Norwegian Red Cross, 1988).

4. Observations about control from Dr. Malcolm Potts, "Preparing for the Battle," *People* (London), Vol. 14, No. 4, 1987; incubation period from Roy M. Anderson and Robert M. May, "Epidemiological Parameters of HIV Transmission," *Nature,* June 9, 1988; observation about progression to AIDS from Institute of Medicine, National Academy of Sciences, *Confronting AIDS, Update 1988* (Washington, D.C.: National Academy Press, 1988).

5. World Health Organization (WHO), "Global Programme On AIDS: Progress Report Number 3," Geneva, May 1988; role of prostitutes from Don C. Des Jarlais et al., "HIV Infection and Intravenous Drug Use: Critical Issues in Transmission Dynamics, Infection Outcomes, and Prevention," *Reviews of Infectious Diseases,* Vol. 10, No. 1, 1988, and from Bruce Lambert, "AIDS Among Prostitutes Not as Prevalent as Believed, Studies Show," *New York Times,* September 20, 1988.

6. Until recently, researchers commonly cited 5–20 percent of sexually active adults infected in major urban areas of East and Central Africa; see Jonathan M. Mann et al., "The International Epidemiology of AIDS," *Scientific American,* October 1988. New data from urban centers in the Kagera region of Tanzania reveal 32.8 percent of adults (aged 15–54) infected; see J. Killewo et al., "The Epidemiology of HIV-1 Infection in the Kagera Region of Tanzania," abstract of paper presented at the Third International Conference on AIDS and Associated Cancers in Africa, Arusha, Tanzania, September 14–16, 1988 (hereinafter cited as Arusha Conference). Prostitute observation from Peter Piot and Michel Caraël, "Epidemiological and Sociological Aspects of HIV-infection in Developing Countries," *British Medical Bulletin,* Vol. 44, No. 1, 1988.

7. Dr. Jonathan Mann, "Global AIDS: A Status Report," Testimony before the Presidential Commission on the Human Immunodeficiency Virus Epidemic (hereinafter cited as Presidential Commission), April 18, 1988.

8. Nancy S. Padian, "Heterosexual Transmission of Acquired Immunodeficiency Syndrome: International Perspectives and National Projections," *Reviews of Infectious Diseases,* September/October 1987; Sabatier, *Blaming Others.*

9. J.O. Ndinya-Achola et al., "Co-Factors in Male-Female Transmission of HIV," abstract of paper presented at Arusha Conference; Mann et al., "International Epidemiology of AIDS"; Michael Specter, "Herpes Found to Increase Susceptibility to AIDS Virus Infection," *Washington Post,* June 16, 1988; D. Zagury et al., "Long Term Cultures of HTLV-III-infected T-cells: A Model of Cytopathology of T-cell Depletion in AIDS," *Science,* February 21, 1986.

10. WHO computer printout and Mann et al., "International Epidemiology of AIDS."

11. Dr. James Chin, Chief, AIDS Surveillance Unit, WHO, Geneva, private communications, September 27 and October 21, 1988.

12. U.S. estimate from William L. Heyward and James W. Curran, "The Epidemiology of AIDS in the U.S.," *Scientific American,* October 1988; European estimate from J.B. Brunet, "Aids and HIV Infection in Europe," abstract of paper presented at Stockholm Conference; Latin American estimate from Pan American Health Organization (PAHO), "The Epidemiology of AIDS in the Americas," Testimony before Presidential Commission, April 18, 1988; Asian estimate from Chin, private communication.

13. Rural outbreaks from Dr. Samuel Ikwaras Okware, "Towards a National AIDS-Control Program in Uganda," *The Western Journal of Medicine,* December 1987, and from William Lyerly, Jr., AIDS Coordinator, Bureau for Africa, U.S. Agency for International Development (AID), Washington, D.C., private communication, October 10, 1988.

14. The percentage of European cases involving drug injection has leveled off in 1988 and includes cases where there are risk behaviors in addition to IV drug use; see Don C. Des Jarlais, "HIV Infection Among Persons Who Inject Illicit Drugs: Problems and Prospects," paper presented at Stockholm Conference.

15. *Report of the Presidential Commission on the Human Immunodeficiency Virus Epidemic* (Washington D.C.: U.S. Government Printing Office, 1988).

16. Cases in American children from James W. Curran et al., "Epidemiology of HIV Infection and AIDS in the United States" *Science,* February 5, 1988; IV drug link to cases in American women from Donald R. Hopkins, "Aids in Minority Populations in the United States," *Public Health Reports,* November/December 1987; prostitutes' IV drug link from Dr. June E. Osborn, "Aids: Politics and Science," *New England Journal of Medicine,* February 18, 1988.

17. J.W. Pape et al., "Epidemiology of AIDS in Haiti (1979–1987)," Testimony before Presidential Commission, April 18, 1988.

18. PAHO, "Epidemiology of AIDS in the Americas"; C. Bartholomew et al., "Transition From Homosexual to Heterosexual AIDS in Trinidad and Tobago," abstract of paper presented at Arusha Conference; observations about Dominican Republic, Honduras, Equador, Brazil, and Mexico from Renée Sabatier, *AIDS and the Third World,* Panos Dossier 1 (Philadephia: New Society Publishers, for Panos Institute, 1988).

19. Figures on Haiti, Mexico, and Rwanda from Ruth Leger Sivard, *World Military and Social Expenditures 1987–88* (Washington, D.C.: World Priorities, 1987); Swedish figure refers to per capita health spending in 1984,

as cited in ibid.; U.S. number refers to 1986 spending, from National Center for Health Statistics, U.S. Department of Health and Human Services, *Health, United States 1987* (Washington, D.C.: U.S. Government Printing Office, 1988); United Nations Children's Fund (UNICEF), *State of the World's Children 1988* (New York: Oxford University Press for UNICEF, 1988).

20. Hesio Cordeiro et al., "Medical Costs of HIV and AIDS in Brazil," paper presented at the First International Conference on the Global Impact of AIDS, London, March 8–10, 1988 (hereinafter cited as London Conference); Renée Sabatier, "The Global Costs of AIDS," *The Futurist,* November/December 1987.

21. AZT costs from Fred J. Hellinger, "Forecasting the Personal Medical Care Costs of AIDS from 1988 Through 1991," *Public Health Reports,* May/June 1988; anemia observation from Sabatier, *AIDS and the Third World.*

22. Relationship between GNP and cost of treatment from Mead Over et al., "The Direct and Indirect Cost of HIV Infection in Developing Countries: The Cases of Zaire and Tanzania," paper presented at Stockholm Conference; Mama Yemo hospital example from Thomas C. Quinn, "AIDS in Africa: An Epidemiologic Paradigm," *Science,* November 21, 1986; observation about quality of care from Sabatier, *AIDS and the Third World.*

23. Hospital bed rates from Mann et al., "International Epidemiology of AIDS," and from Sabatier, *AIDS and the Third World;* patient discharge from J. Wilson Carswell, "Impact of AIDS in the Developing World," *British Medical Bulletin,* Vol. 44, No. 1, 1988, and from Raisa Scriabine-Smith, unpublished manuscript prepared for the Hudson Institute, Indianapolis, Ind., 1988.

24. Over et al., "Direct and Indirect Cost of HIV Infection."

25. Slutkin et al., "Effect of AIDS on the Tuberculosis Problem and Programmes."

26. Sabatier, *AIDS and the Third World;* R. Colebunders et al., "HIV Infection in Patients with Tuberculosis in Kinshasa, Zaire," abstract of paper presented at Arusha Conference.

27. United Nations, *Mortality of Children Under Age 5: World Estimates and Projections, 1950–2025* (New York: 1988).

28. Figures on pregnant women from Carswell, "Impact of AIDS in the Developing World"; mother-to-child infection rate from T. Manzila et al., "Perinatal HIV Transmission in Two African Hospitals: One Year Follow-Up," abstract of paper presented at Arusha Conference; impact on child survival from Mann et al., "International Epidemiology of AIDS," and from Rodolfo A. Bulatao, "Initial Investigation of the Demographic Impact of AIDS in One African Country" (draft), World Bank, Washington, D.C., unpublished, June 15, 1987.

29. John Bongaarts, "Modeling the Demographic Impact of AIDS in Africa," paper presented at the Annual Meeting of the American Association for the Advancement of Science, Boston, February 11–15, 1988; Philip J. Hilts, "Aids Impact on Population," *Washington Post,* May 24, 1988.

30. Carswell, "Impact of AIDS in the Developing World."

31. "Mining Companies Face Increasing Burden," *New Scientist,* March 17, 1988; Copper Belt study from Renée Sabatier, *AIDS and the Third World,* 2nd ed. (London: Panos Institute, 1987).

32. Indirect costs from Over, "Direct and Indirect Cost of HIV Infection," and from David E. Bloom and Geoffrey Carliner, "The Economic Impact of AIDS in the United States," *Science,* February 5, 1988.

33. Over, "Direct and Indirect Cost of HIV Infection."

34. Ibid.

35. F. Davachi et al., "Economic Impact on Families of Children with AIDS in Kinshasa, Zaire," paper presented at London Conference.

36. Sharon Kingman and Steve Conner, "The Answer is Still a Condom," *New Scientist,* June 23, 1988; Marilyn Chase, "AIDS Virus in Infected People Mutates At a Dizzying Rate, Two Studies Show," *Wall Street Journal,* August 4, 1988.

37. Dr. Jeffrey Harris, AIDS Coordinator, AID, Washington, D.C., private communication, October 8, 1988.

38. Sabatier, *AIDS and the Third World* (1988).

39. European booklet mailings from Scriabine-Smith, unpublished manuscript; Canadian poll from a study conducted by the Alberta provincial government, as cited in Sabatier, *AIDS and the Third World* (1988); American data from the National Health Interview Survey of August 1987, as cited in Institute of Medicine, *Confronting AIDS, Update 1988.*

40. Steve Conner and Sharon Kingman, "The Trouble with Testing," *New Scientist,* January 28, 1988; number of countries with travel restrictions from the Panos Institute, as cited in "AIDS Said to Claim a Victim a Minute," *Washington Post,* September 28, 1988.

41. Alan M. Brandt, "AIDS in Historical Perspective: Four Lessons from the History of STDs," *American Journal of Public Health,* April 1988; Sandra G. Boodman, "Premarital AIDS Testing Annoying Many in Illinois," *Washington Post,* July 30, 1988.

42. Hungarian testing information from Radio Free Europe, February 23, 1987, as cited in Scriabine-Smith, unpublished manuscript; Bill Keller, "New Soviet Law Makes AIDS Testing Mandatory," *New York Times,* August 27, 1987; "Mandatory AIDS Test on Basis 'of Slight Suspicion' in Bavaria," *Nature,* June 10, 1988; Wayne D. Johnson, "The

Impact of Mandatory Reporting of HIV Seropositive Persons in South Carolina," abstract of paper presented at the Stockholm Conference; for evidence that voluntary and anonymous testing and partner tracing are successful, see Nancy Padian et al., "Partner Notification as a Means to Prevent Further HIV Transmission," M.L. Rekart, "A Modified System of Contact Tracing for HIV Seropositives—A Year's Results," and J.E. Kristoffersen, "Case Contact Tracing and Testing in HIV Infection," all abstracts of papers presented at Stockholm Conference; see also Institute of Medicine, *Confronting AIDS, Update 1988.*

43. Sabatier, *AIDS and the Third World* (1988).

44. Marshall H. Becker and Jill G. Joseph, "Aids and Behavioral Change to Reduce Risk: A Review," *American Journal of Public Health,* April 1988; Office of Technology Assessment (OTA), U.S. Congress, *How Effective is AIDS Education?* Staff Paper, Washington, D.C., May 1988; Robert R. Stempel and Andrew R. Moss, "Changes in Sexual Behavior By Gay Men in Response to AIDS," abstract of paper presented at Stockholm Conference.

45. Rates in San Francisco from Dr. Warren Winklestein, School of Public Health, University of California, Berkeley, private communication, September 13, 1988; M. Paalman et al., "Condom Promotion in the Netherlands: Evaluation," abstract of paper presented at Stockholm Conference; Finland information from S. Valle, "The Occurrence of STD's in a Cohort of Homosexual Men Prior To and After Repeated Personal Counselling," abstract of paper presented at Stockholm Conference; C.A. Carne et al., "Prevalence of Antibodies to Human Immunodeficiency Virus, Gonorrhoea Rates, and Changed Sexual Behavior in Homosexual Men in London," *The Lancet,* March 21, 1987; G. von Krogh et al., "Declining Incidence of Syphilis Among Homosexual Men in Stockholm," *The Lancet,* October 18, 1986,

as cited in the Scriabine-Smith, unpublished manuscript; Asmus Poulsen and Susanne Ullman, "AIDS-Induced Decline of Incidence of Syphilis in Denmark," *Acta Dermata Vernereologica*, Vol. 65, No. 6, 1985, as cited in ibid.

46. R.R. Stempel et al., "Changes in Sexual Behavior by Gay Men in Response to AIDS," R. Stall et al., "Intravenous Drug Use, the Combination of Drugs and Sexual Activity and HIV Infection Among Gay and Bisexual Men: The San Francisco Men's Health Study," and M. Miller et al., "Relationships Between Knowledge About AIDS Risk and Actual Risk Behaviour in a Sample of Homosexual Men," all abstracts of papers presented at Stockholm Conference; Valle, "The Occurrence of STD's in a Cohort of Homosexual Men Prior To and After Repeated Personal Counselling." See also OTA, *How Effective is AIDS Education?* and C. Beeker et al., "Gay Male Sexual Behavior Change in a Low-Incidence Area for AIDS," abstract of paper presented at Stockholm Conference.

47. Treatment capacity for addicts from Dr. Roy Pickens, Associate Director for AIDS, National Institute on Drug Abuse, Rockville, Md., private communication, August 23, 1988; coupon data from Joyce F. Jackson, AIDS Community Support Unit, New Jersey Department of Health, Testimony before Presidential Commission, December 18, 1987.

48. OTA, *How Effective is AIDS Education?*

49. Pilot programs have been approved in New York City and Portland, Oregon, according to Don C. Des Jarlais, New York State Division of Substance Abuse Services, private communication, August 18, 1988.

50. Doug Lefton, "Nations Report on Needle Distribution," *American Medical News*, March 4, 1988; "European Countries Develop Programs to Fight AIDS," *AIDS Patient Care* (New York), June 1988; E.C. Buning, "The Evaluation of the Needle/Syringe Exchange in Amsterdam," abstract of paper presented at Stockholm Conference; decline in Dutch drug users from Lefton, "Nations Report."

51. OTA, *How Effective is AIDS Education?;* three fourths figure from Des Jarlais et al., "HIV Infection and Intravenous Drug Use."

52. Centers for Disease Control (CDC), "Weekly Surveillance Report," Atlanta, Ga., August 1, 1988; 19 percent figure from Martha F. Rogers and Walter W. Williams, "Aids in Blacks and Hispanics: Implications for Prevention," *Issues in Science and Technology*, Spring 1987; rates for children and women from Dr. James Mason, Opening Address of the National Conference on the Prevention of HIV Infection and AIDS Among Racial and Ethnic Minorities in the United States, Washington, D.C., August 15, 1988.

53. "Needle Sharing and AIDS in Minorities," *Journal of the American Medical Association*, September 18, 1987; Rogers and Williams, "Aids in Blacks and Hispanics"; black HIV infection outside cities from Lytt I. Gardner et al., "Race Specific Trend Anaysis of HIV Antibody Prevalence in the United States," abstract of paper presented at Stockholm Conference.

54. "CDC Spends Over $30 Million to Prevent HIV Infection Among Minorities at Risk," press release from CDC, Atlanta, Ga., September 6, 1988; fiscal year 1989 funding information from Debbie Mathis, Budget Office, CDC, Atlanta, Ga., private communication, October 21, 1988.

55. WHO, "Global Programme on AIDS: Proposed Programme & Budget for 1989," Geneva, September 1988.

56. Tom Netter, Public Information Officer, WHO, Geneva, December 12, 1988; sub-Saharan countries from William Lyerly, Jr. et al., "Impact of Epidemiology and Demographic Patterns on Regional HIV/AIDS Control Strategies in Africa," abstract of paper presented at Arusha Conference.

57. "Kenyans Respond to Red Cross Alert," *People* (London), Vol. 14, No. 4, 1987; Susan Allen et al., "AIDS Education in Urban Rwanda: Change In Knowledge and Attitudes From 1986 to 1987," abstract of paper presented at Stockholm Conference; Edward C. Green, "AIDS and Condoms in the Dominican Republic: Evaluation of an AIDS Education Program," paper presented at the Annual Meeting of the American Association for the Advancement of Science, Boston, February 11, 1988.

58. Guatemala and Mexico examples from Kathryn Carovano, AIDSCOM project, Washington, D.C., private communication, August 30, 1988; Uganda example from Robin Le Mare, Ugandan desk officer, Action AID, London, U.K., private communication, September 16, 1988.

59. Infection rates from Quinn, "AIDS in Africa"; percentage of cases attributable to AIDS from Piot and Caraël, "Epidemiological and Sociological Aspects of HIV-infection."

60. "HIV Screening in the Americas," PAHO, Washington, D.C., unpublished mimeograph, January 19, 1988; "Strategy for Countrywide Screening of Blood Donors in Zambia," abstract of paper presented at Stockholm Conference; Zimbabwe from "A Specially Prepared Update of the Panos Dossier 'AIDS in the Third World'," London, unpublished mimeograph, October 1987; Mexico from Dr. Gonzales Pacheco, PAHO, Washington, D.C., private communication, August 15, 1988; new blood tests from T. C. Quinn et al., "A Rapid Enzyme Immunoassay for the Detection of Antibodies to HIV-1 and HIV-2," and from J. P. Galvin et al., "HIV-CHEK—A Sensitive, Rapid, Manual Test for the Detection of HIV Antibodies," abstracts of papers presented at Arusha Conference.

61. Malcolm Potts, "The Imperative Intervention: Targeting AIDS Control Activities Toward High-Risk Populations," unpublished discussion paper from Family Health International (FHI), Research Triangle Park,

N.C., undated; B. Auvert et al., "Characteristics of the HIV Infection in Kinshasa as Determined By Computer Simulation," abstract of paper presented at London Conference.

62. Chin, private communication.

63. Ghana data from Sharon Weir, Program Coordinator of AIDSTECH, FHI, Research Triangle Park, N.C., private communication, August 29, 1988 (based on a pilot project conducted by FHI among 72 prostitutes between June 1987 and January 1988); Francis Plummer et al., "Durability of Changed Sexual Behavior in Nairobi Prostitutes: Increasing Use of Condoms," and E. Antonio De Moya and Ernesto Guerrero, "The Breaking of the Condom Use Taboo in the Dominican Republic," abstracts of papers presented at Stockholm Conference.

64. In mid-1988 the total population in Burundi, Central African Republic, Congo, Kenya, Rwanda, Tanzania, Uganda, Zaire, and Zambia was an estimated 122.1 million, according to the Population Reference Bureau, Washington, D.C. In these nine countries, women of childbearing age (15–49) constitute on average 22.5 percent of the total population, according to age distributions available in United Nations, *World Demographic Estimates and Projections, 1950–2025* (New York: 1988). Thus the total number of people needing condoms is 27.5 million. Condoms cost about 4.4¢ apiece and an average couple uses 100–144 per year, according to Carl Hemmer, Chief of Commodity and Program Support Division, AID, Washington, D.C., private communication, October 12, 1988. Shipping adds 20 percent to cost and subsidizing their sale through commercial channels adds another 70 percent, making total costs roughly $12 per couple, according to Jerald Bailey, Deputy Division Chief of Research, Office of Population, AID, Washington, D.C., private communication, October 12, 1988. Community-based distribution or programs that actively promoted condom use through education, advertising, and so on would cost considerably more.

65. W. Parker Mauldin and Sheldon J. Segal, *Prevalence of Contraceptive Use in Developing Countries: A Chart Book* (New York: Rockefeller Foundation, 1986); condom use in Africa applies to married women of reproductive age, from John W. Townsend and Luis Varela, The Population Council, Testimony before Presidential Commission, April 18, 1988.

66. Estimate of funding available for AIDS control in developing countries from Harris, private communication. No one has yet compiled data on funds available for AIDS control in the Third World so this number is necessarily a ballpark estimate. WHO's budget for AIDS control in 1988 was $66 million and AID gave an additional $15 million in bilateral aid. World military expenditure in 1987 from Sivard, *World Military and Social Expenditures, 1987–88.*

67. Harvey V. Fineberg, "The Social Dimensions of AIDS," *Scientific American,* October 1988.

68. Kenneth Presitt, "AIDS in Africa: The Triple Disaster," in Norman Miller and Richard C. Rockwell, eds., *AIDS In Africa: The Social and Policy Impact* (Lewiston, N.Y.: The Edwin Mellen Press, 1988).

69. Clare Ansberry, "AIDS, Stirring Panic and Prejudice, Tests the Nation's Character," *Wall Street Journal,* November, 13, 1987; Colombian example from Sarita Kendall, "Latin American Conference Increases AIDS Awareness," AIDS Watch No. 1, 1988, supplement to *People* (London).

70. For an excellent discussion of these issues, see Sabatier, *Blaming Others.*

71. Dr. Jonathan Mann, "Worldwide Epidemiology of AIDS," Address to London Conference; "London Declaration on AIDS Prevention," World Summit of Ministers of Health on Programmes for AIDS Prevention, January 28, 1988; *Report of Presidential Commission.*

72. Fineberg, "Social Dimensions of AIDS"; Ghana example from "Family Planners Define Their Role in Preventing Viral Spread," *New Scientist,* July 21, 1988.

73. Bill Keller, "New Soviet Law Makes AIDS Testing Mandatory," *New York Times,* August 27, 1987.

74. Bulgaria from Sophia Miskiewicz, "AIDS in Eastern Europe and the Soviet Union," Radio Free Europe Research Report No. 24, February 23, 1987; registration of addicts from United Press International, B Wire, Moscow Bureau, "Soviet Scientist Says 'Positive Results' in AIDS Research," February 11, 1987; Poland from Radio Free Europe Research Report, Poland No. 3, February 19, 1986; all broadcasts cited in Scriabine-Smith, unpublished manuscript.

75. Bloom and Carliner, "Economic Impact of AIDS in the United States."

76. New York hospital bed data from Paul S. Jellinek, "Case-Managing AIDS," *Issues in Science and Technology,* Summer 1988; San Francisco funds for AIDS from Mona J. Rowe and Caitlin C. Ryan, "Comparing State-Only Expenditure for AIDS," *American Journal of Public Health,* April 1988; New York data from Robert Blake, Budget Officer, New York City Budget Office, private communication, September 13, 1988; cost per resident from Bloom and Carliner, "Economic Impact of AIDS in the United States."

77. Bloom and Carliner, "Economic Impact of AIDS in the United States"; P.S. Arno and R.G. Hughes, "Local Policy Response to the AIDS Epidemic: New York and San Francisco," *New York State Journal of Medicine,* May 1987; Robert T. Chen et al. "Hospital Utilization by Persons with AIDS in San Francisco, January 1984-June 1987," abstract of paper presented at Stockholm Conference; Ian Douglas Campbell, "AIDS Care and Prevention in a Zambian Rural Community," paper presented at London Conference.

Chapter 8. Enhancing Global Security

1. Carolyn Stephenson, "Alternative International Security Systems: An Introduc-

tion," in Carolyn Stephenson, ed., *Alternative Methods for International Security* (Lanham, Md.: University Press of America, 1982).

2. Gene Sharp, *Making Europe Unconquerable: The Potential of Civilian-Based Deterrence and Defense* (Cambridge, Mass.: Ballinger, 1985).

3. Rita Tullberg, "World Military Expenditures," *Bulletin of Peace Proposals,* Vol. 17, No. 3–4, 1986; Ruth Leger Sivard, *World Military and Social Expenditures 1987–88* (Washington, D.C: World Priorities, 1988).

4. Sivard, *World Military and Social Expenditures 1987–88.* On arms production capabilities, see U.S. Arms Control and Disarmament Agency, *World Military Expenditures and Arms Transfers 1987* (Washington, D.C.: U.S. Government Printing Office, 1988).

5. Sivard, *World Military and Social Expenditures 1987–88.*

6. Ibid.

7. Ibid.; Miroslav Nincic, *How War Might Spread to Europe* (Philadelphia: Taylor and Francis, 1985).

8. More than half the civilian deaths in current hostilities, as in Afghanistan, Ethiopia, Mozambique, and the Sudan, resulted from war-related famine; Sivard, *World Military and Social Expenditures 1987–88.* Boulding quote in Greg Mitchell, "Real Security. What Is It? How Can We Get It?" *Nuclear Times,* May/June 1986.

9. Soedjatmoko, "Patterns of Armed Conflict in the Third World," *Alternatives,* Vol. 10, No. 4, 1985; Center for Defense Information, "A World At War—1983," *The Defense Monitor,* Vol. 12, No. 1, 1983.

10. Mohammed Ayoob, "The Iran-Iraq War and Regional Security in the Persian Gulf," *Alternatives,* Vol. 10, No. 4, 1985.

11. Robert C. Johansen, "Toward a Dependable Peace: A Proposal for an Appropriate Security System," World Policy Paper No. 8 (New York: World Policy Institute, 1983).

12. Lloyd Jeffry Dumas, *The Overburdened Economy* (Berkeley, Calif.: University of California Press, 1986).

13. Sivard, *World Military and Social Expenditures 1987–88;* Eisenhower quote is from his address to the American Society of Newspaper Editors, Washington, D.C., April 1953.

14. Rita Tullberg, "Military-Related Debt in Non-Oil Developing Countries, 1972–82," *Bulletin of Peace Proposals,* Vol. 17, No. 3–4, 1986; Michael Brzoska and Thomas Ohlson, "The Future of Arms Transfers: The Changing Pattern," *Bulletin of Peace Proposals,* Vol. 16, No. 2, 1985; Lloyd J. Dumas, "Economic Conversion: The Critical Link," *Bulletin of Peace Proposals,* Vol. 19, No. 1, 1988.

15. Private communication, February 3, 1988.

16. Cumulative military spending from U.S. Department of Defense, *National Defense Budget Estimates for FY 1988/1989* (Washington, D.C.: Office of the Assistant Secretary of Defense (Comptroller), 1987); Seymour Melman, "An Economic Alternative to the Arms Race: Conversion from Military to Civilian Economy," Presentation at Rayburn House Office Building, Washington, D.C., November 1986.

17. Mary Acland-Hood, "Military Research and Development," *Bulletin of Peace Proposals,* Vol. 17, No. 3–4, 1986; Dumas, *The Overburdened Economy.*

18. Acland-Hood, "Military Research and Development"; Dumas, *The Overburdened Economy;* Ulrich Albrecht, "Rüstungsforschung und Dritte Welt," *Informationsdienst Wissenschaft und Frieden,* December 1984/January 1985.

19. Dumas, *The Overburdened Economy.*

20. Ibid.

21. Simon Ramo, *America's Technology Slip* (New York: John Wiley & Sons, 1980).

22. David Noble, *Forces of Production: A Social History of Automation* (New York: Oxford University Press, 1986).

23. Dumas, *The Overburdened Economy.*

24. Michael Dee Oden, *A Military Dollar Really Is Different: The Economic Impacts of Military Spending Reconsidered* (Lansing, Mich.: Employment Research Associates, 1988).

25. Dumas, *The Overburdened Economy.*

26. Lloyd J. Dumas, "University Research, Industrial Innovation, and the Pentagon," in John Tirman, ed., *Militarization of High Technology* (Cambridge, Mass.: Ballinger, 1984); *Economic Report of the President* (Washington, D.C.: U.S. Government Printing Office, 1988); Mario Pianta, *New Technologies Across the Atlantic: U.S. Leadership or European Autonomy?* (London: Wheatsheaf Books, 1988).

27. Dumas, *The Overburdened Economy;* Pianta, *New Technologies Across the Atlantic.*

28. Military expenditure from Executive Office of the President, Office of Management and Budget, *Historical Tables: Budget of the U.S. Government, Fiscal Year 1989* (Washington, D.C.: U.S. Government Printing Office, 1988); U.S. pollution abatement figures from *Survey of Current Business,* May 1988.

29. Wendell Berry, *Home Economics* (San Francisco: North Point Press, 1987).

30. World Commission on Environment and Development, *Our Common Future* (New York: Oxford University Press, 1987).

31. "Environment and Conflict," Earthscan Briefing Document 40, International Institute for Environment and Development, London, November 1984.

32. Ghali quote from Lloyd Timberlake, *Africa in Crisis: The Causes, the Cures of Environmental Bankruptcy* (London: International Institute for Environment and Development, 1985). For description of international water disputes, see "Environment and Conflict," Earthscan; Norman Myers, *Not Far Afield: U.S. Interests and the Global Environment* (Washington, D.C.: World Resources Institute, 1988); "Where Dams Can Cause Wars," *Economist,* July 18, 1987; "Canadian Ban Covers Water Diversions to US," *Journal of Commerce,* November 6, 1987; John Tagliabue, "The Rhine Struggles to Survive," *New York Times,* February 15, 1987; Fernando Ortiz Monasterio, "Confronting Environmental Degradation: A Problem Without Borders," *Ceres,* September 1987; "West Germans Look For Ways to Clean Elbe River, Seek Cooperation With East Germany, Czechoslovakia," *Multinational Environmental Outlook,* September 15, 1988.

33. Narul Huda, "Bangladesh Blames Neighbors for its Floods," *Panoscope* (London), December 1987.

34. Philip P. Micklin, "Desiccation of the Aral Sea: A Water Management Disaster in the Soviet Union," *Science,* September 2, 1988; James Critchlow, "Aral Sea Vanishes as Cotton Fields Expand" (letter to the editor), *New York Times,* September 25, 1988.

35. Emanuel Somers, "Transboundary Pollution and Environmental Health," *Environment,* June 1987.

36. Michael Weisskopf, " 'Toxic Clouds' Can Carry Pollutants Far and Wide," *Washington Post,* March 16, 1988; Monasterio, "Confronting Environmental Degradation."

37. Worldwatch Institute, calculated from U.S. Environmental Protection Agency, *Regulatory Impact Analysis,* Vol. 1 (Washington, D.C.: 1987), and from Matthew Wald, "Fighting the Greenhouse Effect," *New York Times,* August 28, 1988.

38. Christopher Flavin, *Reassessing Nuclear Power: The Fallout From Chernobyl,* Worldwatch Paper No. 75 (Washington, D.C.: Worldwatch Institute, March 1987); "Czech/Austrian Nuclear Disagreement," *Financial Times European Energy Economist,* July 1, 1988; "Chilean Group Opposes Argentine Nuclear Waste Dump," *Ecoforum,* June 1988.

39. Patrick Smith with Alan George, "The Dumping Grounds," *South,* August 1988.

40. Tagliabue, "The Rhine Struggles to Survive."

41. Robert C. Johansen, "The Failure of Arms Control," *Sojourners,* March 1981; Johansen, "Toward a Dependable Peace."

42. Robert S. Norris et al., "START and Strategic Modernization," *Nuclear Weapons Databook Working Papers 87–2* (Washington, D.C.: Natural Resources Defense Council, 1987).

43. For a more detailed discussion of independent initiatives, see Robert C. Johansen, *Toward an Alternative Security System,* World Policy Paper No. 24 (New York: World Policy Institute, 1983); Mark Sommer and Gordon Feller, " 'Independent Initiatives': Better Than Arms Control?" *New Options,* October 27, 1986.

44. Michael G. Renner, "Disarming Implications of the INF Treaty," *World Watch* (Washington, D.C.), March/April 1988; Philip Taubman, "Soviet Proposes Arctic Peace Zone," *New York Times,* October 2, 1987.

45. For a detailed presentation of these proposals, see the set of articles on "Nonoffensive Defense" in *Bulletin of Atomic Scientists,* September 1988.

46. Hal Harvey, "Defense Without Aggression," *Bulletin of Atomic Scientists,* September 1988; Bernard E. Trainor, "Soviet Arms Doctrine in Flux: An Emphasis on the Defense," *New York Times,* March 7, 1988; Dmitri Yazov, "The Soviet Proposal for European Security," *Bulletin of Atomic Scientists,* September 1988; "Der Warschauer Pakt Bietet Gleichgewicht der Konventionellen Streitkräfte in Europa an," *Süddeutsche Zeitung,* July 18, 1988; Paul Lewis, "Soviet Offers to Adjust Imbalance of Conventional Forces in Europe," *New York Times,* June 24, 1988.

47. For a brief account of these events and the text of the Joint Statement and the treaty outline, see Robert Krinsky, "An Introduc-

tion to Disarmament," Briefing Paper No. 2, National Commission for Economic Conversion and Disarmament, Washington, D.C., May 1988, and Lawrence D. Weiler, "General Disarmament Proposals," *Arms Control Today,* July/August 1986.

48. Marcus Raskin, "Draft Treaty for a Comprehensive Program for Common Security and General Disarmament," Institute for Policy Studies, Washington, D.C., July 1986.

49. Cost estimate is reported in Robert C. Johansen, "The Reagan Administration and the U.N.: The Costs of Unilateralism," *World Policy Journal,* Fall 1986.

50. John Tirman, "International Monitoring for Peace," *Issues in Science and Technology,* Summer 1988; Owen Thomas, "Nations Keep an Extra Eye on Each Other," *Christian Science Monitor,* September 28, 1988. For text of Rep. Mrazek's bill, see H.R. 4036, "The International Security and Satellite Monitoring Act of 1988," introduced on February 29, 1988. The bill will be reintroduced in the next Congress, and hearings are planned for 1989; personal communication with Robert Katula, Special Assistant to Robert Mrazek, October 3, 1988.

51. Johansen, "The Reagan Administration and the U.N."; "The Requirements for Stable Coexistence in United States-Soviet Relations," *Congressional Record,* May 9, 1988; Jonathan Steele, "Superpowers: Beyond Arms Control," *END, Journal of European Nuclear Disarmament,* Summer 1988. Philip Taubman, "Gorbachev Offers Disputed Radar for Peaceful Exploration of Space," *New York Times,* September 17, 1988.

52. Hilary F. French, "Restoring the UN," *World Watch* (Washington, D.C.), July/August 1988.

53. The United Nations has had previous success in such cases; see Johansen, "The Reagan Administration and the U.N." Paul Lewis, "Soviets Say U.N. Peacekeeping Effort Should Emphasize Prevention," *New York Times,* October 18, 1988.

54. Nicaragua's proposal from Johansen, "The Reagan Administration and the U.N."; Honduras' proposal from Wilson Ring, "Honduras Holding U.S. Responsible for Contras," *Washington Post*, October 23, 1988; Pentagon estimate from Joanne Omang, "Policing a Latin Peace Projected to Cost Millions," *Washington Post*, May 11, 1985; U.S. spending from Joshua Cohen and Joel Rogers, "Central America Policy: The True Cost of Intervention," *The Nation*, April 12, 1986; Central American spending from Arms Control and Disarmament Agency, *World Military Expenditures and Arms Transfers 1987*.

55. Robert C. Johansen, "For a Permanent UN Police Force," *Christian Science Monitor*, October 13, 1982; Paul Lewis, "Soviets Urge Nations to Provide a U.N. Army," *New York Times*, October 3, 1988.

56. For 1988, expenditures totaled about $250 million; the sum of $380 million is arrived at by annualizing the initial three-month cost of keeping U.N. observers in Iran and Iraq ($37.5 million), based on George D. Moffett III, "Peacekeepers Win Peace Prize," *Christian Science Monitor*, September 30, 1988.

57. "Questions and Answers About Economic Conversion," Corliss Lamont Program in Economic Conversion, Columbia University, New York, May 1987; military payroll figure is a Worldwatch estimate.

58. H.R. 813, "The Defense Economic Adjustment Act," by Rep. Ted Weiss; for a brief characterization of the bill's main provisions, see Seymour Melman, "Law for Economic Conversion: Necessity and Characteristics," *Bulletin of Peace Proposals*, Vol. 19, No. 1, 1988.

59. Jonathan Feldman, "An Introduction to Economic Conversion," Briefing Paper No. 1, National Commission for Economic Conversion and Disarmament, Washington, D.C., May 1988; Herbert York, "Some Possible Measures for Slowing the Qualitative Arms Race," *Proceedings of the 22nd Pugwash Conference on Science and World Affairs*, Oxford, U.K., September 7–12, 1972 (Oxford: 1973).

60. William E. Saxe, review of Ellis Joffe, *The Chinese Army After Mao* (Cambridge, Mass.: Harvard University Press, 1987), in *Friday Review of Defense Literature*, September 16, 1988; "China Invents the Entrepreneurial Army," *Economist*, May 14, 1988.

61. Samuel S. Kim, "The United Nations, Lawmaking, and World Order," *Alternatives*, Vol. 10, No. 4, 1985.

62. Sandra Postel, "Protecting Forests from Air Pollution and Acid Rain," in Lester R. Brown et al., *State of the World 1985* (New York: W.W. Norton & Co., 1985); "European Nations Ratify Sulfur Reduction Pact," *World Environment Report*, September 17, 1987; Warren E. Leary, "Reagan, In Switch, Agrees to a Plan on Acid Rain," *New York Times*, August 7, 1988; "12 Nations Agree to Cut Pollution," *Washington Post*, November 1, 1988.

63. Hilary F. French, "Industrial Wasteland," *World Watch* (Washington, D.C.), November/December 1988; "Ostblock Schlägt Europäische Umweltkonferenz Vor," *Süddeutsche Zeitung*, July 18, 1988.

64. "West Germans Look For Ways to Clean Elbe River, Seek Cooperation With East Germany, Czechoslovakia," *Multinational Environmental Outlook*, September 15, 1988; "East, West German Officials Struggle With Environmental Cooperation on Elbe," *Multinational Environmental Outlook*, August 4, 1988; "U.S. and Soviets Spur Scientific Collaboration," *Conservation Foundation Letter*, 1988:1.

65. "U.S. and Soviets Spur Scientific Collaboration"; Cass Peterson, "U.S., Soviet Scientists Open Dialogue on 'Greenhouse Effect'," *Washington Post*, May 12, 1988.

66. John B. Oakes, "Greening Central America," *New York Times*, April 20, 1988; "Peace Through Parks: A Proposal for Biological Reserves for the Protection of Unique Natural Areas on the Border Between Nica-

ragua and Costa Rica," Nicaraguan Institute of Natural Resources, National Park Service of Nicaragua, Managua, mimeographed, Spring 1986.

67. Philip Shabecoff, "Parley Urges Quick Action to Protect Atmosphere," *New York Times,* July 1, 1988.

Chapter 9. Mobilizing at the Grassroots

1. In addition to the particular sources given in these notes, this chapter is based on visits to dozens of grassroots development projects in Bolivia and Brazil in the summer of 1988, as well as previous trips to other parts of Latin America.

2. Estimates of global participation in grassroots movements for sustainable development are of necessity highly speculative. One attempt to calculate a rough figure for rural Third World grassroots initiatives came to 100 million; Bertrand Schneider, *The Barefoot Revolution: A Report to the Club of Rome* (London: Intermediate Technologies Publications, 1988).

3. Sheldon Annis, "Re-organization at the Grassroots," *Grassroots Development,* Vol. 11, No. 2, 1987; cultural transformation discussed in Richard Critchfield, "Science and the Villager: The Last Sleeper Wakes," *Foreign Affairs,* Fall 1982, and *Villages* (Garden City, N.Y.: Anchor Press/Doubleday, 1981).

4. Independent groups discussed in *World Development* (supplement), Fall 1987; Schneider, *Barefoot Revolution.*

5. Table based on James Tarrant et al., "Natural Resources and Environmental Management in Indonesia: An Overview," U.S. Agency for International Development (AID), Washington, D.C., October 1987; Philippines from Jason DeParle, "The Slum Behind the Sheraton," *Washington Monthly,* December 1987; all other countries discussed elsewhere in text with citations given.

6. Terry Alliband, *Catalysts of Development: Voluntary Agencies in India* (West Hartford,

Conn.: Kumarian, 1983); Mathew Zachariah, *Revolution Through Reform: A Comparison of Sarvodaya and Conscientization* (New York: Praeger, 1986); Aloysius P. Fernandez, "NGOs in South Asia: People's Participation and Partnership," *World Development* (supplement), Fall 1987; D.L. Sheth, "Grass Roots Initiatives in India," *Development: Seeds of Change,* No. 2, 1984; Centre for Science and Environment, *The State of India's Environment 1984–85, The Second Citizen's Report* (New Delhi: 1985).

7. *ADAB News* (Dhaka, Bangladesh), May/June 1987; Joanna Macy, *Dharma and Development: Religion as Resource in the Sarvodaya Self-Help Movement,* rev. ed. (West Hartford, Conn.: Kumarian, 1985); "Mosquito Control without Pesticides," *Panoscope* (London), October 1987; Denis Goulet, "Development Strategy in Sri Lanka and a People's Alternative," in Donald Attwood et al., eds., *Power and Poverty: Development and Development Projects in the Third World* (Boulder, Colo.: Westview Press, 1988).

8. Annis, "Re-organization at the Grassroots"; Penny Lernoux, *Cry of the People* (New York: Penguin, 1980); Rubem César Fernandes and Leilah Landim, "Um Perfil das ONGs no Brasil," *Comunicaçõqoes do ISER* (Rio de Janeiro), November 1986; Jane Kramer, "Letter from the Elysian Fields," *New Yorker,* March 2, 1987; Sheldon Annis and Peter Hakim, eds., *Direct to the Poor: Grassroots Development in Latin America* (Boulder, Colo.: Lynne Rienner, 1988).

9. Robert Wasserstrom, *Grassroots Development in Latin America & the Caribbean: Oral Histories of Social Change* (New York: Praeger, 1985); Albert Hirschman, *Getting Ahead Collectively: Grassroots Experiences in Latin America* (New York: Pergamon, 1984); Leon Zamosc, *The Agrarian Question and the Peasant Movement in Colombia: Struggles of the National Peasant Association, 1967–1981* (Cambridge: Cambridge University Press, 1986); David Francis, "Colombian Official Develops Innovative Plan to Protect Environment," *Christian Science Monitor,* June 27, 1986; Peter Rosset and

John Vandermeer, eds., *Nicaragua: The Unfinished Revolution* (New York: Grove, 1986).

10. Lloyd Timberlake, *Only One Earth: Living for the Future* (New York: Sterling, 1987); Paul Harrison, *The Greening of Africa* (New York: Viking/Penguin, 1987); Barbara Thomas, *Politics, Participation, and Poverty: Development Through Self-Help in Kenya* (Boulder, Colo.: Westview Press, 1985); Simon Muchiro, "The Role of African NGOs as a Tool for Change," *Development: Seeds of Change,* No. 4, 1987; Pierre Pradervand, "Self-Reliance for Survival in Africa: Peasant Groups Key to Continent's Future," *Christian Science Monitor,* March 9, 1988.

11. Hilary F. French, "Industrial Wasteland," *World Watch* (Washington, D.C.), November/December 1988; Helsinki Watch, *From Below: Independent Peace and Environmental Movements in Eastern Europe & The USSR* (New York: 1987).

12. U.S. environmental movement from Peter Borrelli, "Environmentalism at a Crossroads," *Amicus Journal,* Summer 1987, and from Will Collette, "Citizen's Clearinghouse on Hazardous Wastes," *Environment,* November 1987; Horst Mewes, "The Green Party Comes of Age," *Environment,* June 1985; Saral Sarkar, "The Green Movement in West Germany," *Alternatives,* April 1986.

13. Role of African women from Harrison, *Greening of Africa;* Population Reference Bureau, *World Population Data Sheet 1988* (Washington, D.C.: 1988); Peter Wanyande, "Women's Groups in Participatory Development: Kenya's Development Experience Through the Use of Harambee," *Development: Seeds of Change*, No. 2/3, 1987; Kathryn March and Rachelle Taqqu, *Women's Informal Associations in Developing Countries: Catalysts for Change?* (Boulder, Colo.: Westview Press, 1986); Sally Yudelman, *Hopeful Openings: A Study of Five Women's Development Organizations in Latin America and the Caribbean* (West Hartford, Conn.: Kumarian, 1987); Zubeida M. Ahmad, "Women's Work and Their Struggle

to Organize," *Development: Seeds of Change,* No. 4, 1984.

14. Sithembiso Nyoni, "Indigenous NGOs: Liberation, Self-Reliance, and Development," *World Development* (supplement), Fall 1987.

15. Bangladesh Rural Advancement Committee, "Household Strategies in Bonkura Village," in David Korten, ed., *Community Management: Asian Experience and Perspectives* (West Hartford, Conn.: Kumarian, 1986).

16. Hirschman, *Getting Ahead Collectively.*

17. Lori Heise, Senior Researcher, Worldwatch Institute, private communications with organizers in various regions of India during visit in Fall 1986.

18. Indian community development experience from Gerrit Huizer, "Harmony vs. Confrontation," *Development: Seeds of Change,* No. 2, 1984; AID community development experience from Erik Eckholm, *The Dispossessed of the Earth: Land Reform and Sustainable Development,* Worldwatch Paper 30 (Washington, D.C.: Worldwatch Institute, June 1979).

19. Paulo Freire, *Pedagogy of the Oppressed* (New York: Continuum, 1970); popular education from Patrick Breslin, *Development and Dignity* (Washington, D.C.: Inter-American Foundation (IAF), 1987); Ariel Dorfman, "Bread and Burnt Rice: Culture and Economic Survival in Latin America," *Grassroots Development,* Vol. 7, No. 2, 1984.

20. Francis Mulwa, "Participation of the Grassroots in Rural Development: The Case of the Development Education Programme of the Catholic Diocese of Machakos, Kenya," *Development: Seeds of Change,* No. 2/3, 1987; Albert Hirschman, "The Principle of Conservation and Mutation of Social Energy," in Annis and Hakim, *Direct to the Poor.*

21. Eileen Belamide, "Building Self-Help Groups: The Philippine Experience," *Ideas and Action* (U.N. Food and Agriculture Organization, Rome), November 1986; Devendra Kumar, Centre of Science for Villages,

Wardha, India, private communication, May 23, 1988.

22. Macy, *Dharma and Development.*

23. Dorfman, "Bread and Burnt Rice."

24. Barber B. Conable, "Address to the Board of Governors," Berlin, September 27, 1988; World Bank, *The World Bank's Support for the Alleviation of Poverty* (Washington, D.C.: 1988).

25. Incentives to organize discussed in Sheldon Annis, "Can Small-Scale Development be a Large-Scale Policy? The Case of Latin America," *World Development* (supplement), Fall 1987.

26. Céline Sachs, "Mutirão in Brazil, Initiatives for Self-Reliance," *Development: Seeds of Change,* No. 4, 1986; Julie Fischer, "Creating Communities: Squatter Neighborhood Associations in Latin America," *Grassroots Development,* Vol. 6, No. 1, 1982; Manila from Walden Bello, "The ZOTO Experience," *Christianity and Crisis,* November 9, 1987; Bangkok from Bertha Turner, ed., *Building Community: A Third World Case Book* (London: Building Community Books, 1988).

27. Paz quoted in Turner, *Building Community;* Sheldon Annis, "What is Not the Same about the Urban Poor: The Case of Mexico City," in John Lewis, ed., *Strengthening the Poor: What Have We Learned?* (New Brunswick, New Jersey: Transaction Books, 1988).

28. Fischer, "Creating Communities"; Eliana Athayde, Centro de Defesa Rubião, Rio de Janeiro, Brazil, private communication, June 14, 1988; Gilson Cardoso, president, Associação de Moradores de Santa Marta, Rio de Janeiro, Brazil, private communication, June 15, 1988; author's visit to Santa Marta, June 15, 1988.

29. Timberlake, *Only One Earth;* Turner, *Building Community;* Pino Cimò, "Managing Local Food Supplies: Activism in Peru," *Ceres,* September 1987.

30. Alan Riding, "Brazil's Northeast, Misery Molded by Man and Nature," *New York Times,* May 3, 1988; Valdemar de Oliveira Neto, Director-President, Centro Luiz Freire, Olinda, Brazil, private communication, June 21, 1988; Suzana Cavalcanti, Co-Director, Centro Luiz Freire, Olinda, Brazil, private communication, June 22, 1988; Maria Lucia Prazeres Farias, Director, Escola Maria Conceição, Recife, Brazil, private communication, June 22, 1988; author's visit to community schools, June 22, 1988.

31. John Briscoe and David de Ferranti, *Water for Rural Communities: Helping People Help Themselves* (Washington, D.C.: World Bank, 1988); "We Can Solve It: An Alternative by the Community," video by UTTHAN-Mahiti, Development Action Planning Team, Ahmadabad, India, 1987.

32. "We Can Solve It."

33. Sandra Huffman et al., "Community Designed Interventions to Prevent Malnutrition in Peru: Community Kitchens and Neighborhood Childcare" (draft), Center to Prevent Childhood Malnutrition, Bethesda, Md., May 20, 1988; Alan Riding, "Hunger Spreading in Peru Inflation," *New York Times,* October 30, 1988.

34. United Nations Children's Fund (UNICEF), *The State of the World's Children 1988* (New York: Oxford University Press, for UNICEF, 1988).

35. Marilynn M. Rosenthal, *Health Care in the People's Republic of China: Moving Toward Modernization* (Boulder, Colo.: Westview Press, 1987); Golam Samdani Fakir, "The Role of NGOs in Health and Family Planning in Bangladesh," *ADAB News* (Dhaka, Bangladesh), May/June 1987.

36. South Korea and Indonesia from Bruce Stokes, *Helping Ourselves: Local Solutions to Global Problems* (New York: W.W. Norton & Co., 1981); Thailand from Norman Uphoff, *Local Institutional Development: An Analytical Sourcebook with Cases* (West Hartford, Conn.: Kumarian, 1986).

37. Jodi L. Jacobson, *Planning the Global Family*, Worldwatch Paper 80 (Washington, D.C.: Worldwatch Institute, December 1987).

38. Harrison, *Greening of Africa;* Sonia Correa, SOS Corpo Mulher, Recife, Brazil, private communication, June 21, 1988.

39. Judith Tendler et al., "What to Think About Cooperatives: A Guide from Bolivia," in Annis and Hakim, *Direct to the Poor;* Sheldon Annis, "The Next World Bank? Financing Development from the Bottom Up," *Grassroots Development,* Vol. 11, No. 1, 1987.

40. Shoaib Sultan Khan, General Manager, Aga Khan Rural Support Program, "Successful Rural Development in the Mountains of Pakistan," presentation at International Forestry Seminar, AID, Washington, D.C., February 2, 1988; Operations Evaluation Department, *The Aga Khan Rural Support Program in Pakistan: An Interim Evaluation* (Washington, D.C.: World Bank, 1987).

41. Khan, "Successful Rural Development in the Mountains of Pakistan"; Operations Evaluation Department, *Aga Khan Rural Support Program.*

42. Taiwan and South Korea from Uphoff, *Local Institutional Development;* Michael Bratton, "Farmer Organizations and Food Production in Zimbabwe," *World Development,* March 1986; Norman Uphoff, "Activating Community Capacity for Water Management in Sri Lanka," in Korten, *Community Management;* Philippines from Benjamin Bagadion and Frances Korten, "Developing Irrigators' Organizations: A Learning Process Approach," in Michael Cernea, ed., *Putting People First: Sociological Variables in Rural Development* (New York: Oxford University Press, 1985); India from V. D. Deshpande et al., "Water for People," in Korten, *Community Management.*

43. Judith Tendler, "What Ever Happened to Poverty Alleviation?" Ford Foundation, New York, March 1987.

44. Ibid.; Medea Benjamin, "SEWA: Indian Women Organize," *Seeds* (Oakhurst Baptist Church, Decatur, Ga.), August 1986; Jennefer Sebstad, *Women and Self-Reliance in India: The SEWA Story* (London: Zed, in press).

45. Muhammad Yunus, Managing Director, Grameen Bank, Bangladesh, speech to 1988 Conference of Society for International Development—Washington Chapter, April 22, 1988.

46. Ibid.; Clyde Farnsworth, "Micro-Loans to the World's Poorest," *New York Times,* February 21, 1988; Staff of the Select Committee on Hunger, "Access and Availability of Credit to the Poor in Developing Countries and the United States," U.S. House of Representatives, Washington, D.C., 1988.

47. Bhoomi Sena from Guy Gran, "Learning from Development Success: Some Lessons from Contemporary Case Histories," National Association of Schools of Public Affairs and Administration, September 1983, and from Anisur Rahman, "Some Dimensions of People's Participation in the Bhoomi Sena Movement," United Nations Research Institute for Social Development, Geneva, 1981; Seth Mydans, "In the Big Manila Land Plan, Steps are Small," *New York Times,* October 18, 1987; Tom Barry, *Roots of Rebellion: Land & Hunger in Central America* (Boston: South End, 1987); Alan Durning, "Brazil's Landless Lose Again," *World Watch* (Washington, D.C.), September/October 1988; Amnesty International, *Brazil: Authorized Violence in Rural Areas* (London: 1988).

48. Paul Kurian, "Commercialisation of Common Property Resources, Kusnur Satyagraha," *Economic and Political Weekly,* January 16, 1988.

49. Robert Wade, "Why Some Indian Villages Co-operate," *Economic and Political Weekly,* April 16, 1988; Joshua Bishop, "Indigenous Social Structures, Formal Institutions, and the Management of Renewable

Natural Resources in Mali" (draft), Sahelian Department, World Bank, Washington, D.C., August 1988; J. Arnold and Gabriel Campbell, "Collective Management of Hill Forests in Nepal: The Community Forestry Development Project," and Donald Messerschmidt, "People and Resources in Nepal: Customary Resource Management Systems of the Upper Kali Gandaki," both in Board on Science and Technology for International Development, *Proceedings of the Conference on Common Property Resource Management* (Washington, D.C.: National Academy Press, 1986).

50. Brazil from various private communications during author's visit, June 1988; "Philippines: 50,000 Strong National Fisherfolk Organization Demands Genuine Aquarian Reform," *IFDA Dossier*, May/June 1988; Sandeep Pendse, "The Struggle of Fisherfolk in Goa," *Development: Seeds of Change*, No. 2, 1984; K.G. Kumar, "Organising Fisherfolk Cooperatives in Kerala," *Economic and Political Weekly*, March 19, 1988; Centre for Science and Environment, *State of India's Environment 1984–85*.

51. Julie Sloan Denslow and Christine Padoch, *People of the Tropical Rain Forest* (Berkeley, Ca.: University of California Press, 1988); Stephen Schwartzman and Mary Helena Allegretti, "Extractive Production in the Amazon and the Rubber Tappers' Movement," Environmental Defense Fund, Washington, D.C., May 28, 1987; Stephen Schwartzman, Environmental Defense Fund, Washington, D.C., private communication, April 13, 1988.

52. Private communications with various members and officers of rubber tapper union, Acre, Brazil, June 23, 1988; Mary Helena Allegretti and Stephen Schwartzman, "Extractive Reserves: A Sustainable Development Alternative for Amazonia," Environmental Defense Fund, Washington, D.C., 1987.

53. Allegretti and Schwartzman, "Extractive Reserves"; Alan Durning, "Violence in the Brazilian Jungle—A Global Concern," *Christian Science Monitor*, August 23, 1988.

54. Margaret Scott, "Loggers and Locals Fight for the Heart of Borneo," *Far Eastern Economic Review*, April 28, 1988.

55. Mark Shepard, *Gandhi Today: A Report on Mahatma Gandhi's Successors* (Arcata, Calif.: Simple Productions, 1987).

56. Vandana Shiva, "Fight for Survival in India," *Earth Island Journal*, Spring 1988; "Protecting Doon Valley's Eco-System, Problems and Limitations," *Economic and Political Weekly*, October 10, 1987; Jayanta Bandyopadhyay and Vandana Shiva, "Chipko: Rekindling India's Forest Culture," *Ecologist*, January/February 1987; Shobhita Jain, "Women and People's Ecological Movement: A Case Study of Women's Role in the Chipko Movement in Uttar Pradesh," *Economic and Political Weekly*, October 13, 1984; observations of Lori Heise, Senior Researcher, Worldwatch Institute, during visit to Chipko eco-development camp, Garhwal, India, Fall 1986.

57. Harrison, *Greening of Africa;* Sandra Postel and Lori Heise, *Reforesting the Earth,* Worldwatch Paper 83 (Washington, D.C.: Worldwatch Institute, April 1988); Elizabeth Obel, "Maendeleo Ya Wanawake Organization," *Panoscope* (London), October 1987.

58. Harrison, *Greening of Africa.*

59. Ibid.; Bernard Lecomte, *Project Aid: Limitations and Alternatives* (Paris: Organisation for Economic Co-operation and Development (OECD), 1986); "Can Outsiders Play a Positive Role in Strengthening Grassroots Movements?" *Food Monitor* (World Hunger Year, New York), Spring 1986; Peter Wright and Edouard Bonkoungou, "Soil and Water Conservation as a Starting Point for Rural Forestry: The Oxfam Project in Ouahigouya, Burkina Faso," *Rural Africana*, Fall 1985/ Winter 1986.

60. Spreading networks traced in "NGO Networker" (newsletter), World Resources Institute, Washington, D.C., and in *Panoscope*, Panos Institute, London; environmental

movement in Africa from Paula Williams, "Evolving Concerns," Letter/Report to Peter Martin, Institute of Current World Affairs, Hanover, N.H., October 1987; Nalim Ladduwahetty, Editor and Founding Member, Sri Lankan Environmental Congress, Colombo, Sri Lanka, private communication, February 10, 1988; Brazilian environmental movement from private communications during author's visit, June 1988.

61. Annis, "The Next World Bank?"

62. Ibid.; Annis, "Can Small-Scale Development be a Large-Scale Policy?"

63. Steven Greenhouse, "Third World Tells I.M.F. that Poverty has Increased," *New York Times*, September 29, 1988; international debt payments from World Bank, *World Debt Tables: External Debt of Developing Countries, 1987–88 Edition, Volume I. Analysis and Summary Tables* (Washington, D.C.: 1988); development assistance from Joseph Wheeler, *Development Co-operation: Efforts and Policies of the Members of the Development Assistance Committee, 1987 Report* (Paris: OECD, 1988).

64. Stephen Hellinger et al., *Aid for Just Development* (Boulder, Colo.: Lynne Rienner, 1988); Kurt Finsterbush and Warren Van Wicklin, "The Contribution of Beneficiary Participation to Development Project Effectiveness," *Public Administration and Development,* 1987.

65. Robert Cassen and Associates, *Does Aid Work?* (Oxford: Clarendon, 1986); charities as "growth field" from Joseph Wheeler, *Development Co-operation: Efforts and Policies of the Members of the Development Assistance Committee, 1986 Report* (Paris: OECD, 1987); Brian Smith, "U.S. and Canadian PVOs as Transnational Development Institutions," in Robert Gorman, ed., *Private Voluntary Organizations as Agents of Development* (Boulder, Colo.: Westview Press, 1984); Hendrik van der Heijden, "The Reconciliation of NGO Autonomy, Program Integrity and Operational Effectiveness with Accountability to Do-

nors," *World Development* (supplement), Fall 1987.

66. Robert Chambers, *Rural Development: Putting the Last First* (Essex: Longman Scientific & Technical, 1983).

67. Problems of overfunding based on numerous private communications in United States and Latin America, especially Kevin Healy, Bolivia Representative, Inter-American Foundation, Arlington, Va., September 29, 1988.

68. AID comment at "Rethinking U.S. Foreign Assistance," Forum held by Society for International Development—Washington Chapter, Washington, D.C., September 16, 1988; Bengali example from Charles Elliott, "Some Aspects of Relations Between the North and South in the NGO Sector," *World Development* (supplement), Fall 1987.

69. Cernea, *Putting People First;* Lecomte, *Project Aid.*

70. On new assistance compact, see Anne Gordon Drabek, "Development Alternatives: The Challenge for NGOs—An Overview of the Issues" and numerous other articles, *World Development* (supplement), Fall 1987.

71. Lecomte, *Project Aid;* Kingston Kajese, "An Agenda of Future Tasks for International and Indigenous NGOs: Views from the South," and Brain Smith, "An Agenda of Future Tasks for International and Indigenous NGOs: Views from the North," *World Development* (supplement), Fall 1987.

72. Breslin, *Development and Dignity;* IAF, "The Inter-American Foundation: Report of the Evaluation Group," Washington, D.C., March 1984; Office of Technology Assessment, U.S. Congress, *Grassroots Development: The African Development Foundation* (Washington, D.C.: U.S. Government Printing Office, 1988); Oxfam from Ben Whitaker, *A Bridge of People* (London: Heinemann, 1983); Michael Gallagher and Miriam Parel, Ashoka, Washington, D.C., and Lenny Silverstein, Ashoka, Rio de Janeiro, private communications, Spring and Summer 1988.

73. Hellinger et al., *Aid for Just Development;* Chambers, *Putting the Last First.*

74. Annis, "The Next World Bank?"

75. Pierre Pradervand, "Traveling in a Mammie Wagon—or a Range Rover," *Food Monitor* (World Hunger Year, New York), Spring 1986.

76. Annis, "Can Small-Scale Development Become a Large-Scale Policy?"

77. Zimbabwe from Jacobson, *Planning the Global Family,* and from Timberlake, *Only One Earth;* Valerie Miller, *Between Struggle and Hope: The Nicaraguan Literacy Crusade* (Boulder, Colo.: Westview Press, 1985); Burkina Faso and Kenya from Harrison, *Greening of Africa.*

78. Philippine National Irrigation Administration from Benjamin Bagadion and Frances Korten, "Developing Irrigators' Organizations: A Learning Process Approach," in Cernea, *Putting People First;* David Korten, "Third Generation NGO Strategies: A Key to People-Centered Development," *World Development* (supplement), Fall 1987.

79. Bello, "The ZOTO experience."

80. Dexter Chavunduka et al., *Khuluma Usenza: The Story of O.R.A.P. in Zimbabwe's Rural Development* (Bulawayo, Zimbabwe: Organization of Rural Associations for Progress, 1985); People of God from author's visit to *Povo de Deus,* Recife, Brazil, June 1988; Shelton Davis, "The Ayoreode-Zapocó Communal Sawmill: A Social Forestry Project in Eastern Bolivia," *Grassroots Development,* Vol. 9, No. 2, 1985.

81. Quoted in DeParle, "The Slum Behind the Sheraton."

Chapter 10. Outlining a Global Action Plan

1. Christopher Flavin, *Nuclear Power: The Fallout From Chernobyl,* Worldwatch Paper 75 (Washington, D.C.: Worldwatch Institute, February 1987).

2. Bill Keepin and Gregory Kats, "Greenhouse Warming: Comparative Analysis of Nuclear and Efficiency Abatement Strategies," *Energy Policy,* December 1988; Christopher Flavin, "The Case Against Reviving Nuclear Power," *World Watch* (Washington, D.C.), July/August 1988.

3. U.S. Department of Energy, Energy Information Administration, *Monthly Energy Review,* July 1988; Christopher Flavin and Alan B. Durning, *Building on Success: The Age of Energy Efficiency,* Worldwatch Paper 82 (Washington, D.C.: Worldwatch Institute, March 1988); International Energy Agency, *Energy Conservation in IEA Countries* (Paris: Organisation for Economic Co-operation and Development (OECD), 1987); carbon emission figures are Worldwatch estimates based on Gregg Marland, Environmental Science Division, Oak Ridge National Laboratory, Oak Ridge, Tenn., unpublished printout and private communication, September 9, 1988.

4. Michael Renner, *Rethinking the Role of the Automobile,* Worldwatch Paper 84 (Washington, D.C.: Worldwatch Institute, June 1988); automobile growth of 3 percent annually, or a 75-percent increase by 2010, is consistent with recent trends. Carbon emission figures are Worldwatch estimates based on carbon emissions produced by different fuels derived from Gregg Marland, "The Impact of Synthetic Fuels on Global Carbon Dioxide Emissions," in W.C. Clark, ed., *Carbon Dioxide Review 1982* (New York: Oxford University Press, 1982); unless otherwise noted, all carbon estimates are based on this source. Deborah Bleviss, *The New Oil Crisis and Fuel Economy Technologies: Preparing the Light Transportation Industry for the 1990's* (New York: Quorum Press, 1988).

5. World electricity breakdowns are based on ICF Inc., Fairfax, Va., private communication, October 21, 1988; estimate of electricity share of fossil fuel use is Worldwatch estimate; energy efficiency potentials are de-

scribed in Flavin and Durning, *Building on Success.*

6. Lighting electricity figures are Worldwatch estimates based on U.S. figures and on United Nations, *1985 Energy Statistics Yearbook* (New York: 1987); projected growth is based on an assumed 3-percent annual growth rate, with carbon emissions based on replacing coal-fired generation through efficiency improvements; Arthur H. Rosenfeld and David Hafemeister, "Energy-Efficient Buildings," *Scientific American,* April 1988.

7. Office of Technology Assessment, U.S. Congress, *Industrial Energy Use* (Washington, D.C.: U.S. Government Printing Office, 1983).

8. Robert H. Williams and Eric D. Larson, "Steam-Injected Gas Turbines and Electric Utility Planning," *IEEE Technology and Society Magazine,* March 1986; carbon emissions projections are Worldwatch estimate based on a 30-percent improvement in the efficiency of plant with an 80-percent capacity factor; carbon emission figures for 1 million megawatts of coal-fired capacity are based on an assumed 44-percent capacity factor derived from United Nations, *1985 Energy Yearbook.*

9. Carbon emissions in 1988 from Marland, unpublished printout; the 3-billion-ton figure is based on the difference between constant energy intensity of a world economy growing 3 percent annually and a 2-percent annual reduction in intensity for 20 years; degree difference range derived from Irving Mintzer, *A Matter of Degrees: The Potential for Controlling the Greenhouse Effect* (Washington, D.C.: World Resources Institute, 1987).

10. Cynthia Pollock Shea, *Renewable Energy: Today's Contribution, Tomorrow's Promise,* Worldwatch Paper 81 (Washington, D.C.: Worldwatch Institute, January 1988).

11. ICF Inc., private communication; Shea, *Renewable Energy;* carbon emissions based on replacing coal-fired generation with renewables.

12. International Energy Agency, *Renewable Sources of Energy* (Paris: OECD, 1987); carbon displacement projections based on an assumed capacity factor of 20 percent for future wind and photovoltaic systems.

13. U.S. Department of Energy, *Budget Highlights, FY 1989* (Washington, D.C.: 1988); John Holusha, "Government Agrees to Relaxation of Auto Mileage Standard for '89," *New York Times,* October 4, 1988.

14. William U. Chandler et al., *Energy Efficiency: A New Agenda* (Washington, D.C.: American Council for an Energy Efficient Economy, 1988); gasoline tax projections are Worldwatch estimates.

15. Flavin and Durning, *Building on Success.*

16. Appliance efficiency from Flavin and Durning, *Building on Success;* fuel economy target from Chandler et al., *A New Agenda.*

17. Marland, private communication; World Bank, *China: The Energy Sector* (Washington, D.C.: 1985); Christopher Flavin, *Electricity for a Developing World: New Directions,* Worldwatch Paper 70 (Washington, D.C.: Worldwatch Institute, June 1986); José Goldemberg et al., *Energy for a Sustainable World* (Washington, D.C.: World Resources Institute, 1987).

18. "Global Environmental Protection Act of 1988," S. 2666, U.S. Senate, introduced by Senator Robert Stafford, July 28, 1988; "National Energy Policy Act of 1988," S. 2667, U.S. Senate, introduced by Senator Timothy Wirth, July 28, 1988; "Global Warming Prevention Act of 1988," H.R. 5460, U.S. House of Representatives, introduced by Representative Claudine Schneider, October 5, 1988.

19. "Conference Statement," The Changing Atmosphere: Implications for Global Security, Toronto, June 27–30, 1988; William U. Chandler, Battelle Pacific Northwest Laboratory, "An Energy Efficiency Protocol for Reducing the Risk of Global Climate Change," background paper for Project Blueprint, Washington, D.C., June 15, 1988.

20. Brazil figure from Alberto W. Setzer et al., "Relatório de Atividades do Projeto IBDR-INPE 'SEQE'—Ano 1987," Instituto de Pesquisas Espaciais, São Paulo, Brazil, May 1988; 11.3 million figure from FAO, *Tropical Forest Resources,* Forestry Paper 30 (Rome: 1982); new estimate for Brazil is 6.5 million hectares greater than previous estimates (see World Resources Institute/International Institute for Environment and Development, *World Resources 1986* (New York: Basic Books, 1986)), which leads to conclusion that the FAO estimate is probably at least 50 percent too low; for discussion of forest damage in industrial countries, see James J. MacKenzie and Mohamed T. El-Ashry, *Ill Winds: Airborne Pollution's Toll on Trees and Crops* (Washington, D.C.: World Resources Institute, 1988).

21. Sandra Postel and Lori Heise, *Reforesting the Earth,* Worldwatch Paper 83 (Washington, D.C.: Worldwatch Institute, April 1988).

22. For an analysis of the effects of government forest policies, see Robert Repetto, *The Forest For the Trees? Government Policies and the Misuse of Forest Resources* (Washington, D.C.: World Resources Institute, 1988).

23. Peter Truell, "Latin American Debt Prompts Action," *Wall Street Journal,* September 22, 1988; "G-7 Summit Leaders' Endorsement of Sustainable Development Welcomed," *International Environment Reporter,* July 13, 1988.

24. Marlise Simons, "Brazil Acts to Slow Destruction of Amazon Forest," *New York Times,* October 13, 1988.

25. Terence Hpay, *The International Tropical Timber Agreement: Its Prospects for Tropical Timber Trade, Development and Forest Management* (London: International Union for Conservation of Nature and Natural Resources/International Institute for Environment and Development, 1986); Richard House, "Timber Producers, Users Talk of Saving Forests," *Washington Post,* July 23, 1988.

26. Postel and Heise, *Reforesting the Earth.*

27. Ibid., with one important change: the carbon-fixing rate was reduced from 6.5 tons per hectare per year to 5.5 tons based on analysis of data in Sandra Brown et al., "Biomass of Tropical Tree Plantations and Its Implications for the Global Carbon Budget," *Canadian Journal of Forest Research,* Vol. 16, No. 2, 1986.

28. Area in Conservation Reserve from Lester R. Brown, "Breakthrough on Soil Erosion," *World Watch* (Washington, D.C.), May/June 1988. Calculation assumes a carbon-fixing rate of 5 tons per hectare per year, although higher rates—for example, with American sycamores—have been achieved; see Gregg Marland, Oak Ridge National Laboratory, Testimony before the Committee on Energy and Natural Resources, U.S. Senate, September 19, 1988. A 500-megawatt coal-fired plant emits 946,000 tons of carbon per year, according to calculations by Worldwatch.

29. Postel and Heise, *Reforesting the Earth.*

30. Daniel J. Dudek, *Offsetting New CO_2 Emissions* (New York: Environmental Defense Fund, 1988).

31. Louise Sweeney, "The Greening of Kenya," *Christian Science Monitor,* October 7, 1986; "Power Company to Fund Reforestation to Offset Carbon Dioxide Emissions, Slow Greenhouse Effect," press release, World Resources Institute, Washington, D.C., October 11, 1988; Philip Shabecoff, "U.S. Utility Turns to Guatemala to Aid Air," *New York Times,* October 12, 1988; Gary Moll, Vice President of Programs, American Forestry Association, Testimony before the Committee on Energy and Natural Resources, U.S. Senate, September 19, 1988.

32. Information on forest assessment from Robert W. Harrill, Woods Hole Research Center, Woods Hole, Mass., private communication, October 6, 1988.

33. Robert W. Herdt, *Technological Potential for Increasing Crop Productivity in Developing Countries,* paper presented to the meeting of the International Trade Research Consortium, December 14–18, 1986; Lester R. Brown with Erik P. Eckholm, *By Bread Alone* (New York: Praeger Publishers, 1974).

34. Francis Urban and Philip Rose, *World Population by Country and Region, 1950–86, and Projections to 2050* (Washington, D.C.: U.S. Department of Agriculture (USDA), Economic Research Service (ERS), 1988); USDA, ERS, *World Grain Harvested Area, Production, and Yield 1950–87* (unpublished printout) (Washington, D.C.: 1988).

35. USDA, ERS, *World Grain 1950–87;* Herdt, *Technological Potential.*

36. USDA, ERS, *World Grain 1950–87;* U.N. Food and Agriculture Organization (FAO), *FAO Fertilizer Yearbook 1986* (Rome: 1986).

37. J. Dawson Ahalt, "Argentine Agriculture Struggles With Policy Changes," *Choices,* First Quarter 1988.

38. Milton J. Esman, *Landlessness and Near-Landlessness in Developing Countries* (Ithaca, N.Y.: Cornell University Center for International Studies, 1978); R. Albert Berry and William R. Cline, *Farm Size, Factor Productivity and Technical Change in Developing Countries* (draft, June 1976), summarized in Schlomo Eckstein et al., *Land Reform in Latin America: Bolivia, Chile, Mexico, Peru and Venezuela,* Staff Working Paper No. 275, World Bank, Washington, D.C., April 1978; Erik Eckholm, *The Dispossessed of the Earth: Land Reform and Sustainable Development,* Worldwatch Paper 30 (Washington, D.C.: Worldwatch Institute, June 1979).

39. Gary Lee, "Soviets Allow Land Leasing for Farmers," *Washington Post,* August 27, 1988.

40. Edward C. Wolf, *Beyond the Green Revolution: New Approaches for Third World Agriculture,* Worldwatch Paper 73 (Washington, D.C.: Worldwatch Institute: October 1986).

41. Ibid.

42. Ibid.

43. Kenneth Tull, "Bio-Intensive Gardening in the Philippines: An International Institute for Rural Reconstruction and UNICEF Project," in Kenneth Tull et al., *Experiences in Success: Case Studies in Growing Enough Food Through Regenerative Agriculture* (Emmaus, Pa.: Rodale International, 1987).

44. M. Rupert Cutler, "The Peril of Vanishing Farmlands," *New York Times,* July 1, 1980.

45. OECD, *Land Use Policies and Agriculture* (Paris: 1976).

46. Norman A. Berg, "Making the Most of the New Soil Conservation Initiatives," *Journal of Soil and Water Conservation,* January/February 1987; USDA, ERS, *Cropland, Water, and Conservation Situation and Outlook Report,* Washington, D.C., September 1988; "Sixth CRP Signup Adds 3.4 Million Acres," *Agricultural Outlook,* August 1988.

47. Sandra Postel, *Conserving Water: The Untapped Alternative,* Worldwatch Paper 67 (Washington, D.C.: Worldwatch Institute, September 1985).

48. Consultative Group on International Agricultural Research, World Bank, *Annual Report 1987–88* (Washington, D.C.: 1988).

49. International Monetary Fund (IMF), *International Financial Statistics,* Washington, D.C., various months.

50. USDA, Foreign Agricultural Service (FAS), "Reference Tables for Wheat, Corn, and Total Coarse Grains: Supply-Distribution for Individual Countries," *World Grain Situation and Outlook,* Washington, D.C., January 1987; USDA, FAS, "Reference Tables on Rice: Supply-Distribution for Individual Countries," *World Grain Situation and Outlook,* Washington, D.C., August 1986.

51. IMF, *International Financial Statistics Yearbook* (Washington, D.C.: 1988).

52. Brown with Eckholm, *By Bread Alone.*

53. Population Information Program, "Population and Birth Planning in the People's Republic of China" *Population Reports,* Series J, No. 25, Johns Hopkins University, Baltimore, Md., January/February 1982; USDA, ERS, *World Grain 1950–87.*

54. Barber B. Conable, President, World Bank, "Address to the Board of Governors," Berlin, September 27, 1988; USDA, ERS, *World Grain 1950–87;* World Bank, *World Development Report 1988* (New York: Oxford University Press, 1988).

55. United Nations, Statistical Office, *Monthly Bulletin of Statistics,* New York, September 1988.

56. Carl Haub, Population Reference Bureau, Washington, D.C., private communication, October 17, 1988.

57. Quote from Economic and Social Commission for Asia and the Pacific, *Population of Japan,* Country Monograph Series No. 11 (New York: United Nations, 1984); Haub, private communication. See also Irene V. Taeuber, *The Population of Japan* (Princeton, N.J.: Princeton University Press, 1958).

58. Population Information Program, "Population and Birth Planning in the People's Republic of China"; Haub, private communication.

59. United Nations, *Monthly Bulletin;* Haub, private communication.

60. United Nations, *Monthly Bulletin.*

61. Jodi L. Jacobson, *Planning the Global Family,* Worldwatch Paper 80 (Washington, D.C.: Worldwatch Institute, December 1987).

62. Population Information Program, "Population and Birth Planning in the People's Republic of China"; Pi-chao Chen, "11 M Chinese Opt for Only One Child Glory Certificate," *People* (London), Vol. 9, No. 4, 1982.

63. Population Information Program, "Population and Birth Planning in the People's Republic of China"; Chen, "11 M Chinese"; World Bank, *World Development Report 1988.*

64. Department of International Economic and Social Affairs, *Fertility Behavior in the Context of Development: Evidence from the World Fertility Survey* (New York: United Nations, 1987).

65. Judith Jacobsen, *Promoting Population Stabilization: Incentives for Small Families,* Worldwatch Paper 54 (Washington, D.C.: Worldwatch Institute, June 1983).

66. Lester R. Brown and Edward C. Wolf, "Reclaiming the Future," in Lester R. Brown et al., *State of the World 1988* (New York: W.W. Norton & Co., 1988).

67. Thomas E. Lovejoy, "Will Unexpectedly the Top Blow Off?" Plenary Address to the Annual Meeting of the American Institute of Biological Sciences, University of California at Davis, August 14, 1988.

68. Eduard A. Shevardnadze, Minister for Foreign Affairs, Union of Soviet Socialist Republics, Statement before the Forty-third Session of the U.N. General Assembly, New York, September 27, 1988.

69. United Nations Children's Fund (UNICEF), *The State of the World's Children 1989* (New York: Oxford University Press, for UNICEF, 1989).

70. For Ghana and Peru, see World Food Council, *The Global State of Hunger and Malnutrition;* Michael Griffin, "Harsh Times for Madagascar's Growing Numbers," *People* (London), Vol. 15, No. 2, 1988.

71. Ruth Leger Sivard, *World Military and Social Expenditures 1987–88* (Washington, D.C.: World Priorities Inc., 1987).

72. "Conference Statement," The Changing Atmosphere.

Index